The Zionist Paradox

The Schusterman Series in Israel Studies

EDITORS
S. Ilan Troen / Jehuda Reinharz / Sylvia Fuks Fried

The Schusterman Series in Israel Studies publishes original scholarship of exceptional significance on the history of Zionism and the State of Israel. It draws on disciplines across the academy, from anthropology, sociology, political science and international relations to the arts, history and literature. It seeks to further an understanding of Israel within the context of the modern Middle East and the modern Jewish experience. There is special interest in developing publications that enrich the university curriculum and enlighten the public at large. The series is published under the auspices of the Schusterman Center for Israel Studies at Brandeis University.

For a complete list of books in this series, please see www.upne.com

Yigal Schwartz
The Zionist Paradox: Hebrew Literature and Israeli Identity

Tuvia Friling
A Jewish Kapo in Auschwitz: History, Memory, and the Politics of Survival

Anat Helman
Becoming Israeli: National Ideals and Everyday Life in the 1950s

Motti Golani
Palestine between Politics and Terror, 1945–1947

Ilana Szobel
A Poetics of Trauma: The Work of Dahlia Ravikovitch

Anita Shapira
Israel: A History

Orit Rozin
The Rise of the Individual in 1950s Israel: A Challenge to Collectivism

Boaz Neumann
Land and Desire in Early Zionism

Yigal Schwartz

The Zionist Paradox

Hebrew Literature and Israeli Identity

Translated by Michal Sapir

BRANDEIS UNIVERSITY PRESS
Waltham, Massachusetts

BRANDEIS UNIVERSITY PRESS
An imprint of University Press of New England
www.upne.com

© 2014 Brandeis University
All rights reserved
Manufactured in the United States of America
Typeset in Garamond Premier Pro by
Integrated Publishing Solutions

For permission to reproduce any of the material in this book, contact Permissions, University Press of New England, One Court Street, Suite 250, Lebanon NH 03766; or visit www.upne.com

Library of Congress Cataloging-in-Publication Data
Shvarts, Yig'al.
[Ha-yada'ta et ha-aerts sham ha-limon poreah. English]
The Zionist paradox : Hebrew literature and Israeli identity / Yigal Schwartz ; translated by Michal Sapir.
pages cm. — (The Schusterman series in Israel studies)
Includes bibliographical references and index.
ISBN 978-1-58465-894-8 (cloth: alk. paper) —
ISBN 978-1-61168-601-2 (pbk. : alk. paper) —
ISBN 978-1-61168-602-9 (ebook)
1. Zionism in literature. 2. Hebrew fiction—History and criticism. 3. Israeli fiction—History and criticism. 4. Jews—Israel—Identity. 5. National characteristics, Israeli, in literature. I. Sapir, Michal. II. Title.
PJ5030.Z55S5813   2014
892.4'093585694—dc23   2014013635

5 4 3 2 1

PUBLICATION OF THIS BOOK IS SUPPORTED BY
*Michael Liberman (Brandeis '85) and Polina Liberman
in honor of Professor Jacob Cohen beloved mentor of
generations of Brandeis University students*

Contents

Preface & Acknowledgments
ix

Introduction
1

1. Avraham Mapu, *The Love of Zion* (1853)
The Beautiful Daughter of Zion, the (Faux) Shepherd
Boy and the Cutting Up of the Monster
13

2. Theodor Herzl, *Altneuland* (1902)
Shall These Dry Bones Live
49

3. Yosef Luidor, "Yoash" (1912)
The Taste of Freedom and Space
97

4. Moshe Shamir, *He Walked in the Fields* (1948)
It Turned Out It Was All Fake...
142

5. Amos Oz, "Nomads and Viper" (1963)
A Short, Patched European Jacket
over a White Desert Robe
221

Notes 289
Bibliography 315
Index 329

Preface & Acknowledgments

The writing of this book would not have been accomplished without the aid of dozens of illuminating observations garnered from the writings of scholars in various disciplines, mainly in literary studies, humanistic geography, and comparative mythology—a great and diverse array from which I tried to derive a unified methodological framework with a clear logic.

Especially important for me were the wonderful historical journeys through Western literature and culture taken by Erich Auerbach, Georg Lukács, Mikhail Bakhtin, Northrop Frye, Arnold Hauser, Franco Moretti, and Zygmunt Bauman, and the wonderful historical journeys made by my teachers along the paths of modern Hebrew literature. Particularly important for this book were the historiographical journeys of Baruch Kurzweil, Gershon Shaked, Dan Miron, and Nurit Gertz.

No less important and fascinating were the explorations of mythologies and "primitive religions" made by J. G. Frazer, Joseph Campbell, and, in particular, Mircea Eliade, whose great studies—chief among them "Eternal Return"—fired up my thoughts. A major contribution was made by the works of scholars who studied the "religion of nationality": Benedict Anderson, George L. Mosse, David Biale, Oz Almog, Maoz Azaryahu, Yael Zerubavel, and others. In addition, my work would not have been achieved without what I learned from the studies of humanistic geographers, most notably David Harvey and Douglas C. D. Pocock. I also, I believe, acquired real insights from studies with a postcolonial orientation, especially those written by Edward Said, Homi Bhabha, and Lennard Davis.

In my attempt to create a methodological framework that would allow me to move in the time-space-culture that it was my aim to identify and describe, I repeatedly relied on the excellent work of Zali Gurevitch and Gideon Aran, Gabriel Zoran, and Rachel Elboim-Dror.

To all these scholars, and to the scores of others from whose writings I drew knowledge, joyful discovery, moments of cautious optimism, and also a few moments of doubt and even despair—I wish to extend my deep gratitude and appreciation.

The book's theoretical framework is of great importance to me, but it is not there for its own sake. Its aim is to serve the attempt to decipher texts, and through them a complex and changing psychocultural experience. Furthermore, in all the theoretical segments, as well as—and I tried to make this distinction—in the ideological-political ones, I steered as clear as I could of dogmatic arguments. I shall be satisfied if a few of the readers become convinced that in the writing of this study I tried, even if I did not succeed, to follow a work plan similar to the one drawn up by the writer Toni Morrison in the preface to her 1992 book of essays *Playing in the Dark:* "These chapters put forth an argument for extending the study of American literature into what I hope will be a wider landscape. I want to draw a map, so to speak, of a critical geography and use that map to open as much space for discovery, intellectual adventure, and close exploration as did the original charting of the New World—without the mandate for conquest. I intend to outline an attractive, fruitful, and provocative critical project, unencumbered by dreams of subversion or rallying gestures at fortress walls" (3).

This study would not have seen the light of day, certainly not in its present form, without the welcomed help of many people. I would like to express my gratitude to my teachers and friends who read early drafts of the manuscript or heard my lectures on various sections of the study and made wise and useful remarks: the late Prof. Gershon Shaked, Prof. Menachem Brinker, Prof. Ruth Kartun-Blum, Dr. Tamar Hess, and Tali Artman from the Hebrew University in Jerusalem; Prof. Arnold Band from the University of California, Los Angeles; Prof. Avraham Holtz from the Jewish Theological Seminary in New York; Prof. Nili Gold from the University of Pennsylvania; Prof. Edna Amir Coffin from the University of Michigan, Ann Arbor; Prof. Avner Holtzman from Tel Aviv University; and Dr. Anat Weisman, Dr. Ma'ayan Harel, and Dr. Shlomit Zaarur from Ben Gurion University of the Negev.

This is also the place to thank Prof. Shlomo Hasson from the Geography Department and Prof. Alon Kadish from the History Department of the Hebrew University—the seminars for advanced students we taught together helped me to sharpen my focus on some of the issues discussed in this book. Thanks are also due to the students at the seminars I taught at the Hebrew University, the University of Michigan, Ann Arbor, and Ben Gurion University of the Negev, whose remarks made me go back and examine my conclusions and formulate them more clearly.

I wish to extend my heartfelt thanks to the wonderful research assistants I had the privilege of working with during the long years I dedicated to this study: Dr. Shai Tzur, Dror Mish'ani, Yo'ana Gonen, Dana Ben-Zaken, Yael Hazan, Dr. Svetlana Natkovich, Rina Baruch, and last but certainly not least Chen Strass, who also took on the difficult task of preparing the book's indexes and bibliography.

I also wish to thank the staff at the Amos Oz archive at Ben Gurion University, especially Ruti Kalman; my friend the writer Gabriela Avigur-Rotem; and Hila Blum, a great friend and a fantastic editor who prepared the Hebrew edition.

I wish here to thank those individuals and institutions who had a hand in the English edition. My friend and editor Shimon Adaf abridged the Hebrew edition so that it would not prove too unwieldy in English; Michal Sapir was thorough and exacting and still produced an elegant translation that retained the original melody. Sylvia Fuks Fried was a wonderful editor: I continue to be impressed by her wisdom, fine sensibility, and superb taste. Special thanks to my Ben Gurion University colleagues President Rivka Carmi, Rector Zvi Hacohen, and Dean David Newman for their collegiality and support, and to the Rothschild Caesarea Foundation, which provided generous resources to translate and produce the English edition. I am grateful that my book received additional support from the Schusterman Center for Israel Studies at Brandeis University and that it appears in its Series in Israel Studies.

Finally, a giant thank you to my extraordinary children: Ben, Yoav and his spouse, Liron, and Zohar. And to Galit, my wife and beloved, heartfelt thanks for your warmth, infinite patience, and love, for which I hope I am worthy.

NEVE SHALOM, *Spring 2014*

Introduction

*The principle of "Here we stand and from here we shall not move!"
is completely missing from the biography of this people—*
—Y. H. BRENNER, *Our Self-Evaluation*

This book was born from a combination of existential distress and intellectual curiosity. It is rooted in an attempt to understand the nature and the origins of the unease we Israelis feel about our identity and about the place we define as our national home.

Why do we keep complaining that this is not the state we dreamed about: small, crowded, hot, sweaty, surrounded by enemies, situated at the heart of the "Levant," far from the cultural centers of the modern world and yet standing at the forefront of "the battle of civilizations"?

Why do we keep feeling disappointed in our Israeliness and are sometimes even embarrassed to be Israelis, and when we travel around the world, which we do perhaps more than any other people, then over there, abroad, we are drawn to meet our fellow countrymen, but also, and at least to the same degree, we try to avoid meeting them?

And at the same time, what is the origin of our gnawing doubt about the future of our national home—a doubt we take the trouble to nurture devotedly and which, we must admit, is hardly reconcilable with the phenomenal objective success of the Zionist project?

Why are we at times seized by the thought that maybe we, the Jews, "are not made" to live in a state of our own . . . ? And when we calm down we wonder to ourselves or to our friends whether we should start all over again from scratch, and this time in a different place, a greener, less hot one, with plenty of water. And preferably with different neighbors, more "enlightened" and "civilized," or maybe with no neighbors at all, on some island . . .

In this context I cannot but be reminded of the immortal dialogue between Dorothy and the Scarecrow in *The Wizard of Oz*, a dialogue that deals, like this foundational American book, with the questions of what makes a place a home and how a habitat becomes a national home. Here: "'Tell me something about yourself and the country you came from,' said the Scarecrow, when [Dorothy] had finished her dinner. So she told him all about Kansas, and how gray everything was there, and how the cyclone had carried her to this queer Land of Oz. The Scarecrow listened carefully, and said, 'I cannot understand why you should wish to leave this beautiful country and go back to the dry, gray place you call Kansas.' 'That is because you have no brains' answered the girl. 'No matter how dreary and gray our homes are, we people of flesh and blood would rather live there than in any other country, be it ever so beautiful. There is no place like home.' The Scarecrow sighed. 'Of course I cannot understand it,' he said. 'If your heads were stuffed with straw, like mine, you would probably all live in the beautiful places, and then Kansas would have no people at all. It is fortunate for Kansas that you have brains.'"[1]

The Scarecrow thinks with universal "common sense": rational creatures are supposed to live in the prettiest, greenest, most pleasant place they know. In contrast, Dorothy thinks the "American way." Her concept of place is based on one single idea: "There's no place like home." Or in Y. H. Brenner's words, in the epigraph I have chosen for this book, "Here we stand and from here we shall not move."

Dorothy's concept of place can also be described—following some of Zali Gurevitch and Gideon Aran's suggestive observations in their essay "On the Place"—as that of the daughter of an immigrant society who adopts a "native" concept of place. According to Gurevitch and Aran, "The native is always in place. He was born in the place and from it, and has resided in it ever since—in the cradle, at home, in the grave. The place is like an extension of his body. The native maintains a natural connection, a practical overlap between the place in the physical sense (the 'place') and the place as a world of meanings, of language, memory and faith (the 'Place')."[2] By contrast, the immigrant is never in place. He is born in one place and aspires to another, and when he arrives "at the promised land," he has to bridge the gap between dream and reality. His basic existential experience is based on the existence of a (temporary/perennial) gap between the place in the physical sense (the place) and the place as a world of meanings, of language, memory and faith (the Place).

For Dorothy, who in this context is supposed to represent all American immigrants-settlers, the clear advantages of the Land of Oz over Kansas—Oz is greener, it summons amazing adventures and wonderful friends, there is no trace in it of the representatives of a harsh Calvinistic tradition or of hunger and want—are totally irrelevant to the question of why she wants to go back to Kansas. "Home" is "home." Period. And any other place, as beautiful as it might be, is another country and, in her words, "a queer country."

In other words, L. Frank Baum created an American heroine whose fundamental existential experience can be defined, in Gurevitch and Aran's terms, as a fundamental experience that is based on an overlap between the place in the physical sense (the place) and the place as a world of meanings, of language, memory and faith (the Place). "Naturally," a heroine with this fundamental existential experience cannot understand the Scarecrow's simple and wise miscomprehension. Moreover, she even deems it stupid ("That is because you have no brains").

Dorothy answers the Scarecrow on behalf of "we people of flesh and blood," but her answer applies, if it applies at all, to the members of the American nation, who believed and still do believe, at least according to Jean Baudrillard, that they have fulfilled "the American dream"—that is, that they have managed to realize the vision of the founding fathers: to turn the masses of immigrants into a great nation, and the wild, untamed landscape into a model civilized environment.

As for the members of the revived Hebrew nation, who starting in the middle of the eighteenth century have returned to "the Land of the Fathers," where they tried to fulfill "the Zionist dream" in its various forms, physically and/or through the writing of essays, impressions and stories—here the situation is a lot more complicated.

True, many among the Jewish people participated in the planning of the Zionist project; a considerable number of them took part in the attempts to realize it; and thousands gave their lives for it. Yet despite the enormous effort and the phenomenal objective successes, the Zionist endeavor down the generations, in its various areas of activity, has been accompanied with a sense of a missed opportunity, an experience of a broken dream, which is slowly turning into a kind of general agreement that there is, probably, an unbridgeable gap between our Place and our place.

In this book I have tried to point to and describe what I see as important literary junctures in the journey of the attempt to fulfill the Zionist dream. My choice to focus on the subject of Hebrew literature rests on two simple reasons. First, this is the area I know better than any other area of Hebrew creativity. Second, Hebrew literature played a major part in the construction of modern Hebrew culture. As is well known, a considerable part of the characteristics of modern Hebrew culture was thought up and shaped in the feverish minds of Hebrew writers, who from the end of the eighteenth century on gained among large publics a status enjoyed in the distant and recent past by the nation's great intellectuals and spiritual figures: prophets, priests, rabbis, and tzadikim (righteous people).

I have marked the historical-literary journey I wish to make here with five junctures, to which I dedicate five chapters. First chapter: 1853—*The Love of Zion*, Avraham Mapu. Second chapter: 1902—*Altneuland*, Theodor Herzl. Third chapter: 1912—"Yoash," Yosef Luidor. Fourth chapter: 1948—*He Walked in the Fields*, Moshe Shamir. Fifth chapter: 1963—"Nomads and Viper," Amos Oz.

The book opens with a discussion of *The Love of Zion*, which, to my mind, is the foundational text of the vast historical-literary course of development I wish to describe here. The second chapter, *Altneuland*, and the third chapter, "Yoash," look at narrative texts that—again, to my mind—reflect the two central utopian Zionist models that for several decades competed for the hearts and minds of Hebrew readers. The two final stories, the first of which, *He Walked in the Fields*, was written just before the founding of the state of Israel, and the second, "Nomads and Viper," was written when the state was fifteen years old, represent in my view the two essential literary responses of the "native sons" to the Zionist project, of whose realization they themselves, as the "first Israelis," were supposed to be the ultimate proof.

This study encompasses a period of over a hundred years. It is a hefty historical-literary chunk, which includes the majority of modern Hebrew literature. However—and this is a fundamental caveat in this study—the fact that we are dealing with a large literary corpus, created over a lengthy period of time, does not mean that it can be discussed in isolation from the basic assumptions of premodern Hebrew literature, written from the Bible onward and centering its attention on issues of nation building and land settlement. In this context, crucial importance should be accorded, as I will show later on, to several basic assumptions that underpinned Hebrew culture during the first period in which the people of Israel inhabited their land—that is, from the period of the Patriarchs, the first of whom, Abraham, immigrated to Eretz Israel from Aram-Naharaim; through the period of the settlement of the twelve tribes that returned from Egyptian exile; through the kingdoms of Judah and Ephraim; and up to the destruction of the kingdom of Ephraim and the Babylonian exile, the destruction of the kingdom of Judah, and the scattering of the people of Zion to the four corners of the world.

Since the people of Israel were exiled from their land, about two thousand years ago, they have dreamed about returning to Zion. These dreams are expressed in thousands of literary works. Theirs is a huge, extremely diverse corpus, yet it is founded on what can be termed "a vector of desire" with two distinct characteristics, which Yehuda Halevi, the great Spanish Hebrew poet, wonderfully defined and wedded together in one dense sentence: "My heart is in the East and I in the uttermost West."

The first distinct characteristic implied in this sentence, which has become a kind of motto for Jewish existence in exile, is the direction of the desire: from the Diaspora to Eretz Israel. The second distinct characteristic is the great, seemingly irreparable rift between the two organs belonging to the very same entity: the heart, representing the higher human sphere, man's emotional, mental, and ideological existence, which is in the farthest East, and the body, representing the earthbound, corporeal, lowest human sphere, which is in the uttermost West.[4]

Avraham Mapu in *The Love of Zion* did not change the direction of this vector of desire—from the Diaspora to Eretz Israel—but he changed the identity of the element that generates and drives it.

In all the thousands of texts that preceded *The Love of Zion*, the dream of returning to Zion is linked to the messianic (millennial) utopia, a utopia whose principles have been ordained by a supreme authority, the God of Israel, who alone can turn it into a reality. In other words, the rift between life in the Diaspora (the "place," the body) and life in the ideal realm (the "Place," the heart) was seen as unchangeable and permanent.

In *The Love of Zion*, on the other hand, the dream about *Shivat Zion* (returning to Zion) is linked to a human utopia, a utopia whose principles are determined by the thoughts, drives, and interests of human beings, who are the ones charged with turning it into a reality. This means (and this is the start of a great revolution that, unfortunately, as I shall show again and again, has never reached its full realization in the portrayed world of Hebrew narrative fiction) that *The Love of Zion* proclaimed (and this is how this slender book was understood by thousands of human beings) that the great, supposedly perennial rift between the place and the Place can be mended.

The "realistic" affinity of the Jews with their historic homeland was actualized by Mapu by developing and enhancing a "cultural narrative"; that is—and I am relying here on the succinct definition from Nurit Gertz, who in turn relied on Jean-Francois Lyotard's famous observations in his essay "The Postmodern Condition"—by developing and enhancing an interpretive narrative configuration according to which people are called to think, feel, live, and die.[5]

Cultural narratives—which are always the products of a combination of the three great narrative modes: mythology, history, and literary fiction[6]—are required, concocted, and most evident mainly in times of crisis. Natural disasters, epidemics, great military defeats, pogroms, genocide, and other collective traumas—these exacerbate the human need for all-embracing interpretive narrative frameworks.[7]

Various scholars have emphasized the kinship between narrative and identity. In this context, Shlomith Rimmon-Kennan argues that "we lead our lives as stories, and our identity is constructed both by stories we tell ourselves and others about ourselves and by the master narratives that consciously or unconsciously serve as models for ours."[8] These master narratives, or, more in line with our discussion here, these cultural narratives, are the medium through which, and only through which, as Fredric Jameson claimed, we are able to understand our past, our present and our future.[9]

In order to understand we therefore need to tell a story, "and to tell a story means," as Rimmon-Kennan beautifully puts it, "to model it on previous stories."[10] The modeling of stories on previous stories is thus an essential human trait, and it has existed for a long time. The interpretation of stories from this point of departure is also not new, since it too, just like the work of storytelling, is based on the modeling of (interpretive, critical) stories or narratives on previous (interpretive, critical) stories or narratives. What is new is the conscious and systematic reading of stories through the prism of the cultural narrative, and this area has seen an impressive development in recent years. This is true both for the discussion of single works or groups of works that have sociological and psychological common ground and, and this is particularly relevant to the present study, for the discussion of single works or groups of works that deal with "the biography of a people."

The cultural narrative that Mapu developed and enhanced will be called here the story of the renaissance of the people of Israel in the Land of Israel. This cultural narrative, which has become the dominant narrative matrix in the corpus of Hebrew texts devoted to re-imagining the people and the land in the last hundred and fifty years, is based on a reenactment of biblical metanarratives—biblical cultural narratives that have become habitual and fixed in the nation's memory—dealing with the "birth" phase/the mythical phase of the nation's formation (Abraham's journey from Ur Kaśdim [Ur of the Chaldees] to Canaan, the Exodus from Egypt, the Akedah [the binding of Isaac], etc.), and the "End of Days" phase in its different versions.[11]

This story of national renaissance unfolds around two intertwining axes: the axis of "human engineering" and the axis of "landscape conceptualization." The axis of human engineering is based on a conceptual plot mechanism, which centers on presenting a possible inventory of potential male and female mates from which will be eventually selected, after a long series of tests, the chosen couple—the one suitable to serve as the first couple in the revived leading dynasty of the people of Israel. The axis of landscape conceptualization is based on a similar mechanism. It centers on presenting an inventory of forms of settlement, from which is determined, after a long series of tests, the model fit to serve as the framework for the renewed existence of the people of Israel in its land.

In other words, *The Love of Zion*'s innovation and importance stem not only, as many of its readers thought, from a story about the love for Eretz Israel (Ahavat Zion means "the love of Zion") or about a couple's love that takes place in Eretz Israel, but rather from creating the dramatic encounter between the narrative imagining of a couple who are supposed to restart the national dynasty and the narrative imagining of a place in which they and their descendants and their descendants' descendants are supposed to live, think, feel, and die.

Theodor Herzl and Yosef Luidor followed the artistic and conceptual path outlined by Mapu. But their divergences from his model, and the obvious differences between the fictional landscapes they created and the human types they both portrayed, stem from the specific identity of the generators of the vector of desire in their works; that is, from the specific identity of the factors that generate the movement that is supposed to bring about the pairing of the preferred representatives of the imagined nation and direct them to the creation of a new life.

In the construction of *The Love of Zion*, Mapu relied on the two utopian archetypes that had taken root and thrived in the secular branch of the Western utopian tradition (the one dealing with human utopias): the "garden utopia" and the "city utopia." The garden utopia deals, as Rachel Elboim-Dror succinctly puts it, "with the primordial, pastoral golden age, the ancient Arcadia, a time when man lived simply and harmoniously with nature."[12] And Elboim-Dror elaborates: "These images are based on the myth of the Garden of Eden, the myth of origin and creation, and the breach of contract that resulted in man's expulsion from the garden. It is one of the ancient and basic myths, which have continued to exist in human consciousness and have been preserved in the utopian genre as an ideal model for human life within nature. Each generation creates its own 'garden'; some wish to return to the garden of the primordial past, and some locate it in the future."[13] On the other hand, notes Elboim-Dror, the city utopia "is related to the myth of end and destination."[14] "As opposed to the heavenly city above, 'the city of God,' which is made by divine hands, the [city] utopia wished to direct the earthly ideal city by human hands, without the intervention of a higher power—yet following a heavenly model—since in human society there is a profound need to live according to transcendental precedents."[15]

The distinction between the two human utopian archetypes (the garden utopia and the city utopia) parallels the famous distinction made by the German sociologist Ferdinand Tönnies between "community" and "society."[16] According to Tönnies, the driving force behind the community (Gemeinschaft) is man's "natural will" (Wesenwille), which is reflected in acts that are "made for their own sake" ("scratching," "eating," "loving"). The driving force behind the society (Gesellschaft) is man's "rational will" (Kürwille), which is reflected in his decisions—in the conscious choice he makes between alternatives that can further his goals. Community is based on blood ties, geographic proximity, and religious affiliation. Society is based on common interests (social, cultural, etc.) and contractual agreements in defined areas.[17]

Mapu, who as I will show in detail was "a conservative revolutionary," tried to create an imagined nation based on a balance between defining characteristics of the garden utopia on the one hand and the city utopia on the other, and, respectively, between the elements typical, according to Tönnies, of community on the one hand and society on the other.

Mapu's version of the story of the renaissance of the people of Israel in the Land of Israel is based on a reenactment of the biblical story that deals with the beginning of the establishment of the people of Israel as a kingdom—the story of Saul being taken "from tending the flock" to be anointed as king in Jerusalem—in a toned down and sterilized form. The choice of Saul, the rustic herdsman, to be king in Jerusalem was a doubly revolutionary act. First, it announced the shift from a community (a group of human beings whose connection is "tribal," based on blood ties, geographical proximity, and religious affiliation) to a society (a group of people whose connection is "stately," based on common interests [social, cultural, etc.] and contractual agreements in defined areas). Secondly, it clearly drew a revolutionary vector of desire, imposing the rule of the representative of the rural periphery (the garden utopia) on the sanctified urban sphere (the city utopia).

The story of Amnon, Mapu's protagonist, being brought from the Bethlehem fields to Jerusalem recreates the story of Saul being crowned as king, but only on the manifest level. This can be clearly inferred—and I will elaborate on this issue in the first chapter—from Amnon's "pedigree": we are dealing here with a "false herdsman," who in actual fact belongs to the old Jerusalemite elite. In other words, rather than breaching the Jewish elite's "purity of descent," Mapu settled for a symbolic act—"a rejuvenating journey" made by the members of this urban elite to their rural estates, where they meet their mates, who are rural in appearances only.

Herzl and Luidor were more audacious. The imagined nations they created are based on clear—and opposing—decisions about the nature of the appropriate relationship between the defining characteristics of the garden utopia and the city utopia, and, respectively, between the typical elements that constitute, according to Tönnies's distinctions, community and society.

Herzl's story of the renaissance of the people of Israel in the Land of Israel is based on a reenactment of three biblical stories of nation founding: the Exodus from Egypt, Isaiah's End of Days prophecy, and Ezekiel's vision of the Valley of the Dry Bones.

In his cover version of these biblical stories there is almost no trace of communal elements (ties of kinship and geographical proximity), whereas there is a significant densification of social elements (common interests and contractual agreements in defined areas). And respectively, in this strictly modern cover version (Herzl envisioned a kind of improved combination of the Europe and America of his time), anything that has to do with nature and the natural (the garden utopia) must be subordinate to anything that has to do with civilization (the city utopia). No wonder, then, that *Altneuland*'s protagonists, the men and women who will join one another to create a new dynasty, have studied in institutions of higher education—European ones, of course.

The story of the renaissance of the people of Israel in the Land of Israel created by Luidor is virtually opposite in its teleology to the one created by Herzl. It is based on a reenactment of the biblical Akedah story in a way that takes away its religious values (the covenant between the people of Israel and "Hamakom," the Place, God) and recharges it with values of the religion of nationality, in its extreme-romantic guise (the covenant between the people and the place, the land of Eretz Israel).

In Luidor's cover version of the biblical story, there is a significant densification of communal elements (ties of kinship and geographical proximity) and a significant exclusion of social elements (common interests and contractual agreements in defined areas). And respectively, in the "native-primitive" cover version, everything that has to do with civilization—again, the Western one (the city utopia), except perhaps the weapons—must be subordinate to nature and the natural (the garden utopia). No wonder, then, that the story's ultimate hero, Yoash, is described as someone who has grown out of the land (as a "native," an autochthonous creature), as someone who rejects any kind of social organization (school, public committee, democratic elections, etc.), and as someone whose short life's climax is the moment in which he unites with his beloved land.

Moshe Shamir's and Amos Oz's reenactments of the story of the renaissance of the people of Israel in the Land of Israel represent, in my view, the two fundamental existential positions dividing Israeli society.

Shamir's *He Walked in the Fields*—written, let us not forget, by a complete "sabra" (native Israeli)—zealously preserves the Diasporic vector of desire: from the Diaspora to Eretz Israel. This emerges, among other things, from an examination of Shamir's two cover versions of the Akedah story, which form the basis for the story of Uri Cahana, the sabra protagonist (and Shamir's peer) in the novel.

As we shall see, Shamir puts Uri on the spot twice—once in Luidor's extreme-romantic vein, as someone who sacrifices his life for the "place," Eretz Israel, rather than for the "Place," the sanctification of the name of God. However, and here lies the dramatic innovation, this sacrifice is also described as a farce. Shamir leads us to understand that "it turned out that it was all a fake,"[18] that what we are dealing with is, in fact, the suicide of a weak boy who is running away from his life's tasks toward a carefully planned and staged death. In other words, after presenting the sabra as the crowning glory of Zionism, Shamir shows him up as a balloon and pricks him with the pin of irony.

The motive for this surprising move becomes clear when we notice that Uri, the handsome sabra who dies, like Agnon's Yitzhak Kumer, "in a sorry affair," is replaced by the new immigrant Mika, who at first dislikes the Zionist project yet later successfully passes all its entrance examinations—including those in which Uri had failed.

At the basis of Shamir's reenactment of the Akedah story in *He Walked in the Fields* is the idea of a continuous Zionist revolution. Its essence is the assumption that the Jewish people will only have a chance of surviving in Eretz Israel if the gap between the place, the "real" place in which we live, and the Place, the ideal, "whole" (greater) Land of Israel, is preserved. This gap, Shamir believes—and this, in my view, is the fundamental position of the Israeli Right—must be preserved by any means necessary, including that of "murdering" the sabra, since the sabra is the most prominent proof of the success (and completion) of the Zionist attempt to erase the gap between the place and the Place.

In other words, according to Shamir, if we as a nation wish to live, we must consistently renew the pool of national tasks that will enable the "new recruits" to sacrifice their lives for the conquest of the land and the building of the nation, thus gaining the desired entry permit to the imagined community—and at the same time "making room" for new recruits. This represents an infinite replication of the blood covenant rite between man and land, which Luidor had dramatized in "Yoash" sixty years earlier—in the early period of Eretz-Israeli fiction—as a one-off event!

By contrast Oz, in his first collection of short stories, suggested a no less dramatic existential option. In Oz—the writer who together with A. B. Yehoshua played a crucial role in the creation of Israeliness—Shamir's replication and perpetuation of the Zionist rite of the Akedah is replaced by a complete reversal in the direction of the vector of desire that had dominated Hebrew literature from the destruction of the First Temple onward, excluding, as I already noted, certain sections of Hebrew literature written in the period of the Haskalah.

In these stories Oz adopted Yehuda Halevi's Diasporic split between the body and the heart, which as mentioned had assumed the existence of an irreparable rift between the place and the Place—with one "small" change. In Oz—and he represents here, to my mind, a considerable part of the Israeli Left, which was in fact already "post-Zionist" in the 1960s—the body (the "home") is in Israel, but the heart (the "Home") is "elsewhere," in Europe.

"Nomads and Viper," the story at the center of the fifth chapter of this volume, tells a renaissance story based not on biblical metanarratives dealing with the beginning phase or the end phase of the people of Israel in the Land of Israel, but rather on a universal story: that of the Garden of Eden.

The story raises a poignant central question—which re-emerges in many of Oz and A. B. Yehoshua's formative stories: how and why was/will be the Israeli Garden of Eden destroyed. Or, to refer to the plot of the specific story I chose to discuss—why does the story's heroine, a sabra kibbutz member called Geula (redemption), die? Or why does she only manage to achieve her (sexual) redemption by being bitten by a viper, which represents here, clearly and even explicitly, the "ultimate Arab other," a kind of Arab super phallus?

The answers to these questions are reflected in the story's thematic structure, which is based on an assimilation of the two utopian models to which Zionist literature has adhered—the garden utopia (the community) on the one hand, and the city utopia (the society) on the other—and on an intensified actualization of the contradiction between them; a fundamental contradiction that Mapu, Herzl, Luidor, and even Shamir tried to soften and blur.

Oz assumes that the Zionist project is the product of contrasting and hostile motivations, and he expresses this, among other ways, through the strange, inherently impossible status of the "home": the kibbutz. On the one hand, this home is clearly marked by the rural, romantic, and social Zionist utopia (the Luidor option), which means turning one's back on the urban West and trying to merge with the "Orient," the "Levant." On the other hand, this home is clearly marked by the modern, urban Zionist option (the Herzl option), in which the main goal is to establish a society that would be "an improved Europe."

The Israeli existence, according to Oz, is therefore a strange hybrid: primitive-modern, tribal-social, merging into the environment and fencing itself off from it. Oz's kibbutzim (like those in Israeli reality) are located in the midst of nature yet surround themselves with ordinary and electric fences—a hybrid existence destined to be destroyed because of the sharp contradiction built into its constitutive elements.

Oz's stories of the renaissance of the people of Israel in the Land of Israel, as well as A. B. Yehoshua's, almost always end with a colossal crash that comes to pass, again, almost always, with the help of the heroes who represent the writers' peers, that is, the "first Israelis."

Geula and her friends, the kibbutz youths, are seen as inviting the invasion of the kibbutz by the Bedouins. Geula fantasizes that the Bedouin Arab rapes her and "invites" "an act of retaliation." Her friends comply and go out "to even the score with the nomads . . . , carrying short, thick sticks,"[19] and thus, with an act of vengeance driven by primitive urges and blood ties, they disturb the delicate equilibrium between society and community on which the kibbutz is based and also, respectively, the delicate equilibrium between the garden utopia and the city utopia that underpins the Jewish-Israeli existence in its geopolitical environment.

The origin of the self-destructive desire that characterizes Geula and her male and female friends in "Nomads and Viper" and in Oz's earlier and later stories (for instance in the novels *Elsewhere, Perhaps*, and *My Michael*, and of course, albeit with a certain reversal, in the novella *Unto Death*) is their craving for "otherness," for other people and other places. The human beings the protagonists long for are distant others (Europeans) or proximate others (Arabs or Mizrahi Jews). The proximate others are observed here from a quasi-colonialist position, which situates those observing them—and this is the crucial point in this phenomenon—in a quasi-European position. Accordingly, the landscapes that the protagonists are nostalgic for are always "beyond" and over: over the border, overseas, etc.

I

The Love of Zion,
Avraham Mapu, 1853

The Beautiful Daughter of Zion, the (Faux) Shepherd Boy, and the Cutting Up of the Monster

> *Had a talented writer seen us on that fine morning, he would have found ample material for a poem. This would have been a poem about four married Jews and how they lay unbuttoned on the grass, enjoying the day in silence. Also included would be a sun and its warm rays, a sky, nature, dewdrops, songbirds and horses, each prettier than the last. Such a writer should, of course, be generous enough to add some products of his own imagination too: a flock of sheep grazing in the meadow, a clear running brook at which "Jews do break their thirst." He would doubtless place flutes in our mouths on which we would trill a song of praise to the beloved bride in the Song of Songs, just like the shepherds of yore. We had our own baskets of food, thank God, so that we would not have to impose upon the writer for refreshments.*
>
> —MENDELE MOCHER SFORIM, *Fishke the Lame*

The Legend of the New Age

The Love of Zion (*Ahavat Zion*) is the first Hebrew text to consistently and systematically rebel against the basic assumption that has underlined traditional Hebrew literature. This is the first text to describe an Eretz-Israeli imagined landscape from a position that assumes that it is possible to erase the "perennial gap" between the "place" and the "Place"—between the "earthly Jerusalem" and the "heavenly Jerusalem."

The Love of Zion's originality in this context was noted by the critic Shlomo Tzemach. In an essay entitled "A Conversation,"[1] written in the form of a debate held by several participants about the question, What is the use of still teaching *The Love of Zion* in Israeli schools? S. Tzemach's representative in the discussion, "an old writer," states that *The Love of Zion* is the first text in Hebrew literature to feature landscape description "as a self-contained form of art." True, "an old writer" says, "This is certainly not the landscape of Zion and Jerusalem. These are the gardens of the Lithuanian capital Kaunas, with its mountain ranges and the banks of the Nemunas; it is there that Mapu built his arbor, under whose shade he wrote these words. But it matters not. In Witz's first landscape painting, 'The Miraculous Draught of Fishes,' it is also not the sea of Tiberias and its banks that are depicted, but the Swiss lake. The main thing is the urge to refer to outdoors views and transfer them from the realm of nature to the realm of art. Here in this passage, mute nature is metamorphosed by man into a world entirely expressive of the human spirit."

The obvious question—why we had to wait until 1853, the year of *The Love of Zion*'s publication, before we could read landscape descriptions in Hebrew literature "as a self-contained form of art"—is answered by Tzemach through the words of the "teacher," another participant in the fictional discussion about *The Love of Zion*'s relevance: that in that period a new individual was created, "an individual with a new feeling, which he had not felt [before], or which he had felt very vaguely, and it is this clear feeling which revealed to him the secret of the landscape's beauty." And he adds that "[this] new feeling that was attached to nature and colored it with its world [is] the love for the homeland, for the Land of the Fathers."

Tzemach ties the appearance of landscape descriptions in *The Love of Zion* to the emergence of "a [Jewish] individual with a new feeling," a Jew feeling a new kind of "love for the homeland."[2]

Like Tzemach, I also believe that *The Love of Zion* is the first attempt in Hebrew literature to create a new Jew and a new national landscape. Like him, I also think that *The Love of Zion* is a book that should be seen as a foundational text, both on the socio-ideological level (that is, the level that concerns the plans and actions of many people [in our context, Jews] from different places across the world) and on the artistic/literary level (that is, the level that deals with the ways in which the imagined Eretz-Israeli landscape is portrayed and described).

The Love of Zion's status as a foundational text can be deduced from hundreds of testimonies. Many Jews who emigrated to Eretz Israel in the first Aliyot reported that "this little book" captured their hearts, provoking an emotional turmoil that made them decide to pack their belongings and leave for Eretz Israel. *The Love of Zion*'s importance in the lives of its contemporaries can also be inferred from the thoughts and memories of famous public figures, writers, and essayists. Here, for example, is a passage from a piece by Ya'akov Fichman:

> This naïve story became not only a primordial vision, but also a clarion call for a new life, a wake-up call to leave the dark narrow alleyways for the lush open land. The smell of fields and gardens arose from its pages and the voices of vine growers and farmers filled all its corners with joy. A longing for the grace of youth and love sang from all its chapters, and a kind of yearning for happiness, for a full life, for a generous sun—that filled the young hearts with warmth and intoxication.
>
> It was the book of the time, its instructive and rousing work. It reopened our eyes to see the greenness of the land, it soothed our hearts, it carried us away from the surrounding ugliness and pettiness; and it also taught us to loathe the swarm of flatterers and hypocrites who stood between us and the fountains of life.
>
> We today have no sense of the great revolution that this little book brought about at the time.... Anywhere it arrived it carried the spirit of the coming days. In every corner it reached it was received as the harbinger of a new gospel. Hope spoke through its lines—the hope of days to come.... [Mapu] created the legend of the new age, a legend that anticipated redemption and that paved the way for it.[3]

The Love of Zion's status as a foundational text in the artistic sense—as a source of inspiration for many writers and a literary and stylistic model for imitation (both from an admiring and a disparaging position)—was pointed to by Dan Miron:

> The short description of the town of Bethlehem and its environs in the beginning of chapter 4 of "The Love of Zion" left its mark on several generations of readers. First, from the novel's publication in 1853 to approximately the end of the 19th century, this description—the first landscape description in the first Hebrew novel—served as both an admired stylistic model and a descriptive, picturesque "topos." Both as a basic literary scene of the ideal Hebrew countryside, and as a perfect example of an elegant use of the language of the scriptures adapted to contemporary taste, the description was often imitated in literary and other texts (Eretz-Israeli travel literature, Zionist opinion journalism, the flowery correspondence of Hebrew-speaking *maskilim* and *Hovevei Zion*). Sentences such as "this beautiful landscape shall grow fresh olives and red vines with their first succulent bunches" or "its hills girded with joy and its dales embroidered with flowers and roses" seemed to flow spontaneously from the quills of writers and other purveyors of poetic phrases, intertwined with verses from Amos and Isaiah and with the poeticisms of Job and the author of Psalms. The influence of the Bethlehem description was especially evident in early Eretz-Israeli prose, which started ap-

pearing in the later decades of the 19th century, with the emergence of the "new *Yishuv*" ... [the writers of the period] sidestepped the Eretz-Israeli reality as it was then ... [drawing] instead ... an idyllic-ideal picture of a renewed Hebrew life in the land of the Fathers [in Mapu's style]. [Or, as Brenner claimed in his ironic introduction to "From Here and There" (Mi-Kan U-Mi-Kan), 1911] "wonderful poetic scenes of the glorious splendor of the Carmel and the Sharon, of work in the Bethlehem fields, of the courage of those born and bred in Eretz Israel—of the love of the daughters of Zion and Jerusalem."[4]

The plot of this foundational book, published in 1853 and reprinted many times since, takes place in the kingdom of Judah, at the time of Ahaz and Hezekiah. It is a period marked by a crisis of faith, and later by a religious, social-moral, and economic resurgence. This resurgence is put under threat by an external force (Assyria), but eventually the threat is removed by divine intervention (the epidemic in Rabshakeh's army).

The story centers on the love affairs of two young couples, Tamar and Amnon and Peninah and Teman. Tamar and Teman are siblings, as are Amnon and Peninah. Their families belong to the upper socio-economic and political echelon of Jerusalem.

These love affairs begin with a symbolic event between the family patriarchs, Yoram and Yedidiah. Yoram, who is about to go to war against the Philistines, meets Yedidiah in his country house on the Mount of Olives and persuades him to pledge on a handshake that their children will get married when they come of age. The handshake between the patriarchs is complemented by two symbolic events related to Hananeel, the father of Yedidiah's wife Tirzah, and the only representative of the grandparents' generation in the story. The first event: Hananeel, who is present in Jerusalem at the time of Tamar's birth, entrusts his daughter with a ring "made by an artist,"[5] which she is supposed to pass on to his granddaughter when the latter grows up. Tamar is supposed to wear the ring once becoming an adult, the ring serving her as "a testimonial that Tamar shall be an equal heir with my children to all my wealth."[6] The second event: Hananeel, who was one of the noblemen of Israel and is now among the exiles traveling on foot to Assyria, writes to Tirzah about a dream he had during a night's stopover on the banks of the river Chebar. Here it is: "And I saw ... a tall youth of a comely face, beautifully attired, a sword girded to his side, and wearing an open helmet. He had raven locks crowning his brow, and rosy cheeks; his forehead was as white as the driven snow; his jaw was firmly set and he had pearly teeth; he was astride a beautiful black steed. When I looked upon his handsome face, I cried bitterly and called: 'Oh, God, my God, I too had sons as handsome as he, and now none are left to close my eyes in death nor to inherit my wealth.' As the youth heard my cries, he alighted from his horse and took my right hand, saying in his gentle voice, 'Why, I am he who is in love with thy grandchild, Tamar, and I am seeking thee in the land of thy captivity so that I may release thee and take thee to Zion to thy beloved children.' And I asked him his name and that of his father, and he said, 'This I cannot tell thee now, because some deep mystery enshrouds it, but it will come to light in the near future.' He showed me the ring which I gave to Tamar, and he said, 'Tamar gave it to me as a sign of her love for me.' Then I awoke, and, alas, it was only a dream" (LZ, 29–30).

The plot thickens due to a series of intrigues, which forces Naame, the wife of Yoram, who has been taken captive in the war against the Philistines and exiled to the island of Kapthar (Crete), to run away with her children and wander around the villages, drawing their livelihood from seasonal work. Amnon and Peninah's (temporary) poor financial situation and their apparently low social status do not deter Teman and Tamar, who travel to their parents' rural estates (Teman to Carmel and Tamar to Bethlehem) and desperately fall in love with Amnon and Peninah.

The plot then continues to thicken, not only on the familial/private level and the national/political level (the Assyrian siege of Jerusalem and a group of the city's residents—including Zimri, who is responsible for the plots against the two eminent families—who wish to discourage the besieged Jerusalemites and surrender to Sennacherib), but also on the symbolic level (the changing fortunes of the ring).

These complications, however, which are all interconnected, are soon resolved. The plots are discovered, the siege is removed, the bad guys get punished, and the lost ring is restored to its rightful owner, Tirzah's father, Hananeel, and Yoram and Amnon return from their place of captivity, and the members of both families—and with them Hadoram, the family's loyal friend from the city of Tyre—are united in a dual wedding celebration (Amnon and Tamar, Teman and Peninah) in the country house on the Mount of Olives that Yoram gave Yedidiah at the beginning of the story, when the two made the pact agreeing to the marriage of their offspring.

Topography at the Service of Ideology

We can learn about Mapu's new position with regard to Jewish culture from a methodical examination of *The Love of Zion*'s topographical plane, that is, the work's spatial organization, which is perceived by the reader as a kind of geographical map. One of the ways to perform this examination is to describe and interpret the structural and thematic link between the "central area" of the portrayed world's map (the area that serves as the setting for the events that are crucial to the plot) and the "surrounding area" of this map (the area that serves as the setting for the plot's background events).[7] This distinction between the central area and the surrounding area is of great importance in the context of discussing the work's status in terms of its historical reception. The surrounding area represents the "old" worldview—the one that was customary and common in the author's time. The central area, on the other hand, represents the "new" worldview—the one that the author espoused and which he tried to disseminate to his readers.[8]

The surrounding area in *The Love of Zion*—which in cartographic terms can be likened to a large-scale map—is demarcated by six points: Jerusalem in the center; Nineveh in the northeast; the kingdom of Ephraim (Israel) and its destroyed capital Samaria in the north; the island of Kapthar, where Yoram and later Amnon are exiled, in the northwest; Botzra, where Tirzah and Tamar and later Amnon are exiled; and Echron, the Philistines' city, in the southwest. The "central area"—which can be likened to a small-scale map—is delineated by four points: Jerusalem in the center, the Dead Sea in the southeast, Bethlehem in the south, and Carmel in the southwest.

The waypoints of the surrounding area were chosen according to a thematic coordinate system, underpinned by two binary oppositions. The first opposition is between homeland (Judah) and places of exile (the island of Kapthar and Nineveh, and the stations on the way to them, Botzra and Echron). The second opposition is between the city of God and faith (Jerusalem) and pagan, power-worshipping cities (the great Nineveh on the one hand and Samaria, the capital of the kingdom of Ephraim, on the other).

As a frame of reference for his story, an author can choose the present in which he lives or, more precisely, sections of this present. He can also choose segments from any period in the past. And he can also choose sections from the future as he imagines it. Whichever way, the author's choice of anchoring his narrative's events in a particular segment on the extra-narrative temporal plane is significant, since this choice links his story to a defined group of metanarratives that suggest several basic mytho-historical interpretive positions, each giving rise to certain worldviews with which the author has to contend. The crucial importance of a decision of this kind is clearer in works that turn to a defined period in the distant or near past that is routinely mediated in the collective consciousness through a specific metanarrative.[9]

Mapu's choice of anchoring his story in the time of Ahaz and Hezekiah creates a sharp historical analogy between the location and situation of the author and his immediate readers (exiles in eastern Europe) and the location and situation of the story's protagonists (the citizens of the sovereign kingdom of Judah). The writer enhances this analogy by giving the topic of exile and expulsion a special status in the novel's plot structure: a considerable number of the story's events take place under the strong influence of one exile (the exile from the kingdom of Ephraim) and the threat of another (the exile from the kingdom of Judah). The events on the collective plane have a direct influence on the events on the private plane. Many of the central characters are exiled from their country (Yoram, Hananeel, Amnon, Zimri) and some from their home (Naame, Amnon, Tamar). Furthermore, the exile of some of the characters (Yoram, Hananeel) dictates the exile of other characters (Naame, Amnon, Peninah). And this, among other things, is because another exile, Zimri (who is exiled from Ephraim to Judah), consistently uses the spatial rift between the characters to further his own manipulations, which, among other things, cause some of the characters to be exiled from the central area of the story's portrayed world to its surrounding area.

The tension between homeland and exile in *The Love of Zion* has a clear moral dimension. This is due to the link Mapu made between the historical period in which the fictional events are anchored and the metanarrative that may be called the Nebuchadnezzar Syndrome. It is a symmetrical moral plot model that says that whoever does what is good in the eyes of God shall live peacefully on their land, and whoever does what is bad in the eyes of God shall be exiled from their home and land. This mytho-historical conditional pattern is reflected in *The Love of Zion* insofar as all the characters that come from the "sinful" Samaria are permanently exiled from their land (a course of events that is also orchestrated symmetrically and morally—Zimri, the bad character from Samaria, is exiled to Jerusalem and murdered there, whereas Hananeel, the good character from Samaria, is exiled to Nineveh and later returns to Israel, but to Jerusalem rather than Samaria), whereas all those exiled from Jerusalem return, sooner or later, to their city and home.

The second opposition around which the surrounding area in *The Love of Zion* is structured is, as already mentioned, the one between the city of God and faith (Jerusalem) and the pagan power-worshipping city (Nineveh); the same opposition, on a smaller scale, is created between Jerusalem, the capital of the kingdom of Judah, and Samaria, the capital of the kingdom of Ephraim. We explicitly learn about the status and importance of these two pairs of oppositions in the novel from two monologues: the one included in a letter sent by Amnon to Tamar from Nineveh, and Zimri's soliloquy as he escapes from Samaria to Jerusalem. Here, first, is a passage from Amnon's letter, which reads like an excerpt from an ancient tourist guide: "In the land of Nimrod, in Nineveh, in the city of a mighty nation, am I . . . [It is] a big city in the land of Assyria, a land of corn and wine, and from her skies the dew falls in abundance. Now I want you to know about the great city of which so much is spoken: In the time of the first creation, when God created the mountains and the people, cities were built, and the City of Nineveh was erected on her foundations from the very beginning of the centuries, after the mountains were created. The hands of Ashur built the city, and, to establish forever the name of his son, Nin, he called the city Nineveh. The city is built on both sides of the River Hiddekel; it is three days' journey through this city. A high wall surrounds it. A channel brings the water from the river to the city, and fills the brooks and valleys" (*LZ*, 150–51).

Immediately following is a passage that abandons the seemingly objective description in favor of a description entirely built on a comparative geographical/demographical study: "Such is the strong city [of Nineveh], built so many years back. But do you think it can be compared with the beautiful Zion, even though it is young? Nineveh's brooks are not like those in Zion. A pure light is spread over everything in Zion, while a gloomy light is over the waters of Nineveh. You do not see joyful faces here; the people are dull and their eyes are dim with tears of the oppressed. Every day captives are brought here in battleships and fisherboats. Not like the Mountains of Zion, Mt. Moriah and the Mount of Olives, crowned with a bold splendor. Not to them can you compare the smoky mountains of Assyria, which shoot out flames of fire and burn all the surroundings. Zion is the dwelling of our Creator, and Nineveh is the abode of lions. I call Nineveh, therefore, a sweet and fearful city. It is like a leopard adorned with a fine skin—pleasant to look at and fierce with the roar issuing from its mouth. From this city, King Sennacherib comes forth like a lion from the heights on the Jordan and darkens the surface of the earth . . . His arm is ready to strike the Holy Mountain" (151–52).[10]

And juxtaposed with those is the first impressions of the fugitive Zimri—having just escaped the "King of Assyria, with his mighty army [that] overspread [Samaria] like an overflowing river" (25)—of the city of Jerusalem: "Zimri came to Jerusalem through the gate of Ephraim at nightfall. A beautiful sight met his gaze. It was a glorious night. The sky was clear and the stars shone in their splendor. Everything there was life. The palaces were aglow with light. On the piazzas men and women in evening attire were promenading, and laughter and music could be heard from all directions. People were going hither and thither. Carriages and chariots, with the young lords and their wives, could be seen driving in all directions. Some few pedestrians were also seen going to the home of some friend. It is no wonder that Zimri forgot for a while his purpose in Jerusalem. The sight overwhelmed him, after living for three years in the besieged city, where everything had become one vast wasteland. 'How gloomy and desolate is Samaria,' he said, 'and how beautiful and bright is Zion! Samaria has gone to her decline, while Zion is blooming in the splendor and glory of the king who rules there. Ephraim has fallen and the land of Judah is rising in her beauty. A new earth and a new heaven I see here—a peaceful land where the inhabitants are enjoying peace under the blue dome of heaven, for the King has established law and justice'" (26–27).

The waypoints of the central area in *The Love of Zion* also create, through their reciprocal relations, two binary oppositions. The first opposition is between life in a bustling city of government and a tranquil life in the bosom of nature. The second opposition is between Jerusalem as a lively and vibrant city, and the Dead Sea. Jerusalem is seen in this context as a source of life (in several senses: the spiritual, the religious, the institutional/administrative, and so forth), whereas the Dead Sea is portrayed as a landscape of death and destruction, a landscape hostile to any form of life.[11]

In his novel, Mapu structured and developed the opposition between town and country—which he inherited from the two archetypes of utopian literature: the garden utopia and the city utopia, most probably through the mediation of Rousseau's writings and Moshe Chaim Luzzatto's shepherds plays[12]—in numerous ways, including some clear proclamations by the two representatives of the country in his story: the authentic representative (Sisry, Yoram's confidant, under whose protection Naame and Peninah find refuge in Carmel) and the false representative (Amnon, who tends to the sheep and goats of Avicha, his father Yoram's overseer, in Bethlehem and "who was looked upon as a shepherd boy") (*LZ*, 38). The Carmelite Sisry refers to this issue several times. One is when he responds to the defamatory words of Azrikam, Yoram's (false) urban son, who claims decisively and arrogantly that only city people are truly faithful to God, while "the farmers and shepherds . . . are ignorant and do not even know God." Sisry says, "Honor may dwell in the palaces, the knowledge of God in the dwellings of the righteous, God's glory in His Holy Temple, but the fear of God dwells in the villages. Though they are far from the house of God, God is in their hearts and the name of God is ever on their lips. They feel God's hand upon them in all seasons of the year, when they sow and when they reap, in want and in plenty. Sometimes, when they are in need of rain, they raise their eyes toward heaven and pray that God will send rain to refresh the dry fields; and again, when the fields are covered with the crops and they can see a year of plenty, you hear the prayer of thanksgiving in every home. In the time of harvest and the gathering in of the fruits, they rejoice over the gifts of God. They have plenty for themselves and the poor" (70).

Sisry links life in the countryside with closeness to faith (because of the villagers' dependency on the forces of nature), human modesty, and social sensibility. But he goes further, comparing life in the countryside with life in the city also in terms of man's physical, sexual, mental, and moral health. Here we go:

> If you would spend the night in the village you would see how early the shepherds and the farmers are awake. When the quiet of night is still over the earth, and the hills and mountains are just beginning to grow light after the heavy mire of the nights, the men go to their work, and their handsome, buxom wives spin the wool and flax for clothes for the household. And later on, when the sun rises on the mountaintops and the birds, awakened by the great light, chirp and sing from their nests, the farmer also sings his song of praise to his God and Maker, and his prayer ascends like incense to heaven. Then they return to their homes, and their wives, with beaming countenances, meet them on the threshold, and their children, already awake, greet them with joy and gladness. They eat of the plenty of God, and are thankful. Then back to work again they go, and the women busy themselves with the household duties, and the children, after their work is done, play in the fields.
>
> In the cities it is vastly different; there, he who calls himself the son of Zion is still asleep in his ivory bed, and at noon, when he does awake, he calls for his servants, who hasten to carry out his slightest wish. They bathe him and anoint him with perfumed oils; they adorn him like a helpless idol. When he looks at himself and at his costume, his face changes; he is dissatisfied with himself; he thinks the material in his garments should be brought from Egypt and his linen should be woven from the flax growing near the Black Sea. (70–71)

The waypoints of the central area in *The Love of Zion* outline a further binary opposition: that between populated places, represented by the vibrant Jerusalem, and a place presented as hostile to any form of life, the Dead Sea. This can be seen, for example, in the scene in which the love pact between Tamar and Amnon is sealed:

> Mt. Olive! The name brings to our mind a most beautiful picture. It is synonymous with peace and rest. There, under the shade of its olive branches, one finds at this season of the year the keenest pleasure in nature . . . It was to this most favored of all nature's nooks that Tamar, Amnon and Teman directed their steps . . . It was Tamar who broke the silence by saying, "In three days we shall be living here. How I love this place!"
>
> "How curious," said Amnon, "are the desires of the different people! In the villages they long for the din of the large cities, as a change from their continual

quiet. They think they would reach the haven of their desires if they could but leave the country and live amidst the bustle and noise of the city. On the other hand, the city folks weary of the excitement amidst which they live and are anxious to come to some quiet spot to be away from the tumult around them. How dear is this Mount in which both the tumult and quiet are combined! To the east lies the Salt Sea Plain, for centuries a sight of utter desolation, and a death-like quiet dwells there. From the west of Mt. Olive can be seen the city of Jerusalem in all its beauty."

"Did you ever see that Salt Sea Plain?" asked Tamar.

"Yes, I saw it," said Amnon, "on my return from Botzra. Our fathers tell us that before Sodom and Gomorrah were destroyed by the hand of God, because of their iniquities, it was like the Garden of Eden, and now it is the most fearful spot on God's universe. In its depth there is brimstone, sulfur, salt, and the atmosphere is full of the odor of burning tar. It is a pathetic waste; nothing grows upon its surface, not even grass. You cannot hear the song of birds, because the winged creatures will not nestle there. Even the wild beasts shun it, because God's curse rests over it ever since Sodom and Gomorrah were wiped off its surface. Over the whole Plain the echo of that mournful dirge can be heard. Satan hovers over it on the wings of darkness. And the King of the Satyrs dwells in the ruins of Sodom and Gomorrah, overlooking the Salt Sea waste. There is not a breath of life on this Plain. To the border of that Salt Sea Plain the Jordan overflows its banks, and the fish, which are left after the ebb of the tide, die on its surface. It looks as if the Inferno had opened its monstrous jaws and swallowed every living thing on or about this place."

"Turn from that gloomy sight," interrupted Tamar, "and look to the west and behold the City of God. How pleasing is the tumult of the people gathered there! See the beautiful eastern gate and the water gate covered in the evening with the water carriers who come for a supply for the home. See yonder the rush at the gate of the horse-market, where the lords and the wealthy merchants ride in beautiful chariots and carriages. And turn your eyes to the driveway leading to the Temple; you can hear the echoes of the carriage wheels upon the road even here, and how pleasant is the sound!" (100–101).

It is worth noting the vocal orchestration that introduces us to the opposition between Jerusalem and the Dead Sea. First the narrator tells us briefly about the Mount of Olives. Then Amnon speaks about the fundamental opposition between the countryside and the city, from which he turns, with Tamar's encouragement, to a different opposition: that between Jerusalem and the Dead Sea. He talks at length about the Dead Sea with all its terrors—until Tamar stops him, asking him to look at the city of God and the hubbub of its daily life.

This vocal orchestration is important, since it highlights two characteristics of the surrounding area. First, that the opposition between town and country is part of a more comprehensive opposition: the opposition between the representative of death—the desolate, annihilating landscape, albeit very impressive in itself (and it is easy to see the similarity between the Dead Sea and the "gloomy light . . . over the waters of Nineveh") (151)—and the representative of life—the landscape of civilization, where life is the result of an intensive human effort. This suggestive basic opposition gives *The Love of Zion* a dimension of a metaphysical drama. Secondly, the distribution of roles between Amnon and Tamar—she speaks about Jerusalem and he about the Dead Sea—hints at the existence of a sharp tension between the positive force that connects the two and the force that threatens to separate them. It creates a delicate and fragile, fertile and dangerous, erotic/thanatic equilibrium, which is a central element in the story's force field.

When we examine the map of the surrounding area against the map of the central area, one fact stands out: Jerusalem keeps its status in both maps. In both, it is situated in the center, in two senses: on the geographical plane as a point of intersection for all the traffic routes, and on the thematic plane as a point of encounter and intensification of the central oppositions (homeland versus exile, awe of God and a moral stance versus paganism and power worship, life in the city versus life in nature, and a vibrant human landscape versus a landscape of eternal desolation). In other words, Mapu did not question—as many writers and intellectuals after him would—Jerusalem's status as the regulative ideal of Jewish society and culture. His Jerusalem, like the one in the Hebrew Bible, is the center of the country and the center of the world, and moving nearer to it or farther from it has clearly defined normative implications.

This geothematic fact, however, should not lead us to conclude that Mapu accepted the normative foundation that had granted Jerusalem its status in the past as a necessary given. On the contrary, he questioned Jerusalem's traditional, sacred foundation, replacing it with a new ideological foundation that he tried to establish and validate through his story. In topographical terms, this pioneering move can be described as follows: Mapu shifted to the story's surrounding area, the oppositions that represent the basic values of traditional Judaism—homeland versus Diaspora, faith and spirituality versus paganism and power worship—oppositions that are merely different guises of the same traditional Jewish tension: the tension between the place and the Place, between the secular and the sacred. In their place, in the central area, he situated oppositions that represent supranational and universal human tensions: the tension between a rural and an urban existence, and the tension between vibrant human life and an annihilating landscape.

This shift in the power relations between the two pairs of oppositions, which represent differing and competing worldviews, is also reflected in the spatial composition of Jerusalem itself. This site, which symbolizes the heart of the nation, is divided into places frequented mainly by those who cling to the Torah and support the Davidic kingdom (the Temple, Yedidiah's house, etc.), and places that are the haunts of those who have abandoned the Torah and betrayed the Davidic kingdom (Carmi's wine house, Azrikam's house, etc.). The split between these places and between those who frequent them is underlined by a group of natural spatial oppositions. For instance, the places where the positive characters congregate are high and/or well lit and/or open to visitors from all peoples and social classes, whereas the places where the negative characters congregate are cellar-like and/or dark and/or closed to occasional visitors. The (temporary) blurring of boundaries and disruption of hierarchy between these realms are highlighted by the infiltration of negative characters into the spaces of the positive characters, and the infiltration of positive characters into the spaces of the negative characters. The resumption of order is underlined by the return of all the characters in the novel, be they positive or negative, to their natural spaces. Thus, for example, Azrikam, the son of the lowly servants Uchon and Hella, infiltrates Yoram's residence and almost takes it over by trying to marry Tamar. Zimri similarly infiltrates all the elite's strongholds in Jerusalem (Yedidiah's house, the Temple, etc.). On the other hand, Naame and Peninah, and consequently also Amnon, Tamar, and Teman, are dragged into spaces where an honest person dares not tread: the Tent of Defilement, or, more precisely, what looks like the Tent of Defilement at the gate of the valley, and the nocturnal journeys to it through the River Kidron, described as a place "where all the refuse is thrown," and the Valley of Tophet (inferno), the place "where they used to sacrifice their children to Moloch" (176). The resumption of normal order manifests itself in the death or imprisonment of the negative characters, but not before they gather once more in the "negative" spaces: Carmi's wine house and the Tent of Defilement at the gate of the valley. By contrast, all the positive characters are reinstated in both senses: to their proper status and to their proper space.

The relations of center and periphery, which characterize the spatial representations of the central thematic oppositions in *The Love of Zion* reflect the tension between the worldview that was conventional in Mapu's time and the view that was unique to Mapu himself. The fact that the common view is placed in the background, whereas the writer's view, which undermines the former, is placed in the foreground, has a crucial poetic, as well as reception-related function. Let me explain:

The writer, any writer, knows that readers tend to identify with stories that are set in a concrete space-time much more than with stories set in a generalized space-time. Therefore, and in keeping with their ideological intentions, writers frequently realize the traditional-common worldview of their time in the surrounding area of the portrayed world, whereas they realize their own, new worldview in the central area of the portrayed world.

The readers, who follow the writers' "reading instructions," therefore have at their disposal two maps whose relationship is clearly valorized: the "background map" or the "map of the old world," which is anachronistic and irrelevant, and the "foreground map" or the "map of the new world," which is up to date.

This literary device, which can be described as the exploitation of the readers' normative attitude to one object (here the way in which events in the fictional world are portrayed) in order to change their stance regarding another object (here the desired character of the New Jew and the new homeland), is a basic device used in all literary texts—especially those whose manifest intention is to persuade us to believe in something, do something, change something, that is, texts whose purpose is to spur us into action. No wonder, then, that in the texts under discussion—which are close in spirit to the genre of the thesis novel, a hybrid genre that, as Susan Suleiman compellingly showed,[13] combines realistic literature with didactic literature—this device becomes predominant.

This device also plays a predominant role, as we shall see in detail in the next subsection, in the way Mapu constructs the story's chronotopic plane—the one that deals with the specific character of the portrayed world's system of movements and actions—including also, and for our discussion here mainly, the specific nature of the reenactment (the cover version) of the biblical metanarratives (those cultural narratives that have become habitual and fixed in the nation's memory) that focus on the birth phase, the mythical phase of the nation's creation.

The writer—again, any writer—knows that in the same way that readers tend to identify with stories that are set in a concrete space-time, they also tend to identify with concrete, unique characters. These characters' personal stories attract readers more than the description of what happens to large groups of people.

Therefore, and in accordance with their ideological intentions, writers represent the traditional common worldview of their time in the "collective plotline"—the one that deals with what happens to large groups of people, whereas they represent their own, new worldview in the "private plotline"—the one that deals with the personal stories of unique characters.

The dominant worldview in a given time will therefore always, or almost always, be presented as part of the collective plotline, through a demonstratively outdated and manifestly irrelevant rewriting of one of the biblical metanarratives that deal with the mythical phase of the nation's creation. By contrast, the writer's worldview will always, or almost always, be presented as part of the private plotline, through an innovative reenactment, often based on importing and adopting fashionable European cultural narratives, of one of the biblical metanarratives that deal with the mythical phase of the nation's creation or, as we shall see below, in cases of a real revolution, through an innovative reenactment of other biblical metanarratives.

A Conservative Revolution—Mapu's Force Field

The collective plotline in *The Love of Zion* is historical and national in nature and is based on the metanarrative of the End of Days according to Isaiah's vision. This metanarrative, which links a religious and social/moral situation— the whole world's recognition of Jacob's God and its agreement to renounce war ("They will beat their swords into plowshares and their spears into pruning hooks")—with a specific spatial configuration in both the topographic and chronotopic sense ("the Mountain of the Lord's house shall be established as the highest of the Mountains, and shall be raised above the hills; all the nations shall stream to it"),[14] was repeatedly revalidated in the ancient Hebrew historical and cultural landscape by way of a cyclical ritual movement: the annual pilgrimages to the Temple in Jerusalem.

In the traditional Hebrew and Jewish cultural landscape, this metanarrative is also represented—including by modern commentators who approached this landscape from different ideological standpoints—through the reward narrative, which connects the people of Israel with the God of Israel and the Land of Israel. It is a mytho-historical narrative founded on a clear and well-defined conditional pattern: if the people of Israel do what is good in the eyes of God, they will live peacefully on their land and enjoy its blessings; if they do what is evil in the eyes of God, they will be exiled from their land.

The Love of Zion's national/historical collective plotline reenacts the metanarrative of the End of Days in its two classical/biblical versions. First, there are numerous mentions of the pilgrimage to the Temple during the three festivals;[15] second, the conditional pattern of the reward narrative is fully confirmed. The people of Ephraim, who do what is evil in the eyes of God, are exiled from their land, whereas the people of Judah, who do what is good in the eyes of God, live securely on their land. This moral/religious/spatial dichotomy is particularly noticeable, both because the two kingdoms are threatened by the same foreign kingdom, used as "a staff in God's hand," and because Mapu highlights this dichotomy through his omniscient narrator:

> It came to pass in the fourth year of the reign of Hezekiah, King of Judah, and in the seventh year of the reign of Hosea, King of Israel, that God, in his anger against the Ephraimites, who had reached the last stage of corruption, sent against them Shalmaneser, King of Assyria, with his mighty army. They overspread the land of the Ephraimites like an overflowing river. After a siege of three years the King of Assyria conquered them. All the captives were sent to Halah and Habor, cities near the river Gozan, and also to the Cities of the Medes. He removed the high places designated for the altars of worship, broke their images and banished their priests and prophets.
>
> Judah, her sister country, seeing that Israel, because of her wickedness, was punished by the hand of God, took it as a lesson to themselves and turned their hearts to God, followed the teachings of their prophets and loved God's chosen king, Hezekiah, in whose reign they lived in peace, while Israel was in much disgrace (*LZ*, 25).[16]

The message to all the gentiles, included in Isaiah's End of Days prophecy, is fulfilled in *The Love of Zion* through the figure, the story, and the actions of Hadoram, the traveling merchant from Tyre. Hadoram plays the role of the "approving other"; someone who serves as an objective witness and as the representative of those readers who are "still" skeptical about the validity of the re-enacted metanarrative—a typical narrative function in texts that reflect a solid ideological agenda (particularly in various kinds of utopias).[17]

Indeed, at the end of the story we are told that Hadoram—who played a central role in the reunification of Yedidiah and Yoram's families—has become an ally. During the final gathering of all the (positive) major characters on the Mount of Olives, Hadoram says: "I brought thee from the distant lands to be near thy loved ones. So I want to be near thy God, whose glory became known to all the inhabitants of the world. The clash of swords and the roar of shots have ceased everywhere, and peace has returned to all the nations far and near. Therefore, I will attach myself to the people, for the God of Zion is greater than all the gods of other nations, and to Him belong the greatness, the strength and the glory. Let us go to God's house and let us approach Him with praise and offerings.... And all present congratulated him, and called him 'One of us,' and they said, 'May the God of Jacob, who was favorable to His children, favor you forever and unite you to the House of Jacob'" (266–67).

The private plotline in *The Love of Zion* is based on two different metanarratives. One comes from the biblical inventory and can be called "from tending the flock": the story of a simple herdsman (Moses, Saul, David) being selected as leader. The other belongs to the European inventory: the metanarrative called the holy grail. The loss of a sacred object marks a period of drought for the land and barrenness for the royal family (an old dying king and his unmarried daughter). The finding of the sacred object marks a period of prosperity for the land and fertility for the royal family (the king's daughter gets married to the knight/prince who has found the grail, and they give birth to a son who becomes an heir to the old king). The "from tending the flock" story is alluded to here in the story of the shepherd (or the so-called shepherd) Amnon, who is taken from tending the flock in the Bethlehem fields to the financial, political, and spiritual elite in Jerusalem.[18] The holy grail plot—a typical Romance metanarrative—is alluded to here through Hananeel's signet ring and its changing fortunes. This magical object is given by Hananeel to Tirzah (paralleling the handshake between Yoram and Yedidiah), and later by Tamar to Amnon, in acts that signify the sealing of a love pact. The loss of this object is interpreted as a breach of trust, signifying love's deceptions and lies. The final return of the lost object to its rightful owner marks the completion of the magic circle and love's final triumph.

The comparison between the private and the collective plotlines in *The Love of Zion* clarifies the structure and logic of the book's chronotopic plane, which resemble the structure and inner logic of its topographic plane. In its two maps—the one that represents the traditional, conventional position and the one that represents Mapu's special new position—Jerusalem is situated at the center. In other words, the writer preserved the city's status as a regulative ideal. The same conclusion is reached when we examine the story's directions of traffic and its orientations, since all the traffic in *The Love of Zion* proceeds to Jerusalem and from it—a fact that makes the city the novel's central junction and the site in relation to which the readers form their interpretation and judgments about the work's world.

The similarity between the structuring of the novel's topographic plane and the structuring of its chronotopic plane also finds expression in the way Mapu diverged from the traditional modes of portraying the Eretz-Israeli landscape. On the topographic plane he created a new ideological order of priorities by displacing the thematic foci that captured most of the attention in the traditional Jewish community to the surrounding area (Diaspora versus homeland, Judaism versus paganism, and so forth) and replacing them with new and universal thematic foci (city life versus country life and so forth). On the chronotopic plane, Mapu created a new order of priorities by changing the status and importance of the directions of traffic on the central route of the novel's roadmap.

Both the collective and the private plotlines feature substantial movement to and from Jerusalem. But the movement in the private plotline (the plotline that represents Mapu's worldview) differs in orientation from the movement in the general plotline (the plotline that represents the common, dominant worldview), and the motivations behind the two types of movement is fundamentally different.

As already mentioned, Mapu's Eretz Israel is divided into two kinds of areas: an urban area (Jerusalem), identified with the authorities, the economic power, and also with a hub of corruption and intrigue, and a rural area (Carmel, the Bethlehem fields), identified with a simple and wholesome lifestyle. The traditional traffic in the Eretz-Israeli landscape—the annual one of the three festive pilgrimages, and the future one of the End of Days—is from the periphery to the holy center: from the rural areas to Jerusalem. Essentially, this is a religious/moral direction of traffic. Although this traditional movement is mentioned in *The Love of Zion*, it serves as the backdrop for another kind of movement: the representatives of the urban elite go out to the rural area, some for a longer period (Amnon and Peninah) and some for a shorter one (Tamar and Teman), later returning to the city. This movement—the representatives of the elite leaving the city for the countryside—is the most significant in the novel. This is the movement that makes possible the encounter between the Romeos and the Juliets of the fictional world, an encounter that results in an act of "racial improvement": improving the "urban species," which is in danger of depletion and atrophy, by "crossbreeding" it with the vigorous "rural species." This biological "crossbreeding" is supplemented by sociocultural "schooling" (the periods of study and training that Amnon undertakes in the army and among the prophet's sons), the final result being the restoration of former glories in a reinforced and revamped version, or in other words, the budding of a national renaissance.[19]

Mapu's reversal of the vectors of desire's status in the novel's chronotopic configuration—by increasing the importance of the route leading from Jerusalem to the countryside at the expense of the importance of the route leading from the countryside to Jerusalem—contains a revolutionary kernel. This reversal suggests that the author prefers the biological/erotic motivation over the religious/moral one, and the universal Romance worldview over the sacred/historical/national one. This conclusion, which is based on an analysis of the novel's chronotopic plane, finds further support in the rationales that motivate the major characters—both Amnon and Tamar clearly subordinate their commitment to the people and the people's destiny to their love affair.[20] Yet it must be added that the revolutionary kernel in *The Love of Zion*, as it is suggested by the story's chronotopic plane, is small and neutered. The book's author recognizes that something is rotten in the Kingdom of Judah, points to the infected area (the city), and even offers a solution for renewal in the shape of another area (the countryside). In Mapu, however, and here he resembles Charles Dickens rather than Jane Austen or the Brontë sisters, "everything stays in the family": the chosen couples all represent the same group, privileged and rich; and Mapu lets this group keep its status, as long as its future generation (Tamar, Amnon, Teman and Peninah) experiences a brief invigorating stay in the open and healthy expanses of the countryside. What counts here is the class/family pedigree rather than the change of place.

The Symbolic Place, the Chosen Couple, and Type Scenes

According to what we have seen so far, Mapu tried to reduce the gap between the "Place" and the "place" by alluding to two biblical metanarratives and re-enacting them conservatively and secularly. From another direction we can say—and here I am joining the fascinating debate held by several scholars on Mapu's scholastic orientation[21]—that Mapu's landscape conceptualization combines romantic and neoclassical tendencies. The combination of these tendencies finds its most impressive expression in what I will call the novel's symbolic places.

Let me preface by saying, following John Kirtland Wright,[22] that places and landscapes in literature reveal the most fascinating Terra Incognita: the one that resides in the human psyche. The fundamental inability to look directly at the "Atlantis of the mind," and therefore to describe it "as it is," forces writers to use spatial patterns that serve a symbolic function. Places in literature are charged with symbolic value, asserts the humanistic geographer Douglas C. D. Pocock— and I embrace his assertion—in the following two major ways: a) by co-opting the symbolic meanings that a certain place has in the mother culture or in other cultures, which the author, whether knowingly or not, adopts[23] (these are meanings that are already implied, to return to Lennard Davis's terminology,[24] by the concept of the Terrain, and they are implied by many of the "terrains" that surround us—for example, the glut of symbolic meanings implied by the terrain "Jerusalem": Jerusalem in the Jewish tradition, in the Christian tradition, in the Islamic tradition, and so on); and b) as a result of the principles underpinning the author's construction of the fictional world. One such principle, especially pertinent to our discussion, is the principle of repetition, in which the same places are repeatedly mentioned in different parts of the work. Due to these mentions—which are the result of plot twists, the speech or recollection of the narrator and the characters, and/or of the fact that this place forms the desired destination of the work's central characters and/or is strategically placed within the narrative sequence (the place where the story begins or ends; the place where the most dramatic scenes occur, etc.)—this place becomes the "symbolic place," a crossroads both on the work's reality-simulating map and on the spatial/metaphorical level, as a semantic prism through which the work's interpretive dimension is woven.

The symbolic place can be represented by one point in the story's reality-simulating landscape—for example, the battlefields where lie Prince Andrei in Tolstoy's *War and Peace* and the protagonist of Yoram Kaniuk's novella *Eagles*; the tree struck by lightning in Charlotte Brontë's *Jane Eyre*, and the mound that Hartmann climbs and falls from in S. Y. Agnon's *Another Face*. It can also be created from the web of interrelations among several secondary landscapes. Groups of writers who have had the same formative basic experiences and have fed on the same cultural traditions will often construct in their works similar interrelations between the same secondary landscapes.[25]

Furthermore, symbolic spaces are always anchored in a specific historical-cultural context. In other words, every symbolic place, every spatial focus for the energy flow of the work's force field, to use G. Zoran's suggestive definition,[26] is a new spatial creation, born from the merging of two positions. On the one hand, the symbolic place reflects the perception and importance of that place in the cultural map in relation to which the writer operated, and on the other hand, because of the innovative portrayal of that place in the specific work—and there is always innovation, even in the most epigonic reenactments—it challenges the common and conventional ways of perceiving and portraying that place in the given period, as well as the nature and makeup of the map archive of the landscape in which that place is contained.[27]

Mapu's relationship with the map archive of Eretz Israel—and it should be reemphasized that this is a region that gave rise to a vast archive of maps down the generations—is of particular importance, as he is the first to describe landscape "for its own sake," that is, as part of a clear descriptive and conceptual approach. This approach is sharply and lucidly expressed in the way the symbolic places in *The Love of Zion* are characterized.

In his previously mentioned essay on *The Love of Zion*, D. Miron refers in detail to the status and the importance of the "Bethlehem Scene," which appealed to several generations of readers. He breaks the poetic scene down to its components, while—and one is dependent on the other—wishing to answer the question of why Mapu chose the Bethlehem fields as a preferred object of description. In his answer, Miron examines this scene in two contexts: in the artistic context in terms of genre and school, and in the context of the national-historical metanarrative. With regard to the first context, he claims that the Bethlehem Scene follows a conventional format: "The love meeting between the nobleman's daughter and the shepherd (or vice versa) must, according to its traditional contexts in Romance literature, take place 'in nature.' 'The pleasant place' (*locus amoenus*, in the conventional terminology of the tradition of pastoral and Romance literature), the remote corner far from the 'tumult of the city,' 'from the city and the dead,' surrounded by grass and trees and steeped in natural tranquility, is the customary site for such a love meeting. It is not only the aesthetic associations habitually connected with it (beauty, youth, gentleness) that make it suitable for this role (they turn it into an ideal, stereotypical backdrop for love meetings of any kind), but also the social associations, implied by its remoteness from the center of the sociocultural life and by its 'naturalness.' 'The pleasant place' boasts a seemingly 'egalitarian' essence, beyond social classes. It is where the barriers between rich and poor fall, and the young lovers are equal before the law of nature."[28]

After determining the literary tradition on which Mapu relies in his Bethlehem scene, Miron presents this conclusion as a fact, claiming that it is "a fact that must be considered as one of the distinct signs that, despite the widespread mistakes about the matter (Mapu's conventional portrayal as a 'romantic'), in terms of both its ideas and its aesthetics, his work belongs to the realm of neoclassicism."[29] As for the national-historical context, Miron claims that Mapu chose Bethlehem because it is the cradle of the legitimate royal dynasty. As in the biblical story, in *The Love of Zion* too the direction of the kingship's development is from the rural area to the urban area, from Bethlehem to Jerusalem.

I would like to supplement Miron's important observations about the Bethlehem scene with a few remarks, in the spirit of C. D. Pocock's assertions,[30] about the ways in which places in literature are charged with symbolism. Here we go:

The central status of the Bethlehem scene stems also, and perhaps mainly, from the fact that it is a further reenactment, innovative for its time, of what Robert Alter calls a type scene. By the term type scene Alter refers to "certain prominent elements of repetitive compositional pattern that are a conscious convention."[31] These type scenes, Alter claims, "are dependent on the manipulation of a fixed constellation of predetermined motifs. [And] since biblical narrative characteristically catches its protagonists only at the critical and 'revealing' points in their lives, the biblical type scene occurs not in the rituals of daily existence but at the crucial junctures in the lives of the heroes, from conception and birth to betrothal to deathbed." And I would add that since in biblical narrative the protagonists' personal histories characteristically represent the history of the nation, the critical and revealing moments in the lives of these protagonists, dramatized in those type scenes, represent crucial junctures in the history of the people of Israel.

Alter lists the following biblical type scenes: the annunciation of the birth of the hero to his barren mother, the encounter with the future betrothed at the well, the epiphany in the field, the initiatory trial, danger in the desert and the discovery of a well or other source of sustenance, the testament of the dying hero.[32]

To our concern here—that is, the interrelation between human engineering and landscape conceptualization within a corpus whose ultimate aim is to reestablish the nation in an old-new country—the type scene of the encounter with the future betrothed at the well has enormous importance. For, in the Bible, this descriptive pattern framed the joining together, in ceremonial, symbolic, and fateful events, of the mothers and fathers of the nation or their representatives, on the one hand, and the promised land, on the other. Remember the encounter at the well in Aram Naharaim between Eliezer, Abraham's slave, and Rebecca, whom Eliezer brings to Eretz Israel to be Isaac's wife; Jacob and Rachel's encounter at the well, which ends with Jacob's return to Eretz Israel as the leader of a great tribe; and the encounter at the well between Moses and the daughters of Reuel the Midianite, which precedes the exodus from Egypt—the definitive metanarrative of the Israelite nation's reestablishment. Parallel biblical type scenes occur at places that are other sources of life, for example the encounter between Boaz and Ruth in the field in which Ruth gleans after the reapers.

The Hebrew writers from the Haskalah period on, whose aim was to create an old-new people in an old-new land, repeatedly reimagined such encounter scenes between their chosen couples at a place-life source in Eretz Israel (well, wheat field, vineyard, orchard, and so forth) that repeatedly conversed with the type scenes in the Bible.

The first detailed appearances of such conversations in modern Hebrew literature are the encounter scenes that Mapu created between his chosen couples in *The Love of Zion*, an overtly pseudo-biblical work. As already mentioned, over time Mapu's encounter scenes themselves became type scenes. Scores of Hebrew writers and artists followed them by creating hundreds of encounter scenes between a young man and a young woman near a place-life source in Eretz Israel. This practice had both an imitative, deferential, and admiring strain, and an ironic, sarcastic, or grotesque one.

The attitude of the imitating (portrayed) scene toward the imitated scene finds its expression on two levels: in the presence or absence of fixed elements of the type scene and in the way these elements are represented. The classical biblical scenes include the following elements: the couple, or the representative of one of them, who belong to the same people; a place-life source (well); animals (sheep and goats); a hostile/competing human element (local shepherds, etc.); a vector of desire—"Aliyah" to Eretz Israel. Modern writers from Mapu on subtracted from the classical biblical scene's collection of elements and added to it according to their worldview. In Mapu's Bethlehem scene, for instance, in the encounter between Tamar and Amnon, the well is replaced by a proper stream (with no extra-literary referent), which "enables" Amnon to cross it as he sinks "up to his neck" in his attempt to bridge the class gap ostensibly separating him from Tamar. In the parallel scene at Carmel, however, in the encounter between Teman and Peninah, there is no trace of such a stream, and naturally neither Teman nor Peninah are able to perform a parallel symbolic act of crossing.

Bethlehem's symbolic status in *The Love of Zion* also derives from the city's status in the book's specific spatial configuration. A systematic examination of this status is crucial for understanding Mapu's landscape conceptualization in the work under discussion, for as we shall see, a systematic analysis of the chronotopic plane in *The Love of Zion* suggests a more complex configuration than the one sketched out by Miron. In actual fact, this configuration features not one "pleasant place," but four: the Bethlehem fields, Carmel, Yoram's summer home on the Mount of Olives (which is handed over to his friend Yedidiah), and Yedidiah's *succa* (arbor) in the garden of his house in Jerusalem. Each of these four pleasant places plays an important role in the story's landscape conceptualization, and together, as a spatial whole, they reflect fundamental aspects of Mapu's worldview.

The pleasant places in Bethlehem and in Carmel are given a relatively peripheral status in *The Love of Zion*'s plot. These places are the scenes of the first encounters between the two central couples, and no more. A much more central status is given to the pleasant place on the Mount of Olives. This is the scene of some important events: the two pacts that dictate the development of the plot—between Yoram and Yedidiah and between Amnon and Tamar—as well as the book's concluding events, which fulfill and confirm the validity of the two pacts: the reunion of Yoram's family, and the quadruple wedding in the presence of Hadoram, which concludes the tale.

The fact that the Mount of Olives holds a more central status than Bethlehem and Carmel in the book's force field is consistent with what we saw earlier. Mapu prefers the private (human/secular, love) plotline—which unfolds in intimate spaces (the scenes on the Mount of Olives include two participants [Yoram and Yedidiah], three participants [Amnon, Tamar, and Teman], and at the most two families and one guest: the double family reunion at the end of the story)—over the collective (religious/traditional) plotline, some of whose events feature numerous people who are not related to the nuclear units of affiliation (the shepherds and the daughters of Zion in the Bethlehem fields, and the male and female vine growers in Carmel). As for Yedidiah's arbor, it can be seen as a mirror image, reflecting, inside Jerusalem, the large pleasant places that are outside Jerusalem.

Furthermore, a comparison between the novel's four pleasant places reveals a clear difference between, on the one hand, the Bethlehem fields, the Mount of Olives and the arbor in Yedidiah's garden—the pleasant places that are the sites of plot-driving encounters between Tamar and Amnon—and, on the other, Carmel, the pleasant place that is the site of the encounters between Teman and Peninah. Amnon and Tamar's meeting places are always invaded by a threatening element: a predatory/poisonous animal, representing intensified interrelations between Eros and Thanatos. This happens in Bethlehem, during the lovers' encounter across the stream, when there suddenly appears "a lion; his aspect was fearful; his hair stood up on his shoulders like bristles; his eyes were shooting fire; his jaws were yawning like an open grave; his tongue was as red as fire" (*LZ*, 43). And on the Mount of Olives, when during Tamar and Amnon's encounter they see "an ossifrage, with outspread wings and open beak, with iron-like claws protruding from behind him like spikes . . . chasing a beautiful dove." And also in Yedidiah's arbor, when Tamar almost drinks from the wine pitcher which Amnon supposedly spiked with snake "poison" (207).

The pleasant façade of these three places, designed to recall, as D. Miron remarks, a neoclassical garden, thus conceals a mighty power possessing two sides: an intense erotic side (the lion, the vulture, and the snake—potent masculine creatures, chasing after a beautiful feminine creature, Tamar herself, the dove as her fixed metaphorical metonym, and again Tamar) and a menacing thanatic side. These two sides are most clearly reflected in the figurative configuration of the encounter with the lion in the Bethlehem fields, which juxtaposes metaphors and metaphorical metonyms from the semantic fields of both death and Eros: the lion's aspect "was fearful," "his jaws were yawning like an open grave," and "his hair stood up on his shoulders like bristles." As for its tongue, which "was as red as fire"—it refers us to both mortal danger and erotic seduction.

On the other hand, Carmel, where Teman and Peninah meet, is a real pleasant place. The fearful lion that threatens Tamar's life and obliges Amnon to raise his bow, shoot an arrow, and kill him, is replaced by a pleasant deer.

The different characters of the animals that feature in the two courting scenes is in line with the different characters of another background element—the local bucolic culture. Both scenes take place in a Dionysian atmosphere, yet in Bethlehem, the shepherds' realm, it is a permissive secular atmosphere, whereas in the Carmel, a place of vineyards and wine that seems to invite bacchanalia, it is a religious atmosphere complete with a series of meticulously conducted rites and ceremonies. The different characters of the two sites—which invite comparison because, among other things, we are dealing with two sibling couples and the courting scenes take place at the same time—are explained by the different bio-erotic characters of the two couples: Tamar and Amnon are a libidinal couple, and Teman and Peninah are an anemic couple. This difference is manifested in all the areas of comparison: when comparing the brother and the sister in each pair of siblings, when comparing the development of the relationships of the two couples, and also—and here there is a deliberate deviation from the pattern in the analogous structure—when examining the triangle Tamar-Amnon-Teman (which has no parallel in the form of another triangle: for example, Teman-Tamar-Peninah) or, more precisely, Teman's relationship with Amnon.

The bio-erotic difference between Tamar and Teman is obvious. Tamar is a vibrant, erotic young woman who is resolutely opinionated. Teman, conversely, comes across as a gentle, honest and conscientious boy, but less energetic and possessing feeble erotic power and charisma. The difference between the two becomes clear when we compare their reactions in scores of similar events. Let me demonstrate: Tamar initiates her own move from the city to the countryside. In contrast, Teman is dragged into the rural adventure as if against his will. Mapu highlights these facts through the opening sentences of the two courting chapters. Chapter 4 (Tamar and Amnon's courting chapter) opens thus: "It was one of the first spring days, when the birds seemed to be calling to everyone, 'Come out! Come out! Enjoy this glorious day! See, the flowers are peeping forth and the trees are clothed all anew to greet you!' It was on just such a day as this that Tamar asked permission of her father to leave the tumult of the city and go into the country with the other maidens of Zion. Tamar's father, who always granted her slightest wish, sent her" (37), whereas chapter 5 (Peninah and Teman's courting chapter) opens thus: "When Teman arrived at Carmel [following his father's orders], he was gladly received by Sisry" (47). Similarly, Tamar refuses to accept the words of the grownups, who tell her that she must subjugate her personal grief over the loss of Amnon to the national grief—the fear that Jerusalem would fall. In other words, she refuses to accept the decorum. Teman behaves differently. We see this when he denies himself a meeting with his beloved Peninah—even after the plot has been exposed and the negative characters have been punished—choosing to obey his mother, who claims that this denial would benefit Peninah and Tamar, who fear for Amnon's safety.

There is also an obvious bio-erotic difference between the twins Peninah and Amnon. During most of the narrated time they seem to have an inferior class status. Peninah accepts her situation and obeys all her mother's subsequent instructions—including those that involve lies, disguise, and evasions. Amnon does all he can to break through the class barrier, beginning with the fact that despite telling the shepherds in Bethlehem not to desire the daughters of the Jerusalem aristocrats, particularly Tamar ("Oh, foolish lads, how dare you stare at this high-born lady! You would do well to look after your sheep and not aspire to one so far above you"), "notwithstanding this speech, Amnon stood gazing after the fair Tamar long after the other shepherds had gone back to their work" (38). He also tries to escape his supposed class inferiority through formal training. He links up with the prophets' sons hoping to learn the art of rhetoric from them, and later joins the King's army to train as a soldier. In order to achieve his goal he also risks his life: see his journey to Nineveh to save Hananeel—the only person who can rescue him from his lowly status.

The difference in character, temperament, and libidinal intensity between Amnon and Peninah on the one hand and Tamar and Teman on the other has a crucial influence on the development of the two couples' relationships. Tamar and Amnon's relationship begins with tremendous intensity and then undergoes great upheavals, as well as what looks like real shifts in emotional positions. Teman and Peninah's relationship begins with a much lesser intensity. It goes through upheavals as well, but these are less dramatic, and include no personal emotional shifts, not even on the surface.

The difference between these relationships can already be inferred from a comparison between the two courting scenes. Tamar and Amnon's courting scene follows the Taming of the Shrew pattern. As mentioned above, Tamar is the one who initiates the move to the countryside. Later, when she sees "the shepherd boy," "his locks . . . as black as the raven" and "his forehead . . . whiter than snow," and when she hears "how sweet is his voice" and sees that "he carries a bow and arrow" (40), she decides to approach him. Even though Macha, her maid, who also covets the "shepherd boy," explicitly associates approaching Amnon with the danger of "wild beasts" in the area.

The dialogue between Tamar and Amnon starts with a clear indication of Tamar's superiority. She asks Amnon to give her the "garland of roses," which he has just mentioned in a song sung to the accompaniment of the shepherds, those "Roses from the valley for the shepherd's crown, to put on the head of his beloved." On hearing the request (which triggers visible signs of protest on his handsome face), Amnon turns pale, responding modestly as befits the supposed class gap between the two: "If you will stoop to take anything from the hand of your servant, you are welcome to this garland." Tamar persists with her aggressive courting, demanding to learn the identity of Amnon's chosen wife, so she can "repay her for the flowers" that he had kept for her, and that she, Tamar, has taken from his hand. Amnon drops his eyes to the ground and says that he has not found his wife among all the tens of thousands of girls he has seen so far. Tamar welcomes the implied compliment, but detects in it a tint of arrogance, which it is not clear was really there. This is the starting point for an erotic repartee: "Tamar replied, 'Oh, lovely youth, you will seek your beloved among thousands and thy choice shall be more precious than ten thousand.'"

Tamar's challenging retort—left unanswered by Amnon—concludes their first encounter. The second encounter begins with a similar balance of power, but concludes differently. It starts when Tamar—who again ignores the danger of the wild beasts—sees Amnon across the stream, approaches him and shows him the garland of flowers in her hand: "Tamar at last broke the silence with these words: 'I am here, my dear, to pay you my debt'" (43). Amnon, aware of the class gap between them, replies, "You see, fair lady, the stream is between us and I cannot reach the garland." To which Tamar replies, "If your arm is short, mine is not." In other words, she declares her ability to compensate for Amnon's impotence. Here, however, the picture changes dramatically. A fearful lion emerges from among the bushes, and Tamar is gripped by "fright" and later falls "unconscious." This is precisely the moment in which Amnon's masculinity—that is, according to the text's implied norms, his superiority—is tested. Indeed, he quickly pulls himself together and shoots an arrow that pierces the heart of the lion, the animal falling dead just next to the unconscious Tamar. Now, after being "brave enough to fight with a lion" and seeing "Tamar lying in a swoon," Amnon's heart "melts," he leaves his herd, wades "neck deep" through the stream that separates them, revives Tamar with "his strong voice," tends to her, and soothes her.

At this moment—under the impression of the dramatic event—Tamar admits Amnon's masculinity/superiority: "Oh, God, worker of wonders, who can see life and death in the same breath and still live! As young and as frail as I am, I have seen both. Why should not my heart quiver within me? Here lies the lion. Oh, how fearful he is! His teeth are like swords; his eyes look as if he could devour me and crush me." The forceful Tamar, however, does not really change. In the following pages of this courting scene she quickly returns to her characteristic domineering, capricious stance. Amnon on his part also reverts to his old ways. He accepts the class hierarchy and submits to it again, if only outwardly.

The bio-erotic intensity of Tamar and Amnon's relationship is further underlined by the way it is reflected in the parallel relationship, Teman and Peninah's. Unlike Tamar, Teman does not initiate contact with Peninah once he meets her and is ravished by her looks—even though he is the masculine side in the couple. This contact happens by chance, as if it were forced on the pair. Teman goes on a hunting expedition, during which he comes across a "pleasant deer" that flees from him. At some stage Teman loses his way: "He walked on, not knowing whither to turn, whether to the right or to the left" (48). Then he too, like Amnon in the parallel scene, calls out in "his strong voice"—but whereas Amnon uses his voice to awaken his beloved, Teman tries to find his servants so they can rescue him from the wood's thicket. He continues to wander, lost, and then, "as he neared the rocks he saw something white in the distance, and hastening his steps toward it like a gazelle, he was surprised to see the same girl he had seen in Sisry's garden a few days before." Here a dialogue develops between the two—very different from the dialogue between Tamar and Amnon. Instead of a dialogue tinged with strong sexual and class tension, we get a dialogue that is a kind of comic reflection of its predecessor. It is a dialogue in which a young aristocrat is talking to a young woman from a lower class, one who not only does not try to protest against the unequal situation but even reinforces it. In fact, Peninah understands neither the noble boy's language (Teman speaks to her in images, which she deciphers literally), nor what he wants from her: "The girl, not grasping his meaning, was very much confused at his words," and again further down, "the girl looked at him perplexed, and not understanding his meaning" (49).

Teman and Peninah's courting scene contains another element that diffuses its potential for bio-erotic intensity. I am referring to the insinuation about Teman's unclear sexual identity, implied by the use of animal images that Mapu attaches to Peninah on the one hand and Teman on the other. Peninah is linked in our minds with the deer, since Teman follows the deer—and finds her. The link between Peninah and the deer is also made on the linguistic level. The deer "succeeded in reaching the bushes" (48), and Peninah is seen "among the fig trees." This link, which hints at a "problematic" sexuality, since the deer is recognized here first of all by its "big horns,"[33] is reinforced by the idiom with which Mapu chose to characterize Teman as he hurries to check who it is wearing something white in the distance: "and hastening his steps toward it *like a gazelle*" (48, emphasis mine).

Teman's implied femininity becomes overt in his relationship with Amnon. It is an erotic relationship that, in its restraint, recalls the relationship between Jonathan and David. The link is suggested by the words Teman says to Amnon when they are alone in his father's house, after he tells him about the love he has lost, that is, Peninah: "This you shall know—that my love for you is a recompense for that love which escaped me. Let our hearts be united" (85). It is also implied by Teman's invitation to Amnon to go for a walk together on the

Mount of Olives (a known meeting place for lovers [96] and a walk that in the end is taken in a threesome: Amnon, Tamar, and Teman), as well as by Teman's enthusiastic reactions to everything Amnon does—in speech and in physical gestures ("'Behold!' cried Teman enthusiastically, 'Behold, I have heard and seen many things, but never such a sweet song as this!'" [102]).

With Tamar, Amnon, Peninah, and Teman's final union on the Mount of Olives, the novel's magical plot is completed. Hananeel's dream is realized, and the disturbed balance of the Romance is reestablished. Yet now we know a lot more about how Mapu sees the world and the people in it, thanks to all the existential landscapes that have been rejected and the pairing options that have been excluded, and thanks also, of course, to all the existential landscapes that have been endorsed and the pairing option that is presented as the best: the biblical Amnon and Tamar option, but in a very different version—the pairing of an energetic, full-of-libido, and courageous, if somewhat capricious, young woman from a respected urban family, with a man from a no-less-respected urban family, but who has spent his formative educational period in nature's bosom.

Mapu, then, created a text that may be called pioneering but can hardly be called revolutionary, despite all the revolutionary instances I have pointed out, which are complemented by revolutionary turns on the level of language; linguistic turns centering—as T. Cohen has shown[34]—on Mapu's use of idioms which in the Bible are employed to describe God or to describe sites and landscapes in Eretz Israel.

Mapu's conservative side is also reflected in his treatment of two other major issues, which are interlinked and intertwined: man's ability to change and the worldview that emerges from the structure of the narrative plot. Mapu wrote a text that deals with history, but it is a mythical history, or perhaps the twilight zone between myth and history. Genre-wise, his preference for the private plotline (the love axis) over the collective plotline (the axis of events on the national plane) indicates a preference for the Romance over the historical novel. This is a very significant generic decision, for it means choosing a deterministic pattern—one that is dictated by destiny and cannot be changed, only fulfilled. Such a pattern raises a real question, which I already hinted at, about classifying *The Love of Zion* as part of Zionist Hebrew literature, which is marked, as we know, by the assumption that the Jewish individual is the master of his own life and is able to determine his future.

Mapu's conservative side is also reflected in his approach to the characters and in the way he portrays the relationships between them. The characters' nature is determined at birth and never changes. In this, they resemble the characters in the ancient Greek romances brilliantly analyzed by Bakhtin,[35] as well as characters in later romances, and differ fundamentally from the characters in modern European literature, which are predicated on man's ability to change and develop—an ability that underpins, as Franco Moretti has shown,[36] the typical genre of modernity, the bildungsroman. Mapu is not interested at all in the psychology of the individual, much less in tracking the changes in this psychology. For him, the individual's psyche, just like the "nation's psyche," is first and foremost the site of a mighty battle between great and contradicting forces and drives, a battle that is fought with different combinations and different intensities in different people and different nations.

The Cutting Up of the Monster and the Revival of the Nation

Mapu's evident conservatism brings us back to the beginning of our discussion from a different angle. Now the question reasserts itself: What was the source of *The Love of Zion*'s power over its historical readers? How can we explain the tremendous impact this "little book" had on so many human beings? Can that which enchanted scores of readers over several generations be summed up by the book's artistic merit—the landscape descriptions, so fresh for their time, the reconstruction of the golden age of the Hebrew nation, or the noblemen and women's graceful love affairs?

I believe it cannot. The testimonies about "the great revolution that this little book brought . . . anywhere it arrived," about the fact that "in every corner it reached it was received as the harbinger of a new gospel" and that "everyone felt, that [this was] a Hebrew book conceived and born in holiness" and "that its influence on the readers resembled the influence of Holy Books" cannot be explained only by the enthusiasm over its literary quality, especially since this quality had evaporated long before the experience of being enchanted by it faded.

In my view the intense response of *The Love of Zion*'s historical addressees stemmed from a different source, from the revolutionary move that Mapu performed but carefully concealed, so that generations of critics failed to note it: positing a "primitive" metanarrative—foreign to the Jewish tradition—as a potential mytho-historical foundation for the revived Hebrew nation.

Mapu was indeed a social conservative, perhaps because this was his character or perhaps because he was well acquainted with the character of the Jewish community of his time for which social mobility could pose a danger—an assumption also held by subsequent great Jewish writers, for example, Chaim Nachman Bialik, as can be seen in several of his works, including the great poem "Metei Midbar" (The Dead of the Desert) and his first story, "Arie Ba'al Guf"

(Brawny Arie). Mapu's social conservatism, however, did not prevent him—and in this Bialik also resembles him, as do less conservative writers such as David Frishman, Y. L. Peretz, and Micha Josef Berdichevsky—from being fascinated by mythical sources, the connection with which, he felt, could add vitality to his community, which in his eyes was in a bad state of stagnation, and lead it toward a new beginning.

In this sense, the Romance served him as the perfect tool because the world of the Romance is situated in the twilight zone between the mythical and the historical—the ultimate creative space for new communities and new normative systems; and also because it is a genre based on an aesthetic mechanism that leads to an abstraction and distancing of idiosyncratic features—that is, features that highlight the differences between one person and another—thus giving an outlet to what Gillian Beer called "the particular [and inherently subversive] desires,"[37] which the conservative/dominant forces in the community do not allow a free, uncensored outlet. In other words, I wish to argue that Mapu's revolutionary energy, which he did not dare or wish to express on the sociohistorical level, was expressed—through features special to the Romance—differently: by bypassing history.

I have already mentioned the role of the animals as Tamar and Amnon's metaphorical representations. The animals reflect and intensify the bio-erotic tension between the members of the chosen couple, who are charged with preserving the race and improving it, as well as renewing an establishment facing atrophy and extinction.[38] However—and here we shift to the novel's mythical axis—the animals in *The Love of Zion* have another role.

Dan Miron wonderfully traced what he called "the polyphony of the flowery phrase" in Mapu,[39] those shards of biblical verses that Mapu generously scatters around his text and that Miron reassembles to form an impressive mosaic—including, and especially, in the context of our discussion here, the fragmentary allusions to the animal world. Miron devotes much attention to the dove, the lion, and the vulture, but barely discusses the snake, which, or at least the poison it produces, "cobra venom" (*LZ*, 207),[40] has a crucial role in portraying Tamar and Amnon's relationship. Moreover, in keeping with his aesthetic approach, in his interpretation of Mapu's art of flowery phrases Miron emphasizes the uniting function, that is, the way in which the patching together of the shards of verses creates meaning. I wish to do the opposite: I wish to explore the meaning of the fact that Mapu alludes to one entity—a monster—and then cuts it up.

Miron highlights the link that connects the predatory animals that take part in the two first dramatic encounter scenes between Amnon and Tamar. This link is created in terms of place—places that are outside the "tumult of the city" (the Bethlehem fields and the Mount of Olives); in terms of time—the encounters are separated by exactly one year; and in terms of the way the two predatory animals are described: "The youths see on the mountain 'an ossifrage, with outspread wings and open beak, with iron-like claws protruding from behind him like spikes'"; "a vulture which," Miron adds, "is a clear extension of the lion, whose jaws are also 'yawning like an open grave' and whose hair stands up 'like bristles,' [and who also] represents the invasion of 'the pleasant place' by wild, predatory nature."[41]

Miron also leads us—and this time unintentionally—to contemplate the link between the lion and the vulture and a third poisonous animal that takes part in another dramatic scene. It is the scene following which Tamar and Amnon part for good, at least as they understand it, and which climaxes in the moment when Zimri offers Tamar, ostensibly on behalf of Amnon, the wine pitcher spiked with the "cobra venom" that is supposedly meant to kill her.

Miron links this encounter scene between Amnon and Tamar—which includes a cobra snake, a typical representative of wild nature invading the "pleasant place" (here, the garden of Tamar's house in the heart of Jerusalem)—with previous encounter scenes between the two that follow the same format when he analyzes the second scene: the vulture's pursuit of the dove and the eagle that comes to the dove's rescue. In this context Miron claims, justifiably, that "the whole scene is clearly based on the midrash of Shir ha-Shirim Rabbah,[42] relating to verse 14 in chapter 2 of *Song of Songs*: 'My dove in the clefts of the rock, in the hiding places on the mountainside' . . . [a midrash that includes the following allegorical story]: Rabbi Ishmael teaches us the following: When the nation of Israel left Egypt, what were they like? They resembled a dove fleeing from a hawk into a crevice where it sees a nestling snake. It entered but could not go any further because the snake was still nestling. It also could not go back, because of the hawk outside. What did the dove do? It started screaming and flashing its wings so that the owner of the dovecote would come and save it. This is what Israel looked like on the seashore.'" The midrashic story from *Song of Songs* has three meanings relevant to our discussion. First, it reinforces the connection between the story of *The Love of Zion*'s protagonists and the collective story of the people of Israel. The protagonists' trouble—and in particular, as Miron points out, that of Tamar, who resembles the dove—is identified with the particular historical trouble of the people of Israel: Sennacherib's siege of Jerusalem. Second, through the allusion to the midrashic story, we learn that Mapu is not interested in another reenactment of the metanarrative that can be summed up by the verse "In every generation they rise up against us to destroy us. And The Holy One, blessed be He, delivers us from their hands"—the hands of Pharaoh, Nebuchadnezzar, Titus and the like—but rather in describing a mytho-historical narrative whose importance parallels in his eyes that of the narrative to which the midrashic story alludes. I am referring to the Exodus from Egypt: the ultimate foundational narrative of the people of Israel, in the course of which they turn from a people of slaves into a free people meriting national independence and their own land.[43]

The midrashic story has another explanatory function. It highlights and homes in on the additional and most important role that the wild animals have in Mapu's pioneering work: connecting the imaginary community that Mapu creates to the mythical plane. The animal parable in Mapu's story—unlike the animal parable in the midrashic story on which it is based—is disassembled and told in three separate scenes. The scenes, as can be learned from the scores of essays and articles by scholars and critics who have tried to prove the work's unity,[44] are linked through dozens of interconnections—but what intrigues me is precisely the unequivocal fact that Mapu chose to separate those scenes, and sharply so. The separation of these three bodies of description, which are linked by dozens of threads, is so decisive and striking that the obvious assumption is that this is one descriptive body that belonged to one imaginary entity that has been cut up into three parts.

If we think of the three scenes' figurative, zoological fabric in this way, a fascinating picture emerges. Before being broken up into three separate creatures, the lion, the vulture, and the snake were one creature. This monstrous creature was as spectacular as it was terrifying: an imaginary creature the likes of which are known from the mythologies of various peoples—possessing the body of a lion, the wings of a bird, and a tail that is a snake.[45]

An essential characteristic of this creature—the one that makes it monstrous—is its hybridity. Its hybrid quality, the fact that it belongs to several zoological classes at once and yet to none, makes it—in all mythologies, including the modern ones[46]—the representative of the chaos that preceded the establishment of any cosmic or social order. Another essential characteristic of these monsters is the fusion of great creative and destructive powers—powers that always have a colossal range of influence, anchored, on the descriptive plane, in the fact that they are enormous creatures and also, and especially, creatures that are reptile, mammal, and bird all wrapped up in one—and often it is the king of the reptiles (crocodile, snake), the king of the mammals (lion, ox), and the king of the birds (eagle, vulture) united in one figure. Some of the monsters also feature, in addition to their zoological hybridity, a combination of abilities partly associated with human or superhuman entities—a typical example is the dragon's ability to produce fire; an ability that, as we learned from Gaston Bachelard, was seen in the history of human culture as both material and immaterial and as one of the most notable manifestations, both in nature itself and in the human imagination, of the fascinating, menacing combination of tremendous creative powers on the one hand, and terrible destructive powers on the other.[47]

Two questions suggest themselves here: a) Why does Mapu need a monster, and b) Why did he cut it in three? The answer to both questions is that Mapu performed a literary rite parallel to the rites that appear in many "primitive" myths, rites that describe the creation of a new existential order through the rending apart of a primeval entity that potentially contains all the ingredients of the new existential order, but in an amorphous, chaotic form—in an all-embracing and limitless unity.

Many creation myths, and there are hundreds of variations, unfold in the same way: one of the "young" gods, signifying the new order, fights an all-embracive primeval entity, slays it, tears its body to pieces, scatters its parts in a limitless expanse, and thus the world with its different components is created. Sometimes the creation of the world occurs as if of its own accord after the act of tearing, and sometimes the act of tearing is also an act of insemination that creates the world.[48] It will suffice, I believe, to mention here only a few creation myths in which this sequence unfolds. In the Egyptian creation myth, according to some versions, Set murders his brother Osiris, cuts his divine corpse into pieces and buries them in various sites all across Egypt. Here the cutting up of the corpse is likened to the annual harvest and threshing of the wheat and the barley, and with the growth of the new crop, Osiris is resurrected, and the whole cycle begins again. In the Babylonian myth, Marduk is chosen to eliminate Tiamat, the ocean of salt water. He slays her and cuts her body in two: one half creates the sky, the other the earth. In the Ugaritic myth, Ba'al kills Yam (also called "river," "dragon," "serpent," and "leviathan"), who like Tiamat represents raging chaotic forces, rends him to pieces, and scatters his remains—thus proving that he is able to dominate the oceanic entity, prevent flooding, and regulate the rainfall, so that there is no overflowing and the agricultural land is watered in the correct measure. I shall also mention Purusha, the primordial creature or the cosmic personality, whose cut up body, according to an Indian hymn, goes on to form the universe's entities. Also, of course, there is Quetzalcoatl, the poetic and fascinating god who symbolizes the eternal combination of the forces of death with the forces of life, known as the "feathered serpent" (combining a reptile and a bird), who burns himself to death in the Gulf of Mexico. As birds fly out of the flames, his heart can be seen shooting up into the sky to become the planet Venus, the morning star.

In Mapu's text, as in the ancient creation texts, the act of cutting the monster to pieces signifies the end of a chaotic, oceanic space—an all-embracive and limitless space with no inner demarcations, according to the Jungian interpretation—and the beginning of a new existential and social order. This order comprises two main elements: a renewed settlement in an old-new land, and an act of coupling between a man and a woman. These two human acts—considered, as Mircea Eliade shows,[49] in different and distant cultures as equivalent to an act of creation—are supposed to coincide, thus ensuring the harmony between man and the world, that is, the only option that ensures survival and continuity. In other words, cutting the monstrous hybrid creature to pieces, settling the land, and crossbreeding the representatives of the two sexes, man and woman (from the same community and/or from different communities), are symbolic acts that are inextricable from one another.

The connection made in *The Love of Zion* between the imaginary act of settling the new homeland, the cutting up of the monster, and the moments of union between the chosen young couple, which take place in nature or in places that simulate nature, and particularly in the spring—this complex connection strongly suggests an intention to fashion a "primitive"-modern creation myth. However, there is a significant difference between Mapu's move and the move made by "primitive" narrators: Mapu cuts up his three-person monster through literary fragmentation and only then ensures the eradication of each of its components. First Amnon kills the lion, then the eagle kills the vulture, and finally Azrikam kills Zimri, while Teman clearly spells out what the latter represents: "'Oh, Zimri,' exclaimed Teman, 'You are still gazing at me, oh, you poisonous reptile! Shortly . . . your serpent tongue will become dry in your throat, and you will cease hissing, like the snake that you are!'" (*LZ*, 225)

Moreover, the midrashic story that Mapu's text alludes to highlights and homes in on the role of the predatory animals in *The Love of Zion* from another direction. In the midrashic story, the allegorical relation is clear as day: the dove is the people of Israel, the hawk and the snake are the enemies of Israel (Pharaoh and Co.), and the dovecote owner is the Holy One, who delivers us from their hands. In Mapu the allegorical meaning of the animal story is much more complicated, interesting, and subversive—a subversiveness for which the Romance serves as the perfect conduit.

Had Mapu stopped at the second animal scene—at the Mount of Olives—he would not have diverged from the path of the *Song of Songs* midrash, that is, from the traditional, conventional zoologization of the people of Israel's relationship with their god. Then it would have been possible to interpret the drama among the birds—the dove, the vulture, and the eagle—as did all the critics who addressed this scene, as an allegory of the relationship between the people of

Israel (the dove/Tamar), those who try to harm them (the vulture/Azrikam), and their savior (the eagle/the Holy One). However, as I have tried to show, this scene is merely one piece torn from a larger descriptive body, and therefore the allegorical meaning suggested by it in isolation should be posited as an option that, as far as I can judge, has an inferior status compared to the "primitive" option suggested by the assembling together, and especially by the tearing apart, of the literary organs seemingly comprising an ancient, primeval descriptive body, from which they have been torn to be placed in the foundational story before us.

2

Altneuland,
Theodor Herzl, 1902
Shall These Dry Bones Live

The plan is the generator.
Without a plan, you have lack of order and willfulness.
The plan holds in itself the essence of sensation.
The great problems of tomorrow, dictated by collective necessities,
put the question of "plan" in a new form.
Modern life demands, and is waiting for, a new kind of plan,
both for the house and the city.

—LE CORBUSIER, *Towards a New Architecture*

If You Will It, It Is No Dream

Of all the literary texts closely examined in this book, *Altneuland* is the clearest case of a sociocultural foundational text and thus also the one whose aesthetic merit stands in the most overt and tough competition with its ideological importance.

Altneuland's foundational intentionality can already be detected in its paratext: in the title, the epigraph, and the epilogue. A perusal of these three units, designed to direct the readers' positions before they immerse themselves in the fictional world and after they leave it, clarifies the story's distinctly conative nature: the fact that it is a text that tries to stir the readers by means of a certain literary configuration (genre, plot structure, rhetorical web, etc.) to do real things in the world.

Herzl's intention of writing a foundational text is suggested by some explicit words he wrote in his diary and in letters to various addressees, by the striking similarities between this book and his programmatic book *The Jewish State*,[1] and by the literary genre he chose: the utopian novel. For, as Rachel Elboim Dror argues, the utopian novel always includes a biting social critique.[2] Yet alongside the critique of the present, it also shows a belief in man's ability to build a new and improved social order. "This," as she says, "is a heroic attempt to perform comprehensive and total social engineering."[3]

Herzl predicted that the book would have a great impact, and he was not mistaken. News of the book spread to all the Jewish communities, and it was read, within a very short period, by hundreds of thousands of people. By 1918 six German editions had been printed, and it was translated into numerous languages.[4] Many of its immediate readers—like *The Love of Zion*'s immediate readers—saw it as a holy book, a modern extension of the Bible. Some of them saw Herzl as a messiah, or at least a prophet, and reacted to what happened to him accordingly. Here is a typical testimony: "My father saw Dr. Herzl as the embodiment of the prophets of Israel rising anew toward complete salvation . . . and when Dr. Herzl passed away, profound grief descended on my father and on the entire household. Dr. Herzl's picture was hung in our house and my father used to stand and look at it with deep sorrow in his eyes."[5]

The book was also the focus of a strong debate that quickly turned into the "hot topic" of Jewish public life in the first decade of the twentieth century. Herzl's most consistent and resolute opponent was Ahad Ha'am, who railed against the detachment of Herzl's vision, and Herzl himself, from Jewish culture, and mocked the book's universalist European characteristics, which originated, in his opinion, in a bad tendency for assimilation, an auto-antisemitic syndrome, and a shameful wish to ingratiate himself with the gentiles. Here are selected excerpts from Ahad Ha'am's criticism:

> Because really there is no trace here of the national spirit specific to an ancient people and it is merely an imitation, testifying to a slavishness of spirit and a belittling of the self, as if the Jews were spineless people, who have only recently tasted the flavor of culture and are ready to absorb anything like a sponge, with no previous historical influence. ("Crime and Punishment," 321)

> Everywhere . . . European people, European customs and European inventions. No special "Jewish" character. The mimicry of monkeys without their own national quality, and the smell of "slavery within freedom," characteristic of the Western exile, arises from every direction. ("Altneuland," 319–20)

> *Altneuland*'s tolerance is nothing but deference to "yesterday's master," *and an overt attempt to show him* at every step that we are always ready and willing to make room for him at the top, to drag him toward the ins and outs of our national and social life, even in places where he has no inner connection with this life whatsoever. ("Crime and Punishment," 321–22; emphasis in the original)

And finally, with regard to the idyllic relations Herzl predicts between the Arab population of Palestine and the Jewish immigrants:

> What a lovely idyll! Only it is a little difficult to understand how the new society managed to find enough land for all the millions of Israelites who returned from their exile, if all the land that the Arabs used to cultivate, that is, most of the fertile land in Eretz Israel, still remained in their hands "and nothing was taken from them." ("Altneuland," 317)

Herzl's honor was avenged by Max Nordau, who responded to Ahad Ha'am by presenting him as a provincial man, alien to the entire Western culture, and as an "Old Jew" unable to throw off the shackles of the ghetto. He contests Ahad Ha'am's central arguments one by one, as Ahad Ha'am did with Herzl's main ideas, and tries to refute them, spicing his reasoning with very strong derogatory characterizations (for example, "any moron [can] pretend to be a supreme authority";[6] Ahad Ha'am's words are plagued with "childishness . . . malicious prying"; they are "a nonsense, whose pretentious worthlessness is undefinable," and so on), which attest to the intensity of the argument that emerged in the wake of the book's publication.

As for the content, here are three central quotes from Nordau's response.

ON EUROPEANNESS: "It is true: 'Altneuland' is a European enclave within Asia. Here Herzl showed precisely what we want and what we are aiming for. We want the Jewish people, once liberated and reunited, to continue being a civilized nation, in so far as it has achieved it, and become a civilized nation in so far as it has not yet achieved it . . . The Jewish people will develop its specific essence as part of Western civilization as a whole, like any other civilized nation, but not outside it, not within a wild, civilization-hating Asianness, as Ahad Ha'am seems to wish" (ibid., 112–13).

ON TOLERANCE: "Ahad Ha'am does not want tolerance. The foreigners should perhaps be killed, or, at the very least, driven out, as in Sodom and Gomorrah. The idea of tolerance fills him with disgust . . . Such hatred might have filled us with repugnance, but it is overcome by our feeling of compassion. We feel compassion for the man who is unable to throw off the shackles of the ghetto. The concept of freedom is incomprehensible to him" (ibid., 113–14).

AND ON ZIONISM: "Ahad Ha'am is one of Zionism's sworn enemies. True, he fights it differently than those who crave assimilation, who aspire for the complete disappearance of Judaism; differently than the devout stuck-in-the-muds, who claim that it is a sin to precipitate matters; but he attacks it with a rage no slighter than theirs, and with less honesty. For he dares to present himself as a

Zionist and at the same time talk about the only Zionism that exists with a carefully calculated show of contempt, as 'that Zionism,' 'political Zionism'" (ibid., 115–16).

The debate between Ahad Ha'am and Max Nordau—joined in a later stage by further prominent personalities, including Chaim Weizmann and M. J. Berdichevsky on Ahad Ha'am's side, and Ze'ev Jabotinsky on Herzl and Nordau's side[7]—revealed what Herzl tried to play down, hide, or at least attenuate in his novel's plot: the voices heralding a culture war between the representatives of the eastern European Jewish elite and the representatives of the central European Jewish elite. This discourse, with its attendant emotional baggage—and I shall return to this issue later on—will have fascinating sequels in Jewish and Hebrew literature all through the twentieth century.

The Diaspora—The "Elend" and the "Old-New Land"

The tension between the "place" and the "Place" was expressed by Mapu, on *The Love of Zion*'s topographic plane, as the tension between the "background map," which reflects the prevalent landscape conceptualization of his time, and the "foreground map," which amends the "background map" and presents his own landscape conceptualization, anchored in both neoclassical and romantic sources. Herzl expressed the tension between the place and the Place, on *Altneuland*'s topographic plane by the same method, but he relied on other sources—Haskalah and colonialist sources on the one hand, and romantic, anti-semitic sources on the other—sources whose interrelations create a very different landscape conceptualization.

The division between the background map and the foreground map in *Altneuland* is clearer than in *The Love of Zion*, and this is because *The Love of Zion* is a text written first and foremost with artistic intentions, whereas *Altneuland* was written first and foremost with ideological intentions. Herzl wrote a novel because he thought—like many writers of utopias who were influenced by the Haskalah writers—that it was an attractive and appealing medium that would help him persuade the readers to believe in his vision and in the steps that need to be taken in order to realize it.

Altneuland's background map, the one that reflects the worldview of Herzl's contemporaries, is presented in the novel as a "narrative past." The foreground map, the one that reflects Herzl's new landscape conceptualization, is anchored in the "historical future" (the year 1923), presented in the novel as a "narrative present."

The novel's division on the time-space level is clearly paralleled by its graphic/thematic organization. The novel is divided into five books: the plot of the first book is set in 1902, in Vienna and in Eretz Israel. The plots in the other four books are set in 1923, in Eretz Israel. The novel's two large sections are therefore separated by twenty years. As we find out in the second part, this period (which forms a prolepsis—a fairly common plot pattern, for obvious reasons, in some utopian novels) includes the activity that has enabled the transition from the narrative past to the narrative present; and in my terminology, the activity that has enabled the transition from the background map (the topographic actualization of the worldview that was prevalent in Herzl's time) to the foreground map (the topographic actualization of the new worldview that Herzl offers his readers). The background map, which Herzl draws in the novel's first book, is divided into two secondary maps: the "Jewish map" of central and eastern Europe in the beginning of the century, represented here by the "map of Vienna," and the map of human existence in Eretz Israel at the same time. The Jewish Vienna-Europe is portrayed here as an almost hopeless region. Herzl's map of the city features four representative places—three of them are utterly depressing and dispiriting. The fourth, which is the most impoverished and miserable, holds some hope for the future.

The first place is the Café Birkenreis in Vienna's Alsergrund district. This is the place that, at the beginning of the book, represents Dr. Friedrich Loewenberg, one of the novel's two main protagonists. It is where we are first introduced to him, as well as where the story begins: "Ever since his student days he [Friedrich] had been coming there, appearing every afternoon at five o'clock with bureaucratic punctuality."[8] He "would seat himself at the round reading table, drink his coffee, and read the papers with which the waiter plied him. And when he had finished with the dailies and the weeklies, the comic sheets and the professional magazines—this never consumed less than an hour and a half—there were chats with friends or solitary musings."

The fact that Friedrich is portrayed in a café is not coincidental. It points to the fact that this "Educated, Desperate Young Man" (as in the title of the novel's first part), like the entire human group he represents, is a homeless creature in every sense. He has no place of his own (he is never described in his place of residence), he has no family ties, he is disconnected from his heritage (he is almost completely assimilated), and he has no real deep emotional bond with anyone. Herzl, who has a considerable satirical talent, tinges Friedrich's description at the café with ironic overtones. For example, he creates a semantic clash between the factual remark that Friedrich has been coming to this café for years, since he was a student, and the image "with bureaucratic punctuality" (*ONL*, 3), which he attaches to the factual remark that he always gets there at five. This semantic clash highlights the—ironic—lack of correspondence between the fact that this is a man who has been out of work for many years and his punctuality.

We see here, however, not only irony but also, and perhaps mainly, pathos. For this is a young, twenty-three-year-old young man, who suffers from "an incurable disease"—the disease of the end of the nineteenth century—Spleen. This disease, which is already reported by the narrator in his opening sentence ("Sunk in deep melancholy, Dr. Friedrich Loewenberg sat"), is reflected in the few details that represent the scene of events (the café) and in the description of Friedrich's behavior. The waiter who has been loyally plying him with newspapers for many years is described as "sickly, pale" and as greeting Friedrich "submissively" and without a word. As for his friendly chats, it turns out that these belong in the past, and "now only dreams were left." This is because one of his two friends committed suicide, and the other died of yellow fever in Brazil. Thus, "for several months past Friedrich had been sitting alone at their old table. Now, having worked through to the bottom of the pile of newspapers, he sat staring straight ahead without seeking out someone to talk to. He felt too tired to make new acquaintances, as if he were not a young man of twenty-three, but a gray-beard who had all too often parted with cherished friends" (3).

The second place in Herzl's Vienna that receives literary treatment is the Loeffler household: "The Loeffler family lived on the second floor of a large house on Gonzaga Street, the ground floor being occupied by the cloth firm of Moritz Loeffler & Co." (10). The Loefflers' household is a typical nouveau riche Jewish Viennese home. We learn about the nature of the household and its residents at the time of a festive event, whose content and style serve to testify to the nature of this privileged social group. This is the ceremony announcing the engagement of Ernestina, the daughter of Mr. Moritz Loeffler from Vienna, the owner of the cloth firm Moritz Loeffler & Co., and Mr. Leopold Weinberger from Bruenn, the son of Mr. Samuel Weinberger, the owner of the fabric firm Samuel Weinberger and Sons. This event, in which fabric combines with fabric and money with money, is described in a satirical, sarcastic fashion. The invited crowd is described as a group of philistines: hedonistic, smug, indifferent to their surroundings, and insensitive. The only exception, which proves the rule, is Dr. Weiss, a rabbi from a small Moravian town, who turns out to be a Zionist: a fact that leads to a flood of mocking reactions, sarcastic remarks, jokes, and bursts of laughter from "the Viennese." The only person who does not join in the general ridiculing of Dr. Weiss and his Zionism is Friedrich. Both because he "was indignant at the brutal and unseemly merriment at the old man's expense" (15), and, probably mainly, because he finds himself in a very awkward situation. He has been invited to an event in which he has a personal interest but about which he had no inkling in advance. He is in love with Ernestina, has met with her several times, and has even spent his measly funds on these meetings. And now he finds himself in her engagement ceremony to another man—a man that he feels is unworthy of being her partner. This is because, in his view, she is "slender, graceful ... enchanting" (10), whereas Mr. Weinberger "had a decided squint and very damp palms." After the ceremony at the Loefflers', Friedrich feels that he must "get away, far away, from all these people ... [and feels] superfluous in the room—in the city, in the whole world" (17–18).

The third place that receives literary treatment in Herzl's Vienna is "a certain fashionable hotel on the Ringstrasse" (28). Here, in "a salon on the first floor," Friedrich meets a rich man named Kingscourt, a sworn misanthrope, who has decided to withdraw from the human world to a remote island, and who wants, as he tells Friedrich, "to take a companion back with me—so that I shall not unlearn human speech, and so that there may be someone by me to close my eyes when I die" (31–32).

The hotel, the rich man Kingscourt's metonymic space, has a parallel status to that of the café, Friedrich's metonymic space. These are two places (one rich and showy, the other more modest) that signify a temporary home with temporary guests who are similarly homeless and therefore suited to each other. The suitability of Friedrich—and in fact, as we shall see below, of Friedrich as Herzl's representative—and Kingscourt also pertains to other characteristics of the latter; characteristics we mostly learn about from his words and actions during their first meeting at the hotel. Kingscourt is "a tall and broad-shouldered man," "in his fifties. His full beard was streaked with gray, his thick brown hair interlaced with silver threads that already shimmered white at the temples. He puffed slowly at a thick cigar" (28). The man blessed with this impressive masculine appearance has a remarkable biography: he was born not as Kingscourt, but as Koenigshoff. He is a Prussian aristocrat. He was an officer in the army. Later he emigrated to America, where in twenty years of hard work as an industrialist he made a fortune. Like Friedrich, Kingscourt was also betrayed by a woman and considered killing himself: in America he took in a poor woman and married her, but she preferred his young nephew, whom Kingscourt had also taken into his home, and who also behaved ungratefully. At that stage Kingscourt collapsed, deciding "to end the shabby comedy of my life with a bullet" (30). However, he changed his mind, and decided to become a recluse on a desert island with a companion who had also had enough of life. And indeed, the gentlemen's agreement between the two—Adalbert von Koeningshoff, the rich Prussian aristocrat, and Doctor Friedrich Loewenberg, the poor Jewish intellectual—is

THEODOR HERZL, *Altneuland* (1902)

based on the decision that "You will be dead to [the world], and it will have gone under—as far as you are concerned" (32).

Between Kingscourt's hotel and Friedrich's café there are thus the same reciprocal relations of difference and complementariness that exist between Kingscourt and Friedrich themselves. On the other hand, between the Loeffler family's home, its residents, and its guests, and the home of the Littwak family, the fourth representative site in Vienna, there are relations of complete opposites. The Loefflers' house is full of every luxury, but they have no future. Unlike them, the Littwaks live in a dreary rented room on the fifth floor on Brigittenauer Laende, but they have a future. Their future lies in their children—David and Miriam—who, like Ernestina, symbolize the generation succeeding the "Desert Generation." But Ernestina belongs to the new generation only biologically, whereas David and Miriam also belong to this generation ideologically. The Loeffler family and its associates despise Zionism. David and his household become avid Zionists. The Loeffler family only believes in money; education interests them, if at all, only as a means of getting capital. The Littwak family—led by the young David—believes in diligence, initiative, persistence, and chiefly education. Eventually, the representatives of both families arrive in Palestine, but Ernestina and her circle become parasites, whereas the Littwaks take part in the building of the new society and achieve great things.

The stark contrast between the Loefflers and the Littwaks is based on a variable that has major importance in Herzl's worldview. The Loeffler family is an assimilated Jewish Viennese family. The Littwak family, as its name suggests, is an Ostjuden family that has recently arrived in Vienna. Friedrich, who donates all his money (received as an advance from Kingscourt) to the family patriarch (a peddler whose wares no one wants but who insists on giving them in return for a cash donation because "I am no beggar" [21]), hears his story: "We came here from Galicia. In Cracow we lived in one room with three other families. We had no source of livelihood. Things can become no worse, I thought, and came here with my wife and children. Here it is no worse; neither is it better" (22).

The Littwaks' house is an eastern European Jewish enclave inside Vienna (just as the Zionist rabbi doctor Weiss is a kind of "provincial" Jewish enclave among "the people of the metropolis"). It is a living space characterized by the deepest poverty (the "one-windowed room . . . contained no stick of furniture whatever. Not a chair, table, or cupboard. On the windowsill were a few small bottles and some broken pots" [24]). However, it shows signs of self-respect, vitality, and beauty—a beauty that originates in the past and a beauty that foreshadows the future. We learn this from the details given to us by the narrator: the family matriarch, who "was emaciated and very weak, but [whose] careworn face still showed traces of beauty," sits "upright" on a straw pallet, nursing with her "flabby breast" a "pretty little" baby (36).

Vienna, with its four facets, is thus portrayed as a place where the Jews have no chances of survival. The novel suggests that Europe would never accept the Jews, and justifiably so. For Herzl, Vienna and the Diaspora in general are not only a loathsome and repulsive place relative to an ideal, longed-for destination —the Place. In Herzl—and this is a very important point for our discussion— the Diaspora is a "no place." But not a no place that, like the biblical no place (the desert) and Mapu's no place (Nineveh), contains both destructive and vital forces, a tension between Eros and Thanatos, between tomb and womb, a place that can serve as a "melting pot" for the creation of a new/renewed nation. In Herzl—and in this sense he is the harbinger of a great literary and cultural wave—the Diaspora is an absolute evil, a desolate and barren existential landscape. As he puts it: "Judaism had sunk lower and lower. It was an 'elend' in the full sense of the old German word that had meant 'out-land,'—the limbo of the banished. Whoever was 'elend' was unfortunate; and whoever was an unfortunate sought for himself a nook in 'elend.' The Jews had thus fallen always lower, as much by their own fault as by the fault of others. Elend . . . Golus . . . Ghetto. Words in different languages for the same thing. Being despised, and finally despising yourself" (252).

The situation in Eretz Israel at the time (1902) was also, in Herzl's view, depressing and dispiriting, though it concealed—and it is this that will enable the shift in the second part of the book—a glimmer of hope.

On the way to their remote island, Kingscourt and Friedrich visit Eretz Israel. This, it should be noted, happens following the suggestion of the Prussian aristocrat Kingscourt, who decides to visit the country as a gesture to his Jewish friend. For his part, Friedrich reacts to the gesture with indifference. They spend "several days in the old land of the Jews" (42). Their travel itinerary in the country—and here I am digressing a little to the chronotopic plane—is identical to the typical itinerary of tourists who (like Herzl himself) visited the country at the end of the nineteenth century. I am referring to the itinerary that starts in Jaffa, continues with a ride "on the miserable railway" to Jerusalem and ends with a quick tour of the new Jewish colonies.[9] Here: "Jaffa made a very unpleasant impression on them. Though nobly situated on the blue Mediterranean, the town was in a state of extreme decay. Landing was difficult in the forsaken harbor. The alleys were dirty, neglected, full of vile odors. Everywhere misery in bright Oriental rags. Poor Turks, dirty Arabs, timid Jews lounged about—indolent, beggarly, hopeless. A peculiar, tomb-like odor of mold caught one's breath" (*ONL*, 42).

And this is what the route from Jaffa to Jerusalem looks like: "They hurried away from Jaffa, and went up to Jerusalem on the miserable railway. The landscape through which they passed was a picture of desolation. The lowlands were mostly sand and swamp, the lean fields looked as if burnt over. The inhabitants of the blackish Arab villages looked like brigands. Naked children played in the dirty alleys. Over the distant horizon loomed the deforested hills of Judaea. The bare slopes and the bleak, rocky valleys showed few traces of present or former cultivation" (ibid.).

Jerusalem, as they discover the following day, is no more cheerful: "shouting, odors, a flurry of dirty colors, crowds of ragged people in narrow, musty lanes, beggars, sick people, hungry children, screeching women, shouting tradesmen. The once royal city of Jerusalem could have sunk no lower" (44).

In the nocturnal Jerusalem, however, there is something "alluring." The city's views manage to excite Kingscourt, and even move some hidden heartstring in Friedrich's apathetic being: "'Jerusalem!' cried Friedrich in a half-whisper, his voice trembling. He could not understand why the sight of this strange city affected him so powerfully. Was it the memory of words heard in early childhood? In passages of prayer murmured by his father? Memories of Seder services of long-forgotten years stirred in him. One of the few Hebrew phrases he still knew rang in his ears: *'Leshana Ha-baa be-Yerushalayim,'*—'Next year in Jerusalem!' Suddenly he saw himself a little boy going to synagogue with his father. Ah, but faith was dead now, youth was dead, his father was dead. And here before him the walls of Jerusalem towered in the fairy moonlight. His eyes overflowed. He stopped short, and the hot tears coursed slowly down his cheeks" (43).

The descriptions of the "old" Eretz Israel in *Altneuland* depict a landscape in terminal decline. These descriptions also feature a few important statements that reveal the nature of some of the prejudices that guided Herzl when he came to outline his ideal world: It is without a doubt the text of a man with firm Europocentric views. Poverty is "oriental," and the residents of the Arab villages look like "brigands." Herzl's Europocentric stance is also evident in the attitudes to life in the country expressed by his emissaries in the narrative, Friedrich and Kingscourt. For them, everything in the country is overmagnified: the smells are too strong, the voices are too loud. As for the sights—and this is another projection of a European scale of sensibility on a landscape characterized by a different scale—the sights are either colorful or bothersome to the eye due to a "strange" color coordination. And while we are on the matter of culturally dependent aesthetic sensibilities, we cannot avoid referring to the deforested mountains on the way to Jerusalem, which are a further "picture of desolation," since a pretty mountain is "of course" green.

The problem is that the culturally dependent aesthetic sensibilities serve here, in a narrative/conceptual move presented as natural, as a lever for a quasi-colonialist policy.[10] This becomes clear, for example, when Kingscourt, the practical man, translates the aesthetic sensibilities into a plan of action: "Yes, it's pretty bad," he declares. "But much could be done here with afforestation. If half a million young giant cedars were planted—they shoot up like asparagus. This country needs nothing but water and shade to have a very great future." Then Friedrich asks an invited question: "And who is to bring water and shade here?" and Kingscourt replies: "The Jews!" (*ONL*, 43).

In a similar vein, during Friedrich and Kingscourt's first tour of the country, we come across two enclaves of hope in the barren land. One enclave takes the shape of Dr. Eichenstamm and his daughter, two eye doctors of Russian origin. Eichenstamm hears Friedrich's eulogy about the people and the land ("We have really died dead. There's nothing left of the Jewish kingdom but this fragment of the Temple wall. And though I fathom my soul to its depths, I find nothing in common with these traffickers in the national misfortune" [44]), and corrects him: "More remains of the Jews than the stones of this ancient bit of masonry and these poor wretches here who, I grant you, ply no wholesome trade. The Jewish people nowadays should be judged neither by its beggars nor by its millionaires."

On hearing these words Friedrich remarks, "I am not rich," to which Eichenstamm replies, "I see what you are—a stranger to your people. If you ever come to us in Russia, you will realize that a Jewish nation still exists. We have a living tradition, a love of the past, and faith in the future. The best and most cultured men among us have remained true to Judaism as a nation" (45).

The second enclave of hope in the desolate and barren background map are the colonies of Hovevei Zion (the Lovers of Zion), who also belong to the Russian Jewish community. Friedrich and Kingscourt visit Rishon Le-Zion, Rehovot, and Gedera, "that lay like oases in the desolate countryside" (47).

As already mentioned, the Vienna and Eretz Israel of 1902, described in the first section of *Altneuland* (the first book, "An Educated, Desperate Young Man") serve as the background map for the proper spatial/semiotic model according to Herzl. This model (the foreground map), with which he wishes to erase the gap between the place and the Place, is depicted in the novel's second part (comprising the second book, "Haifa, 1923"; the third book, "The Prosperous Land"; the fourth book, "Passover"; and the fifth book, "Jerusalem") as part of a new travel itinerary, very different from the standard travel itinerary outlined in the novel's first part and in many of the stories from the period.[11]

The new itinerary symbolizes a renaissance and a modern, optimistic spirit. It begins in Haifa, a city without a religiously and ethnically charged past, rather than in Jaffa. Jaffa, it should be noted, has been erased from Herzl's new map of Eretz Israel. From Haifa Friedrich and Kingscourt travel to Tiberias. On the way they pass through several important places: Neudorf, a new village in the Jezreel Valley—"which is typical of innumerable settlements both to the east and the west of the Jordan" (*ONL*, 120). They continue in the fertile valley through the Ginosar dale, from where they have a view of the Sea of Galilee. From here they observe "Magdala, a sparkling, pretty new townlet with beautiful houses and gardens" (159), on the western side of the Sea of Galilee, and the "green wooded heights" of the Golan mountains on its eastern side, and proceed "on to Tiberias without stopping, taking a southerly direction along the lake shore," driving through the city "from north to south" (160).

Tiberias is portrayed as *the* cosmopolitan city of Eretz Israel. It is a city that has "attracted visitors from Europe and America who had always sought perennial spring" (159). It is full of "first-class hotel accommodations [established by] experienced Swiss hotel keepers," teeming with "the cosmopolitan mob that is so typical of fashionable bathing resorts," some strolling leisurely on the promenade along the lake, some watching the "kaleidoscopic traffic on the lake" or playing on the "special tennis courts" or listening to "Hungarian, Rumanian and Italian bands in national costume" (160). Tiberias's cosmopolitan character is also reflected in the marked diversity of its places of worship: "stately mosques, churches with Latin and Greek crosses, magnificent stone synagogues." The tour of Tiberias also includes a visit to the villa rented by the Littwaks for the duration of the treatment needed for the family matriarch, the mother of David and Miriam, who is seriously ill, and a guided tour of the "Steineck Institute," a famous research institute in bacteriology patterned after the model of the Louis Pasteur Institute. The next stop after Tiberias—which is where, not coincidentally, the distinguished group is invited for the Passover Eve dinner—is El-Quneitra, which "as a railway junction between Safed and Damascus, was a town of some commercial importance in Transjordania" (235).

From there they proceed to an area called the "granary," which includes a "model farm" whose workers are rehabilitated prisoners. Afterward they travel in the Jordan Valley, through Beit She'an and Jericho ("now a . . . tropical [and] enchanting health resort" [238]), all the way to the Dead Sea. There they visit the electrical power plant, the "modern Temple," and from there they travel to Jerusalem. Only this time, as the narrator notes, it is from a different direction, a direction opposite to the one "in the routine itinerary," whose essence and purpose the narrator does not conceal: "Twenty years before, Kingscourt and Friedrich had entered Jerusalem by night and from the west. Now they came by day, approaching from the east. Then she had been a gloomy, dilapidated city; now she was risen in splendor, youthful, alert, risen from death to life" (247).

Entering Jerusalem from the east, rather than the west, reflects a new trajectory of movement in Eretz Israel, as well as a new teleology of this journey. This innovation is intensified here through its juxtaposition with binary oppositions that are all connected to the modern myth of revival, the myth of the Enlightenment, with its typical rhetoric: light versus darkness, past versus present, and life versus death. The dramatic change in the country's trajectories of movement has another aspect: Herzl's Jerusalem—unlike Mapu's, and unlike what was typical of the standard itinerary in the literature of the period—is not the final and ultimate destination. After visiting Jerusalem, Friedrich and Kingscourt, and with them the entire group, travel to Tiberias. And it is here, in this cosmopolitan city—rather than in Jerusalem, the "old capital," or in Haifa, the "new capital"— that the novel ends with two grand events that share a strong thematic bond: the engagement of Friedrich Loewenberg and Miriam Littwak, and the news of David Littwak's appointment as the "President of the New Society."

The Dialectic-Reformatory Position and the Revolutionary-Revisionist Position

Between the standard route of travel in Eretz Israel and the new route—and, respectively, between the two parts of the novel—there are two kinds of reciprocal relations. The first kind may be called "dialectic-reformatory," and the second "revolutionary-revisionist."

The Eretz Israel model created by Herzl maintains dialectic-reformatory reciprocal relations (that is, relations of progress toward the new on the basis of a remodification of the old) with two central cultural/spatial models: with the "classical" models of Eretz Israel (the Bible, the Shtetl, Hibbat Zion), and with the model of the industrial, liberal European state.

Herzl's reformatory position with regard to the "classical" model of Eretz Israel finds its expression in many ways, first and foremost in the shift in Jerusalem's status. In the biblical model, as in the Shtetl model and in Mapu's *The Love of Zion*, Jerusalem is the "heart" of Eretz Israel, of the Jewish people, and of the whole world. And it is also—and one is dependent on the other—the moral/ ideological acid test of the Jewish people and humanity as a whole.

Herzl puts Jerusalem's lofty status in question. It is still a significant spiritual center, on the local level, the global Jewish level (it houses the New Society's "Congress" in Eretz Israel [which is multinational and multiethnic], the new Temple and the "Jewish Academy" [260]), and the international level (it houses the world "Peace Palace" [247], whose role is parallel to the future role of the League of Nations and the United Nations). But it is not the country's center, from which all the roads branch out and in which they all meet again. It is a museum city, full of majesty and exaltedness, and at the same time anemic and boring. In contrast, Haifa is a vibrant and lively city. It serves as Eretz Israel's modern commercial/industrial center, as well as its center of (Western) culture, a city that has no binding religious history and is not ethnically problematic (in Herzl's time Haifa was not seen as an Arab or mixed city, unlike Jaffa and Acre). These two characteristics of Haifa, seen by Herzl as advantageous, should be supplemented by two more characteristics that made him choose it: it is close to the Mediterranean (and therefore to Europe), which makes it "a natural international center" (in Herzl's vision it takes the place of the city of Suez as an international maritime center); and it is located on a mountain, which makes it "a high place," both in the visual sense—it affords views far into the distance—and in the ideological sense, which here replaces the religious one. It is a high and elevated place suitable for the establishment of a ritualistic site, defined as both natural (the mountain) and civilizational (the city).[12] Furthermore, in *Altneuland* Jerusalem is given a parallel status to that which Rome had at the time of the novel's writing ("It reminds me of Rome," says the eye doctor Eichenstamm, "A splendid city, a metropolis, could be erected upon these hills once more. What a view from here! Grander than that from Gianiculo" [*ONL*, 47])—that is, a parallel status to the cultural center of the classical world. Haifa's status in the foreground map, on the other hand, parallels the status enjoyed by London in the background map. It is from London, and later from its twin city in the Orient, Haifa, that Joe Levy, the chief administrator of the New Society, who becomes the director general of its Ministry of Industry, runs worldwide businesses.

Balanced reciprocal relations between the spiritual/traditional element and the rejuvenating and innovative element are also reflected in the relation maintained between the novel's two symbolic places. I am referring to the reestablished Temple in Jerusalem on the one hand—the spiritual center of the Jewish people, which, according to Friedrich, lends validity to the Jewish people's return to Eretz Israel ("Because only here had the Jews built up a free commonwealth in which they could strive for the loftiest human aims" [254])—and the power plant at the Dead Sea on the other hand, a plant that produces electricity by utilizing the force of the water that descends from the "Dead Sea Canal" to the Dead Sea.

The narrator directs us in various ways toward making a comparison between these two places through the novel's structural/graphic design: the description of the power plant concludes the novel's third book, and the description of the Temple opens the fourth part, creating "an analogy of juxtaposition" (an analogy that the reader is invited to create because of the juxtaposition of two passages that are seemingly unconnected). The juxtaposition of the two places, emphasized by their special structural status (a concluding unit on the one hand and an opening unit on the other), highlights their common natural ontological elements, a destroyed (the destruction of the Temple) and dry (the Dead Sea) place that has gained new life, as well as their contrasting natural ontological elements, a high and elevated place as opposed to the lowest place in the world, a spiritual place as opposed to an industrial place. However, the most essential component in the implied comparison between these two places is the viewer's point of view, which in both cases mixes the sacred and the profane. The Temple is described through Friedrich's eyes from two intercrossing viewpoints: that of an assimilated Jew, moved at the sight of the most important symbolic place in Judaism, and that of a tourist, who looks at the building from a purely aesthetic standpoint. The same double prism—and here it is more surprising—can be found in the description of the power station at the Dead Sea:

> The iron tubes through which the waters of the Canal beat down upon the turbine wheels reminded Kingscourt of the apparatus at Niagara. There were some twenty of these mighty iron tubes at the Dead Sea, jutting out from the rocks at equal distances. They were set vertically upon the turbine sheds, resembling fantastic chimneys. The roaring from the tubes and the white foam on the outflowing waters bore witness to a mighty work.
>
> They stepped into one of the turbine sheds. Friedrich was overwhelmed by the immensity of the power development shown him, but Kingscourt seemed quite at his ease in the tumult of this industrial apparatus. With all his might he screamed comments no one could possibly hear; but they could see from his face that for once he was wholly satisfied. It really was a magnificent, Cyclopean sight as the waters crashed down upon the huge bronze spokes of the turbine wheels and drove them to furious turnings.
>
> From here the tamed natural forces were conducted into electric generators, and the current sent along wires throughout all parts of the country. The "Old-New-Land" had been fructified into a garden and a home for people who had once been poor, weak, hopeless, and homeless.
>
> "I feel myself crushed by all this greatness," sighed Friedrich, when at last he could speak.
>
> "Not me," responded David earnestly. "We have not been crushed by the greatness of these forces—it has lifted us up!" (244)

The power station is described here as a technological temple—a description that relies on numerous linguistic and thematic elements. The phrases "mighty iron tubes," the "immensity of the power development," "set vertically upon the turbine sheds, resembling fantastic chimneys," "It really was a magnificent... sight"; the enthusiastic excitement over the machine, which curbs and subdues "natural forces," and is itself "Cyclopean"; and of course the speechlessness that overtakes Friedrich, who even after twenty years on the secluded island seems to have still remained "a Diaspora Jew" at heart, who feels "crushed by all this greatness" (I shall return to this point later); and conversely, the response of the gentile and the energetic industrialist Kingscourt, who "for once... was wholly satisfied"; and also, of course, the reaction of the representative of Herzl's type of Zionism, David, who has already "realized the dream" ("We have not been crushed by the greatness of these forces—it has lifted us up!")—all these turn this passage into a futuristically tinted, modern Zionist manifesto, in which the machine takes the place of God. And, in order to understand the full meaning of the change in Herzl's map of Eretz Israel, we would do well to remember here the description of the Dead Sea in *The Love of Zion:* a remote place on the edges of the map, symbolizing eternal death, the result of a divine condemnation following a moral/religious sin.

The difference between the model of Eretz Israel created by Mapu and the one created by Herzl is also reflected in the relative status of the "garden utopia" and the "city utopia" in each of the works and, respectively, in the relative status of the two forms of human congregation according to Ferdinand Tönnies: "community" and "society."[13]

Mapu's *The Love of Zion* is very close in spirit to the "Arcadian utopia," the utopia of the pastoral garden, whereas *Altneuland* is "an urban utopia" par excellence. Although in both books there is room for the city and the country to exist alongside, in *The Love of Zion* the city is overshadowed by the country, which, as in the Bible, is seen as the starting point of the culture of governance and its source of legitimacy. In *Altneuland*, by contrast, the country is overshadowed by the city.

The dominant status of the urban model in Herzl's novel is evident in every variable of the topographic composition. To begin with, all the Eretz-Israeli landscape that Herzl chose to depict in *Altneuland* is settled, and every piece of land is cultivated, so much so that it seems that the book's author had an anxiety about any piece of landscape not bearing the mark of a human hand: "The hillsides everywhere were cultivated up to the very summits; every bit of soil was exploited" (*ONL*, 125); "On either side of the high road were well-tilled fields, vineyards, tobacco plantations, tree nurseries. Nowhere a rod of barren ground" (157); "There were, in fact, as far as the eye could reach around the shore, numerous large manufacturing plants" (244); in addition, the old-new land is crisscrossed with the straight lines of motorways, ground-level and elevated railways, power lines and telegraph lines. These straight lines symbolize the new energy, a modern geometric energy—whose most emblematic expression here is the train[14]—which Herzl posits against the "classical" spiritual energy, whose most emblematic expression here is the "Ship of the Wise," gently winding its way through the Mediterranean; and finally, Eretz Israel in general, and Haifa in particular, are described as the commercial, economic, and transport-communication nerve center of the entire modern world.

It should be stressed that *Altneuland*'s map is the first and last foundational map, for a long period in the history of Hebrew literature, to exhibit a clear preference for urban settlement. Subsequent maps of Eretz Israel displaying a similar prominence of urban settlement would appear in the canonical wing of the local literature only at the end of the 1930s and in the 1940s in poetry (Avraham Shlonsky, Nathan Alterman), at the end of the 1970s in prose and poetry (Yaakov Shabtai, Meir Wieseltier), and then again in prose starting at the end of the 1980s (Orly Castel-Bloom, Etgar Keret, Assaf Gavron).

The model of Eretz Israel that Herzl imagined, as already mentioned, is also linked in dialectical-reformatory reciprocal relations to the model of the industrial, liberal European state of the end of the preceding century. Herzl's old-new land is, first and foremost, an "upgraded" Europe—in the socio-economic, civic-political, and technological spheres. Herzl's reformatory position in the socio-economic sphere requires a separate discussion. As part of our discussion here I will merely say that it is a balanced approach that rejects, with the same degree of decisiveness, both the extreme socialist positions and the extreme capitalist positions. This position—which, as David Littwak says, provides "the mean between individualism and collectivism," that is, "the individual is not deprived of the stimulus and pleasures of private property, while, at the same time, he is able, through union with his fellows, to resist capitalist domination" (86)—is clearly evident in the construction of the new Eretz-Israeli landscape.

Both the new cities and the new small settlements are built according to comprehensive master plans, which maintain a meticulous architectonic balance between the public and the private areas, between the large buildings that serve the large cooperative systems (large department stores, merchandise warehouses, printing houses, and the like), and residential buildings. As for the private buildings themselves, although they share similar basic features, since they are always designed as parallel functional units in a hierarchical, spatial, communal (rural/urban) system, they reflect (especially in their façades and their interior design) national/ethnic styles and personal taste. The only area that is an exception in this sense, and which only serves to prove the rule, is the complex of the Old City of Jerusalem, which is preserved as a kind of museum display—symbolically important but anachronistic for its time.

In the civic-political sphere as well, Herzl created "an upgraded Europe." Unlike most of the Jewish thinkers and writers of his time who imagined a place for the Jews to live, Herzl had no wish for a national space (which is why the moniker attached to him, "the visionary of the Jewish state," is erroneous and misleading). The new-old land is a place with no political borders, and it is the state of all its residents, regardless of religion, race, and sex. Although the Jews are the ethnic/religious majority, and consequently their culture is more prominent and influential than the culture of other ethnic/religious groups, Herzl's imagined settlement in the country is supposed to create "a democratic civic society." In fact, it seems that Herzl describes a political sphere that can be defined, in accordance with his attitude to the political spheres he could see around him, as a multinational and pluralistic political entity, a kind of Austro-Hungarian empire with a democratic regime.

"Altneuland" is "an upgraded Austro-Hungary" first and foremost on the technological level. Herzl devoted the greater part of his landscape conceptualization to technical issues. No wonder then that his key figures in the building and establishment of the New Society are scientists (the bacteriologist professor Steineck, his architect brother, the eye doctors Eichenstamm and his daughter), merchants (David Littwak), and capable administrators, first among whom is Joe Levy, the director general of the Ministry of Industry. No wonder also that Herzl chose to cast in the role of the "stranger"—a figure that serves as the representative of the readers/judges and that appears in any utopia worthy of its name—Kingscourt the Prussian aristocrat, who made his fortune in the American industry (which was then already the strongest and most highly regarded industry) rather than an intellectual or a merchant (like for instance the "stranger" Hadoram in *The Love of Zion*).

Herzl's great interest in technology, and his belief that it has the power to save humanity in general and the Jews in particular from the majority of their troubles—a belief that suggests that he was captivated (like all the writers of utopias in his time) by the spirit of the Haskalah and the Enlightenment—is clearly reflected in the excerpt I have cited above describing the power plant at the Dead Sea. The same belief emerges again each time the book mentions an electrical device, be it great or small, and each time the narrator addresses issues of master planning—especially city planning.

And in this context, the jewel in the crown is Haifa. In Herzl's vision, it is a wonderfully planned and organized city. Its streets are straight, clean and full of light (96), and it contains only large and spacious stores—petty commerce and small stores are out of the question. It is built of neighborhood after neighborhood of brightly lit mansions. The neighborhoods are interspersed with "green lungs" and crisscrossed by broad avenues, in which large trees shade the residents in daytime and hanging lamps light their way at night. Transport takes place either on the ground by means of "automobiles [speeding] noiselessly on rubber tires" (62), or above it by means of "an electric overhead train," and all with exemplary efficiency.

Herzl's metropolis, and likewise the "New Village," and in fact his whole Eretz-Israeli landscape, fulfill the two central conditions of Le Corbusier's landscape conceptualization and human engineering. First, it is a preplanned, rational, and efficient space based on the following principles: a) the mathematical order of the geometric forms it is based on—the conception of science as nature's enhanced extension; b) economy—as opposed to the excessive decorativeness of the Baroque style; and c) welfare—based on rational considerations and submitting the space to sociocultural projects. These three principles are realized in Herzl's community settlements both in a compulsory democratization and in an elitist taste for functional surfaces in a unified international style: large buildings, full of air and light, "softened" by public parks consisting mostly of domesticated nature. Second, it is a decentralized centralist space, that is, a space structured by a generally hierarchical approach, divided into monofunctional areas: residential, commerce and industry, entertainment and culture, and even separate areas for prisoner rehabilitation. The activity of the New Society is based on the holistic vision and centralist planning that are so characteristic of the modern worldview, a worldview that can be more easily realized—as Herzl's fictional tour-guides keep explaining to their two groups of tourists[15]—in an "empty land" such as Eretz Israel. The claim about the "empty land" appealed to Herzl both because of his basic assumptions, which were influenced by the colonialist slogans adopted by most of the Zionist leaders ("making the desert bloom," "a land without a people for a people without a land"), and because he wished to create a place that would have no trace of any way of living that would recall the Diaspora, that confounded Elend.

And so it is that his famous tolerance completely disappears when dealing with types of settlement that remind him of Jewish existence in the Diaspora, both directly (elements of the Shtetl transplanted to Eretz Israel) and indirectly (the model of the Arab village, called here, not coincidentally, the "Old Village"). The thought that these types of settlement and even parts of them would manage to survive as part of his New Society caused the visionary of modern Jewish existence—and the most liberal of all—revulsion and horror.

As mentioned earlier, Herzl describes Jews of eastern European origins as vibrant creatures and Jews of central European origins as feeble people. But vibrancy apart and culture apart, the Jews of eastern European origins are designated a physical role in the building of the land. Culture—opera, ballet, theatre, and the like—is brought by the people of western/central Europe. This dichotomy suggests both a Europocentric position and a (common) stereotyping of the "other"—here the eastern European Jew—as being close to nature, endowed with a strong survivability, a healthy sexuality, and so on.

Herzl displays a similar stereotypical/racist attitude toward the Arabs in Eretz Israel. The difference in his attitude to these two groups can be summarized by Sigmund Freud's famous distinction between culture and civilization. He disrespects the Jews of eastern Europe because they have no culture; in his view, they lack a profound relationship with the "fine arts." He disrespects the Arabs because they have no civilization; they have not managed to develop any "enlightened" mechanisms of governance or acquire advanced technological knowledge. Therefore, the Arab living space is doomed to the same fate as the Shtetl—disappearance from the face of the earth. This emerges from the recurrent comparing and contrasting between the "old" Arab village and the "New Village."

The "old villages"—none of which is mentioned by name—can only be seen on Herzl's background map (the one from 1902), first through the eyes of Friedrich and Kingscourt and then, in the following sentences, through the eyes of (the Arab!) Reschid Bey: "Nothing could have been more wretched than an Arab village at the end of the nineteenth century. The peasants' clay hovels were unfit for stables. The children lay naked and neglected in the streets, and grew up like dumb beasts ... [in] the filthy nests that used to be called villages in Palestine" (120, 123–24).

In the background map, there is no trace of a new village. The colonies Rishon Le-Zion, Gedera, and Rehovot are described as experimental forms of settlement whose chances of survival are unclear. Conversely, in the foreground map, from 1923, all the "old" Arab villages have been erased, replaced by the New Village, "which is typical of innumerable settlements both to the east and the west of the Jordan" (120).

As for the New Village itself, it is described as the polar opposite of the old village: it has "well-built houses and blooded cattle and up-to-date machinery" (142). In this village we find "model agricultural equipment ... chemical experimental station and ... [an] up-to-date engine house ... [an] elementary school ... [and a] public library [which holds, in the best tradition of European Enlightenment] popular scientific works" (155). "On either side of the high road [leading to the village] were well-tilled fields, vineyards, tobacco plantations, tree nurseries ... electric plows were being guided over fields still damp from the winter rain" (157–58).

The fact that the Arabs have no civilization worthy of its name does not preclude them from taking part in the building of the land. On the contrary, they serve (just like the Old Jews from eastern Europe) as an efficient work force: "the natives ... were the first to be employed, and were paid well for their work" (123). And this, of course, is only for their own benefit: "These people are better off than at any time in the past. They support themselves decently, their children are healthier and are being taught something... They have become more prosperous—that is all" (124).

Herzl proceeds to implement the "erasure from the map" policy also in the case of settlements based on the "old models," and in the case of any element in the landscape that might recall the "old" forms of settlement. Thus, for example, in Haifa they encourage only large stores. Small stores are unwelcome. As for peddlers with their mobile stalls—they are loathsome. Although David, the representative of the New Society, remarks that he is not ashamed of his father who made his living in Vienna as a peddler, he also supports the abolition of all forms of petty commerce and peddling. He justifies this position by citing economic reasons as well as a "social-political" one: "both production and consumption required the large bazaar... We had a social-political motive: that is to say, we wanted to cure our small tradesmen of certain outworn, uneconomic, and injurious forms of trade" (100). David, Herzl's authorized representative and the future "President of the New Society," adds that he does not altogether rejects petty commerce. But he points out with satisfaction that "They are by no means all Jews. Greeks, Levantines, Armenians" (101).

Herzl's worldview becomes clear both when we examine his foreground map as a whole, and when we examine demarcated units on this map, for example, the segment defined as the "street level" in Haifa: "the 'Place of the Nations' was thronged with people from all parts of the world. Brilliant Oriental robes mingled with the sober costumes of the Occident, but the latter predominated. There were many Chinese, Persians and Arabs in the streets, but the city itself seemed thoroughly European. One might easily imagine himself in some Italian port. The brilliant blue of sky and sea was reminiscent of the Riviera, but the buildings were much cleaner and more modern. The traffic, though lively, was far less noisy. The quiet was due partly to the dignified behavior of the many Orientals, but also to the absence of draught animals from the streets. There was no hoof beat of horses, no crackling of whips, no rumbling of wheels. The pavements were as smooth as the footways. Automobiles speeded noiselessly by on rubber tires, with only occasional toots of warning" (61–62).

It is an instructive passage. It includes, in a clear and succinct way, most of the characteristics we discussed earlier: the majority of the "materials" in this fictional spatial unit—both those that are mentioned by name and those whose existence the author and reader are aware of without their names being mentioned—are organized in polar oppositions, and all are organized in hierarchical systems, which repeatedly reflect the worldview of their author. The following polar oppositions emerge from this passage: east versus west, Asians versus Europeans, loud behavior versus dignified behavior, and horses versus cars. The elements of the two oppositions—West versus East and Asians versus Europeans—seem equal in status because of the specific words that connect and qualify them: "Brilliant Oriental robes *mingled with* the sober costumes of the Occident"; "was thronged with *people from all parts of the world*"; "*many* Chinese, Persians and Arabs" (ibid., emphasis mine).

But this is a false impression—as a closer examination reveals: the contrasting of the "sober costumes of the Occident" with the "Brilliant Oriental robes" contains a rhetoric excess that highlights the "exotic" component, which as we have already seen the author does not much care for. Neither is the message of equality contained in the words "many," "people from all parts of the world," and "mingled" actually fulfilled. For this mixture in that place includes only Chinese, Persians, and Arabs! Despite which, and maybe in line with which, the Western costumes "predominated," and all the details, with all their cosmopolitan colorfulness, are drowned out by an impression that is "thoroughly European."

The façade of equality therefore conceals a hierarchical, modern attitude with a patronizing colonialist touch. This fact emerges also from the hidden—manipulative—comparison between animals and the people of the Orient. The author explains the fact that Haifa is a quiet city, rather than noisy like an Italian port town, by two "features" described in one conjoined sentence: a) "the dignified behavior of the many Orientals" and b) "the absence of draught animals" and all their attendant sounds. These two features and the features complementing them—the one that is not mentioned and is, as it were, obvious is the dignified behavior of the Europeans; the one that is mentioned is that the cars that have replaced the animals are much quieter and more efficient—suggest an attitude that invites and justifies a political-cultural endeavor: to conquer/civilize the Levant in the European spirit.[16]

Enlightenment and Colonialism, Romanticism and Auto-Antisemitism

Herzl's attempt to unite the "place" with the "Place" on the choronotopic plane is based—like Mapu's parallel attempt discussed in the previous chapter—on redesigning biblical metanarratives that deal with the mythical biography of the people of Israel using European metanarratives. The biblical metanarratives here are the Exodus from Egypt, the Dry Bones prophecy, and the End of Days vision. The European metanarratives are the metanarrative of the Enlightenment or, more precisely, its liberal/universal subnarrative on the one hand, and its colonialist subnarrative on the other, and the romantic metanarrative or, more precisely, its neoromantic antisemitic subnarrative.

The main part of the discussion in this section will focus on *Altneuland*'s various rewritings (cover versions) of the biblical metanarratives, since they form the core of the novel's subject matter and construction, and they offer the clearest reflection of Herzl's ideological/political agenda. However, before I turn to discuss these rewritings and their interrelations, I wish to point to some other narrative options mentioned in the work. As we shall see promptly, these are narrative options of various kinds that have in common being rejected in the novel, either immediately after being mentioned or gradually. In all these cases, this rejection plays the same role: to prepare the way for the emergence and successful reception of the truly important narrative options—those that Herzl believed should serve as the solid foundation for his imagined community.

Two narrative options of this kind are mentioned on the book's first page: the story of the settlement attempt made by Friedrich's friend Oswald in Brazil, which ended with his death from yellow fever—representing the settlement attempt of Jews in South America sponsored by Baron Hirsch[17]—and the story of the suicide of Friedrich's other friend, Heinrich.[18] Two other rejected narrative options that, like Oswald's attempt to settle in Brazil, also represent sociohistorical endeavors are the Prussian aristocrat-industrialist Kingscourt's attempt to settle in the United States, and the attempt by the group of bourgeois-philistine Viennese Jews to settle in Eretz Israel.

The existential option represented by Heinrich's suicide is rejected by Herzl because it does not coincide with the spirit of the basically optimistic period of the Haskala. Herzl refuses to accept the conscious sacrifice of life as an act of legitimization/sanctification of any cause, however lofty, and he certainly refuses to accept suicide as an ideological solution. The attempt to settle in Brazil is rejected because it represents a joining of the "Old World"–Europe with the "New World"—Brazil, which (as far as the Jewish people are concerned) does not realize any real dialectical bond between the historical cultural past and the desirable future, a dialectical bond that, as already mentioned, is fundamental to Herzl's modern, reformatory thinking. A similar logic leads to the rejection of the attempt to settle in the United States, represented here by Kingscourt, who becomes acclimatized in the United States in an economical but not in a cultural or a human engineering sense—as mentioned earlier, his young and poor wife betrays him with a young relative he has taken into his home.

Taken together, all of this means that the solution for the "Jewish problem" must take effect where the joining of the old and the new will come about—that is, in Eretz Israel. This joining itself, however, is not enough. A parallel change must take place in the people intended to live in this space. This, as we shall see below, also becomes clear from the way the "right" narrative options are portrayed—those realized by David Littwak and Friedrich Loewenberg—and from the negation of the other narrative options; one was already mentioned, that is, the settlement attempt of the bourgeois-philistine Viennese Jews, and the other, which has the status of a metanarrative, is the story of Sabbatai Zevi.

The bourgeois-philistine story is represented in *Altneuland* by all the Viennese Jews (except Friedrich himself and his two friends, Heinrich and Oswald, who, as mentioned earlier, are no longer alive): the affluent Loeffler family, led by Ernestina—Friedrich's beloved in Vienna—and their associates, rich merchants, their employees, and various sycophants. Some of the members of this group, including Ernestina, end up in Eretz Israel.

The fact that Ernestina and her group do not receive any training before arriving in Eretz Israel has a clear consequence: they remain decadent Jews, only now they are Jews who are suffering from an old illness in an "old-new" place, which intensifies their disconnection and unsuitability for life. They are presented as Jews without a future. Their attitude toward their new surroundings is cynical and condescending, and to top it all—and this is a turn for the worse compared to their Vienna existence—they become idlers (most of them have no real source of income) who live on the charity of their old acquaintances.

That the bourgeois-philistine Jewry has no future in the new land is made clear by *Altneuland*'s "biological selection": in the past Ernestina rejected Friedrich, the poor intellectual, in favor of Leopold Weinberger, "member of the firm of Samuel Weinberger and Sons of Bruenn," a rich young man, albeit with "a decided squint and very damp palms" (*ONL*, 10). The same Ernestina, who in Vienna was a desired and adored woman ("blond and dreamy, a marvelously sweet creature" [5]), finds herself in Eretz Israel in a hopeless situation: her husband has lost his fortune, and she, now described as "the fat, faded, gaudily dressed woman" (108), tries to improve her situation by receiving charity from the members of her Viennese circle and even by attempting to seduce her former admirer, Friedrich. But he rejects the love of his youth, preferring Miriam of Cracow, also a good-looking woman, but whose appearance—as in any ideological melodrama worthy of its name—is the "opposite" of Ernestina's, a "classic" Jewish appearance: she has black hair and eyes, and is modestly dressed.

Sabbatai Zevi's story in the novel represents the false Jewish messianic metanarrative. We can learn of the importance of this mytho-historic story for Herzl (who was himself accused of being a false messiah) from its central structural status in the book. This traumatic national story is staged as an opera, which all the novel's (positive) protagonists watch at the impressive opera house in Haifa. "The story (the opera) within a story" is a compositional element that creates within the work a mirror world whose implied worldview reflects the worldview that structures the work as a whole. We hear about the worldview structuring the opera *Sabbatai Zevi*—and indirectly, the worldview structuring *Altneuland* —from David Littwak, who plays the role of the instructor-commentator who steers his immediate addressees (Friedrich and Kingscourt) and his more distant ones (the readers that Herzl envisioned) to the "correct conclusions."

At seeing the figure of Sabbatai Zevi on stage, Friedrich says, "It is strange . . . how such adventures are always able to win the people's confidence" (105). To which David replies with an answer that reveals an ounce of the historiosophical approach of his creator, Theodor Herzl, and his early response to the predictable reactions of his various opponents: "There seems to be a profound reason for that . . . It was not that the people believed what they said, but rather that they said what the people believed, They soothed a yearning. Or, perhaps it would be more correct to say, they sprang from the yearning. That's it. The longing creates the Messiah. You must remember what dark days those were when a Sabbatai and his like appeared. Our people was not yet able to take account of its own situation, and therefore yielded to the spell of such persons. It was only at the end of the nineteenth century, when the other civilized nations had already attained to self-consciousness and given evidence thereof, that our own people—the pariah—realized that its salvation lay within itself, that nothing was to be expected from fantastic miracle workers. They realized then that the way of deliverance must be paved not by a single individual, but by a conscious and alert folk-personality" (105–6).

The rehabilitation of the Jewish people must be performed, according to Herzl's vision, through its reintegration into the "society of nations" and the "bosom of history." This vision is clearly evident in the characters populating *Altneuland*'s central plotlines. The plot Herzl created in the novel proceeds, as in *The Love of Zion*, in two central trajectories: the "collective," national/ historical plotline and the "private" plotline, the plotline of the central characters, David Littwak and Friedrich Loewenberg. The collective plotline is based on the metanarrative of the Exodus from Egypt. The private plotline is divided into two subplotlines, based on interpretations of the collective plotline. One plotline is based on a rereading of the Exodus from Egypt through the End of Days prophecy, in the spirit of the Enlightenment. The other plotline is based on a rereading of the Exodus from Egypt through the vision of the Dry Bones, in the spirit of antisemitic neoromanticism.

That the Exodus from Egypt is *Altneuland*'s metanarrative is clear from the words of the novel's central characters,[19] as well as, and especially in terms of our current discussion, from the structure of the book's chronotopic plane. As you may recall, the novel consists of two large parts that refer to two different domains: the first part describes the Vienna and Eretz Israel of 1902; the second part describes the future, utopian Eretz Israel of 1923. Between the two parts, as far as Friedrich and Kingscourt, the main mediators between the readers and the novel's world, are concerned, lies "a dead time-space." This is the period that sees the change, both on the national and the private level, from the old world, represented by the background map, and the new world, represented by the foreground map. This is a gradual change that lasts more than twenty years, which we learn, in retrospect, from some of the other central characters (chiefly David and Miriam), from some secondary characters (the architect Steineck, the bacteriologist Steineck, Dr. Marcus), and especially from a succinct report by Joe Levy—the legendary managing director of the New Society.

Joe Levy's report on the "exodus from Europe" appears in the fourth book, titled "Passover." Of the reason for Levy's report being heard at that particular time we hear from Littwak: "Joe will tell you about the beginning . . . This Seder evening seemed the appropriate time. The old Haggadah, which we read at dinner, has a story about the sages who assembled at Bene Berak on a Seder evening, and discussed the Egyptian exodus the whole night through. We are the successors of Rabbi Eliezer, Rabbi Joshua, Rabbi Eleazer ben Azariah, Rabbi Akibah and Rabbi Tarphon. And this is our evening of Bene Berak. The old passes over into the new. First we shall finish our Seder after the manner of our forefathers, and then we shall let the new era tell you how it was born. Once more there was an Egypt, and again a happy exodus" (*ONL*, 190).

Herzl reinforces the link between the two exoduses from Egypt—a parallelism whose very existence suggests that Herzl did not see Eretz Israel, as he was accused by some of his opponents, only as "a temporary shelter," but also and especially as a destination where it would be possible to try and erase the gap between the "place" (the biblical Egypt and the new Egypt—the Diaspora) and the "Place" (the Eretz Israel of his vision) by use of, among other things, road signs that guide the reader to see Joe Levy as a modern Moses.

Moses, of the tribe of Levi, led the first Aliyah of the Hebrews. Joe Levy is defined as "the man who carried through the new Jewish national project" (ibid.) Other similarities stand out in this light, as well as fascinating differences: Moses's life story ends with his burial on Mount Nebo, an unknown place with a clear geocultural character. It is a high place that connects the desert, the "no place," the place where the nation was founded, to the promised land, the Place. It is a no place from which one can look out and see the unattainable Place (as a kind of "prize"—you will nonetheless see "the land," and "punishment"—"but you will not cross over into it"). Joe Levy's life story will end, as stated in his will, in a way that cannot but be associated with Moses's death on Mount Nebo: "And when I die, lay me ... up there in the Carmel cemetery, overlooking our beloved land and sea." (232). Herzl's modern Moses, the prophet who has undergone a technological transformation, will be buried in a known place: a "geographical" fact emerging from the way the relation between the place and the Place is perceived in a Zionist text, which, as already mentioned, is fundamentally different from the parallel perception in the Hebrew Bible and in Shtetl literature—where the gap between the place and the Place is staunchly preserved. The difference between the landscape conceptualization that emerges from Moses's story and the one emerging from Joe Levy's story also becomes apparent if we compare the geocultural character of their places of burial. Joe Levy's place of burial is also a high place (Mount Carmel) that connects two different regions. One is, as with Moses, "the promised land" ("our beloved land"—which has already been settled and made to bloom"), and the other is different. The desert, the ultimate dry-land no place,[20] is replaced here by the Mediterranean sea, which Joe Levy chooses to name as "our beloved" (*ONL*, 232). Perhaps because the sea, the ultimate aquatic no place, is the region in which, according to numerous cultural traditions,[21] man can undergo significant emotional upheavals but also sink to erotic and thanatic depths, and perhaps also—and the two options can coexist in the same psychocultural context—because the Mediterranean is, or more precisely was (before the invention of airplanes), the most convenient outlet to Europe: a cursed region for the Jews, the Elend, but also, and nevertheless, the subject of great longing.

 The parallelism between the biblical Moses and the modern Moses has another aspect, which concerns that which both have been denied. Moses was able to look over at the Promised Land, but he did not enter it. The place of Moses, the leader and visionary who belongs to the Desert Generation, is taken by Yehoshua Ben Nun, the man of action who belongs to the new generation. Unlike Moses, the energetic Joe Levy will be able to not just see Eretz Israel but also to die and be buried in it. But he has not been able to do another thing to which he aspired all his life, and that is to meet the people of the "Ship of the Wise": that ship called *Futuro* (future), which represents the free, Platonic human spirit, sailing about to and fro in the Mediterranean sea. Levy keeps trying to meet the ship's passengers—the scholars, the writers, and the other artists—but he never succeeds, ostensibly because of the urgent tasks whose performance he must supervise. In fact, however, the reason he never succeeds in this task (the only one he fails in) is that he feels that the gap between himself, the man of action, and the "intellectual aristocracy of the whole civilized world" (ONL, 222) should be preserved. Joe expresses this feeling, that the gap between action and dream (here—between the settled land and the Eretz Israel of the world's/ West's intellectual vision) should be preserved, in an astonishing declaration, which he attributes to one of the writers who sailed as guests on the *Futuro*. This is an "accomplished writer," like all the people on the *Futuro*, but he has an interesting distinction: "He . . . never left the ship [that is, he did not disembark in order to visit the country] for a moment" (225). The declaration made by that writer, according to Joe Levy, is that "this ship is Zion," meaning that the real Zion is not the one that Joe Levy endeavors to settle with the help of all the technological and sociopolitical achievements and innovations of the modern world, but rather the "Ship of the Wise," cruising the (beloved) Mediterranean like a kind of Ahasverus, the eternally Wandering Jew.

The Enlightenment model is realized in the book by David Littwak. The trajectory of his life, like the trajectory of the (ideal) modern society, is characterized by constant improvement. This trajectory contrasts with the model of the circular-cyclical story so characteristic of traditional cultures.[22] Its character derives from Herzl's belief—which is the essence of the Enlightenment spirit— that it is possible to create harmony between two contradicting processes: individuation and socialization.[23] According to Herzl, however, this harmony is the province of only an elect few among the Jewish people in the beginning of the twentieth century. It is upheld in the novel under two conditions: a) when the subject is an eastern European Jewish man who, although poor, maintains strong ties with tradition and is highly driven, and b) when the events take place in Eretz Israel, where, and only where, the New Society—a society that can be defined as an exemplary social-democratic one—can be founded.

When we first meet him, David Littwak is a helpless and pitiful figure. Friedrich, who is on his way from his habitual Café Birckenreise to the Loefflers' residence—to an event at which he will hear of Ernestina's engagement to another man—notices "a ten-year-old boy standing in the outer doorway. The child's shoulders were hunched up in a thin little coat. He held his arms tightly across his body, and stamped on the drifted snow in a sheltered nook. The hopping seemed almost like a pose, but Friedrich realized that with those torn shoes the child must be freezing bitterly" (ONL, 8–9). The second time we meet David is after Friedrich returns from his visit to the Loefflers'. In view of his visit to this affluent home, in which "money was all" (19), we would expect the poor boy, still sitting in front of the café's door, to arouse more empathy. However Friedrich "was so steeped in his own misery that he had no sympathy to spare for the freezing child" (20). Later, inside the café, Friedrich runs into a peddler who tries to sell him some pieces of haberdashery. Friedrich pushes him away rudely but later throws a coin into his peddler's box. The peddler forces Friedrich to take some of his merchandise in return for that coin, because, he says, "I am no beggar" (21). When Friedrich leaves the café, he sees the peddler and the freezing boy together and realizes that they are father and son. He accompanies them, hears their story, visits their miserable room, and is impressed by the familial solidarity that poverty only serves to reinforce, and by the inner strength of the mother, who despite the squalor in which she lives was "sitting upright," and whose "careworn face," despite being "emaciated and very weak . . . still showed traces of beauty" (24). But what impresses him most is the boy David, whose "words and tone [had] something curiously firm and mature about [them]" (25). The two—"the disaffected" doctor, Friedrich, who, finding his life pointless, has just considered committing suicide, and the boy, the son of a beggar, an immigrant who has just recently arrived from the "backward" province (Galicia) to the great capital Vienna—conduct the following dialogue:

> "How old are you?" [Friedrich] asked the boy.
> "Ten, I think."
> "What do you want to be when you grow up?"
> "I want to study. To study very much."
> Friedrich sighed involuntarily. "And do you think that is enough?"
> "Yes. I have heard that one who studies becomes a free, strong man. I shall study, God helping me. Then I shall go to the Land of Israel with my parents and Miriam."
> "To Palestine?" asked Friedrich in amazement. "What will you do there?"
> "That is our country. There we can be happy." (25–26)

The boy David (he has a Hebrew name, unlike his interlocutor) is not sure how old he is, but he has a clear plan for the future, a plan that combines the three elements that characterize all the Jews from eastern Europe in the story: a strong bond with the family and the tribe; a "practical" love for the Land of Israel (as he calls it, rather than Palestine, as Friedrich calls it), that is, Zionism; and the wish "to study very much," which stems from the conviction that "one who studies becomes a free, strong man"—the fundamental principle of the Enlightenment.

The encounter with David leaves a strong impression on Friedrich; it "stirred old and forgotten things within him."[24] This impression intensifies during their second encounter, in which he gives the Littwaks a large sum of money that he has taken from his new "master" Kingscourt. During this meeting the two conduct the following dialogue, which Friedrich initiates after David "stood regarding Friedrich steadily" with eyes that Friedrich defines as "remarkable":

> "Why do you look at me so closely, David?" he asked.
> "So that I may never forget you, sir. I once read a story about a man who helped a sick lion."
> "Androcles," smiled Friedrich. . . .
> Friedrich rose, and said jestingly as he placed his hand on the boy's round head, "And so you are the lion? Judah once had a lion."
> "That which Judah once had, he can have again," replied David almost defiantly." (35–36)

The story about Androcles and the lion was very well known in the aural literature of ancient times, and it is cited from Aulus Gellius in the fifth book of *Wonders of Egypt* by Apion. According to Apion, Androcles was the slave of a Roman consul administering a part of Africa. He escaped to the desert where he came across a wounded lion. He healed the animal, which rewarded him by sharing its prey with him. Afterward, Androcles ended up in Egypt, where he was captured and returned to Rome. Here he was forced to fight wild animals in the circus. In the ring he met the same lion, which, instead of attacking him, licked his hands. The audience was impressed by the strange phenomenon and demanded and was granted a pardon for the pair. This story attests to the hidden power of David and of the (eastern European) Jewish community he represents; the stored power of one who finds himself in an inferior situation, but due only to external reasons (the lion's wound, David's poverty and lack of education). These are reasons that can be dealt with, enabling one—as David argues before the sceptical Friedrich—to restore former glories: renew the glorious past of "the lion cub of Judea," the "king" of all peoples. Indeed, the David we meet twenty years later in Eretz Israel—after having studied and used his studies to improve his and others' situation—is a highly impressive person. When he meets Friedrich and Kingscourt as they disembark from their yacht on the Haifa shore in 1923, he is described thus: "He was a tall, vigorous man of thirty, whose sunburnt face was framed in a short black beard" (60). David lives on the slopes of the Carmel in a mansion called "Friedrichsheim," named after his past benefactor: "Friedrichsheim was a large, pleasant mansion in the Moorish style, set in gardens. Before the entrance lay a stone lion. The cry of the little son of the peddler echoed back to Friedrich through the years. 'What Judah once had, he can have again! Our old God still lives!' And the dream had been fulfilled" (71).

The dream has been fulfilled both economically and sociopolitically. In the New Society David, who like the rest of his family had no chance in the gentile society nor in the central European bourgeois Jewish society, can obtain any role.

What enables and justifies the Jews' escape from the harsh reality in Europe (prevalent in both its parts: the eastern European Shtetl part and the central European metropolitan one) is, according to the logic of Herzl's utopian book, the assumption that this escape is part of the realization of a universal vision. The new exodus from Egypt is not presented "only" as the realization of the legitimate rights of the Jewish people for sovereignty, but as a perfect enactment of the realization of national rights. It is the ultimate Exodus from Egypt—a full realization of the mythological End of Days prophecy in a thoroughly Haskalah-modern enactment.

As we have seen, Herzl's *Altneuland* is not "just another" European state, but a European state as it is supposed to exist according to his modern vision. And it will be able to exist as such because of two principle factors: a) the overcoming of the disorder that has characterized the old European society ("The old society was rich enough at the beginning of this century, but it suffered from ineffable confusion. It was like a crowded treasure-house where you could not find a spoon when you needed one" [78]) and b) the fact that it is "an empty land," empty of "inherited [national] burdens" (87) and of a local civilization (for, as already mentioned, the Arabs, to Herzl's mind, have not established a real civilization).

The belief in the existence of these "factors"—a belief that seems to have characterized settlers' societies in all continents at all times—is supposed to justify here, as in all the foundational texts of other settlers' societies, the settling activity itself and the missionary activity among the "locals," the "natives." "Cultivation [that is, Western culture] is everything!" roars Steineck. "We Jews introduced cultivation here." When Friedrich asks him what he is working on at his bacteriological institute, Steineck replies as "his eyes grew dreamy," "the opening up of Africa." And he explains: "Yes . . . I hope to find the cure for malaria. We overcome it here in Palestine, thanks to the drainage of the swamps, canalization, and the eucalyptus forests. But conditions are different in Africa. The same measures cannot be taken there because the prerequisite—mass immigration—is not present. The white colonist goes under in Africa. That country can be opened up to civilization only after malaria has been subdued. Only then will enormous areas become available for the surplus population of Europe. And only then will the proletarian masses find a healthy outlet. Understand?" (169).

Education in *Altneuland*, it should be emphasized, is a means not only of achieving private salvation (by David and his like—for example, the painter

Isaacs, "a poor Jewboy whose present position in the world was won through sheer grace of talent" [257]) and national redemption, represented by the prisoners working the land of the homeland, but also of achieving global redemption. Eretz Israel is intended to serve as a forward outpost of the Enlightenment in two complementary senses: as a global center, a place of pilgrimage for all the lovers of light, and as a center for the propagation of education all over the world. The fulfillment of the first sense—a center of education/science (instead of a religious center, as in the Bible, or as a moral-aesthetic center, as in Mapu)—is attested to by the "converts," those Christians who were impressed by Zionism, converted, and took part in making the desert bloom (the Swiss-born engineer who converted to Judaism and was renamed Abraham, and of course Kingscourt, the misanthropic Prussian aristocrat, who was won over by the charms of the land and its residents and stayed); and the Muslims, who lovingly and willingly accept the Jewish settlement and integrate in it.[25]

The fulfillment of the second sense—to serve as a center for the propagation of education/science around the world—is attested to by the health services that Dr. Eichenstamm and his daughter disseminate in Asia, as well as by the bacteriologist Steineck's research institute, where they work on, among other things, developing a cure for malaria, which is afflicting Africa; as well as by the administrative and political systems that the New Society in Eretz Israel has imported from Europe, developed and enhanced, and can now export, significantly improved, back to the countries from which it had imported them.

※ ※ ※

"Friedrich's plotline"—the novel's second central plotline—is based on a rereading of the Exodus from Egypt through the Vision of the Dry Bones in the spirit of antisemitic neoromanticism. As in "David's plotline," here too we have a description of a process of individuation and socialization, but with two clear differences. First, the balance between these elements in the two trajectories is different. In David's story there is a great emphasis on individuation—which coincides with Herzl's choice to focus on his formative years, from childhood to early maturity. In Friedrich's story there is a great emphasis on socialization —when we first meet Friedrich he is already a very mature person; at least mentally, he is already exhausted with life, everything around him strikes him as "sickly, pale," as if he were an old man "who had all too often parted with cherished friends" (4). His close friend Oswald states, "You are not fit for life." He also quotes a sentence from Hamlet which serves here as an expression of unfitness for life: "Get thee to a nunnery, Ophelia!" (5). His only reason for living, at least in his own eyes, is Ernestina. And once she deserts him, he despairs of life ("he thought himself superfluous in the room—in the city, in the whole world" [17–18]) and considers two possible solutions: suicide or the monastery. He chooses the "monastery": life on the remote island in Kingscourt's company.

This monastery, where his twenty-year stay parallels the forty years spent by the Israelites in the desert, features—just like its parallel mytho-historical landscape—completely opposing characteristics: harsh living conditions with elements of death on the one hand, and living conditions with elements of abundant vitality on the other.

The first term of admission to the monastery is the effacement of one's personality. The letter of invitation that Friedrich receives prior to his meeting with Kingscourt is signed by "N. O. Body," which Friedrich interprets for his friend Schiffmann, who does not understand the message: "Nobody. Means no one in English." And according to what the "guide" Kingscourt says, we are dealing with a mental experience of total detachment from the "I," a mental experience "without struggle or desire" (30). Kingscourt defines the stay on the island as "a last experiment." And he explains: "The thought crept into my mind to end the shabby comedy of my life with a bullet. But on thinking it over, I decided that there was always time to shoot . . . Only solitude remained as a last experiment. But it must be a vast, unheard-of solitude, where one would know nothing more of mankind—of its wretched struggles, its uncleanliness, its disloyalties. I wanted deep, genuine solitude . . . a full, true return to nature!"

Kingscourt's "full, true return to nature," however, is very different both from the one preached by Jean-Jacques Rousseau and by Mapu. Life on the secluded island ("a rocky little nest in Cook's archipelago" [31]) has clear rules: what is absolutely forbidden and what is allowed, desired, or obligatory.

The first rule is "no newspapers!" Friedrich says that only once, after fifteen years on the island, did he come across some newspapers that reached them from a ship. He was tempted for a moment to read them but immediately changed his mind, collected the newspapers, and burned them. The second rule is abstention from women! The remote island is inhabited by four men: Kingscourt, Friedrich and two servants—one a black servant and the other a Tahitian, whom Kingscourt pulled out of the water after he tried to drown himself "over an unhappy love affair" (ibid.).

But these two abstentions do suggest others. This becomes clear from the appearance and equipment of the ship that takes the companions to their island. This "yacht [is] very cozy, and equipped with all sorts of American conveniences," and it even has "a small, well-selected library" (39). Onboard the yacht they eat nutritious meals and drink fine wines, Kingscourt even indulging in expensive Cuban cigars, and everything is conducted in a pleasant atmosphere and accompanied with "congenial talk."

In the twenty years they spend together on the island, they maintain, as Friedrich says, a similar lifestyle: "hunting and fishing, eating, drinking and sleeping, playing chess" (84). It is a process of convalescence in a gentlemanly military, European, conservative manner—Kingscourt's manner, that of a Prussian aristocrat, a cavalry officer, a conservative, and a skeptic when it comes to human beings, men and women alike.

This "monastery," the secluded island on which Friedrich and Kingscourt spend twenty years, is depicted as an emblematic liminal space, or in Zali Gurevich and Gideon Aran's terminology, as a "no place" typical of rites of passage.[26] It is a place that is totally disconnected from life's ordinary environment and is dominated by vital and destructive forces that take different and often also strange shapes. It is a kind of place that is at once both primordial and final—tomb and womb—serving as a necessary "melting pot" for the passage from one personality and cultural [social?] phase to another. This passage is possible because there is a shift here from ordinary life, from history, to life outside history. "Timelessness begins for us now" (49), Friedrich says to Kingscourt as they begin their journey to the island.

This melting pot is the structural and thematic parallel to the Elend, the Jewish ghetto or the Diaspora as a whole, which, according to Herzl's stated view, is an entirely negative no place—a no place that is so negative, that whoever grew up in it, at least if he is an Austro-Hungarian Jew, must go through "re-indoctrination" in a similar but different no place, a long and intensive re-indoctrination at the end of which, as Kingscourt promises Friedrich, he shall be cured and thus also fit for the New Society.

Kingscourt promises Friedrich to cure him and seems to fulfill his promise. After the long "training period" on the secluded island, we meet a different Friedrich. Kingscourt looks at his "pupil" as he "lean[s] back in his comfortable easy chair, and puff[s] at a large Havana" (54), and sums up the change: "Well, our island did not disagree with you, Fritz! What a green, hollow-chested Jewboy you were when I took you away. Now you are like an oak. You might still be dangerous to the women." Kingscourt is right. Friedrich has been cured in his Prussian aristocrat friend's "monastery" from "his serious illness"—central European Jewish decadence—and has come back to life. The weak signs of vitality he had shown before—signs revealed in erotic circumstances on the one hand (the futile zeal for Ernestina) and national circumstances on the other (the "remarkable encounter" with David Littwak that "stirred old and forgotten things within him" [26], and with Jerusalem, the desolate "strange city" at night, which moved him so much that "his eyes overflowed" [43])—these signs reappear in similar circumstances after the period of re-indoctrination on the secluded island, but this time more frequently and with growing intensity.

While sailing in the Red Sea—this time from the island to Eretz Israel—Friedrich declares, "It's all one to me... In those twenty years on our beloved island, I lost all interest in the doings of the outside world."[27] But shortly after putting down in Haifa, as he watches the view from the height of the Carmel and hears his guide, David, that poor boy who has become an impressive man, telling him "See, Dr. Loewenberg, this is the land of our fathers" (69), his eyes well up with tears, like in the past when he saw the desolate Jerusalem but also differently: "He had looked then upon moonlight Death; now, Life sparkled joyously in the sun."

Friedrich is also moved when he meets Miriam, David's sister, for the first time. First he sees her image in an oil painting hanging in Friedrichsheim: "a painting over the great chimney place which portrayed a slender, black-haired young woman of great beauty" (72). Then he sees Miriam herself, and what attracts him to her—and as we shall see below, this is not a unique case, but part of a trend—is actually her voice: "He felt strongly moved at hearing his name pronounced in her charming voice."

The two catalyzers in Dr. Friedrich Loewenberg's resurrection—the old-new woman (the helpless baby from Vienna turned into a lovely woman) and the old-new place—gradually merge in the novel. This had already happened during Friedrich and Kingscourt's first tour of the country in its idyllic period. During this trip from Haifa to Tiberias, made on a wonderful spring day in "an enormous touring car... a real Noah's ark" (115) led by David and joined by Miriam, Friedrich "was happy, inexplicably happy. He was young again, exuberant. He teased his charming companion. 'How about your school, Miss Miriam? Have you hung your duties on a hook for a while?' 'He knows nothing!' laughed Miriam. 'Absolutely nothing at all about Jewish things. Allow me to inform you, sir, that our Passover vacation began today. We are going to visit my parents at Tiberias because we shall celebrate the Seder there'" (117).

The personal story—Friedrich's revival, for which "his charming companion" is partly responsible—and the national story—the Exodus from Egypt in its new version—merge here (just like in the first and last encounters between Amnon and Tamar and between Peninah and Teman in *The Love of Zion*) with the blessing of nature: the wonderful spring day, as it is observed from the seat of the "touring car," one of the symbols of the modern technological revolution.

The private story, the story of the match between Friedrich and Miriam, which in Herzl's modernist version is always integrated with the story of the national renaissance, comprises four other prominent scenes. The first scene takes place in the holiday home of Miriam and David's parents in Tiberias. The dying Mrs. Littwak smiles wistfully on hearing Miriam talk about her impending recovery and afterward turns Friedrich's attention to the view seen through the window: "Dear child, I am content. I am already at the gates of Paradise. Look at this view of mine, Dr. Loewenberg. The Garden of Eden, is it not?" (161). And further down:

> Friedrich stepped to the balustrade and looked out over the landscape. The shimmering blue waters of Lake Kinneret. The shores and distant heights softly outlined in the spring air. The steep declivities of the Golan hills on the farther side of the lake, mirrored in its depths. The Jordan flowing into the northern end of the lake. In the distance, the majestic, snow-crowned Hermon, a venerable giant overlooking the smaller ranges and the rejuvenated land. To the left, nearer the town, gentle inlets, lovely beaches, the plain of Kinneret, Magdala, Tiberias itself—a new gem set among the dark ruins of the fortress on the hillside. Verdure and bloom everywhere. A young world, and fragrant.
>
> "The Garden of Eden, indeed!" murmured Friedrich to himself. As he felt Miriam standing beside him, he caught her hand and pressed it softly, as if to thank her that life could still be so beautiful.
>
> The invalid saw from her chair, and her heart beat faster for joy.
>
> "Children!" she murmured inaudibly, and sank into reverie." (161–62)

The second scene in the series of revival scenes, which takes place in the Golan Heights, includes the same elements: the rejuvenated land, the spring, the mythological festival of the renewal of growth, and Miriam's proximity. And here, too, a seemingly naturally integrated electric vehicle. Here we are: "The morning sky was glowing with delicate colors as they boarded the electric train that was to carry them through a bewitching spring landscape. Friedrich felt stirrings of the springtides of his boyhood in his blood. And, though he dared hardly admit it to himself, the proximity of the lovely Miriam was not without its influence upon his mood" (237).

The connection between the proper place and the proper woman, which gives rise to a new life/a new masculinity, is also made in the painter Isaacs's house in Jerusalem. In this famous artist's house—described by the narrator as an architectonic space that integrates (neoclassical/Western) culture and (Western) technology in an exemplary way—Friedrich hears Miriam sing for the first time and is again enchanted by her special voice. Here: "[Isaacs] walked down the arcade to the door of the music room, which he noiselessly set ajar. Now the glorious tones were heard in their full strength. Miriam, unconscious of her audience, sang Schumann, Rubinstein, Wagner, Verdi, Gounod, the music of all the nations, for Lady Lillian [Lady Lillian, the aristocratic wife of Lord Sudbury]. The melodies flowed in a ceaseless stream. Friedrich listened blissfully, happy to be among these choice spirits who realized life in Beauty and Wisdom. When Miriam began the wistful song from 'Mignon' that he had always loved, 'Knowest Thou the Land,' he whispered to himself, '*This* is the Land!'" (263, emphasis mine).

The last scene in this series mirrors a previous scene that took place in the same spot. The Littwaks and their close family friends gather around the bed of the dying Mrs. Littwak. The father tells his wife that "Dr. Loewenberg has brought us good news" (293), referring to David's appointment as president of the New Society. The mother calls Friedrich over and stutters:

> "I thought—so—at once. Then . . . when you—on the balcony . . . outside here . . . children! . . . " She groped blindly. "Miriam—has told—me . . . nothing. But a mother . . . sees! Children! Give . . . each other . . . your hand. My blessing—my blessing!"
>
> Miriam and Friedrich had to reach out their hands to each other, but they were so hesitant that she took notice. She looked anxiously from one to the other, and whispered, "Or . . . or? . . ."
>
> "Yes, indeed," said Friedrich fervently, and pressed the girl's hand. "Yes," repeated Miriam softly.

The New Dynasty

Herzl's utopian novel ends, like *The Love of Zion*, with a double family celebration. The elderly Littwaks, who have in the past suffered hunger and humiliations, find out that their son has been appointed as president of the New Society, and their daughter is engaged to be married to the man of her choice, who is also their former beneficiary, the unnamed person thanks to whom the family was saved from its misfortune.

Ostensibly all is well: the two plotlines that feature the cover versions of the Exodus from Egypt myth are concluded and merged. The merging and conclusion of these two plotlines (the one marked by education and colonialism and the other by romanticism and auto-antisemitism) promise redemption on the national level as well. Eretz Israel is transformed from "a barren land" into a thriving one, and from a backward region on the periphery of Asia into the spearhead of modernity. Things, however, are not that simple. This becomes clear when we reexamine the end of the novel, an examination that, together with other examinations bifurcating from it, reveals cracks that reflect unsolved problems in Herzl's vision, and what seems at first sight like a successful attempt to erase the gap between the "place" and the "Place" turns out to be a hesitant and ambivalent attempt. Herzl's hesitancy and ambivalence with regard to the possibility of realizing his vision is fascinatingly revealed in the ambiguous portrayal of the individual plotlines: David's and Friedrich's (both on his own and with Miriam). It is true that, as I have remarked earlier, David—like the painter Isaacs—is an emblem of the mobility and equality in the New Society; a society in which, as in Venice, "every son . . . could become a Doge" (*ONL*, 286). But the fact that it is, of all people, the son of the beggar, "the Littwak," who becomes president requires further analysis because the other candidates for the presidency withdraw their candidacy as a gesture to the person who "made his way up from very modest beginnings," and because of the "suspicious" nature of the elements that the author has chosen for his equation. Although Venice was a (relatively) mobile society, it preserved the division between patricians and plebeians, a dynastically based class division that is revealed again and again as a thread that runs through Herzl's novel.[28]

This division, it turns out, has two sections. One is a section of true aristocrats, that is, Christian aristocrats with documented pedigrees, of whom Kingscourt is the ultimate representative. The second is a section of "second class" aristocrats, which is in turn divided into two groups: "aristocrats by virtue of (Western) culture" (these are the Austro-Hungarian Jews, led by Friedrich) and "aristocrats by virtue of education" (these are the Ostjuden, plebeians by birth, who can be counted as members of the desired class only after years of strenuous dedication). The class dichotomy within the Jewish community—which is always overshadowed by the dichotomy of aristocracy by birth (the foreign nobility) versus the new aristocracy (the different kinds of Jewish nobility)[29]—can be inferred on many occasions in the novel. Here are two examples:

A) In the artist Isaacs's studio, visited by Friedrich and Miriam, the guests are divided into a group of men and a group of women. Friedrich is sitting among the men, looking at Miriam and Lady Lillian—a real English Lady, the wife of a real English Lord: "The two were standing beside the trellis, their slender figures a pleasing sight. Miriam, dark-haired and somewhat the shorter, cut no poor figure in her simple gown beside the tall, blonde Englishwoman whose costume bespoke a Parisian tailor. Friedrich felt a vague pride as he observed the daughter of the Jewish peddler carrying herself so modestly and yet with such dignity beside the great English lady. In the manner of his absent friend he said to himself, 'All the Devils! We've even achieved a modest entrée into Society!'" (258).

No additional words seem necessary: the highly stereotypical contrast between the two women, the (apparent) effacement of this contrast and the interpretation of the "vague pride," formulated in the style of Kingscourt, the Prussian aristocrat, speak for themselves.

B) While touring the New Village, Friedrich is suddenly overtaken by feelings of shame and regret for having wasted his life without making any worthwhile contribution to society. Miriam tries to comfort him. Friedrich insists, explaining to Miriam what is the "natural role" that he and other intellectuals of his kind (that is, Austro-Hungarian Jews with a European education) should have fulfilled in the New Society: "The intellectuals of my time had the duty, similar to the *noblesse oblige* of earlier days, of working for the improvement of mankind" (156).

The Austro-Hungarian Jews, then, bring civilization to Palestine. Conversely, eastern European Jews bring vigor, potency, familial and tribal ties, and a connection with God. Furthermore, the main representative of culture is a man, whereas the representative of nature and naturalness is a woman. It is a typical orientalist, racist, and misogynistic division, and there is no wonder that the book aroused such strong opposition on a variety of fronts—around the time of its publication, the harsh criticism of Ahad Ha'am, M. J. Berdichevsky, and M. Buber; and in our time, the strong criticism of intellectuals and scholars who have in different ways linked *Altneuland*'s discrimination against eastern European Jews with its discrimination against women and Arabs.[30]

These attacks, it should be said, are essentially understandable and justified, although—and this is an important point in my view—they are exaggerated. This becomes clear from the comparison, ignored by the book's critics, of Herzl's attitude toward the "Jews of the Orient" and his attitude toward central European Jews and their possible rehabilitation.

In *The Love of Zion*, center stage is taken by Amnon and Tamar, two young people who are making their way toward each other in a trajectory influenced by powerful erotic and thanatic forces. Herzl's chosen couple—or to be precise, as shall become clear below, his formal chosen couple—is very different from the chosen couple in *The Love of Zion:* here the "Romeo," Friedrich, is a man in his mid-forties, who has long ago given up life in this world in general, and ties with women in particular. Herzl's "Juliet," Miriam, is younger, but she is also not a libidinous creature, like Tamar. Miriam is a modest woman who has chosen to devote her time and energy to the teaching of young children. The relationship that develops between the two is marked by a weak vitality, already hinted at in their first physical encounter: the one that takes place before Passover at the Littwak's home in Tiberias. This encounter is entirely colored by the initiative of Miriam's mother, who "pushes" the "children" into each other's arms.

A similarly anemic and even more ridiculous situation occurs at the same place at the end of the novel. As already mentioned, the family members and their close friends gather around the mother's deathbed, and only when faced with the dying woman's embarrassment do Friedrich and Miriam muster the courage to declare their commitment to each other. The narrator adds, as if to highlight the lackluster character of this match, "Thus a mother, even when weak and helpless, can always create happiness for her child" (*ONL*, 293).

The way Friedrich and Miriam are brought together in these two scenes coincides with the choice of the site that serves as the backdrop for these scenes, Tiberias. For, in contrast to what one may expect from Herzl's manifest landscape conceptualization, the final coupling does not take place in the book's "Place"; that is, in a place that (like the Mount of Olives in *The Love of Zion*) is the clear symbolic topographic representative of the stated and/or implied ideological intention of the author. This event does not take place in Haifa, the new capital of the old-new land, nor in the New Village, where, according to Herzl, one finds the right combination of nature and civilization. Rather, the event announcing the engagement of the novel's "chosen couple" takes place in Tiberias, a town that in Herzl's vision has a distinctly cosmopolitan character; in other words, in Herzl's mind there is no real connection between the "genetic engineering" of the New Hebrew person and the ultimate representations of settlement in the Eretz Israel of his vision, Haifa and the New Village.

The same conclusion is reached, with greater force, when we examine the characteristics of the event in which the spark of love for Miriam is ignited in Friedrich's heart: the refined/civilized encounter at the painter Isaacs's "studio," during which Friedrich hears Miriam sing. Miriam's repertoire includes "the music of all the nations" (263)—that is, following the Europocentric logic that prevails in the book, a selection of works that were considered at the time European classics: "Schumann, Rubinstein, Wagner, Verdi, Gounod." This repertoire fits in wonderfully with the style of Isaacs's house, a classicist-modernist mixture completely alien to the local styles. And the house is separated from its surroundings by a wall.

It is precisely there, in the house dubbed "the palace of a prince of art" (257), Herzl's "pleasant place"—a neoclassicist building (with a certain kitschy touch) set in "a natural environment" that is controlled by a concealed and effective technology—that the event, and perhaps the novel as a whole, reaches its climax. Friedrich hears Miriam sing a piece "that he had always loved," namely, "the wistful song from 'Mignon' . . . [:] 'Knowest Thou the Land'" (263).

> Knowest thou the land where bloom the lemon trees,
> And darkly gleam the golden oranges?

> A gentle wind blows down from that blue sky;
> Calm stands the myrtle and the laurel high.
> Knowest thou the land? So far and fair!
> Thou, whom I love, and I will wander there.
> Knowest thou the house with all its rooms aglow,
> And shining hall and columned portico?
> The marble statues stand and look at me.
> Alas, poor child, what have they done to thee?

The fact that the climactic moment of the chosen couple's relationship in this utopian novel is associated precisely with "Mignon's Song"—Goethe's text from "Wilhelm Meister," whose famous musical renderings (Ludwig van Beethoven, 1809; Franz Schubert, 1815; Franz Liszt, 1842; Robert Schumann, 1849; and Hugo Wolf, 1888) were probably familiar to Herzl—raises questions, at least on its own. For the land of the lemon of which the song speaks is not Eretz Israel but . . . *Italy!* Yet when this fact is linked to similarly problematic facts—for instance, the fact that the spark of love is ignited of all places in Isaacs's neoclassicist-modernist garden, which is pronouncedly separated from the whole "Levantine environment"—the surprise diminishes.

It seems that in the marriage between Friedrich and Miriam, Herzl created what he considered to be the best match in the Jewish "gene bank," a match that is supposed to ensure the merging of physical and sexual potency; vigor; and familial, tribal, and religious ties identified with a woman from eastern Europe with the intellectualism and culture identified with an Austro-Hungarian man. This, however, as already mentioned, is not the novel's ultimate match. A match of this kind requires biological and mental qualities that can be found, according to Herzl, only in the gentile "gene bank," more precisely, in the "gene bank" of the old Christian gentile aristocracy.

This far-reaching conclusion emerges from a close inspection of the status and role of the complex link Herzl made between two central elements in his narrative: the "external witness," Kingscourt on his own, and the pair, Kingscourt and the child Friedrich, who, in my view, are the novel's perfect couple.

Like Hadoram in Mapu's *The Love of Zion*, Kingscourt in *Altneuland* plays the role of the "external witness," who provides the utopian vision with its final validation. Kingscourt, however—and this points to a fundamental difference between Mapu and Herzl—is a much more important and significant figure than Hadoram. In fact, he—"Adalbert von Koeningshoff, a royal Prussian officer, and Christian German nobleman" (85)—is the most highly regarded character in the novel, as far as Herzl is concerned.

This seems like a surprising statement. But when we examine its supporting evidence, it becomes unavoidable. Kingscourt is behind all the central turning points in the plot: he is the "mysterious philanthropist" thanks to whom the Littwak family is rescued from its troubles; he is the one who prevents Friedrich's suicide; he is the one who insists that the two make a stop in Eretz Israel before embarking on their journey to the secluded island; he is the one who makes Friedrich become "like an oak"; he is the one who insists that they visit Eretz Israel again before traveling to Europe. Kingscourt, more than anyone else, should also be credited with little Friedrich's recovery from his serious illness. And it is only thanks to him that the novel ends happily, with a closure that validates Herzl's vision. For Kingscourt is the one who decides to stay in *Altneuland*—whereas Friedrich, the central European Jew, is ready to renounce everything (both Miriam and the land!) and go back to Europe. Kingscourt's crucial status in the plot[31]—a veritable deus ex machine in this strictly secular novel—coincides with another ostensibly surprising phenomenon: the intense connection between him and little Friedrich, who is named after Dr. Friedrich Loewenberg. Between the two—the elderly Prussian nobleman, who keeps declaring that he is a misanthrope, and the only Eretz-Israeli child in the novel—there develops a proper love story, with all its rules and regulations.

It is a story of love at first sight. On first seeing Kingscourt's white beard, young Friedrich prefers it over his meal; he "crowed loudly, and reached out his little arms to the old man" (*ONL*, 73). Kingscourt, for his part, becomes inseparable from the child and, claiming that "the fellow won't let me go," stays with him for another whole hour. The narrator adds: "From that moment dated the friendship between the old misanthrope and the youngest Littwak."

Kingscourt becomes so attached to the boy that in the middle of a lively adult conversation he is "losing himself for a moment in a vision of the nursery" (75). He even lies in order to be with him (115). And little Littwak returns his love. For example, during the trip to Tiberias, the narrator reports that "Once, however, Fritzchen was in Kingscourt's arms, he refused absolutely to go back to his nurse. David, entering the car last, tried to exert his parental authority. In vain."

The intensifying connection between the two is not missed by Sarah, little Fritz's mother. When Friedrich confides in her that he envies those who are lucky enough to live in the New Society, she tells him that he too has this right, adding that if he believes that Kingscourt will stand in his way and demand that he fulfill his commitment to go back to the secluded island with him, she has the perfect solution to the problem: "'We'll arrange all that. You both belong to us—you as the savior of our family, and he as your friend. You'll see, I'll soon have you settled here. You're not to contradict me, please! I've a word to say in this too. As for the old growler-bear, I'll chain him with bonds of love.' 'Do you mean to marry him off?' cried Friedrich, highly amused. 'I could if I cared to,' she declared.... 'A man is never too old to marry... But I was thinking of other bonds of affection for Mr. Kingscourt. He's enchanted with my Fritzchen... I've noticed that'" (215).

The ultimate test of the relationship between the Prussian nobleman and the Eretz-Israeli boy takes place in the days of Fritz's serious illness. The child "clung to him as to no one else... From no one else would he take his medicine. No one else was allowed to croon him to sleep" (265). At some point everyone loses hope, including the father, David. Only Kingscourt keeps humming his songs. At the critical stage of the disease, Kingscourt manages to put Fritz to sleep, vowing, "If that worm recovers, I'll stay here forever. That's a solemn promise. I offer this sacrifice for his recovery" (269). Indeed Fritz recovers, and since Kingscourt has "sworn an oath, and it stands," he stays in the country.

The love story between Kingscourt and Fritz sheds an illuminating light on Herzl's human engineering. The fact that this is the most impressive match in terms of its emotional force, as well as the crucial match in terms of the plot, obliges us to see all the alternative matches differently. In light of such a lovely and vivacious match as the one between Kingscourt and Fritz—a match that crosses boundaries of race, language, and age; breaks through a barrier of misanthropy; and even overcomes death—the match between Miriam and Friedrich seems even more anemic. Whereas the parallel match, that of David and Sarah, to which the author does not pay much attention, seems like a match whose main function is to facilitate the match between Kingscourt and little Fritz. In other words, the Littwak family serves as a kind of surrogate family because Fritz absolutely prefers Kingscourt.

The bond between Kingscourt and Fritz also sheds new light on the relationship between Kingscourt and the elder Friedrich—the novel's central masculine alliance, at least outwardly. This human alliance, the match between the elder Friedrich and Kingscourt, has drawn the attention of Daniel Boyarin and Michael Gluzman.[32] Both examined this relationship closely and came up with a few brilliant, albeit partially hasty and unfounded, remarks.

Both assume—Boyarin implicitly, Gluzman in a more explicit and reasoned fashion—that the relationship between Kingscourt and Friedrich is of a homoerotic nature. This claim is supported by the fact that Kingscourt, the gentile-Prussian-noble-military man (who is identified with the large cigar that protrudes from his lips) and Friedrich, the Jewish-pale-sickly man, identified by his friend with none other than Ophelia, make a bond that is supposed to be maintained forever in "a rocky little nest" (*ONL*, 31). It is "a lifelong obligation"

(32), and every time a crack appears in it—in the shape of Miriam, in the shape of the new life in Eretz Israel—it is immediately sealed with a ratification of that obligation, accompanied by the typical elements of a lovers' dialogue.

Thus, for example, when the two are sailing from the secluded island back to Europe, Friedrich laughs after Kingscourt tells him that he might now be dangerous to women:

> "You are quite mad, Kingscourt . . . I think too much of you to infer that you're dragging me to Europe to marry me off."
>
> Kingscourt was convulsed with laughter. "Carrion! Marry you off! You don't think me that kind of an ass, I hope! What should I do with you then?"
>
> "Well, it might be a delicate way of getting rid of me. Haven't you had enough of my society?"
>
> "Now the carrion's fishing for compliments," shouted the old man, who expressed his good humor best through epithets. "You know very well, Fritzchen, that I can no longer live without you. Indeed, I arranged this whole trip for your sake. So that you would be patient with me a few years longer." (54)

Little Fritzchen, however, quickly takes the elder Fritzchen's place in Kingscourt's heart. And in fact, in light of all that we have said here, it is no wonder. For little Fritz is an enhanced and improved version of the elder Fritz—and for obvious reasons. Fritz Loewenberg spent all his formative years in the degenerate and corrupting Diaspora, in the Elend. His "rehabilitation" on the secluded island, as successful as it might have been, probably still does not turn him, in Herzl's eyes, into a worthy candidate for establishing a new dynasty in the old-new land. Fritz, on the other hand, was born in Eretz Israel, and receives the right education: the (both bodily and mentally) wholesome norms of the New Society, with a crucial addition—the acquisition of the modes of behavior of a German-gentile-military nobleman.

We should therefore take note of the "strange" nature of the "genetic dynasty" suggested by the novel: Sarah and David's son is called Friedrich—meaning he is a kind of heir to the elder Friedrich (whom David was convinced had died long ago), an interesting status in light of the fact that the central couple, Friedrich and Miriam, have no children and as things stand will probably not have any.

Little Fritz, however, does not go from his parents' care to the care of "his spiritual father" but rather to that of "an adopted grandfather." In this Herzl tells us, either wittingly or unwittingly, that his proper dynasty is passed on from the gentile grandfather to the Eretz-Israeli grandchild, while making an astonishing oedipal leap over the parent generation—the generation of Friedrich, Miriam, David, and Sarah. This is a move that erases, from the starting point of the nation's future—again, either knowingly or unknowingly—all the Jews born in the Diaspora (the Desert Generation), wishing to start everything here, in Eretz Israel, from a match between "Sabra"-Hebraism and Prussianism.

Herzl's human engineering and landscape conceptualization therefore differ considerably from those of Mapu, who, as you will recall, did not dare to deviate from the national "gene bank"—despite hinting at the fundamental legitimacy of a move of this kind (Naame and Peninah disguise themselves as Philistine women and walk behind the harvesters, like Ruth the Moabite in her time)—or even from the "gene bank" of the ruling class (the urban nobility owning properties in the rural periphery).

Herzl, it should be emphasized, envisioned first and foremost a new society rather than a new community; that is, according to Tönnies, a human congregation whose typical characteristics are common interests (social, cultural, and the like) and contractuality with regard to predefined areas. This explains the central status given in the New Society to the social covenant, its multinational and multiethnic character, and the (striking) absence of political borders. An ideological platform, however, is one thing, and existential anxieties are another. A close inspection of Herzl's human engineering suggests that he too was in thrall to the notion of a genetic engineering that would save the Jewish tribe, a notion that was anchored in racial stereotypes: the distinction between weak genes (the Jews, mainly the men from central Europe), strong genes (the Jews, mainly the women from eastern Europe), and the really strong genes (gentiles from ancient aristocratic families).

Animals, Machines, Nature, and Civilization

Unlike in Mapu's work, Herzl's *Altneuland* does not feature even a single real wild or predatory animal. On the other hand, it mentions a number of domestic animals (horses, sheep, cows, donkeys, dogs, etc.), all of which are described as working efficiently in the service of man.

The peripheral status given in the novel to wild animals and predators becomes evident—at least in relation to what exists on the novel's surface—when we compare the participants in versions of the "at the well" scenes in Mapu and in Herzl. The terrible lion, the menacing vulture, and the poisonous snake, which in *The Love of Zion*'s version of the biblical scenes serve as representatives of wild nature, where great forces of fertility and destruction mix with one another, are replaced in *Altneuland* by technological inventions: "a touring car" (115), "an electric train" (237), "a movable . . . trellis" (257), and "a telegram" (291). This difference leads us to conclude that Herzl believed that the fruits of modern civilization can serve as an alternative existential anchor for the connection with nature and the natural. This conclusion coincides with a central intratextual analogy, the one made between Androcles's control of the lion in the story told to Friedrich by the poor boy David, and the control exerted by the turbine sheds, the technological Temple, over "tamed natural forces" (244).

The salient characteristic of *Altneuland*'s fauna—the fact that all the animals are domesticated—coincides with the salient characteristic of the book's flora. While adorning the country with few wild trees and plants, Herzl fills it with plots of fruit-bearing trees and shrubs ("luxuriant orange and lemon groves" [120]), terraces ("with vines, pomegranate and fig trees as in the ancient days of Solomon" [125]), and plants used for industrial production (fields "thickly sown with wheat and oats, maize and hops, poppies and tobacco" [132]; "summer crops . . . maize, sesame, lentils, vetches" [257]). He also repeatedly notes that the entire country (from the Dead Sea Canal northward) is cultivated by the hands of man.

The status given in Herzl's imaginary world to the domesticated elements, however—chief among them the animals—is more complex. This complexity, which the modern technology-craving author seems to have been only partially aware of, is first reflected in the visit made by Friedrich, Kingscourt, and their entourage to the Steineck Institute, the bacteriological research institute. At the beginning, this visit, guided by the Institute's director Professor Steineck, proceeds calmly. The Institute itself is spacious and functional: it was built on the south bank of the Sea of Galilee, "an unpretentious building of moderate size" (165). It occupies a relatively small area, and the professor explains to his visitors why: "We don't need a large building for our purpose . . . Microbes don't take up much room. My stables are in those annexes over there. I use many horses and other creatures. Understand?" But Kingscourt, the Prussian cavalry officer, does not understand:

> "Ah! You ride a great deal," said Kingscourt. "I can understand that—in this magnificent country."
>
> "Country nothing! I use horses and donkeys and dogs—in brief, the whole menagerie—for serum."

The comic misunderstanding between the aristocrat, the man of the Old World, and the scientist, the hero of the New World, has a serious side as well. The world Herzl has created is a world in which nature is erased; a world enslaved to the god of progress—an extreme modern world harboring the danger expressed by Kingscourt in a confrontation with professor Steineck that climaxes with Kingscourt calling the professor a "most esteemed horse-poisoner"

(165). In fact, the disagreement between Steineck and Kingscourt revolves around their view of man's status in the universe. Steineck—like a thoroughly modern man—sees man as the crown and glory of creation and as its purpose. Kingscourt, on the other hand, is as resolute and self-professed a misanthrope as he is a lover of animals (and especially horses). To return to our discussion, the fact that the disagreement between the two remains unresolved, coupled with the great appreciation that the author feels toward both characters, who represent contradicting positions, suggests that Herzl's attitude toward the animal world as representing primeval forces is ambivalent.

Herzl's ambivalence on this issue is fascinatingly reflected on the novel's lexical level and, more precisely, in the characteristics of its reservoir of images. He created "a dynasty of images" that connects the "grandfather," "Adalbert von Koeningshoff, a royal Prussian officer and Christian German nobleman," with the "father," David Littwak, the chosen representative of the "Shtetl Jewry," and the "grandson," Fritz, David's son and an enhanced version of Friedrich.

As for Kingscourt—he, as already mentioned, loves animals much more than human beings and is willing to help them more than he does his own kind. He tells Friedrich, who reports that he has given the large sum of money he received from Kingscourt to the needy, "If you had told me you wished to do something for dogs or horses or other respectable creatures, you could have had my help. But for humans, no! Don't bring that kind around. They're too vile. Wisdom consists only in recognizing their baseness" (37). Kingscourt's strong affinity for animals is also reflected in his language, which is full of vivid images taken from the animal world. Here are a few examples. Of Friedrich he says, "Now the carrion's fishing for compliments" (54) and "What silly-billy notions you have" (85). For himself he uses the terms "an old donkey" (84) and "an old ass" (94), and he says, "If you think me such a donkey . . . you're very much in error" (199). For professor Steineck: "horse-poisoner" (165) and "beloved begetter of microbes" (256).

David is also "caught" using animal imagery, albeit only once. He likens himself, as you will recall, to the lion cub of Judea—an image that Friedrich, and through him the author, reinforces and confirms. When the analogy between David, the representative of the Ostjuden, and the sick lion in Androcles's story is first mentioned, Friedrich laughs, though he is highly impressed by the child beggar's resolute words. The libidinal energy of the representative of the Ostjuden is reflected in this single association with the animal world. Conversely, the bond between Kingscourt, the "grandfather," and little Fritz, the "grandson"— an as it were "Diaspora-bypassing genetic link"—resides almost exclusively in the animalistic semantic field. A central motif here is the "riders' bond." Kingscourt was, as already mentioned, an officer in the Prussian cavalry. The skills he acquired there are passed on to little Fritz. Already in their first meeting, he sits him astride on his shoulders and sings to him antiquated German songs (74). When Friedrich catches Kingscourt in this "shameful situation," Kingscourt tells him, "That fellow will certainly become a cavalryman" (216).

When little Fritz becomes seriously ill, Kingscourt tends to him day and night, sitting by his bed and singing his antiquated German hunting song to him over and over again. When the boy is in critical condition, Kingscourt makes a vow that includes, what else, an element from the animalistic semantic field: "if that worm recovers, I'll stay here forever" (269). And when the "worm" does recover, and Kingscourt is forced "to rationalize" "his love for Fritzchen [that] could no longer be denied," he does so on the basis of "his principles" (269–70). Here: "He admitted that he could stand the little boy well enough, just as one is fond of any innocent creature. Fritzchen was not yet a man, and a hater of mankind [such as Kingscourt] sacrificed nothing of his principles when he took a fancy to such a little fellow" (270).

Upon examining the fauna in Herzl's landscape conceptualization, the fundamental features of his worldview come into sharp focus again: an innovative modern worldview, which at the same time is tied with bonds of admiration and longing to the old hierarchical world; a worldview that erases any trace of the old ways of life—the Shtetl on the one hand and the Arab village on the other—yet is accompanied with a vague fear of getting too far away from nature and the natural. It evinces a longing for romantic values: land, family, tribe, nation, and so forth, yet also a distaste for them; an admiration for modernity, liberality, cosmopolitanism, etc., and at the same time a distrust in them as sufficient for the survival of any people, including the Jewish people.

It is a worldview plagued with strong ambivalence toward the Romantic narrative on the one hand, and the Enlightenment narrative on the other. An ambivalence of this kind, originating in the fin de siècle spirit in Europe, is common to Herzl and to other Jewish writers who grew up in the Austro-Hungarian landscape of the 1860s and 1870s (Joseph Roth, Arthur Schnitzler, Stefan Zweig, and others). This ambivalence, as we shall partially see in the next chapters, was passed on to younger writers, both those who grew up in the same cultural landscape (David Vogel, Aharon Appelfeld, and others), and those who grew up in a different cultural landscape (A. B. Yehoshua, Amos Oz, and others).

3

"Yoash," Yosef Luidor, 1912

The Taste of Freedom and Space

> *Openly I pledged myself to the grave and suffering land,*
> *and often in the consecrated night, I promised to love her faithfully*
> *until death, unafraid, with her heavy burden of fatality, and*
> *never to despise a single one of her enigmas. Thus did*
> *I join myself to her with a mortal cord.*
>
> —FRIEDRICH HÖLDERLIN, *Death of Empedocles*

The Writer behind the Ghostly National Imaginings

The Love of Zion and *Altneuland* are central texts in the history of modern national Jewish imaginings. Most of the scholars of modern Hebrew culture would probably agree on that. The same scholars would probably also agree, in the same context, on the centrality of Moshe Shamir's novel *He Walked in the Fields* and Amos Oz's stories in *Where the Jackals Howl*, which will form the focus of this book's last two chapters.

As for the centrality of Yosef Luidor's stories in the context of our discussion —here there may be some disagreements, since this is a writer whose name, let alone works, are known to few people, mainly to graduates of Hebrew literature departments in universities. Luidor is a writer who wrote only a few stories and a small number of literary essays, some of which have been lost, the rest collected only fifty-five years after his death in the little book *Stories* (1976), in which literary scholars and critics showed little interest.[1]

My choice to focus on Luidor's stories may also raise eyebrows in view of the status given them in the literary world of his time: the period of the Second Aliyah. Anyone familiar with the literature of that time knows that there were better texts written then, by much more acclaimed and well-known writers than Luidor, including texts that describe themselves, or that were seen by their readers, as "period novels"[2]—in particular the three great novels of the time: Y. H. Brenner's *Breakdown and Bereavement*, Aharon Reuveni's *Even to Jerusalem*, and S. Y. Agnon's *Only Yesterday*.

Why therefore have I chosen the somewhat immature stories of an author who is to a large extent unknown? The reason for this choice is that this is a paradigmatic corpus at least on three levels. First, Luidor's texts reflect the inventory of subjects and the sociocultural tensions typical of the literature of his generation, albeit, as I will try to show, sometimes with his own unique dispositions. Second, I chose Luidor from a wish to question one of the basic assumptions according to which Hebrew readers and critics have read and judged Eretz-Israeli literature from the beginning of the twentieth century onward; a basic assumption that, in my view, has allowed them to ignore the psychological and ideological landmines hidden in this corpus, with all its various parts.

I am referring to the famous dichotomy between "genre fiction" and "anti-genre fiction," which has become commonplace following a famous essay by Y. H. Brenner.[3] Genre fiction, or in Gershon Shaked's terminology,[4] "naive fiction," is a body of work that ostensibly describes life in Eretz Israel under the assumption that the Zionist dream has become a reality; that is, that the gap between the "Place" and the "place" has been erased, has evaporated and disappeared. On the other hand, anti-genre fiction, or in Shaked's terminology, "ironic fiction," is a body of work that, again ostensibly, describes life in Eretz Israel under the assumption that the Zionist dream has not been fulfilled; that is, that the "diasporic" gap between the Place and the place still remains.

I wish to claim that the situation in Hebrew literature is more complicated, among other reasons because the genre writers were not really naïve. This fact clearly emerges from the Luidor case. A close and careful reading of his work, to which I shall devote the present chapter of this book, suggests that even he, who in the eyes of the few who discussed him was considered the ultimate native writer, did not really believe the Zionist dream to be realizable.

Third—and this is the level of discussion with which I would like to begin—I chose Luidor precisely because of the issue of anonymity that is raised by his case: the anonymity of the author and of his literary corpus, and the anonymity of his central protagonists. This issue of anonymity, which the Luidor case presents with particular acuteness, is a fascinating cultural issue, which may serve, as I will try to show, both as a key for a fuller understanding of the Second Aliyah literature and as a spotlight shedding light on obscure corners in the history of human engineering and landscape conceptualization in modern Hebrew culture.

In his influential book *Imagined Communities*, Benedict Anderson writes:

"No more arresting emblems of the modern culture of nationalism exist than cenotaphs and tombs of unknown soldiers. The public ceremonial reverence accorded these monuments precisely *because* they are either deliberately empty or no one knows who lies inside them, has no true precedents in earlier times. To feel the force of this modernity one has only to imagine the general reaction to the busybody who 'discovered' the Unknown Soldier's name or insisted on filling the cenotaph with some real bones. Sacrilege of a strange, contemporary kind! Yet void as these tombs are of identifiable mortal remains or immortal souls, they are nonetheless saturated with ghostly *national* imaginings."[5]

Mapu and Herzl were well-known and admired public figures, both during their lifetime and posthumously. Luidor, by contrast, was a peripheral figure in the history of Hebrew literature and culture—during his lifetime as well as after his death. However, and this is a point that I would like to stress here, the anonymity of Luidor, his writings and his native protagonists—that is, those born in Eretz Israel, who emerge, as we shall see, from the fog of myth only to return and disappear in it—is a defining characteristic of the Hebrew literature that was written in Eretz Israel and marked by the national/Zionist revolution, beginning with the literature of the Second Aliyah (to be precise, beginning with the First Aliyah, many of whose achievements the Second Aliyah members appropriated, while ignoring its members and other inhabitants and immigrants[6]), and, later, because of the formative status of the Second Aliyah, is also a defining characteristic of large sections of Eretz-Israeli and Israeli literature.

Luidor himself, the limited corpus he managed to leave behind, and many of his protagonists were seen during his lifetime and after his death as entities whose significance was due to the great project for which they served as building materials. Luidor and many of his friends who arrived in Eretz Israel at the time of the Second Aliyah did not withstand the tests presented to them by the period's ideological elite. A considerable number left the country straightaway or after a short while, and some survived there in various ways.[7] All, however, were seen as collaborators in a historical-cultural project, and thus gained everlasting fame. The outstanding among them had their names engraved in the pantheon of the new national literature and culture, and the less outstanding gained eternal life through the powerful invention of the national age: the monument for the anonymous pioneer/fighter/author.[8] One of the more astonishing characteristics of this phenomenon is the fact that the people of the period were aware of it and articulated it in almost every work they wrote about life in Eretz Israel. For example, the three great novels of the Second Aliyah—*Breakdown and Bereavement, Even to Jerusalem*, and *Only Yesterday*—can and should also be read as "memorial stories" to the anonymous pioneer/fighter/author; that is to say, stories that pay respect to the human beings whose role in the grand historical plot may have been minute, but without whom it would not have happened or have been documented.

In *Breakdown and Bereavement*, as in all of Y. H. Brenner's Eretz Israel stories, the author makes a great effort to undermine the pomposity that was part and parcel of the Zionist ideology of his time. But at the same time he devotes a separate and exalted place to Hanoch Hefetz—the Hebrew watchman who is killed in the line of duty and for his naïve Zionist conviction in a godforsaken place. Brenner endeavors to tone down the pathos of Hanoch's description by various means (including hinting at his sexual incompetence); the pathos, however, is still patently apparent, and the reader cannot avoid associating Hanoch Hefetz, who is considered as one of the "world's mute," with the biblical Hanoch, who was taken by God because he was innocent.

Meyer Ponek, the central character in Devastation (*Shamot*), the third part of A. Reuveni's trilogy *Even to Jerusalem*, the meaning of whose name, "the bright spark," hints at Reuveni's attitude toward him, comes from nowhere and disappears into the mist of myth. He commits suicide in the desert—the ultimate dry-land liminal space—"as befits" a member of the transition generation, the Desert Generation, and is eaten by its representatives: three hungry jackals. It is instructive that Reuveni chose to center the concluding novel of his trilogy on Ponek—a simple guy, one of many who left no real mark on Zionist history —rather than on other characters, which he modeled on some known leaders of the time: David Ben-Gurion (Givoni), Yitzhak Ben-Zvi (Chaim Ram), and others.[9]

S. Y. Agnon in *Only Yesterday* also gives center stage to "an anonymous Zionist soldier"—Isaac Kumer. Kumer is a "simple" man who finds himself entangled with great forces with which he is powerless to contend. He is a typical representative of the national revolution's foot soldiers, whose "prototypes"—their historical "equivalents," the "common people"—we would never have reflected on if the author had not turned the spotlight on them.

Agnon, Brenner, and Reuveni, and likewise Luidor and his colleagues, the lesser-known Second Aliyah writers, thus committed what B. Anderson defined as a "sacrilege of a strange, contemporary kind": they "discovered" the names of the unknown soldiers, and they refused to settle for "ghostly national imaginings," insisting instead on sketching the portraits and life stories of characters who immortalize the concrete, daily existence of tens of thousands of people whom official history has abandoned.

It is the same refusal to settle for "ghostly national imaginings" that has guided me in sketching the biographical and literary portrait of Yosef Luidor—

"an unknown author" who is so representative of his time, not least because of his anonymity.

❧ ❧ ❧

And here is what the entry "Yosef Luidor" says in Gezel Kressel's *Lexicon of Hebrew Literature in Recent Generations*:

> Luidor, Yosef (Galicia[10]—1 May 1921)
> Made aliyah at an early age and worked in various places as an agricultural hand, amongst other places in Rehovot and Tel Hai. Became especially close to Brenner and met his death with Brenner and his friends in the Jaffa Riots of 1921.
> Published some of the first stories on the life of Second Aliyah workers, in "Hatzfira," "Hashiloach," "Hatoren," "Hapoel Hatzair" and so on, as well as several essays of criticism. His writings have not been collected to this day. Left behind a few large-scale stories that were lost with him (his body was never found)."[11]

It seems that the entire drama of the unknown soldier/writer is encapsulated in this brief summary, which Kressel devotes to Luidor in his lexicon—a lexicon that is a kind of national literary antiquities museum (not to say cemetery).[12] This official lexicographical entry for Luidor offers several astonishing details, which together create a story that is most conspicuous by what it doesn't tell, and that begs completion. For the most elementary details are missing: we do not know when Luidor was born, where he was born (there are two versions), or when he immigrated to Eretz Israel. The only clear biographical detail is the date of his death—and that, as can easily be inferred from the list, is because he "met his death with Brenner and his friends in the Jaffa Riots of 1921."

That being murdered with Brenner served Luidor as an entry ticket to the national/Zionist pantheon—at least for a short while, after which he returned to being an "unknown soldier"—is clearly attested to by the following excerpt from Ya'acov Rabinovich's tribute, which has become part of a semi-literary corpus that can be called the "national memorial genre."[13] Here: "Because all of them—Yosef Luidor, Zvi Shatz and little Nunik (the student worker) who died with him, and the farmers Yitzkar junior and senior, who ventured out to this dangerous corner because they could not find any land in a quieter corner, among us—all were worthy of dying with Brenner, worthy of lying together with him. One next to the other, grave-fellows among all the sacred victims and bodies."[14]

What this excerpt from Rabinovich's "official" tribute plays down, however, is the horrific fact mentioned in parentheses by Kressel: "his body was never found." For, in that incident, six Jews were murdered,[15] but only five bodies were brought to burial. Luidor's body, which immediately after the murder lay a little way away from the bodies of his friends, later disappeared, never to be found again.[16] Mordechai Kushnir believes that the only gun the residents of the house in the orchard had was in Luidor's hands, and he may have wounded or killed one of the Arabs, which is possibly why they mutilated his body and disposed of it.[17]

From the meager official biographical data we have on Luidor, it is impossible to learn a great deal about his character and his personality. This gap is filled, at least partially, by the testimonies of several people who knew him or, better—since we are dealing with Luidor—people who had some contact with him. The picture that emerges from these testimonies is of a strange person, very different from the "typical pioneer"; a person whose strangeness was mainly reflected in his characteristics as a social creature. As opposed to the typical pioneer of the Second Aliyah, for whom "the group" and "togetherness" (with all their attendant mutual support and criticism and "rebuke"[18]) were a fundamental part of life, Luidor was a solitary person, whom the thought of a crowd of any kind filled with terror. This emerges, for example, from the sensitive portrait sketched by Ya'acov Ya'ari-Polskin:

> Luidor's orphan-like shyness and loneliness were as strange and uncommon as he himself, with his odd lifestyle and gait. Most of the time he didn't walk on the sidewalks, but in the middle of the road—in an agitated manner, flapping his long arms in the air, like a person escaping a fire or fighting a multitude of invisible pursuers.
>
> For moments on end, like a coquettish and frivolous young girl, he would be stuck in front of the mirror looking at his gloomy portrait, to see if his face did not reveal, heaven forbid, some line, sketch, or shadow from the inner world hidden in the depths of his being. . . .
>
> He always thought he was being laughed at, watched, or pursued, and it caused him untold sorrow and mental suffering.
>
> Often he would vanish from town for several days and nights—and no one, not even those close to him, knew where he had disappeared to. Once, in such a case, some of his friends went out to look for him on the roads and couldn't find him. Finally, after much toil and exertion, they found him on the road between Jaffa and Petach-Tikva, lying in a dark cave, with a loaf of bread and a flask of water beside him, lying and reading an old book.[19]

Luidor's unusual character, his lonely streak and his compulsion for seclusion coupled with his need for an audience and for literary recognition, are described by S. Ben-Zvi in the book *The Second Aliyah*, as part of a piece entitled "Ein Hai in the Old Days":

At that time a group of five workers came over from Rehovot, including Ben-Dor, the late Luidor (who was murdered with Y. H. Brenner on 1 May 1921) and some others. . . .

When the Rehovot group came, our family grew larger in number and richer in spiritual powers. They started gossiping about Luidor, that he wasn't just an ordinary worker, but a writer, who has already had some works published. He himself neither confirmed nor denied this. In general it was difficult to get any words out of him. He was shy and reticent. Limping in one leg—he would drag it in a strange way and was always busy bandaging it, never letting anyone see the wounds. His face was handsome, his small eyes black and striking, and when someone asked him a question, he immediately turned red all over, a shy smile spreading over his face. There was some hidden secret about him. Working in a group was hard for him and in time he committed himself to a farmer from Petach-Tikva for a certain job and would work there on his own, at different hours, which was not the custom among us. He arranged it so he would leave work before us, wishing to use his free time for writing. He chose to place his bed in a corner, where he installed a board that he used as a desk—it was the only table in the whole of Ein-Hai. He had a heavy suitcase full of papers, but no one got to see what was inside. Furtive glances revealed that it contained some neatly arranged newspapers and various papers. He was meticulous about his Saturday visits to Petach-Tikva and sometimes took the time to go there in midweek as well. They whispered that he had a "star" there, a young poetess, and when once someone told him that, he turned even redder than usual, lowered his face to the ground and gave no reply. On rare occasions they managed to make him talk during a debate on a literary subject, but usually he didn't participate in debates frequently. After a week of talking, he would set himself a week of silence, and then wouldn't utter a word. Despite the comrades' efforts and tricks, we didn't manage to break his silence. His eating habits were also odd. He gulped down the food without bread, and after a short while was hungry again. Since the kitchen was closed, he would climb over the boards that were used as a partition between the kitchen and the living room (for some reason the boards didn't go all the way up to the ceiling), jump into the kitchen, take out some bread and onion, dip it in oil and chew. Because of the structure of his teeth, his chewing sounded like the nibbling of a mouse, and when it was heard the comrades would joke and say, "There's a mouse in the kitchen."[20]

Ben-Zvi's piece suggests that Luidor's life among his comrades was not easy. The society he was part of, which in the main consisted of individuals who were themselves unusual in the society from which they emigrated to Eretz Israel, did not welcome those who were unusual within it. Luidor's lonely streak was both self-chosen and forced upon him. This streak can be found, as we shall see below, in all his "alienated" protagonists.[21] It can also be found, according to Luidor, in the main characters in Knut Hamsun's *Pan* and Daniel Defoe's *Robinson Crusoe*—two books that Luidor loved very much and to which he even dedicated enthusiastic reviews.

Luidor characterized Thomas Glahn, *Pan*'s protagonist, thus:

> The lieutenant Thomas Glahn . . . is a universal symbol for all those inspired, lonely, strange spirits . . . who are superior to all those around them but also inferior to them, who provoke both astonishment and disdain, who are exceptional both in the good and bad moments of their lives: those around them will never grasp them, and even if someone thinks he has fathomed them, he will realize in a moment of clarity that he has been entirely wrong. The murderer is an equal among murderers. The foreigner an equal among foreigners. The savage who has no place in civilized society is accepted among the savages. But these types have no place in any kind of human society. Neither among human beasts nor among any kind of respectable and decent people. They solve the enigma of their lives in a different way than the other multitudes. This is the type Dostoyevsky tried to depict in *The Idiot*. But Prince Myshkin is of limited value; he only testifies to himself. Thomas Glahn expresses a universal type. He takes up only a little space and he is great and vast. He is beautiful, wonderful when alone, but in the company of others he is alien, he stands out, he is askew, he disrupts the friendly harmony, disrupts the pleasant idyll of uncomplicated people. He not only secludes himself in the woods. He is lonely even when speaking to people. His loneliness is strange but also magnificent, like the loneliness of that immense oak standing alone in the wilderness. He does not have one of those ordinary human occupations; he is not after profit. He is as free as a bird. He is savage, not savage like a brutish person, but with a soul.[22]

It is easy to detect in this excerpt the traces of Friedrich Nietzsche's "Übermensch" (superman), seen in all his magnificence in isolation and derided in the company of the mob. The savage-with-a-soul, who exists only unto himself and whose actions are important in and for themselves, is the object of Luidor's yearning: that primordial man, who is exempt from the oppressive world of society and its laws and who has no desire or use for its manners and luxuries.

It is the same type of man and existential state that Luidor yearns for in his review of *Robinson Crusoe*. Luidor, who calls it "the book of books in adventure literature,"[23] sees this book as "a tremendous life-project" owing to three "artistic points of merit."[24] Two of those are named and described in detail in the review: "the scope of the adventures" and "the self-reliance story." The third point of merit may be called "the beauty of loneliness," and its traces are felt in each and every line. Here is an excerpt from the review, in which the self-reliance story and the beauty of loneliness are highlighted:

> The self-reliance story is so valuable that it should be counted, as such, among one of the precious gems in world literature ... Robinson Crusoe's self-reliance exceeds the limits of its literary value. It has become a tremendous life-symbol with an educational, ethical value. And this life-symbol is not just expressed in elevated phrases, that is, as a nice symbol in the pages of the book, but rather the story's artistic power is so huge, that the life-symbol penetrates our hearts, overwhelms them, and there is no doubt that in the years of the book's existence, there have been many people for whom it has been a sign, a sign of vigor and power, their potential power to act, a cue to break out into the world of actions. Incidentally, the idea of action runs through the whole book: this man Robinson Crusoe cannot sit idly, an immense power constantly drives him into action, from youth to old age, it is the driving power that is the loftiest in man on earth, and that has never left the greater people throughout their lives. The desire for action in this book is just a primitive desire for action, without an ideal, without a goal; and maybe this is why it affects us so strongly, because it is elementary, naked. The life-symbol in the self-reliance story has such a pure, unspoiled foundation that while other adventure stories may rouse some of the youths of various peoples to embark on any sort of adventure, including sometimes criminal ones, this story can only rouse one to perform humane, sometimes ideal actions.
>
> A primordial moment takes us over when in our imagination we walk with Robinson Crusoe on his desert island. Absolute loneliness. Human language, as well as golden coins, has become useless! We see before us a kind of Adam. A mood of infinite loneliness prevails. Freedom. Oneness. No disruption. Man is king over his beautiful, desolate island. Absolute, unlimited domination in eternal loneliness. Forgotten, forgotten are world and man all around. Only toil is the marker of time; man works for himself and his time passes without the boredom of idleness.[25]

It is amazing to realize what Luidor took from Daniel Defoe's story and what he left out. The civilizing act, which turns nature into civilization, or, in Lennard Davis's terminology, the act of colonialist conquest that this classic book dramatizes and legitimizes,[26] has been completely left out, and with it all the "incriminating evidence"—Crusoe's European rituals, the existence of "natives" on the island, and also, of course, the "educational" and "socialization" processes undergone by the "savage native" Friday. All of these Luidor, the "European colonizer" in "barbaric" Asia, completely overlooked—and in this he differs greatly from Herzl, who always kept his colonialist, proselytizing agenda firmly in view. What appealed to Luidor was a "primitive" desire for action—"only toil," "without an ideal, without a goal" on the one hand, and "Freedom. Oneness. No disruption," "infinite-loneliness," and "eternal-loneliness"[27] on the other.

Luidor, then, was not one of the favored sons of the Second Aliyah period, certainly not one of its acclaimed and well-known writers, whose writings (especially those of Y. H. Brenner) served as a kind of compass for many readers. However, despite his striking distinctness, Luidor was a product of his generation. His basic experiences as an emigrant and a pioneer resembled the basic experiences of the other Second Aliyah immigrants, and as a writer he faced the social, ideological, and artistic problems that were faced by all the writers and poets of the time.

The profound common denominator shared by the writers of this formative wave of immigration probably stems from the fact that they were facing a novel situation that offered a new artistic challenge. They were the first writers who both wrote about Eretz Israel and lived in it.[28] Mapu sat on a mountain in Lithuania and imagined—and many critics noted this phenomenon, which even became a critical truism[29]—that he was sitting on the Mount of Olives. Herzl toured the country hastily and returned to Europe to conduct his worldwide diplomatic campaigns in an attempt to realize the new exodus from Egypt. Once he failed, he settled for a literary fantasy. Luidor, on the other hand, emigrated to Eretz Israel and worked on its land: in Rehovot, in Ein Hai, and in Kfar Saba and so on. He earned his livelihood with difficulty, and did not always have a place to spend the night. His reading and writing were done, as we learn from the testimony of his acquaintances, on remote sites: the basements of abandoned buildings, dark caves, and the like.

In his stories Luidor tried, like all the members of his generation, to reconcile the glowing dream of Eretz Israel he had woven while still in his parents' house in the Diaspora with the Eretz-Israeli reality in which he lived and worked. He also tried to grapple with the very likely possibility that he would die in the country in which he had chosen to live, but not in old age like the "Old Jews" who came to be buried in the Land of the Fathers, but in his youth and violently: in a clash with Arabs, of malaria or another disease, and maybe even of hunger. These existential issues, which preoccupied all the writers and playwrights of that generation, whether naïve or ironic, genre or anti-genre, whether they wrote "affirmative plays" or "doubting plays,"[30] and consequently most of the Israeli writers and playwrights as well as most of the Israeli poets of the later generations[31]—did not preoccupy Mapu and Herzl at all. In the former, all the "good" heroes, those who represent the correct combination of his human engineering and his landscape conceptualization, survive; this includes both the parents and the sons who are intended to take their place (the reunion of the members of the two elite families on the Mount of Olives). In the latter, the parents, the "good" members of the Desert Generation (those who embraced the Zionist vision), die in Eretz Israel (the mother of David Littwak, the first president of the New Society), but not before they give their blessing and support to their worthier sons-successors.

In the writings of Luidor and the other authors of his generation there are (almost) no parents, probably both for mimetic-historical reasons (the Second Aliyah consisted mostly of single men and women), and also it seems for a profound psycho-cultural reason: in a place populated by "pioneers," by settlers in the vein of Robinson Crusoe, there is no room for parents and family relations, nor for neighbors. As for the settlers themselves, the sons' generation, they mostly die young, almost always a violent death—a chilling combination of circumstances that the Second Aliyah writers tried to articulate and give meaning to.

And when we are talking about Yosef Luidor, it is very hard not to connect the violent way in which the young lives of many of his protagonists end, with the fact that he himself had a passionate love affair with death,[32] and ended up being cruelly tortured and dying in the prime of his life.

※ ※ ※

Luidor's attempt to erase the gap between the Place (the Eretz Israel of his dream) and the place (the Eretz Israel in which he lived and worked) was conscious and deliberate. Like the majority of the Second Aliyah writers, Luidor was aware of the proselytizing role of his work. He knew that his stories would be read by recipients who were mostly situated in the Diaspora, and that the images they conveyed of the Eretz-Israeli reality were supposed to reinforce these readers' hopes and dispel their fears, consequently making them take action and immigrate to Eretz Israel. In Luidor's stories, as in many of the other stories of the period, this recruitment purpose takes two major forms: a structural/generic one, and a linguistic/rhetorical one.

In terms of genre, these stories integrate the format of an initiation story—or more precisely an acclimatization story—on the one hand, and of a picaresque romance on the other. They contrast two types of protagonists, whose different life trajectories meet and complement each other. One trajectory is the trajectory of the new immigrants of the Second Aliyah, who are getting acclimated in Eretz Israel and plan to live in it, and the second trajectory is the trajectory of the "natives," the descendants of the immigrants of the First Aliyah, the sabras, who serve as models for the new immigrants, and who, when their role is finished, die and unite with their beloved land.

The acclimatization trajectory is supposed to reflect the new immigrants' successful attempt to erase the gap between the image of the country as they had envisioned it in the Diaspora (the Place), and the image of the country that they are going to see on arriving in Eretz Israel (the place). In many stories this psychocultural move is foreshadowed by an emblematic scene that appears already in the exposition.

The second plot trajectory, which is contrasted with the acclimatization story and complements it, adheres to a romance-picaresque format. The central figure here is the "native," who serves as guide/mentor for the protagonist who is trying to acclimatize. Unlike the new immigrant, the native—and this is a very important point in the context of our discussion—does not develop at all. He is "born circumcised" and dies flawless. In his short life he fulfills two different functions, which affiliate him with two rarely combined generic traditions: on the one hand he is a monumental, larger-than-life figure, belonging to the twilight zone between the historical and the mythical; on the other hand he is a nomadic figure, a quality that turns him (like the Picaro, who, in contrast to the literary native, belongs to a low, morally and aesthetically flawed social sector) into a kind of mirror that reflects the flaws and ills of the local society. This mythification of the "New Hebrew Man"—presenting him as a monolithic unit and as enigmatic and mysterious, as well as, and the two presentations are interconnected, turning him into an artistic object to be walked around and admired—paved the way for the turning of thousands of young men into memorial monuments.[33]

The recruiting intention in Luidor's stories is also, and more explicitly and unambiguously, reflected in their rhetorical composition: in the essayistic/ideological units that Luidor attached to almost every central event in the four stories under discussion, be it in the form of a soliloquy, in the form of a dialogue between two or more of the central characters, or in the form of an explicit generalizing reflection by the omniscient narrator, or by "reflecting" the thoughts of secondary characters from various social groups. Either way, the fictional addressers and addressees merely represent the truly important participants in this dialogue: on the one hand, the contemporary readers who cling to the old sociocultural model, and on the other hand, the author Yosef Luidor who tries to disseminate his new sociocultural model.

A typical example is the following dialogue between the native Yoash and the new immigrant David:

Another time David talked about the pogrom that took place in his hometown a few years earlier.

—Explain to me what is a "pogrom"—said Yoash.—Is it a kind of war between two enemies? And a fight between two people, is that also a "pogrom"?

David stared at Yoash. A Jew—and doesn't know what a "pogrom" is!... But a moment later his eyes lit up and he looked at Yoash like at a superior creature. This is indeed a "free Hebrew man," who never tasted Diaspora in his life and doesn't even know what a pogrom is!

—The name "pogrom" denotes a rampaging attack by one part of the population on another, rioting, killing and destroying lives and properties—David explained briefly.

—Such pogroms can also sometimes happen in this country. A while ago someone from another village was killed in the village next to our moshava, and the people of the first village came to avenge the death of their fellow-villager, and then the people of the neighboring village came toward them and beat them back, but they came back a second and a third time, and a lot of blood was spilled on both sides, until they were tired of fighting and called the dignitaries of our moshava and the dignitaries of other villages to make peace between them.

—You can't compare this attack to the pogroms suffered by the Jews of Russia. Here there was a war between two enemies, and the attackers put themselves in mortal danger.

—And there, in Russia, this is not the case? Do the Jews never hit back at their enemies?

—They don't stand up to their enemies at all, because they are afraid of the gentiles. And David began describing to Yoash the whole affair of the pogrom that happened in his town, from start to finish.

Yoash heard David's stories with calm and equanimity, as if these horrific events happened to the remote tribes of the Druze rather than to the Jews, his brothers and his people. And David did not spare him the horrific and terrifying facts of shattered brains, hacked bellies, cut off breasts and children's bodies torn apart. But suddenly Yoash called out in a voice full of rage:

—Disgrace! Disgrace! I never heard of such a thing, that people should hide in their homes and wait for the rioters to come and smash in their skulls like you smash the skulls of snakes! And you feel pity for them? Such despicable people don't deserve pity!

—But, Yoash, if you had been in Russia and had known the situation of the Jews there–

—It makes no difference!—Yoash cried furiously—Even the snake defends itself! And the Jews of Russia are humans, they are Jews! If, at least, they weren't Jews! What a disgrace! Woe to these Jews!

David stood there distraught, and his face was very pale.

—Why is the disgrace bigger because they are Jews?

—Because I am a Jew as well!

—But the Jews in the Diaspora are not living on their own land . . .

—I see no difference between the countries of the Diaspora and Eretz Israel—Yoash interrupted him—There too the Jews are living on their own land. Any place a man lives in, is his country and his land. I love Eretz Israel and I shall never leave it, because I was born and raised here—and I am used to it and I love it. But if I had been born and raised in a different country, there is no doubt, I would have loved it as much as I love our country now. Although Eretz Israel is where our Fathers were born and raised and where they spilled their blood, with all the love that a man's heart feels for the land in which his forefathers were born, he will love more the land in which he himself was born. And as for the persecutions that the Jews are suffering in their countries, the Jews must respond and fight for their honor and for their right to the land on which they live. Otherwise—you mustn't feel sorry for them, because they are like worms trampled underfoot!

David opened his mouth and started teaching Yoash about loving the Land of the Fathers and about matters of Diaspora and Eretz Israel, but Yoash didn't respond and seemed uninterested in all of that.[34]

This, it seems, is the first native manifesto in Hebrew literature, a manifesto that conforms to almost all the demands and caveats of the definition of the "native" as it is formulated by Zali Gurevich and Gideon Aran. "The native," Gurevich and Aran claim, "is always in place. He was born in the place and from it, and has resided in it ever since—in the cradle, at home, in the grave. The place is like an extension of his body. The native maintains a natural connection, a practical overlap between the place in the physical sense and the place as a world of meanings, of language, memory and faith."[35]

Luidor's "nativeness" is well reflected in this manifesto's rhetorical structure. The dialogue between Yoash and David begins with a partial breakdown in communication and ends with a full breakdown. Yoash simply cannot understand the concept of a pogrom, even after lengthy explanations by David, who has experienced a pogrom personally. This concept of a pogrom does not exist in Yoash's existential lexicon. And likewise, the concept of Diaspora is simply absent from his mental geography.

This breakdown in communication also explains Yoash's disinterested, almost indifferent reaction to David's sermon about "loving the Land of the Fathers" and "about matters of Diaspora and Eretz Israel." Yoash's deafness to the Zionist phraseology should not be taken lightly. It brings into sharp focus the position of Yoash and of Luidor himself as deniers, not only of the possible existence of a mental gap between a Diaspora Jew and an Eretz-Israeli Jew (for, as Yoash argues, "Any place that a man lives in is his country and his land"), but of the very existence in principle of the soteriological tension that had nurtured the Jewish conception of place for many generations and would return to nurture it from the generation of Moshe Shamir onward.

This is a revolutionary statement: for the first time in Hebrew literature, an identity is declared between man, place, and world. Moreover, the physical place replaces both a religious spiritual essence (the "Place" in traditional Judaism) and any alternative spiritual essence—an aspiration for beauty and enlightenment (as in the Haskalah literature) or for a full emotional life and physical and mental health (as in the Revival literature).

This revolution means a rejection of any dialectical position in relation to the Land of the Fathers. No longer a partial acceptance of past tradition, with some modification or other, as we have seen in Mapu and Herzl (for example, in the acceptance in principle of the special status of Jerusalem, including the acknowledgement of the necessity of the Temple), but an extreme (oedipal) rebellious position of "self-proclaimed orphans," "frontiersmen"[36] through which everything returns to the "starting point," to a "primitive Judaism," which is far removed from the historical Judaism of Ahad Ha'am.

Any Place That a Man Lives in Is His Country and His Land

Luidor's extreme, oedipal position is reflected in all the elements of his stories' topographical plane: in the scope and boundaries of each story's actualized space (the location), in the nature of the relations between the "central area" ("foreground map") and the "surrounding area" ("background map"), and in the relations his "portrayed map" maintains with the classical maps of Eretz Israel—those of the Bible and those of the eastern-European Jewish town (the Shtetl) and so on.

Luidor, and like him many of the Second Aliyah writers (especially the genre/naïve ones)—and consequently many of the Third Aliyah writers, some of the writers of the Palmach Generation,[37] and "even" some of the members of the State Generation in their formative years (the sixties and early seventies)[38]—created a relatively limited Eretz-Israeli landscape, which usually consisted of one or two rural/colonizing units and the area between them. The stories before us describe sites in a single *moshava* and a few sites that are a walking distance or a short ride away from that moshava.

It is interesting to note that the background map in "Yoash" and in other stories by Luidor includes allusions to places in the Diaspora (in "Yoash" it is the town from which David came to Eretz Israel; in "Malaria" it is "the bustling town" in Eliahu's "country of residence"), but these places are not named. The background map also includes places from the heroic past of the people of Israel in the land of Israel (for example, in "Yehuda the Orchard Keeper": "the high Tabor ... and the towering Hermon, whose heights overlooked Yoav Ben Zruya and Yehuda Hamaccabi as they fought their enemies" [*Stories*, 61]). On the other hand, there is no mention in the stories of the central places on the implied map of Eretz Israel, that is, the one that the readers of Luidor's time would have envisaged. I am referring to the four holy cities: Jerusalem, Hebron, Safed, and Tiberias. There is also no mention of other major towns on the "Old Yishuv" map: Acre, Haifa, Jaffa, and Beersheba.[39] And finally, in the rare cases in which one of the customary places on the implied map is alluded to in a Luidor story, it is designated only by a neutral, distancing moniker such as "the coastal town" (*Stories*, 94), and no more.

On the other hand, in all of Luidor's stories, and in this he diametrically differs from Herzl, there is a prominent reference to Arab communities—both permanent settlements and tent encampments of Bedouin clans. Thus Luidor has created a "primordial" existential landscape, which includes only recently founded Hebrew settlements. The historical Hebrew settlements—both those identified with the traditional Jewish existence and those not identified with it—have all been erased from the map.

Luidor's extreme, oedipal position can also be detected on the topographical plane when we examine the foreground map of his central characters in relation to the foreground map of the central character in the "Shtetl literature," the literature of the Jewish town in eastern Europe. The latter keeps cropping up (as a kind of return of the repressed), only to be systematically erased.

According to the studies of sociologists and literature scholars, life in the Shtetl revolved around three foci: the home, the synagogue, and the market.[40] Each of these foci represented a central component of the life of the Jewish man/child in the Diaspora. The home represented its intimate and safe space, and the familial/traditional/patriarchal framework (with its unique Jewish characteristics); the synagogue (and in parallel, the *heder* and the *yeshiva*) represented the connection to the Place/God and the community; and the market (and in parallel, the street) represented the connection to the everyday world—a world of economic difficulties and of real physical dangers in the encounter with the gentiles.

The lives of Luidor's protagonists, and of many other central characters in the stories of the period, are led in a similar semiotic landscape, at least from a structural formal standpoint. It is a landscape that includes the same spatial subcategories: the sphere of the home, the communal Jewish sphere, and the everyday sphere (the world of work and the encounter with the gentiles). This spatial-structural overlap—which in itself should come as no surprise, since the plots are set in a First Aliyah colony at the beginning of the century, that is, in a landscape in which the "old" Jewish framework still holds—highlights the innovative nature of the places that actualize these spatial categories and their different specific gravity.

The first element in the Shtetl map to be reconfigured by Luidor is the parental home. Here this space has in fact no role or importance. From a very young age Luidor's native protagonists feel comfortable only in the spaces outside the home. This change can also be discerned in the relationships between parents and children. In the Shtetl map, the home has a crucial significance, mainly because of the binding connections between father and son. These connections, with all their psychological and cultural implications, undergo in Luidor's stories an astonishing transformation. In the stories in which all the main characters are immigrants—veterans or new—there is no mention of the nuclear family. Neither in the present—which makes sense, because these are immigrants who have mostly arrived in Eretz Israel on their own—nor in the characters' memories! The sphere of the home is replaced here by spheres that feature some—minimal—alternative aspects of home. In "Malaria," the protagonist Eliyahu finds refuge in "a 'hotel' where, once or twice a year, a guest comes and stays for a few days" (*Stories*, 95). What turns this "hotel" into a kind of home is the landlady's daughter, who takes care of Eliyahu when he is sick with malaria. In "Yehuda the Orchard Keeper," Shlomo finds temporary shelter with his older and strong brother Yehuda, who lives in "a small building" inside the orchard he is guarding. After some Arabs attack Shlomo and beat him up, he hurries to Yehuda's house "and tells ... [him] everything that happened to him, behaving like a small child in front of his father" (58).

The immigrant protagonists, then, do not mention their family home, but, without acknowledging it, they do need an alternative space. By contrast the native protagonists require no substitute. They ignore their homes in the moshavot and often erase them from their existential map altogether, because—and I shall return to this—their creator believed that a home is not necessary for those who claim the land as their home. This clearly emerges when we trace Yoash's "biography," from this native's attitude toward his family members in particular and toward the parent generation in his colony in general, and from the latter's, and especially his father's, reaction to him.

From the age of three Yoash has spent only short periods of time at home. He prefers "the Bedouins' tents outside the moshava" (65). Yoash has no sense of respect for his elders. He scorns the idea of democracy and claims that voting rights should only be given to those who know what's what—regardless of their age. For example, he claims that if they are adults who "have no brains" (71), they should be denied voting rights, whereas a child, if he is clever, should be entitled to these rights.

The spatial foci in Luidor's stories that parallel the heder, the yeshiva, and the synagogue, which in the "old landscape" signify the connection between the individual and his community and God—that is, a double focus, both social and religious—also undergo a significant transformation. This transformation (like that of the status of the home) takes place in two versions. One relatively subtle version pertains to the spaces inhabited by the immigrants; another, more extreme version, pertains to the spaces inhabited by the natives.

In the "immigrants' version" there is no mention of religious community institutions. These are replaced by Zionist community institutions with a similar semantic status. In "Yehuda the Orchard Keeper" this is the status of the kitchen, the communal dining room (where the samovar has a parallel status to that of a Torah scroll in the synagogue) and the "communal store" (53). In "Malaria" it is the status of . . . the pharmacy—the source of quinine: the medicine that serves here as a kind of "sacramental bread."[41] In the "natives' version," the erasure of the status and importance of the public institutions is absolute. This emerges most clearly from Yoash's attitude to his school: "At school he felt out of place. He couldn't submit to order and discipline and refused to accept authority. The teacher, an expert pedagogue, who knew the qualities, inclinations and natural talents of each of his pupils and also allowed each of them to develop according to his inclinations and talents, failed to fathom the boy Yoash, who remained an enigma to him" (*Stories*, 66).[42]

The erasure of the parental home and the school from the existential map in "Yoash" and in other stories by members of that generation has social and cultural implications that can hardly be overestimated. First, the only significant category in the portrayed semiotic landscape is open space—the outdoors, nature. As we know, the parallel category in the old spatial model is the street and the market—where the Jews (so problematically) encountered the world of action and the gentile world. Second, Luidor rejects any process of socialization. Yoash is a "nature boy." As such, his character is formed not by some cultural establishment or by the representatives of such an establishment, but solely and exclusively in an encounter with the representatives of nature: the sun, the wind, the rain, the soil, the trees and the shrubs, toads, snakes, donkeys, horses, and ... Arabs. Thus—to return to Gurevitch and Aran's definition—in "Yoash," as in any "native" text, the place dictates the thought, rather than—as in traditional Judaism, for hundreds of years, as well as in pre-Zionist utopias such as *The Love of Zion* and Zionist utopias such as *Altneuland*—the thought dictating the place. Third, Luidor's "portrayed map" marks a dramatic shift in the composition of what may be called the "inventory of national phobias." Diasporic Hebrew literature was a distinctly agoraphobic literature. This is true for classical Shtetl literature (Shalom Aleichem, Mendele Moykher Sforim), which erased the street and the market—the "outer," "gentile" space—as well as for postclassical Shtetl fiction in Hebrew (Micah Joseph Berdichevsky, Y. D. Berkovich, Chaim Nachman Bialik), in which, although everything outside the "Jewish space" was (intellectually, culturally, erotically) attractive and seductive, it was always also, and at least to the same extent, foreign and hostile.[43]

In this regard as well, "Yoash" marks a complete shift. This is a distinctly claustrophobic story. The space here is divided into gradually widening circles. And the farther the circle is from the human-civilized center—the moshava and its various institutions—the more it is considered significant! Like the protagonists of "frontier stories" in the corpuses of other colonizing societies, Yoash only feels free, at peace with himself and the world, in a primordial, entirely virgin space.[44] No wonder, then, that his favorite place—which is the story's "symbolic place"—is described as a holy place, a place of "communion"—"far ... from the whole world." It is a place akin to Robinson Crusoe's island, as Luidor saw it, a place displaying no traces of human presence and its civilizing/technical and cultural/social projects. It is a place reserved solely for true natives, who are "like the animal in the field, the bird in the sky and the wind in the sea" (*Stories*, 76). Entry to this place is forbidden—and this a crucial point for our discussion to which I shall return later—for ordinary human beings, including new immigrants, be they even as brave and truly Zionist as David: "—Now, David—Yoash turned to his friend in a muffled voice that gradually became louder—now I take leave of you for a short while. Look: all this space is in my heart. We are far from the whole world, from the world of people. We can see neither a ploughed field nor a fruit-bearing tree, nor anything that can remind us of the presence of man. We are free from everyday life, liberated from any work or burden, as are our horses. I am as free as the animal in the field, the bird in the sky, and the wind in the sea. Look: clouds are gathering in the sky; soon it will pour down with rain—it too is a blessing for me, it too is one of the forces of nature, and how I love the forces of nature! I have tasted the taste of freedom and space again—and savage man has risen in me. Whirlwind torrential rain! Gather all around, and spin and dance wildly—with me in your midst!" (ibid.).

Notice that in the symbolic place in "Yoash," there is not even a hint of the equilibrium between town and country that had characterized the symbolic places in *The Love of Zion* and *Altneuland*. This is a monolithic space: primordial nature with no trace of civilization. This is the space of "savage man" (as in Nietzsche), a space of romantic, pantheistic merging, and no more.

Furthermore, Mapu and Herzl portrayed living spaces that are in many ways connected to the world around them. Luidor, by contrast, portrayed a limited, minimal space, manifestly detached from everything that surrounds it: from the "Old Yishuv" and the "New Yishuv" in Eretz Israel, from the countries of origin of the immigrants who arrived in Eretz Israel at the time (Russia, Galicia, Yemen, and so forth), from the Middle East in general, as well as from the Old World (Europe) and the New World (The United States of America). Thus Luidor created a paradoxical fictional world. On the one hand, his existential landscape is very far from the Shtetl. But on the other hand, it is precisely his extreme, oedipal spatial actualization that reconnects with the Shtetl. For although the preferred landscape here is primordial nature—a clearly anti-agoraphobic, anti-shtetl-diasporic preference—the fact that the entire scene of events (the foreground map) is completely detached from the total landscape (the background map) reflects a new kind of agoraphobia.

The Taste of Freedom and Space

Mapu and Herzl tried to abolish, or at least narrow, the gap between Eretz Israel as the Place and Eretz Israel as the place, by rewriting biblical metanarratives that deal with the birth phase of the people of Israel. Luidor and his generation, conversely, presented a much more aggressive position in relation to the national religious heritage, a position that they passed on to several subsequent generations of writers. Many of the Second Aliyah writers—and in this issue Luidor stands at the forefront—tried, as already mentioned, not only to abolish the gap between the Place and the place, but to deny the very possibility of a soteriological tension.

On the chronotopic plane, this revolutionary approach is expressed in a paradigmatic change in the identity of the metanarrative that they chose to reshape.

The rewritings of the metanarratives that deal with the birth and/or rebirth of the people of Israel are replaced in this generation by rewritings of a metanarrative that deals with the very existence—or at least the question of the eternal validity—of the covenant between the people of Israel and their God: the story of the Akedah (the binding of Isaac).

The attitude of the members of that generation to the story of the Akedah is succinctly evoked by the concluding scene of the story "Yoash":

> Yoash lay lifeless, his arms and legs spread, as if he meant to defend his land with his body even after his death. In one semicircle stood the Hebrew youngsters, and in the other semicircle—the members of the commission and those of the committee... The people stood and looked silently at the face of the dead youth, and it seemed that the heart of each of the spectators was moved by a special thought.
>
> Who knows? Perhaps on seeing the blood pouring out of the breast of the dead youth and streaming and flooding and permeating the soil of the land, a thought occurred to one of them, that the new blood is mixing in the bottom of the earth with the blood that had been spilled in these places two thousand years ago... A different thought, however, occurred to the young man, the member of the moshava committee. Or so it seemed from these words, that absently escaped from his lips:
>
> —Reckless boy!
>
> These words expressed both reproach and sadness.
>
> The land has been established in perpetuity as the moshava's. If the commission didn't find working Jews on the land, it found a dead Jew on it, and if the moshava members didn't claim ownership of it through their sweat, they claimed it through the blood of one of their brothers" (*Stories*, 89–90).

This excerpt is a crucial landmark in what would crystalize as the tradition of martyrdom for the land in Hebrew culture. Here, and in scores of parallel passages in the Hebrew fiction, poetry, and drama of the Second Aliyah, we see the institutionalization of the revolution that centers around converting the covenant between Jewish man and the Place in the sense of God, into a covenant between Jewish man and the Place in the sense of Eretz Israel.[45] This revolution involved far-reaching, conscious and unconscious, mental and sociocultural choices.

In this scene Yoash is "at the center of attention"—everyone surrounds him and looks at him. But we should remember that this is a status he gains only after his death. In his life he fails to conquer the center—that is, to influence the people of the moshava to accept his views. At the age of thirteen, for the first time, he "invades" the committee house, demanding, in a dramatic scene, to become keeper of the granary, but is driven out in a humiliating rite (*Stories*, 67–68).[46] Later, as a young man, he "invades" the committee house again. This time he conquers the center, but only in the spatial sense and only for a short while. First we are told that he came to the meeting "uninvited," and that he stands "in one of the corners of the room," "totally . . . forgotten . . . , pushed to the corner" (*Stories*, 82). But "suddenly he stood in the middle of the room, erect and seemingly much grown in stature, stretched out his hand like a ruler and a leader, and his large eyes dominated the room and those assembled in it like the gaze of a commander of a warring army on the battlefield" (83). Despite his impressive performance, hinting at a mythical element (he is seemingly much grown in stature), Yoash's words fail to get through to the moshava members. Some pretend they agree with him, some do not hear him at all, and the rest silence him. His words are "heard" only after his death. Only when dead does he take up his proper place in the author's eyes, at the center of the circle—the center of the world.

It follows that death in battle over the homeland is a crucial element in the continuation and "correct" construction of life. It is Yoash's death in the battle over the contested land—rather than the cunning of the members of the moshava committee, or the work done in the contested area—that gives the moshava its rights over the land. It is a clear act of appropriating the individual's death for the sake of the nation, which was so typical, as George L. Mosse ably showed in his book *Fallen Soldiers*, of hundreds of texts produced in Europe on the eve of the First World War—the period in which Luidor wrote his stories, and also in which the "Yizkor Culture" (memorial culture) started being created in Eretz Israel, in slogans ("It is good to die for one's country," "In their death they bequeathed us our lives," "The silver platter" [*magash hakessef*], etc.), in ceremonies, coins and stamps, and in hundreds of books and memorial monuments. In Luidor's stories, moreover, the death of the individual is seen not only as part of life (the life of the nation), but as its pinnacle. In their real death (Yoash) or symbolic death (David in the battle with the Arabs; Efrat in his battle with malaria, etc.), Luidor's protagonists live their lives to the fullest.

This concept, which can be found in most of the Eretz-Israeli stories of the writers of the period, whether naïve or ironic—from Moshe Smilansky's "Zmira" and "Hawaja Nazar," through Shlomo Tzemach's "The First Grave" and "Fallow Land," to Y. H. Brenner's *Breakdown and Bereavement*, A. Reuveni's *Even to Jerusalem* and S. Y. Agnon's *Only Yesterday*—this concept established itself in Eretz-Israeli literature (written in the land of Israel before the founding of the state) and in Israeli literature (written in the land of Israel after the founding of the state). This was true in the thirties and forties, due to the formative status of the corpus discussed here, as well as in the following decades, due to the same acclaimed literary output and to literature created subsequently—chiefly, certainly in terms of its literary power and the depth of its influence, Nathan Alterman's "Living Dead" poetry, its personal early section (some of the poems of *Stars Outside* and *Joy of the Poor*), its public/national section (*Plague Poems*, some of the poems of *City of the Dove*, some of the poems of *The Seventh Column*, and so on).[47]

The essence of this concept—first actualized, I emphasize again, in Luidor's "Yoash"—in relation to Alterman's poetics was summed up by Moshe Dayan, the former IDF commander in chief and Israeli defense minister, in a preface he wrote for the IDF edition of "The Silver Platter": "Alterman's fighting . . . is the fighting that was part of life—fighting until the end—until death, although this death is not the end of fighting but its climax, and since fighting is part and sometimes the whole of life, when it is the climax of fighting, it is not the cessation of life, but rather its full powerful expression. . . . This is the death at whose price future is bought for the next generation."[48]

And indeed, at the price of Yoash's death in battle, the moshava buys "its rights over the land." His death also creates a temporary bond between all the representatives of the (Jewish) sectors taking part in the story. His body is surrounded by a circle—the mythical symbol of perfection—created by two semicircles. It is a human circle that turns Yoash into an aesthetic and moral object. He is not "only" a person who has died, but an object that undergoes a process of aesthetization and immortalization.

A very similar scene describes Yehuda in "Yehuda the Orchard Keeper." The narrator likens Yehuda's stance to that of "a solid rock rooted in the ground or a firm marble statue"; it is such an impressive rock/statue, that "the people around him could not take their eyes off this picture" (*Stories*, 55). In both cases there is an aesthetization, fetishization, and fascistization of the "New Hebrew Man," but in "Yoash" it is also a move that stems from dying while fighting for the homeland, an aesthetic/moral/political link that is at the very heart of the cult of the fallen soldiers.

And since we are dealing with the aesthetization, fetishization, and fascistization of death, we might want to take note of the fact that only Yoash's heart was injured in his death—the rest of his body and his face remain as pure and intact as before. This description, which brings to mind the icons of Christ, coincides with the way the murder itself is reported: "Suddenly emerged an Arab youth, who had until know stood further away, and after making his way through the people surrounding Yoash, attacked him with his knife—and stabbed him in the heart." The suddenness of the crucial event; the fact that the attacker had stood until that moment, throughout the entire battle, to the side; the way he paved his way into the hostile human circle surrounding Yoash and the fact that this circle would shortly be replaced by the circle of mourning Jews; the fact that the unknown messenger homes in directly on Yoash's heart—all these take the event out of the realm of a cruel result of a violent dispute over property between the representatives of two camps, and turn it into a climactic event in a "memorial story"—an event that has mythological aspects and a ritual/foundational function.

In his death Yoash creates a horizontal link (the circle of mourners around him) as well as a vertical one. The blood pouring out of his breast and permeating the soil—an in-itself-chilling romantic/"primitive" picture, which recurs in dozens of versions in the literature of this and subsequent generations—this "new blood" "is mixing in the bottom of the earth with the blood that had been spilled in these places two thousand years ago" (90). A vertical link of this kind is also attributed to Eliyahu, the protagonists of "Malaria," and to Yehuda and his friends, the watchmen from the Galilee, who help him repel the Arabs' attack on the orchard under his charge. Of Eliyahu it is said "that he had in his blood a lot of the blood of the ancient Jews, the natives of the country from past generations" (98). And in their battle to defend the orchard, the Hebrew watchmen join "with Yoav Ben Zruya and ... Yehuda Hamaccabi" (61), meaning that, in the climactic moments of the plot—during the battle against the Arabs or immediately after it in the gravest moments of crisis of malaria and so on—Luidor's protagonists succeed in enforcing the native approach as formulated by Gurevich and Aran:

> The native situates the world around him and thus situates himself in the world. In order to anchor the world, in his myths and rituals he constructs the place as the center of the world, positing it against chaos, the nothingness that has no center or order. The place, therefore, is the foundation of the world. Fixing the place as the center of world makes it not only the beginning of Creation but also a starting point for any orientation—up and down, middle and sides, near and far ... According to this approach, the place is the basis for identity, because in it the individual becomes connected to the world and through the world to himself. For the native, a holy place is a ritualistic and mythical concentration of his basic experience of the world—his being at home in the world.
>
> The cult of the sacred [and in our context, of the national martyr] becomes, therefore, the cult of the place. In certain points (indicated by a high mountain, a stick, a stone, a turret) there is a magical creation of concentrations of holiness,

and according to the myth, in these points there is a kind of vertical Axis Mundi that threads together and connects heaven, earth and netherworld. Around this axis is concentrated the totality of the world, and through it man connects to what is beyond him. This link with the beyond, with the wholly other, is made through the place itself.[49]

It should be noted, however, that the Axis Mundi created by Luidor's protagonists does not link the earth with the heavens, always perceived in the great religions, as we learned from Rudolf Otto, as divine/spiritual by nature,[50] but rather links the surface of the earth (the heroic struggle for a national territory) with the depths of the earth (the parallel mythological struggle, which the current struggle tries to reenact and replicate, while leaping over the entire "Jewish history").

The connection to the "beyond" through the place is depicted in Luidor—as in other subsequent writers of "land fiction" and also, as Gideon Ofrat showed,[51] in the writers of "land plays"—as a renewal of the tradition of sanctifying the land with blood in German romanticism (as it is expressed in Nietzsche), and as a renewal of this tradition as it is expressed in Tolstoy, whose figure and teachings (propagated both directly and through reworkings by contemporary thinkers, such as A. D. Gordon[52]) had a tremendous influence on the members of the Second Aliyah.[53]

One of the most suggestive sources for this tradition, which Luidor and his friends used for rewriting the rite of the covenant between man and the Place/God, is the myth of Osiris (the killing and resurrection of the Egyptian god, the son of the god of earth and the goddess of heaven—a creature that is inherently Axis Mundi), which, together with similar myths (Adonis, Atis, etc.) are the metanarratives of the cyclical (seasonal/annual) conceptions of fertility and extinction in many of the ancient human societies.[54]

The rereading of the Akedah story and/or the crucifixion story, the two foundational stories of monotheism, through the myth of Osiris—one of the central, and perhaps *the* central myth of "primitive" civilizations, which the monotheistic stories appropriated and "civilized"[55]—takes place in the stories under discussion through covenant rites struck between characters in the fictional world who are linked with mythical time (here, the pre-Diaspora time), and the representatives of the implied contemporary addressee—"the immigrants," the "new Jews" recently arrived in the country.

In "Yoash," the traces of the Osiris myth are clearly evident. Yoash, who represents mythical time, meta-time, makes a love pact with David, the new immigrant. In his death Yoash finally connects (through his blood) with mythical time (the blood of the dead from "two thousand years ago" [*Stories*, 90]), while at the same time connecting in a "blood tie" with his beloved friend David. The story ends with David (who himself almost died in the battle) leaving the hospital, destined to follow in Yoash's footsteps. It is a changing-of-the-guard ceremony: an Old Jew who becomes a New Hebrew in exchange for a native-born New Hebrew.[56]

The acclimatization story or immigration story, and especially the native's story—the two plotlines that are supposed to merge in the corpus before us—were formed from the outset as masculine stories. The romantic relationship in the stories is between the central character, the man, and the land; the woman is absent. If the woman does appear, then her status is peripheral, and she is not perceived as an erotic element. As a rule, the women in the stories of the period have three roles: to serve as alternative mothers and sisters,[57] to represent ideological possibilities between which the hero is supposed to choose (Sonia and Shifra in *Only Yesterday*; the Wettstein sisters in *Even to Jerusalem*; the Hefets sisters in *Breakdown and Bereavement*, and other real or symbolic sisters), and to demonstrate in their behavior the attitude expected of the readers toward the heroic men, the living monuments—an exemplary behavior, which means renouncing independence and femininity.

The new world—open, anti-claustrophobic, anti-Shtetl—belongs to the men. The women must settle for the old world, with its limited scope and its usual places: the kitchen, the clothes storage, and rarely also the vegetable garden and the vineyard.[58] Women thus have no real place in the existential landscape created by Luidor and his friends. On the other hand, it is easy to find in this landscape signs of homoerotic culture. Most of the works describe a pair of men who are intimately close or a group of men who maintain a close-knit male friendship, which highlights the exclusion of women and the extreme, puritan position of the authors, typical of writers-colonizers.[59]

Thus, for example, David and Yoash are portrayed in the image of David and Jonathan or of Amnon and Teman from *The Love of Zion*: "And Yoash and David became attached to each other in bonds of love. Each found in his friend a man after his own heart. David found in Yoash a worthy and exemplary Hebrew young man, work-loving and brave ... and Yoash loved David because he saw in him an ideal young man whose soul is pure" (*Stories*, 70–71).

A truly "perfect match": the (masculine) rude health, rootedness, and power of the native on the one hand, and the ideality and the pure soul (a typically feminine combination) of the immigrant on the other. "Malaria" also portrays the new immigrant and the veteran immigrant as a couple. Granted, the landlady's daughter very briefly disrupts this match, and the new immigrant even prefers her for a short while to his friend (when the friend catches them together in the room, where the young woman is nursing him, he is tacitly angry at him: "He was very upset at that man who came and spoiled his beautiful illusion" [101]). However, very soon the "wrong" couple is dispensed with. The landlady's daughter presents the relationship that is developing between her and the new immigrant as "only a bit of fun," and the new immigrant returns to the "essential thing"—fulfilling the pact between him and his "veteran" friend. And as for Yehuda the orchard keeper, here the masculine group takes the place of the masculine couple.

The heights of Luidor's stories' homoeroticism can be found in the scenes in which there is a merging between a masculine bond and the task of defending the land/homeland (a merging that we shall encounter again, together with the homoeroticism that creates it and stems from it, in all the national pioneers stories, including *He Walked in the Fields* and "Nomads and Viper"). A notable scene of this kind is the battle over the orchard in "Yehuda the Orchard Keeper," in which the New Hebrew Men from Judea and the Galilee unite with the ancient Hebrews in a war against the enemies, the Arabs, over their hold on the land. Another notable scene of this kind comes at the end of "Yoash." Here there is a merging of the battle over the land with the homoeroticism between a pair of men in the narrated present (Yoash and David), and of this pair with the groups of selected men who defended the same piece of land in days gone by. This merging is created through a double blood covenant: Yoash's blood that is "streaming and flooding and permeating the soil of the land" (90), which mixes with the blood of David who "is bleeding all over" (89); and the mixed blood of the "couple," which mixes with the bloods of the "Judean zealots"; that is, "with the blood that had been spilled in these places two thousand years ago" (90).

Yoash, then, Luidor's ultimate hero, dies in an act of self-sacrifice on the soil of his homeland. In doing so he reenacts and ratifies the ancient covenant of the people of Israel and the land of Israel. Such reenactments and ratifications are customary, as we learn from Mircea Eliade,[60] in all "primitive" cultures, cultures in which man is afraid of the present and the future and finds his place and the meaning of his existence only through reenactments of the mythical experience. And since we are dealing with a society of pioneers, the act of colonizing is seen as a repetition of the act of creation and as its equivalent.

In "Yoash," however, as in a considerable part of Hebrew settler literature, the territorial conquest is not made only through working the land. Although working the land is considered a very important precept in the new immigrant writers' conventional set of rules, it alone does not proffer rights over the land.

Nor is entitlement over the land gained through ancestral rights; it is gained only by making a sacrifice and building an altar/monument. Furthermore, the people of the moshava take hold of the contested land through Yoash's sacrificial act—the virginal and pure youth, intact save for his heart, lies with "his arms and legs spread, as if he meant to defend his land with his body even after death" (*Stories*, 89–90), his blood saturating the soil of his beloved land. This mechanism for taking possession over the land, including Yoash's "resurrection" in the figure of David, resembles the possession-taking rites practiced by the Christian, Spanish, and Portuguese conquerors in South America. Here is what Eliade writes in this context: "It was in the name of Jesus Christ that the Spanish and Portuguese conquistadores took possession of the islands and continents that they had discovered and conquered. The setting up of the Cross was equivalent to a justification and to a consecration of the new country, to a 'new birth,' thus repeating baptism (act of creation)."[61]

From what I have said so far, and in light of the models of human engineering and landscape conceptualization in the previous texts I have examined, another conclusion emerges, as fascinating as it is alarming. The matches between women and men, the likes of which we have seen in Mapu and Herzl, are replaced in Luidor by a blood covenant between men, one or all of whom together "impregnate" the land. The clearest fulfillment of this blood covenant, which is described in the concluding scene of "Yoash," creates a communion between a dead youth, pure and virginal and flawless, who died according to all the rules of kitsch nationalistic romantic art,[62] and youths like him, innocent and perfect, who consecrated the "grave and suffering land" at the dawn of history. And meanwhile, love, sex, education, technology, and other elements that create life and build cultural continuity are replaced in Luidor by death, "which bequeaths us life."

The source for the alarm here is that Luidor's human/spatial model, the "land, man, blood" model, as G. Ofrat so aptly put it[63]—which offers no biological continuity! (unless, as the text implies, David will pair up with Yoash's younger sister, "an optional match" that contains more than a modicum of homoeroticism)—enjoyed, as we know, and perhaps still enjoys, a prominent status in the human engineering and landscape conceptualization of the revived Hebrew culture.

The Secret of Life and Death

Mapu's and Herzl's human engineering and landscape conceptualization are not all of a piece. As I tried to show in the previous sections, the two authors produced rewritings of biblical metanarratives dealing with the birth period and the end of days of the Hebrew nation by using European metanarratives that do not entirely coincide with them.

In *The Love of Zion* there is an incongruity between the traditional biblical model and Mapu's alternative model, which is essentially secular, as well as between the neoclassical model and the neoromantic model. In Herzl there is an incongruity between the model that relies on the metanarrative of the Enlightenment and the model that relies on the neoromantic tradition in its auto-antisemitic variety.

In Luidor it is harder to identify this kind of incongruity, and it is no coincidence. Mapu's and Herzl's human engineering and landscape conceptualization are reformatory: Mapu and Herzl observe the recent and distant cultural past from a dialectical and ambivalent position. Luidor's human engineering and landscape conceptualization are revolutionary/radical. And yet—and this is a fascinating point—in Luidor too, as in his predecessors, and despite his desperate attempts to set himself apart from them, the soteriological gap (the gap between the idea and the belief that it can be realized) is ultimately preserved, which means that he has not created a native approach but (only) a fantasy of a native approach, which is at once aware and unaware of its flimsiness and the impossibility of its existence.

The soteriological gap hiding behind the extreme anti-soteriological façade of Luidor's stories is evident mainly in the nature of the relations between the two plotlines running through his stories: the native (the native-born New Hebrew Man) plotline and the new immigrant plotline. This seemingly surprising and instructive phenomenon finds its fullest expression in "Yoash."

I have already pointed out that "Yoash," like Luidor's other stories, integrates two generic formats. One plotline is based on the tradition of stories of acclimatization, and a second plotline is based on the figure of the romance hero—the "bigger than life" hero, who resides on the seam between history and myth and displays a satirical streak that is expressed in his overt or implied social critique of the Old Yishuv and the New Yishuv.

David is the acclimatizing hero. He undergoes a series of site-specific tests, in an ascending order of importance: agricultural work, horse riding, familiarity with open space, a limited conflict with the Arabs, and the final test—a bloody conflict over a piece of land, at the end of which he is found worthy of following in Yoash's footsteps. His worthiness finally becomes clear from the way the story ends. The narrator, who describes the scene in which people are gathering around Yoash's dead body, concludes by pointing out that the people of the moshava gained "their rights" over the contested land "with the blood of one of their brothers" (*Stories*, 90), and later, in a very brief epilogue, displacing time and space, he says of David, who was injured in that bloody battle: "David spent about two months in hospital and was discharged in good health."

The living David is thus crowned as heir to the dead Yoash. It is the format of a "relay race," necessitated by the fact that, ideologically speaking, David "toes the line" with Yoash. In his vigorous, combative reaction to the Arab's violent attack, he proves that the term "pogrom" has become unfamiliar to him as well. Now he has turned, at least ostensibly, into what he himself defined as a free Hebrew man. In other words, from the trajectory taken by David—in isolation from Yoash's trajectory—we could get the impression that we are dealing with a revolutionary Zionist story, a story in which by changing your place you can change your luck. But this impression, shared by all the critics who have written about the story, is wrong.

For although David changes, and although he is found worthy of carrying the baton of the national mission (both as a fighter and perhaps, as hinted by the "pitying gaze" he directs at Yoash's sister [75], as the male component in the first biological link of the revived Hebrew dynasty), David is not Yoash and will never be like him. Between the two, the native and the acclimatizing immigrant, there is a permanent gap. This gap between the two friends and between the existential essences they represent is reflected in the diametrical differences in their attitude to the most important elements in Luidor's portrayed world: time and history, open space, other natives (the Arabs), and animals.

David has a strong connection with history. His Diaspora memories have stamped his consciousness with a conflict between Old Jew and New Jew that he must resolve. In his eyes, "new Hebrewness" is a desired location where one is born, like Yoash, or, if one was unlucky enough to be born in the Diaspora, to which one must immigrate, to Eretz Israel and undergo a harsh (though not necessarily prolonged) evolutionary process, at the end of which one may cross the threshold into the desired destination. By contrast, for Yoash historical time is an empty category, and also—if looked at from the perspective suggested in Eliade's remarks on the native's experience[64]—a threatening and unwanted category. For Yoash, and this is another factor that makes him fit the definition of the native, space rather than time is the definitive category. Even though, as he admits in the difficult conversation with David on the subject of the pogrom, the Jews can be defined by their race, the crucial piece of information for determining the identity of human beings is their place of birth: "—What do I care about your countries of exile?—Yoash called in great anger—I have nothing to do with the 'Diaspora' and the Jews in the Diaspora! I was born here and I never knew any other homeland! If the Jews of Russia are in exile, what does it have to do with me? Why do I always have to be afraid and watch every step and relinquish my right and my honor before these savages?! And you—he turned to the two farmers' boys—how can you speak in the name of a Diaspora that you've never known or seen? Why is your heart full of diasporic submission and why does it not contain even a spark of pride in your homeland? In what way are you inferior to these Arabs?" (*Stories*, 86).

Yoash's affinity with the land and open space is clear and absolute. He and the land and the open space are one. This emerges from the description of his activities in the landscape from infancy to death. This affinity, it should be stressed, never changes along the temporal axis. For Yoash, like all "the heroes from time immemorial," "was born circumcised"—and, as the narrator puts it in the story's opening line, "since childhood Yoash had alienated himself in his actions" (63). What changes in him is not the type of actions he performs but only their intensity, a change that attests to the strengthening of that basic affinity. At the age of three Yoash used to "love going out on rainy days in the Eretz-Israeli winter and run in the pouring rain and dance around like a fleet-footed foal." In his youth, in his journeys through virginal space, he felt "free like the animal in the field, the bird in the sky, and the wind in the sea" (76). And at the high point of his life, that is, in the battle over the land of Eretz Israel in which he loses his life, his blood spills, "mixing in the bottom of the earth with the blood that had been spilled in these places two thousand years ago" (90).

Yoash has a similar basic affinity with the wild animals and the Arabs, who for him are different manifestations of the same being, with all that this entails. Throughout his short life he has many encounters with animals and Arabs, whom he sees as authentic and legitimate representatives of nature, representatives who should be judged by their actions. The only difference that applies in this context, for him—just as in the context of his affinity with the land and the open space—is the size and power of the animal standing before him or the importance and intensity of the confrontation with the Arabs.

Yoash's dialogue with the animals begins in his early childhood, when he "lies for days on end by the swamp outside the moshava, capturing frogs and worms" (63). Later he captures toads, tortures the "terrified creature" a little, and sets it free. In the next stage he already captures snakes; when all the older workers "stand far back ready to attack the snake with their hoes ... voicing their fear loudly," he, Yoash, "stands there calmly, as if it has nothing to do with him ... he measures the snake with a cold and cruel gaze like the gaze of the snake itself. The two enemies seem to be measuring each other up with their gazes" (64).

And then comes the description of the "battle" between Yoash and the snake, which carries great importance for several reasons: because it foreshadows the description of the battle between Yoash and the Arabs at the end of the story, because of the marked difference between Yoash's attitude toward animals and Arabs and David's attitude toward the same entities, and in a more general context, because of the differences and similarities between Yoash's attitude toward the animals and the country's Arabs and the attitude of Mapu's and Herzl's protagonists toward the same entities and the attitude of the protagonists in stories by younger writers, who have absorbed the "Yoash model." Here: "Afterward [after the "battle of gazes" between Yoash and the snake], he [Yoash] goes over to the iron pipe, set up in the orchard to transfer water, and as he rolls the snake he directs it so that its head would hit the iron pipe. The snake sees the danger that awaits him clearly, and it musters its last strength, its mouth foaming, its whole body quivering—but in vain! Two, three more hits with the pipe—and it is lying dead with its head smashed. The eyes of the dangerous creature protrude from their sockets like when it was alive, and it seems that any moment now it might awaken and rise again against its enemy. But its smashed body testifies that there is no more life in it. And little Yoash stands and looks deep, deep into the snake's eyes, as if seeking in them the secret of life and death" (ibid.).

Between Yoash and the snake there is a profound similarity. Both are nature's creatures, both measure the world and their enemies with the same gaze, and both are attached to their territory and defend it as best they can, even till death. In the argument that breaks out between him and David about the reaction of the Jews of Russia to the pogroms, Yoash claims that faced with this reaction, he prefers the snake over his Jewish brothers because "even the snake defends itself" (ibid.). The profound similarity between a (positive) Hebrew hero and a poisonous animal, and moreover one that is seen as so negative, is a new phenomenon in modern Hebrew literature.

As we recall, Mapu and Herzl recognized the animalistic/natural element as vital for their project, which deals with the creation of a new nation, but they balanced and curbed it in various ways. Luidor adopts a completely different strategy. His "hero" has only natural elements. Like Zimri, the bad guy in *The Love of Zion*, so Yoash, the hero of the story that bears his name, combines a tremendous aesthetic power with an absence of erotic potency—the potency without which it is impossible to create a new stage in the dynasty.

No wonder then, and I shall return to this crucial issue, that Yoash dies a virgin. His role in Luidor's tapestry of life is identical to that of the snake. In the same way that the scene with the snake forms one stage in the depiction of Yoash's portrait, so does Yoash form one stage in the evolution of David's development. In the same way that the dead snake is seen by little Yoash as reflecting the "secret of life and death," so the dead Yoash is seen by those looking at him at the end of the story as an undeciphered secret. In other words, when little Yoash "stands and looks deep, deep into the [dead] snake's eyes," he sees himself (his essence) and the fate that awaits him. This mirror-like situation suggests that he is a narcissistic figure, in the profound sense of this term; that is, a figure that plays first and foremost an aesthetic/mythical role, rather than a social role. Yoash, like K. Hamsun's Thomas Glahn and like Robinson Crusoe, as Luidor the critic understood them—lonely, superior heroes, who cannot find their place in human society—is merely a symbolic figure, a concrete human representation of the liminal state between myth and history. In other words, this New Hebrew Man can and is supposed to serve as a guide to human beings who live in the story's reality-simulating world, but he himself has no foothold and can have no foothold in that world.

The "dialogue" Yoash has with his Arab neighbors (whom he prefers over the people of the moshava, like he prefers the wild horse over the domesticated donkey) is similar to the one he has with the animals. First he becomes their leader, and then their rival. And in all these events Yoash represents "a natural and wild force" (66), a monolithic force without doubts or biases, typical of proper natives.

David's attitude toward the land, open space, and the forces of nature (the wind, the sea, etc.) and the representatives of nature (the animals, the Arabs, and Yoash himself) is much more complicated than that of his admired friend. At the beginning of the story David tends to think in ideological terms, and once he even "started teaching Yoash about loving the Land of the Fathers and about matters of Diaspora and Eretz Israel" (74). But he gradually gets rid of this unnecessary baggage, until finally he is released, or that's at least what he believes, from the sense of a gap between the Place and the place.

> Without a thought or idea in his mind the youth lay, enjoying the place's magnificence to the full....
>
> He knows and feels in the depths of his heart, even without promising it to himself again and again, that he is the son of this land, to which his soul is attached and in which he will live until the day he dies. He feels that here he has found a safe haven....
>
> He treats with utter indifference all the quibbling and arguments on the burning questions that reach him from the newspapers and monthlies in the Diaspora. In the Diaspora he used to gulp every word, and here, within beautiful nature, with ample work, in the free air, he has no need for them at all. How boring are these periodicals! Boredom rises from every line, even the most interesting story is hard to read. (78)

The metamorphosis seems complete: David, like Yoash, becomes "a son of this land." He takes everything for granted, and the tension between the Diaspora and Eretz Israel, between the place and the Place, is no longer relevant, and the thousands-of-years-old Jewish soteriological tension is longer in force. However, declarations and wishes are one thing, and an actual mental reality is another. This becomes clear from examining this passage within its context in the text's continuum, in light of what precedes it and what follows it.

The landscape in which David lies "enjoying the place's magnificence to the full" is in fact not the "Place." The Place is the wild expanse that Yoash explores on his own. It is a landscape in which David has no foothold and will never have one; he is forced and will always be forced to settle for a more "inferior" landscape. As mentioned earlier, Yoash, like all the "heroes from time immemorial," lives/dies in the twilight zone between myth and history. He comes from the mythical landscape and returns to it (just like the heroes of the American frontier stories).[65] David is an ordinary, historical mortal, and therefore has no right to enter that landscape, which for him is taboo. This reality is dictated to him by Yoash, who is aware of the unbridgeable gap between him and his friend:

> Look: clouds are gathering in the sky, soon it will pour down with rain—it too is a blessing for me, it too is one of the forces of nature, and how I love the forces of nature! I have tasted the taste of freedom and space again—and savage man has risen in me. Whirlwind torrential rain! Gather all around, and spin and dance wildly—with me in your midst!" . . .
> —Forgive me, David my friend!—Yoash apologized to his friend—Right now you are also superfluous for me. Alone, alone with my horse and with nature I must remain now. (*Stories*, 76)

This stance of the acclimatizing immigrant, standing on the threshold of the "real" landscape—the one preserved for natives alone—appears in another version. Right after David is excluded from entering the dry-land wild expanse, he rides his horse for a while and suddenly finds himself in front of the raging sea.

> David stood face to face with the sea. He—and the great and terrible, raging, and stormy sea, which seemed to wage rampaging war on the land. Along the entire beach the sea billowed in one enormous wave, which like a powerful army regiment assaulted the beach thunderously and noisily and with destructive and devastating force. But the land looks serenely at the furious, raging war of the sea. It knows the sea's soldiers—those immense waves, whose rage is only great until they reach the edge of the shore, when they turn to betray the sea and grovel submissively before the land, licking its soil, and the sea, resenting the betrayal

of its soldiers, continues to send waves, more immense than the first, to take the beach by storm. And the sea never tires of its harsh wars, and its forces are never exhausted.

How wonderful is this sea! You can stand and look at it for hours on end, like at a thing of wonder. It is so simple and seemingly one. But it conceals a great secret. An eternal secret is buried in its depths, and it has the power to attract the eyes that scan its surface and draw the heart of man, who is both afraid of it and admires it. This sea is like a great animal, which has both a consciousness and a free will—and what is man compared to this great animal?

What is man, that he dares to stand alone ten steps away from this sea? And what if it suddenly decides to overflow and flood over one more kilometer? Then it will swallow David together with his horse, leaving no trace . . . And a feeling of submissiveness, of self-surrender before the great force of nature overtook David. Indeed this feeling, like the feeling of nature as a whole in all its beauty and glory, can overtake man only when he is alone, when there is no one else with him to point their finger and say, "How lovely is this tree! How wonderful is this view!" (77–78)

This passage reflects the fragility of Luidor's native's fantasy. David, unlike Yoash, cannot be "in the midst" of nature. He watches it from the outside, a position that is typical, to follow Friedrich Schiller's famous distinction,[66] of the sentimental, "civilized" person, who has lost the unmediated contact with the phenomenal world and is fundamentally different from the naïve/native position.

David, who finds himself near the sea by chance, stands face to face with this force of nature, in approximately the same way that Yoash and the snake "are measuring each other up with their gazes." But unlike Yoash, who "measures the snake with a cold and cruel gaze like the gaze of the snake itself" and then kills it, David feels great terror in front of the sea—which he likens to "a great animal, which has both a consciousness and a free will."

This terror is evident both in the content of his thoughts and in the linguistic associations made between the passage in question and the Bible and the Talmud, and between it and other passages in the story. The relationship between the sea and the land seems to David like a war, and he describes it in explicit terms from that semantic field: "rampaging war," "a powerful army regiment," "the furious, raging war of the sea," "the sea's soldiers," "the betrayal of its soldiers," "to take the beach by storm" and so on.

As opposed to Yoash, the "savage man" who calls the sea and the storm to gather round him, to spin and dance wildly with him in their midst, David is overtaken by "a feeling of submissiveness, of self-surrender before the great force of nature." As opposed to Yoash, who keeps "penetrating" nature until finally he is swallowed by it in order to come back metamorphosed—in line with the Osiris model—David feels that his attempt to "penetrate" nature is an unforgivable act of arrogance against a formidable force. And he is very fearful, as we can gather from the biblical verse fragments that mix with his thoughts, that he will end up like Pharaoh and his chariots, which sank in the Red Sea: "And what if it suddenly decides to overflow and flood over one more kilometer? Then it will swallow David together with his horse, leaving no trace."

The myth of Osiris, which here rewrites the story of the Binding of Isaac in the form of an optimistic relay race, is undermined by another myth—the myth of Tannhäuser, who went into the cave in Venusberg and disappeared, never to be seen again.[67] This myth is seen here as unidirectional/defeatist, and reflects the castration anxiety of the New Hebrew Man. And it should be noted that this castration anxiety—the fear of being swallowed in the ground or drowning in the sea—coincides with the misogyny that is so evident in this literary corpus; that is, with the recurring exclusion, patronization, and disparagement of anything to do with women and femininity.[68]

As another intertext suggests, the mental problematic revealed here also has a sociocultural source: the difficulty of adapting to nature and its representatives, a mental difficulty typical of immigrants who were educated in a cultural community that kept a distance from nature both practically and ideologically. This difficulty is reflected here in the double-edged attempt to cling to the Talmudic verse, alluded to in the phrase "How lovely is this tree!" (*ma na'eh ilan ze*), which originates, as we know, in the Mishnah saying that compares exposure to the landscape and openness to its aesthetic values with idol worship, a comparison that Luidor's ("primitive") landscape conceptualization rebels against and yet, paradoxically, also holds on to because nativeness in its ultimate expression—in the encounter between the native and his defining landscape—is seen by the immigrant/newcomer as a mythical, unattainable, super-human, and inhuman essence.[69]

Settlers and Nomads

The unbridgeable gap in Luidor's stories between the native plotline and the new immigrant plotline has additional aspects, whose identification and examination may enrich our understanding of Second Aliyah literature and shed light on the literary fiction that dealt with imagining the new man and the old-new place in earlier and later periods.

A central aspect in this context is the tension depicted in many of the period's works between the peasant, the farmer, the permanent worker, and the homeowner on the one hand, and the temporary worker, the homeless person, and the itinerant watchman on the other. This tension, which has its origin in the socioeconomic reality of the time,[70] but also, and it seems mainly, in the pioneers' ideological platform—which was based both on biblical models reworked by the Haskalah and Revival literatures (from Moshe Chaim Luzzatto onward), and on models borrowed from Russian culture (the farmer versus the horse-riding Cossack) and Arabic culture (the peasant versus the nomadic shepherd)[71]—recurs in all of Luidor's stories, which in this respect as well represent a very considerable part of Second Aliyah literature.

This tension between homeowners/settlers and homeless people/nomads comes in different guises. At times it is overt and prominent, and at others peripheral. Either way, however, it is always tied in with the gap, seen as unbridgeable, between the situation of the native and the situation of the new immigrant, as well as—and this is the point I wish to stress here—with the split, also detectable in the figures of Luidor's "natives," between recognizing the necessity of the "sumud" (Arabic: persistence, steadfastness, holding on to the land) and the old "Diasporic" wish to keep wandering, this time (only) within the perimeters of Eretz Israel.

I wish to argue that Luidor's protagonists—just like the antiheroes of Y. H. Brenner, S. Y. Agnon, A. Reuveni, and their ironic/anti-genre colleagues—never take root in the land. In fact, they face—again, just like the protagonists of the ironic/anti-genre writers—two existential possibilities: a) to fulfill, with their own bodies, the metanarrative of the Binding of Isaac in a new national version that is performed through a partial adoption of ancient myths; or b) to realize in Eretz Israel the metanarrative of the Diaspora: eternal wandering. That is, to create a new version of the myth of Ahasver[72]—to become the "Cain of the natural landscape," an existential template that will become prevalent, and I shall discuss this fascinating issue in the following chapters, in the foundational poetry of Alterman in the forties and consequently in the foundational fiction and poetry of the Palmach Generation (Moshe Shamir, Yigal Mosinzon, Amir Gilboa, Chaim Guri, and many others), and with amazing deformations, also in the foundational literature of the State Generation, in the early books of A. Oz and A. B. Yehoshua.

Yoash is a man of "freedom and open space." He exists only in a state of motion, especially riding a horse. As a child ("at the age of three") he is described as being "like a fleet-footed foal that suddenly bursts out of its yard and runs wildly and mischievously all across the moshava" (*Stories*, 63); "and when he was... eight he was already climbing onto the horses' backs and riding without a bridle or a saddle... like a tempest and a storm" (64). The tempest and the storm, with their motoric/energetic forces, become realized in the figure of the youthful Yoash's ultimate landscape, which is the only place where, riding his horse, which "broke out like a lion's cub and ran all over the land," he feels like the "savage man" (76). By contrast, the new immigrant and the potential farmer David's attitude to horses is completely different: "And when David started working, it was especially hard for him to get used to the horse. He handled it with too much caution, as if it were a lion, and kept glancing at its hind legs with great fear. Even Yoash's promise that this attentive beast would never kick him couldn't dispel his suspicion of this most honest of horses. When he tended to the horse, his eyes would darken over and his breath would shorten and cold sweat would run down his brow in the expectation that soon the horse would treat him to a nice kick in the belly or the head" (70).[73]

Different attitudes toward the horse also set apart the brothers Shlomo and Yehuda in "Yehuda the Orchard Keeper." Yehuda, the watchman, rides a horse, whereas his little (in both senses of the word) brother, a peasant/settler, rides a donkey. Yehuda, like Yoash, is a man devoted to movement in space, a nomadic spirit. Staying in one place, let alone getting attached to a piece of land, is neither in his nature nor good for him. Here: "Yehuda was also a bit lazy in his work and made no more money than an ordinary worker. Although it was easy for him to do work that would demand a lot of effort from others, when he realized that he had already made his daily wages, he lost all interest in working. He couldn't stand the subordination... nor could he be tied down to a monthly or yearly position. He loved freedom without end or limit, as if great freedom was the purpose of his life. And he only chose daily or contract jobs so that he would always be free and able to move from place to place, from moshava to moshava and from one region to another. From Judea to Samaria and from Samaria to the Lower Galilee and from the Lower Galilee to the Upper Galilee" (56).

Luidor thus has a clear topographical and occupational hierarchy: the Galilee is rated a lot more highly than Judea, temporary work in the field is rated more highly than regular work in the field, guarding is rated a lot more highly than working in the field, and traveling in the Eretz-Israeli landscape (not as part of your job), and in particular on foot, is the most highly rated activity. Yehuda, the "super-traveler," is described by Luidor's narrator as a kind of high priest of the Eretz-Israeli landscape.

Like Amnon and Tamar, Teman and Peninah and their family members, and Hadoram in *The Love of Zion*, and like Friedrich, Miriam, David, and Kingscourt in *Altneuland*—Luidor's Yehuda also follows a geographical itinerary that is a fundamental axis in the history of the national chronotopics: the (on-foot) pilgrimage to the holy sites in Eretz Israel.

However, the (on-foot) pilgrimage made by Yehuda, who counts as "an entire 'caravan,'" differs from those of his predecessors in two major ways. First, it is a spatial ritual independent of any defined time frame. It takes place at least once every year, but not necessarily at times of religious significance (Sukkot, Passover, Shavuot, Rosh Hashanah, Yom Kippur, etc.). Second, Yehuda changes both the destination of the traditional (on-foot) pilgrimage and—and the two are interdependent—its typical itinerary, and therefore also the logic, purpose, and meaning of this national and religious ritualistic movement.

The destination of the (on-foot) pilgrimage here is neither Jerusalem (as in Mapu), nor another traditional local site (the Tomb of the Patriarchs, Rachel's Tomb, etc.). Nor is it a modern site charged with mythological force (for example, the power station at the Dead Sea in *Altneuland*). The destination here is "*Every* moshava, *every* river, *every* sea and *every* mountain" (56, emphasis mine); that is, natural sites (all, rather than one or several of them) and new agricultural settlements (again, all of them). In other words, the purpose here is to wander "from place to place, from moshava to moshava and from one region to another. From Judea to Samaria and from Samaria to the Lower Galilee and from the Lower Galilee to the Upper Galilee."

All of this means that a) we have before us a map that has no destination/ topographical center, neither a traditional center (Jerusalem) nor a modern center (Haifa, the "New Village," etc.), nor a different topographical center; and b) The center here is a "moving center," whose location changes in accordance with the changes in the location of Yehuda, who is likened to "an entire 'caravan.'" Any place that Yehuda comes to becomes a temporary center, which soon becomes the permanent center, that is, the "moving center": the caravan of (on-foot) pilgrims making its way to the place that for a while will become the new temporary center and so forth.

The movement outlined by Yehuda—which recalls the Israelites' movement as they follow the Tabernacle in the desert and the parallel movement that follows the Ark of the Covenant in the book of Samuel, as well as the movements of the natives in the dream maps of "primitive" cultures[74]—is a typical ritualistic act, which highlights the normative superiority of constantly moving in the Eretz-Israeli landscape over any act of taking hold of and settling (in one place) in it.

This normative superiority—a narrative-ideological template characteristic, as mentioned earlier, of many central characters in the fiction of the Second Aliyah period—is also reflected in the structure and content of the thoughts of Luidor's positive protagonists. Sapir, for example, the new immigrant in the story "Harvest Days," receives an offer from Barzillai, the son of First Aliyah immigrants, to work on his plot in the moshava as a permanent worker, and this is how he reacts to the offer: "Sapir was alarmed on hearing this last offer. Until now he had wished with all his heart to be transferred to working in the field, but in the decisive moment he recoiled from the great change that would suddenly occur in his lifestyle. He remembered the great freedom he had enjoyed up till now, working in the orchards as a day worker, and now he would always be enslaved to his master, to his horses, and to the cowshed, day and night, on the Sabbath and on holidays. True, there were many advantages to such a post. Regular meals, a place to stay, and a good bed and no worries about domestic matters. But his freedom, which he loved so much, what would become of it?" (*Stories*, 42).

The repeated appearances of the tension between the homeowner/farmer and the wanderer/nomad, in their more anarchic manifestations (Yoash's wild horse rides, Yehuda's ramblings, etc.) and less anarchic ones (the Galilee watchmen traveling around the country in "Yehuda the Orchard Keeper," the temporary worker Sapir's curbed craving for freedom, etc.), are thus a fundamental element in the landscape conceptualization and human engineering of the writers (and thinkers) of the Second Aliyah.

These compulsively repeated appearances are, in my view, another literary testimony to the profound doubts felt by the writers of the period, including Luidor, about the possibility of erasing the gap between the Place and the place and about the possible emergence of a "new Jew." For, as I see it, the tension between the permanent settler and the nomad in the stories before us is merely an Eretz-Israeli adaptation of fundamental tensions in Jewish culture: the ancient tension between the tent dweller (Isaac, Jacob) and the wandering nomad (Esau, Ismael), and the tension between settling in Eretz Israel and wandering in the Diaspora.

In light of this we can understand Luidor's ambivalent attitude toward his natives, both those who die in defense of a piece of land in the homeland (Yoash) and the nomads (Yehuda, Sapir). For as we have already seen, on the one hand both these Hebrew types are presented as perfect and as figures who can serve as role models for the more human new immigrants, who will become homeowners: farmers, temporary and then permanent workers, etc. However, and this is also something I have already hinted at, these heroes of days gone by have no place in the real-life plot, in the story's pioneering/settling Zionist history. As soon as they have finished their role as mentors to the new immigrants, they must disappear from the story's reality-simulating stage into the mists of myth. Some are destined to die young and beautiful—in the prime of their lives—in battle, and others are destined to continue moving forever on the old-new routes.

Now, it seems to me, it is easier to understand what captivated Luidor so much in the figures of Robinson Crusoe and Thomas Glahn from Hamsun's *Pan*. They have the same strange mix of practical wisdom and extreme asociality that typifies his own protagonists. These protagonists' asociality coincides with the fact that their greatness is not discernible within the human throng, but only in the unpopulated open space—on an island, in the woods, in the Nietzschean wild expanse, etc.—and seems to invite their exclusion from the story's stage once they have finished their role as founders of a new settlement/society/community.

It should be understood that Luidor's typically asocial role models—and Yoash and Yehuda are at the top of this list—pose a clear threat to the ordered society that has gone through its first revolutionary phase: the passage from the mythical realm to the historical realm. This threat and the mechanisms society puts in place in order to remove it were described by Hannah Naveh:

> The inverse character of this literary and cultural hero—["Western literature's hero, who is permanently settled in the city or in the country"[75]]—is the figure of the nomad. The nomad questions in his very existence most of the conventions, values, worldview, culture and existential principles of the permanent settler. For the nomad the journey is a permanent way of life. The nomad doesn't "go on a journey"—his life is a permanent journey, as Deleuze and Guattari noted in their book *A Thousand Plateaus* (1987): "The nomad reterritorializes on deterritorialization itself."[76] The nomad is on the periphery of settled society, and when he touches it, his touch is felt by the permanent settlers more like the infiltration of a foreign tribe, of a foreign and frightening entity of an unfamiliar and incomprehensible kind. This is the conventional perception of gypsy societies, and it also reveals the incompetence of modern welfare society to deal with homeless people who have voluntarily chosen "to live outside," as Stephanie Golden describes in her book *The Women Outside* (1992). The wish of settled society is to domesticate the nomad and subject him to its institutions, just as the anarchism that characterizes the genre of the picaresque has undergone a process of refinement in order to control its chaotic and subversive message.[77]

Another mechanism put in place by society to neutralize the threat posed by the nomad—who is a native because wherever he is, is his home, and home for him is not connected, as Naveh notes in relation to the homedweller, "to a place ... [and] a society that bear the marks of permanence, unified state mechanisms and order, and . . . real estate"[78]—is "use and throw away," a manipulation that every society performs on its "others," often also defined on an ethnic basis.

It is against this backdrop—or more precisely, also against this backdrop—that we should try and understand the intense love affair that most of the protagonists of Second Aliyah writers have with death, and consequently also the love affair with death of younger Hebrew writers.

The Second Aliyah protagonists' love affair with death takes two principle forms. Among the natives it is a passionate love affair, which they immerse themselves in forcefully and almost with relish. In contrast, the immigrant protagonists treat this affair as if they were forced into it and are trying to get out of it in one piece. Thus, for example, the fascination with death that Yoash exhibits from childhood—when he looks "deep, deep" into the eyes of the dead snake—recurs in dozens of versions in all the literature of that generation, and it will suffice if I mention here only two prominent examples, from A. Hareuveni's *Even to Jerusalem* and S. Y. Agnon's *Only Yesterday*.

The protagonist of *Even to Jerusalem*, Meyer Ponek, the New Hebrew Man, has a complex love affair with death—which is embodied for him in the figure of a Bedouin-Arab and various animals. Toward the end of the novel Meyer Ponek fights Hajj Yosef, the childless desert dweller, who brutally rapes the deaf and dumb Nechamkeh. Ponek fights the Hajj, defeats him and kills him, and thus seems to get rid of him. But then, just as in Yoash's case, the death element that had been hidden in the Hajj, the man of the desert, is transferred to Ponek.

From that moment, Ponek loses his way, until finally he shoots himself to death in the desert in a powerfully expressive scene, a scene whose power stems from the chilling perspective through which the sequence of events is reported: the "consciousness" of four jackals that follow Ponek's actions for a long time and with great interest—until the shot is heard. Then they run away "terrified to death,"[79] but come back and devour his flesh, being part of the "great nature" into whose "bosom," in the desert dune, Ponek's bones will disappear.

A parallel role to that of the jackals in *Even to Jerusalem* is given to the dog Balak in *Only Yesterday*. This dog, which gave rise to heaps of interpretations, reflects in my view first and foremost that generation's profound fear of nature, which they identify also (but not only) with a chaotic and annihilating indifference. The dog-bite injury, which is the cause of Isaac's death, is a grotesque parallel of the bite of the mosquito infected with malaria—the Zionist disease—which Luidor and his fellow naïve writers of the period turned into a highly dramatic event; an event that mixes love and death, a kind of Zionist version of Liebestod—the lovers uniting in death (here the beloved mother earth and the son, the sweet youth), which fifty years later would undergo another grotesque remodification in the final scene of the story "Nomads and Viper."

And while we are on the subject of Isaac Kumer, we must return to the mechanism that the Second Aliyah writers—naive and ironic alike—developed as a means of buttressing their ideological revolution. What happens to Isaac Kumer is the paradigmatic story of the Second Aliyah. He is a character who sacrifices himself for the homeland while consciously/unconsciously effacing the generation of his parents. Although Isaac, like all of S. Y. Agnon's other Second Aliyah characters (and his central characters in general), and like all of Y. H. Brenner's Second Aliyah characters (and his central characters in general), is an "antihero," he, like Luidor's protagonists Yoash, Yehuda and Sapir, is regarded with an ambivalent attitude. All of them, as you might recall, are seen through the prism of the myth of Osiris—the spring myth of fertility and renewal—on the one hand, and through the myth of the pessimistic/impotent Tannhäuser on the other.[80] The struggle between these two mythical templates, which runs like a thread through Eretz-Israeli literature, reached its most defining formulation in the final section of *Only Yesterday*, which—as many commentators have noted—is the definitive novel of Second Aliyah literature.

> On the day that Isaac was buried, the sky was covered with clouds. The sun was overcast and a wind came and with it came lightning flashes and thunderbolts. The firmament was shaken with the rumble of their might and began to bring down rare, warm drops. The next day, the clouds scattered and the sun shone, and we knew that all our expectations were in vain. And even the winds we imagined would refresh us didn't bring any gain, as they were hot and piercing as leeches.
>
> But at night the winds cooled and the world began to cool off. And the next day the sun was dull and pressed and squeezed between the clouds. Before it finished its course, it was pushed out of the firmament. That sun, that devouring fire, that had blazed with its strong heat and burned all the grass of the field and parched the trees and dried up the springs of water—darkening clouds pushed her out until there wasn't a corner in the firmament that it wasn't pushed out of. And when we lifted our eyes to the sky to see if the clouds weren't lying, abundant rain began coming down. Only yesterday we had stood in prayer and pleading and we increased the number of Slikhot and we blew Shofars and we recited Hosanna, and today we read aloud the Praising, thanking and singing.
>
> When the rains began coming down they didn't stop coming down by day or by night. The water flowed from above and from below, on the roofs of our houses and underneath our houses, it swept away furnishings and brought down houses. But the cisterns were filled with water. And now we have water to drink and even

to cool our food and to bake our bread and to dip our hands. For six or seven days the rains came down, and when they stopped they started coming down again. Finally, the rains stopped and the clouds dispersed and the sun shone. And when we came outside we saw that the earth was smiling with its plants and its flowers. And from one end of the land to the other came shepherds and their flocks, and from the soaked earth rose the voice of the sheep, and they were answered by the birds of the skies. And a great rejoicing was in the world. Such rejoicing had never been seen. All the villages in Judea and the Galilee, in the plain and in the mountains produced crops and the whole land was like a Garden of the Lord. And every bush and every blade of grass emitted a good smell, and needless to say, so did the oranges. Like a blessed dwelling was the whole land, and its inhabitants were blessed by the Lord. And you our brothers, the elite of our salvation in Kinneret and Merhavia, in Eyn Ganim and in Um Juni, which is now Degania, you went out to your work in the fields and the gardens, the work our comrade Isaac wasn't blessed with. Our comrade Isaac wasn't blessed to stand on the ground and plow and sow, but like his ancestor Reb Yudel Hasid and like some other Saints and Hasids, he was blessed to be given an estate of a grave in the holy earth. May all mourners mourn for that tortured man who died in a sorry affair. And we shall tell the deeds of our brothers and sisters, the children of the living God, the nation of the Lord, who work the earth of Israel for a monument and fame and glory.

> Completed are the deeds of Isaac
> The deeds of our other comrades
> The men and the women
> Will come in the book *A Parcel of Land*[81]

The ending of *Only Yesterday*, like the endings of other Agnon stories and like all the passages in which he deals with Zionist issues, is built of several layers of meaning, the myriad links between which suggest a position that mixes pathos and irony.[82] This complex position, however, does not blur the existence of the profound questions that preoccupied Agnon, who serves here as a faithful representative of his time.

The passage before us raises again the question that was presented at the beginning of the book: the question of Isaac's status as the representative of his generation. This question is inextricably linked to the question of sacrifice: Is Isaac, as Shaked suggested,[83] the Unknown Soldier of his generation? Can we say that *Only Yesterday*, like "Yoash," is a memorial story? Is Isaac's burial rite an incarnation of the burial and resurrection rite of Osiris—for both rites signify a passage from an arid season to a season of plenty and fertility?[84] Or does the rain fall here because of the prayer, the pleading and the Slikhot, the Shofar-blowing and the Hosanna-saying—all customary within Jewish ritual based on the Covenant of Abraham? Or maybe there is a merging of traditions here, which directs us to another pattern of sin and atonement—the one whose definitive embodiment can be found in the story of Oedipus, in which only after the hero stabs out his own eyes, the plague is removed from his town (I have already indicated that the "oedipal sin" is a key component in the culture of the Second Aliyah).

Nor can we ignore the opposite direction suggested by the text, the one that leads us to think that maybe it is Isaac, who "died in a sorry affair," who brought down the rains that almost annihilate the world. Does Agnon imply that the sorry affair is in fact the attempt to "appropriate" the life of this hero/not hero for the sake of building a new nation, and that his positioning as an unknown soldier in the service of the people is a malicious or at least cynical act that is supposed to cover up for the spilled blood of the modern Isaac, who, unlike the biblical Isaac, is not saved by a miracle? Either way, or both ways: that is, if Isaac's story as it has been told to us is indeed the central story, and if the central story is the one that has not been told (the collective settlement story that is supposed to come in the book *A Parcel of Land*, the book that Agnon never wrote and never intended to write), the metanarrative that the writer chose for the central plotline of his period novel is the story of the Binding of Isaac.

This story, which replaces the birth and end of days stories of the people of Israel, on which Mapu and Herzl based their narratives, was reloaded by the Second Aliyah writers with new ingredients, some of which are terrifying. I am referring mainly to the appropriation of the life of the individual for the life of the nation, to the cult of the dead heroes, to the misogyny, to the identification made between nature, predatory animals, and the "other." To the substitution of the link between man and God with the link between man and the land—a substitution that begins with "the religion of labor" and ends with "Greater Israel." And especially, to the fact that the land in the literature of this formative period is not won through a return to nature (as in Rousseau and Mapu), nor through education (for those of eastern European origin) or a "military" re-indoctrination (for those of Austro-Hungarian origin) as in Herzl, nor with manual labor or even "cunning" (as the moshava committee suggests in "Yoash"), but with blood: with the blood of national martyrs, who serve first as role models and then as scapegoats.

4

He Walked in the Fields, Moshe Shamir, 1948

"It turned out it was all fake..."

*The first films I ever saw were Tarzan films.
There wasn't a single Tarzan film shown in Jerusalem
that we, the gang and I, missed. We saw them all... There
were Flash Gordon films too... Death in those films was always
spectacular, noble and beautiful. I never rebelled when at school,
on 11 Adar each year, the anniversary of the heroic death of
Trumpeldor, we were taught to declaim "It is good to die for our
land." Of course it was good to "die for." In the films, whenever anyone ... had to "die for," he was always given a magnificent death,
with weeping beauties, with waves of love from the Sons of Light
who remained in the land of the living, ... and always an opportunity to deliver memorable "last words," in the spirit of "It is good
to die for our land." ... And so we all began to view the
world around us selectively. Jerusalem, Palestine, our street
and our homes all looked to us like an imperfect replica of what
was shown in the films. We all became little Platonists:
reality was merely a partial, imperfect realisation
of a perfect form that existed in a higher world.*
—AMOS OZ, *from the essay "The Lost Garden"*

The Ultimate Novel of the 1948 Generation

He Walked in the Fields, Moshe Shamir's first novel, was written in 1946–47, while he was a member of Kibbutz Mishmar Ha'emek. At that time Shamir was already one of the leaders of a group of writers customarily called the writers of the 1948 Generation, the Palmach Generation, or Dor ba'aretz (the Generation in the Land). The young Shamir, as Hagit Halperin notes, won "great appreciation both from the poet Avraham Shlonsky and from David Hanegbi, who headed the Sifriat Po'alim publishing house, and from the writers of his generation who respected him, asked for his advice and cooperated with him on every important literary project."[1]

Before the novel's publication Shamir edited *Al HaHoma*, the journal of the Hashomer Hatzair movement, in which he published his first stories. He also published his stories in *Yalkut HaRe'im* and *Mishmar*.

The novel was published by Sifriat Po'alim, after some delay, which I shall address shortly, in January 1948 and was enthusiastically received by most of the critics as well as, and even more strikingly, by the readers, who bought it in droves. The novel's first, hardcover edition had a print run of three thousand copies; the second edition included twenty thousand copies and sold out in less than six months. By 1984 there had been seven more printings.[2] Afterward, the Am Oved publishing house acquired the rights for the book and printed it seven more times in the years 1972–1991. In an interview with Moshe Zonder in 2001, Shamir said, "The novel continues to be printed to this day and has reached almost a hundred thousand copies."[3]

In fact, Shamir was the first Hebrew writer whose book became a bestseller. This is true even if judged by contemporary measures, and all the more in terms of the measures used in the early years of the state, when the country's Jewish population numbered about six hundred thousand, of which some were Eretz-Israeli born and old immigrants, and some new immigrants who had only recently arrived in Israel and were not yet fluent in Hebrew.

A powerful promotional tool for the novel was its theatrical production. Shamir adapted his novel for the stage even before it was published, and Yosef Milo directed it. The premiere took place at the Mugrabi Hall in Tel Aviv on 31 May 1948. It was announced as a gala show for the Palmach's seven-year anniversary. The honorary guests were approximately seven hundred members of the Palmach brigade, who arrived at the hall from various places around the country and gave the play, the director, the actors, and of course the playwright-author, an enthusiastic reception.[4]

In its first production the play was shown 171 times—a large number for the nascent Israeli theater, and was seen by 172,000 men and women—about a third of the country's Jewish population at that time![5]

The "hysterical" reception won by *He Walked in the Fields*—it was also awarded, in the year of its publication, the Ussishkin Prize—was, it seems, the result of factors on two different planes: the literary and the social-cultural.

This is how Gershon Shaked explains the enthusiastic response to the book on the literary plane: "[Shamir's] work was to a large extent a novelty on the literary landscape: it was different from the sophisticated novels of writers such as Brenner, Gnesin and Agnon, but also from the ideological melodramas of the Third Aliyah writers (Aricha, Bar-Yosef, Ya'ari, Hameiri). One can say that he wrote well-made novels that described subject matters, protagonists and plots that interested the local audience more than those found in the translated novels, which until then had filled the role of 'the readable novel' in the literary system."[6]

The enthusiasm for the book probably also had another reason, pointed to by Hanoch Bartov, also of the 1948 Generation—that is, Shamir's usage of the Hebrew language. Bartov argues that Shamir's flexible language was an illustration of the fact that "we can write about ourselves." According to him, Shamir had "linguistic intuition." His language was fresh, contemporary, and made good use of dialogue. The significant change that Shamir introduced, asserts Bartov, was linguistic: "He returned the Hebrew sentence to the reader."[7]

But it was not only the book's literary and linguistic characteristics that made it such a draw for tens of thousands of readers. It was also, and mainly, a "foundational text": a work that was perceived by the readers of the time as reflecting a crucial phase in the process of consolidating the "Israeli community."

An uncontestable testimony to the way the novel and the play were perceived as foundational texts was the flood of reviews that accompanied the two works immediately following their publication and, especially, the fact that practically all those reviews focused on the same question: Did Shamir credibly and faithfully represent the descriptive objects that were perceived by the audience of the time as being at the center of the book's interest—the labor settlement movement (more precisely, the kibbutzim); the sabras, the first generation born and raised in the country (more precisely, the youths among them); and the Palmach, the elite fighting force of the Haganah organization, which was founded at the end of the British Mandate? Another feature of this deluge of reviews—and I refer here only to the reviews published in 1948—is the highly emotional stance taken by the writers, which manifested itself in clusters of superlatives or a glut of condemnations and abuses aimed at the novel and the play.

Haim Gamzu, who was actually known as a scathing critic, praises the character of the native Israeli in the novel, a boy who, as he sees it, is lovingly and naturally devoted to his homeland.[8] Gamzu remarks that Uri Cahana, the novel's central young character, expresses the same inherent heroism that characterizes, in his view, all the young members of the generation who are living the Palmach life. The thrilled critic goes on to address the author, Moshe Shamir, directly, and thanks him for having created a genuine sabra hero, ready to realize the ideal.

Those who condemned the author also did so, for the most part, in reference to the question of the mimetic credibility of the artistic representation; that is, in relation to the way the work described, rationalized, and judged characters and plot developments that they perceived as direct representations of human beings and events that they knew firsthand. Y. Achi-Ne'eman believes for example that Shamir the playwright betrayed his vocation: "In wartime, the theater's role is to evoke exemplary edifying figures, and the characters of the Palmachniks in the play are the opposite of that."[9] And David Aran, who wrote about the book approximately four years after its publication, asserts that "Moshe Shamir's novel was undoubtedly an important event in our literature," noting that "it fulfills the great realistic mission: discovering the specific beauty in a certain way of life." However, in the same breath he points to what is in his view "the book's flaw": "the rupture between the plot and the description," a flaw that to his mind "is not merely formal, but is the result of his [Moshe Shamir's] general outlook and of the bad character of the protagonists." And he wonders, like his predecessors, "How will the reader understand the great project he is faced with in view of such protagonists? How will he believe in its future in view of such protagonists?"[10]

On this count the leaders of Hashomer Hatzair, and most notably Ya'akov Hazan and Meir Ya'ari, went furthest. As H. Halperin discovered, the two were in favor of banning the novel,[11] which was supposed to be published by Sifriat Po'alim, their movement's publishing house. The movement's forefathers, Halperin suggests, decided to punish Shamir for having violated two major imperatives: a) he left kibbutz Mishmar Ha'emek, and b) he wrote a novel that is neither "representative" nor "edifying." Ya'akov Hazan, also a member of Mishmar Ha'emek, claimed, according to Shamir, "that it [the book] doesn't contain enough positivity and that he wouldn't be able to give it as a present to his daughter, to read it and be raised on its values."[12] And indeed, the book's printing was delayed by eight months (from July 1947 to February 1948). The ban was apparently called off both because the Cameri Theater started working on the play and the publishers realized that publishing the book to coincide with the play would help sales, and because Eliyahu Shamir, the author's brother, was killed in battle in January 1948—a fact that shed a grotesque light on the whole affair of the ban.[13]

The flood of reviews that accompanied the book's publication and the play's staging, the polarized emotional positions, and the affair of the ban that ended so embarrassingly following the death in battle of Eliyahu Shamir—all these testify to the shakiness of the borderline between art and life in the cultural scene of those turbulent days. The public—first and foremost, but not only, the one that Shamir himself had come from—treated the book and the play as both a mirror and a shaping force. The kibbutzim members, especially the members of Hashomer Hatzair and the enlisted Hachshara (settlement-training) groups, and chief among them the Palmachniks, learned from their predecessors, the people of the Second and Third Aliyah who flew the flag of Zionist pioneering, about the great power of foundational texts. Therefore many of them, including the professional critics, treated the novel and the play as binding historical documents and thus read them with a limited amount of aesthetic distance.

One of the manifestations of this phenomenon was the reaction of the play's spectators, who saw themselves also as its protagonists. One of many examples of this phenomenon is the story told by the actor Yosef Yadin about one of the shows that took place in Jerusalem, on the first day of the first ceasefire during the War of Liberation. The actors arrived in Jerusalem via the Burma Road. At Motza "the shooting started—the actors unloaded the stage set and carried it on their shoulders all the way to Jerusalem . . . an audience of hundreds was waiting at 'Edison' . . . there was no electricity . . . they brought oil lamps from their homes to light up the stage." There was a shortage of water, and "the moment Mika turns on the tap . . . the audience shouts 'Turn it off . . . you mustn't waste water.'"[14]

Another example of the lack of a clear dividing line between imagination and reality, this time on the part of the artists, is offered by the playwright Yosef Milo: "They said at the time that this play was the IDF's secret weapon—and one day they sent us to put it on in [the military camp in] Tzrifin . . . One hour before the show the soldiers came and took all the chairs out of the hall. The empty hall then filled with soldiers with rucksacks, with guns, who sat down on their rucksacks. Immediately after the show they were loaded on trucks and sent into battle in Sha'ar Hagai, and it was a horrible feeling. We saw them going out to battle, but we didn't know how many of them would return."[15]

Other evidence of the phenomenon of a reduced aesthetic distance between *He Walked in the Fields* and its historical recipients emerges from reading many of their notes: most of them read the novel "against the grain"—that is, in opposition to the elementary reading instructions that the text provides. The most striking example is the fact that they read the novel as if it had been set during the War of Liberation, while it was actually set during the end of the Mandate period. Another example is their almost complete disregard for the discordant tones that Shamir appended to the event of Uri's death, which is shaped as a semiconscious suicide and not—as it has been repeatedly read— as a heroic death in battle.[16] A third example is the fact that most of the critics ignored Mika's story, that is, the story of the Holocaust survivors who had just arrived in the country and met its residents—a complex and problematic story that Shamir, in contrast to the usual representational norm of the time, gave a pivotal status in his novel and tried to deal with, as I shall show below, in a new way. The responses of the novel and the play's immediate historical addressees thus prove that *He Walked in the Fields* was a typical foundational text. The most incisive formulations in this context were offered by Emmanuel Sivan and Judd Ne'eman.[17]

In his important book *The 1948 Generation: Myth, Profile and Memory*—a book that is largely dedicated to an enquiry into the myth of the Palmach Generation—Sivan writes: "The terms sabra and 1948 fighter, and even more sabra and 1948 fallen soldier, were presented [in the social and cultural landscape of the early days of the state] as inextricably linked. Undoubtedly, this was also due to the fact that most of the young writers who wrote about the war were sabras, or almost sabras, and that their protagonists were from the peer and origin group they knew best. Because of the monopoly that these writers had in practice over the authentic expression of the war—as members of the generation that came from the firing line—they left a deep imprint on the public consciousness. And of course there is no book in which this imprint is more deeply felt than *He Walked in the Fields*, which, though it was published in 1947, gained special popularity as a novel and a play during and immediately after the war. Its hero, the 20-year-old Uri, was presented by its author . . . as a kind of archetype . . . of the fallen sabra soldier of 1948. His figure became engraved in the public consciousness as if he was the representative figure of the 1948 sabra fighter (and fallen soldier)."[18]

Ne'eman determines the status and place of *He Walked in the Fields* through the concept of the "dominant fiction," which he borrows from the French cinema scholar Jacques Rancière. Rancière, whose aim is to define a society's "self-reflective" discourse, refers by this concept to "the privileged mode of representation by which the image of the social consensus is offered to the members of a social formation and within which they are asked to identify themselves."[19] "When we come to choose an Israeli work that would meet Rancière's definition," writes Ne'eman, "We shall find that Moshe Shamir's novel, and maybe even to a larger extent the film *He Walked in the Fields*, can be considered as Israel's dominant fiction in its early years."[20]

The status of *He Walked in the Fields* as a "dominant fiction" has become clear again in the last decade, which has seen a renewed and innovative reading of the foundational texts of modern Jewish and Israeli culture. In all the texts of this kind, whose focus is the corpus created by the members of the 1948 Generation, the discussion of Shamir's text takes center stage.

Public Territories, Intimate Spaces, and No-Man's Lands

The novel *He Walked in the Fields* is based, as Michal Arbel has shown, on two central double homecomings: the double return of Willie, the father of the Cahana family, and the double return of Uri, his son: "The novel opens with a prologue describing Willie's journey away from home, on his way to the British military base in Egypt after the death of his only son . . . The novel proper opens with a return: Uri returns home to Gat Ha'amakim, from Kadoorie.[21] He has been preceded by his father, who had returned home from a two-year-long mission with the Tehran orphans.[22] The novel's ending also opens with the urgent need for Uri to return home from his Palmach training, to his girlfriend who is carrying his child—a homecoming which does not take place because of the heroic death that in a certain sense Uri brings upon himself. Here too the son's planned return is forestalled by the return of the father, who takes leave from his training in order to say goodbye to his home and to reunite with his wife after years of physical and emotional separation."[23]

The movements of the father and the son, Willie and Uri, are intertwined with the movements of the novel's two central women, Ruthka, Willie's wife, and Mika, Uri's girlfriend, a "Tehran child," who has arrived in the country in the wake of Willie's mission to Iran; as well as with the movements of secondary characters associated with the central characters. Ruthka came to the country with a group of young Zionists from Poland, where she had had a romantic relationship with the group's leader, Biberman, an ideologue, an articulate thinker but a weak doer, a "comfort-loving [person], afraid of new relationships and new encounters . . . [who] protects himself with heaps and heaps of eloquence."[24] Not long after the Polish group has begun establishing itself in the "outpost" which would become Gat Ha'amakim, the book's main setting, it is joined—despite Biberman's reservations, and as an answer to the secret wishes of Ruthka, "who was hoping and eager . . . [for] openings into new worlds" (*HWF*, 51)—by "a group of pioneers from Germany" (50). One of the "German" newcomers was Willie. But Willie—and this, as we shall see, is an important piece of information for understanding Shamir's human engineering—is not German, but rather a Russian who had joined the German group in Berlin, where he had been sent by his father to study.

Willie, unlike the other members of the German group, "immediately started transfusing his blood into the blood of the kibbutz" (53), mainly through the relationship that develops between him and Ruthka, and that leads to marriage, Uri's birth, and the starting of a family. Life in the new outpost is hard and dangerous, especially for the first newborns—one of whom dies—and Ruthka decides to act: she moves with Uri to Willie's parents' house in Tel Aviv to wait out the danger, against Willie's wish and amid the disapproval of the group members, who interpret the act as a betrayal. In Tel Aviv Ruthka is comfortable: her son is safe and the relationship with Willie, who visits his wife and son infrequently, is preserved, but at the same time she finds a substitute in Yossel Brumberg, formerly a pioneer and presently an artist, who declares himself committed to no one, let alone any community or idea. However, when Willie arrives in Tel Aviv and states his mind firmly, and since the situation in the kibbutz has become a little easier, Ruthka decides to return to the kibbutz, and the life of the Cahana family is re-stabilized, despite her "primordial sin" of leaving the kibbutz with Uri (45). With time, the relationship between Willie and Ruthka goes sour again. Willie finds refuge in national missions, most notably bringing the Tehran children to the country, and Ruthka finds refuge in her work in the kibbutz and in the bosom of Avraham Goren, who is a kind of "new edition of Biberman from twenty years ago," and whose appeal is "his refined spirituality which invites pampering, alongside a certain toughness and his manly status as a commander" (69).

Uri only learns of the family crisis when he comes back from Kadoorie, after completing his studies. This crisis and his father's decision to join the Jewish Brigade lead him, along with other factors that I shall touch on later, to connect with Mika on the one hand, and join the Palmach on the other.[25]

Mika becomes pregnant. She tries to talk to Uri about the future of their relationship and in particular about the pregnancy, and runs into a dead end. Uri is incapable of shouldering any responsibility—either as a partner or as a parent —and escapes to his military tasks. The last of these, training new recruits to throw a grenade, is the scene of "an invited accident": of all people, the young commander Uri chooses a new immigrant, probably a Holocaust survivor, with no coordination, to be the first to practice throwing a live grenade. The latter drops the grenade just outside the trench in which the soldiers are standing, Uri jumps, grabs the grenade, and is blown up with it.

The novel ends with another double movement. After Willie finds out about the accident, he sends Ruthka to the hospital in Afula, where Uri's body has been taken. He himself goes to Haifa to meet Mika and prevent her from executing her plan to kill the fetus in her womb—a journey that turns out to be redundant, at least on the practical level, since Mika has already decided to keep the baby.

Shamir's position regarding the status of the tension between the "Place" and the "place" manifests itself on the topographic plane—just as in the works of Mapu, Herzl, and Luidor—in the structural/thematic link between the work's "background map" and "foreground map." The background map in *He Walked in the Fields* is identified with the world of the fathers and is created from the ensemble of relations existing among the central geographical landmarks in the world of the father, Willie. The foreground map in Shamir's novel is identified with the world of the sons and is created from the ensemble of relations existing among the central geographical landmarks in the world of the son, Uri. As I have already hinted, the relation between Shamir's background map and foreground map is fundamentally different from the parallel topographic relation in the works of Mapu, Herzl, and Luidor. In those works, the background map represented the old, flawed order, whereas the foreground map represented the new, correct order. In Shamir it is exactly the opposite, which suggests a conservative revisionist position.

The background map in *He Walked in the Fields* is quite broad, resembling in its scope the background map in *The Love of Zion*. It spreads all the way from Uzbekistan and the Indian Ocean to the United States, from Poland and the Carpathians to Germany and London, from Russia to Australia, and from Tehran in Iran to the northern part of the Sinai Peninsula and Egypt. At the center of this map, as in all the previous maps, stands Eretz Israel, and at the center of Eretz Israel, as in Luidor and his followers among the Third Aliyah writers, stands a small agricultural settlement in the Galilee. In this sense—and this is true also for the foreground map—Shamir's landscape conceptualization, at least in his first novel, suggests a continuing deterioration in the status of Jerusalem. Here it is "the kibbutz in the valley" that serves as the regulative idea: the definitive ideological/moral yardstick of the depicted world.

The central landmarks in "Willie's map," the novel's background map, are Russia, Germany, Poland, Tehran, Egypt, Tel Aviv, the fields in the valley and of course the kibbutz. These landmarks are organized in a clear set of binary oppositions: a) Diaspora (Russia, Germany, Poland) versus homeland; b) the Russian Jewish realm, perceived as vital and practical, versus the German Jewish realm, perceived as spiritual and impotent; c) Holocaust (the refugee camp in Tehran) versus revival (Aliyah to Eretz Israel); d) urban space (Tel Aviv) presented, in the tradition of the Second and Third Aliyah, in a negative light, versus rural space (the kibbutz) presented, in line with the same tradition, in a positive light; e) agricultural space (the kibbutz's cultivated fields) versus military space (Egypt); f) public space (shower rooms, the dining hall, the silo, the tractors' shed, and so on) versus private space (Willie and Ruthka's shared room); and g) annihilating desert space (the Sinai desert) versus populated land.

Among these landmarks and across the story's temporal continuum—and here I am getting ahead of myself and encroaching on the chronotopic plane—

there is harmony. This harmony reflects the years-long attempt by Willie, the representative of the fathers' generation, to find the golden mean between the binary oppositions that demarcate his life. Willie immigrates to Eretz Israel but does not sever his ties with the Diaspora, both by bringing the Tehran children to the country and by volunteering to join the Brigade. In his personality and deeds he combines the noble qualities of Russian Jewry on the one hand and western and central Europe on the other. He connects (and after all he is the designer and builder of the Kibbutz's mythological bridge) the Holocaust survivors with the "seventh million," those immigrants who were fortunate to immigrate to Eretz Israel in time. He divides his time, in small rations, between his private life—Ruthka, Uri, and the family home—and his duties to the demanding collective, and between work in the kibbutz and his contribution to a more universal cause: volunteering to serve in the Brigade. He even agrees to a period of status quo between his beloved kibbutz and the "sinful city" of Tel Aviv. And when he stays in the kibbutz, after separating from Ruthka, he finds a place of refuge: the room of the Tehran children's teacher, located between the kibbutz's permanent houses and the refugees' temporary tents.

Moreover, the range of Willie's movement is very wide relative to that of the other characters in the story. Some of these movements seem contradictory in their purpose. However, and this is the important point, his movements as a whole have a sharp and clear concentric logic: Eretz Israel is the center of the world, at its center there is the kibbutz, and at the center of the kibbutz there is Ruthka.

What is more, and the two are interconnected, Willie—unlike Uri—repeatedly chooses life over a heroic death. This is already suggested by the prologue, "Introduction in Quneitra," to which we shall return, which ends with Willie's journey back from his home, after Uri's death, to his military base in Egypt. This is a difficult journey for him, he is full of questions about his and his family's past, and doubts about the future, and even more about whether there is a point to human life in general. At a certain stage he waits for some kind of signal from above: "Cahana stretched both his hands out the window, as if wishing to catch a gift that would drop for him from the sky. Nothing fell toward him. On the contrary. The newspaper escaped from his grasp and flew along the dark windows, its whiteness still visible for a little while" (*HWF*, 8).

Corporal Willie Cahana loses heart for a moment, a fact signaled by his hope that some gift would fall from the sky. But such a gift does not and cannot fall because Willie, who represents the correct existential position according to Shamir, is a secular person and possibly even an atheist. The proof: the "descent into Egypt" and the passage through the desert, two crucial elements of the revival myth of the Jewish people, provoke in him, at the most, a parodic attitude.[26] For him—unlike for the people of Israel, who during their journey through the desert were awarded the Ten Commandments and the sweet-tasting manna—nothing comes down and nothing can come down from the sky.

A deus ex machina solution is not part of Willie's worldview, which is entirely based on the human and the rational. And to prove it, not only does nothing drop for him from the sky, but the opposite happens: the newspaper, carrying the mourning notices of Uri's death, escapes from his grasp and flies along the windows before disappearing in the desert sands. That is, Willie, again in contrast to Uri, does not hold on to death. He neither represses nor forgets it, but nor does he allow death to reign over him. It is this balanced reaction, which characterizes all his behavior (save perhaps for the outburst about Yossel Brumberg, Ruthka's Tel Aviv suitor), that enables him to cross the annihilating desert again without being swallowed in it, and claim his place in the hearts of Ruthka and of the settled land.

Uri's map, the map of the representative of the sons' generation, the sabras, is much smaller than Willie's. It includes the kibbutz as a desired center, the Kadoorie agricultural school, Har Ha'ayalot where he walks with Mika, the military camps where he serves, which are not far from the kibbutz either, the frontier area, which is located, as he tells Mika, "outside the country's borders" (240), the spot chosen for grenade-throwing practice where he is killed/commits suicide, and the Afula hospital where his dead body is brought.

The landmarks on Uri's map are also organized in binary oppositions but in a configuration that, though much more limited than the one that marks his father's map, is nevertheless much more problematic and dramatic. This configuration is based on the following oppositions: a) home/the kibbutz versus substitute spaces—Kadoorie, the army; b) quasi-intimate spaces versus public spaces inside the kibbutz; and c) wild nature versus domesticated nature.

Uri's existential space is highly reminiscent of Yoash's, and not by chance. For, at least according to the expectations of the novel's historical readers, Uri, the sabra, is the ultimate actualization of Yoash, who is himself the mythological embodiment of the New Hebrew Man. However, a careful examination of the text suggests that these two lived spaces differ in several significant ways, which enable us to explain, at least partially, the different status and fate of the two "natives."

On the level of the "total space" (the overall scope of a specific character's movement) there is a considerable resemblance between the existential maps of the two natives. Both are focused on a small area in a northern part of the country. What is located outside this area does not interest Yoash and Uri at all. Uri, like Yoash and Luidor's other New Hebrew Men—unlike his parents, Ruthka and Willie, and Mika, the Holocaust survivor, who as mentioned before is of the same age—has no regard for the coastal cities of Tel Aviv and Haifa, or the cities of the "Old Yishuv," Jerusalem, Hebron, Tiberias and Safed, let alone for other places on earth. This phenomenon is noticeable in the attitude of the two natives toward stories about the representatives of the Diaspora. Yoash refuses to listen to David's stories about the pogroms in Russia, and Uri is completely impervious to Mika's stories about her meanderings during the Holocaust.

In other words, for the two sabras the birthplace—the moshava in "Yoash" and kibbutz Gat Ha'amakim in *He Walked in the Fields*—is the center of the world, the axis mundi, on three different planes: a) it is located at the topographical center of their "total space"; b) it is the center of the world's "force field"—that is, most of their actual movements and their desired movements take place from and to it; and c) these birthplaces serve in Luidor and Shamir as the novel's regulative idea (like Jerusalem in Mapu and like the link between Haifa and Jerusalem or the link between the Temple in Jerusalem and the technological temple near the Dead Sea in Herzl), that is, as the ultimate yardstick in relation to which are judged all the other places in the fictional landscape and all the protagonists' movements in the desired and actual journeys between these places.

Another similarity between the two can be detected in their attitude toward the "locals," the Palestinian Arabs. While both respect them, they at the same time "talk to them in their own language," the language of power, without feeling that there is any kind of internal contradiction in their behavior.

The similarities between Yoash and Uri's existential maps, and the differences between them, also manifest themselves in the nature of the central points in their lived spaces and the reciprocal relations among these points. As we may remember, in Yoash's world neither the parental home nor educational institutions have any meaning. The only significant space is the open expanse, which represents the new, anti-claustrophobic experience. Nevertheless, as we have seen, Yoash is a capable farmer and a lauded guardsman and fighter. It is true that he, along with the rest of Luidor's protagonists, prefers wandering around the country or at least working as a watchman to working in the fields, but this preference stems from an ideological stance that calls for maximum freedom of movement, rather than from an external limitation, that is, a limitation imposed on him by some person or institution. *He Walked in the Fields* also attaches little weight to the home, but here not because of Uri's character or some ideological principle he espouses, but simply because the option of the home is not available to him.

In fact Uri is homeless from the moment he returns to the kibbutz from the Kadoorie school. This phenomenon is clearly reflected—and I am crossing over to the chronotopic plane again—in the map that outlines his movements. He travels straight from the school to the room of Ethel, "who was his first nursemaid" while he "was the first child she took care of" (16); later he wanders around the kibbutz's public spaces (the dining hall, the kitchen), rides with his father to the fields, and returns to Ethel's room. And again he roams around the kibbutz's public spaces (the laundry room, the clothing storage, and the showers). Then, for the first time, he meets his mother—not in her room, but in the neglected playground near the children's houses; from there he makes his way back to Ethel's room.

In other words, Uri has no home—incidentally, at this stage the reader, in contrast to the naïve Uri, already knows that in his mother's home resides a stranger, Avraham Goren, and that his father lives in a temporary room, which he is also about to abandon—but only a surrogate home, which is itself "regressive": a place that takes him back to the (alternative) home he had when he was five!

Nor is Uri given a room of his own, in which he could have perhaps felt at home in his own kibbutz. Neither the fact that he is the kibbutz's eldest son, nor that he was "an only son" to his parents (33), who belong to the local "aristocracy," stands him in good stead. No one is impressed by the fact that he has graduated from the prestigious Kadoorie (where thanks to his father's connections he studied free of charge), that he has grown and matured and even knows how to state his mind firmly. For the old (male) kibbutz members, represented in this context by Biberman, the housing committee coordinator, Uri is "a transparent being," a kind of "present absentee." And the proof: Biberman responds thus when Uri asks to get an intimate space of his own: "'A private room?' Biberman wondered, his amazement outgrowing his irritation. 'And where will we find you a private room?'" (134).

Uri's displacement from his home provokes in him a counterreaction, which is reflected in the location of his intimate meetings. His first meeting with Mika—to which we shall return—takes place in vineyard B, which Shamir has placed outside the boundaries of the kibbutz. The erotic encounter between the two also takes place in vineyard B. The next encounter happens in the apple grove, and the following one in a hidden clearing in the forest on the way to Har Ha'ayalot.

All of Uri's intimate meetings take place, then, outside the boundaries of his home, the kibbutz.[27] This fact takes on a sarcastic tinge when we notice two additional facts: first, the erotic relations between Uri and Mika intensify in direct proportion to the distance of the encounter from the kibbutz; second, only the meetings in which they quarrel take place in the kibbutz itself—notably the meeting in which Uri informs Mika that he is going to join the army (a meeting that takes place on the public bench near the dining hall) and the last meeting between them (a meeting that takes place in Mika's tent, the only tent among the tents of the Tehran children that has not yet been dismantled), in which Uri fails to hear her plea for him to stay in the kibbutz or at least be more attentive to her troubles.

The educational institutions in "Yoash" and in *He Walked in the Fields* also have different statuses and functions. In "Yoash," the school is superfluous, since Yoash is a nature boy who rejects any socializing contact. On the other hand—and this is a key point for understanding the prose fiction of the Palmach Generation—the gang, or rather the gangs, the Kadoorie one and the army one, are Uri's places of refuge. Even though in this context too he finds himself in a position of loneliness, because it is "in his nature" to be first among his peers, especially in the Palmach, where he always marches ahead of his soldiers, the "Jama'a" [Arabic for "gang"], the masculine-sabra-adolescent group of friends with all that it entails (the pranks, the thefts from kibbutzim, the military training, and even the group-infatuation with the same mythological female support soldier), is the one and only social framework in which Uri feels comfortable.

There is also a difference between Yoash and Uri in terms of their affinity to agricultural work. Yoash cultivates his land and enjoys the fruits of his work. Uri, on the other hand, wishes to work in the fields, a very prestigious branch of work in the kibbutz at the time, but makes only a minimal effort to realize his wish. In fact, the only time he goes to the agricultural fields is on his first day in the kibbutz after returning from Kadoorie. He rides to the fields with his father, surveys them, and returns to the kibbutz a few minutes later, in the same car.

Moreover, Uri, who at Kadoorie specialized in field agriculture, never walks in the fields. This fact receives special significance in view of both the name of the novel in which he is the protagonist, and the fact that his father, Willie, decides to make his way home during his leave from the British army on foot, and through the kibbutz's fields.

It seems that Uri—like Elik in *With His Own Hands*—prefers mechanical tools, including weapons, over the direct contact with the land. But this context too is cast in an ironic light. The first time we meet him, catching a ride in Ilana's truck, he fails to distinguish between a loaded truck and an empty one; and he ends his life and his part in the novel after carelessly handling a frag grenade.

However, it seems that the crucial difference between Yoash and Uri concerns their attitude toward open space. The comparison between the two in this context highlights the gap between the mythological native and his sabra (step) descendant. Many critics have pointed to the vividness of the landscape descriptions in *He Walked in the Fields*,[28] and to the sense of intimacy that Shamir's sabra protagonists feel in the open.[29] Indeed, the writing of Shamir and of S. Yizhar, the two major writers of their generation, represented a leap forward in terms of landscape observation and description, a shift that also manifested itself in their adoption of a deictic position; that is, one that points to defined extra-literary spaces.[30]

All the historical recipients who read *He Walked in the Fields* identified Gat Ha'amakim, the fictional kibbutz, with Mishmar Ha'emek, the kibbutz that was home to Shamir, Ya'akov Hazan, and others, and identified the spatial details of the fictional kibbutz with the spatial details of the real kibbutz. If one detail or another was missing, they filled it in. And if a certain detail was put in the wrong place, they commented on it and even expressed their irritation, or (at best) tried to understand the significance of the change.

In Luidor, on the other hand, we find no "realistic plenitude," let alone a deictic position, but nevertheless his natives and even his old immigrants feel much more comfortable in the open space than the sabras of Shamir and his generation. For Yoash and Yehuda the orchard keeper and their friends wish to be absorbed in and merge with the country's open spaces, whereas the contact that Uri and his friends maintain with the landscape (as well as with the beings that are in it) is the contact of conquest,[31] or more precisely, the contact of temporary conquest. This contact, we might say, paraphrasing a line from Nathan Alterman's poem "Od Hozer Ha-Nigun," is like the caress of a wanderer, a person who is in constant motion: a quick acquaintance and a light demonstration of ownership, followed by the resumption of movement, and so on and so on indefinitely. Always in motion, always making contact in a snatched, possessive, but neither powerful nor entirely committed way.

The obvious differences between Yoash's and Uri's connection with the space around them explain, at least partially, the difference between their death scenes. Yoash lived all his short life on the margins of the community in which he was born and raised, but in his death he becomes, as I tried to show in the previous chapter, the center of a circle, signifying a new wholeness—one whose validity is confirmed by the people of the community as well as those outside it. In other words, the trajectory of Yoash's life is centripetal; his life is led on the margins, but upon ending it becomes the center. By contrast, the trajectory of Uri's life is centrifugal. He was born in the kibbutz but constantly moves away from it in ever widening circles, finally dying an unnecessary death far from its parameters.

The Intelligent, Cunning Man, and the Mimicker

In contrast to the writers discussed in the previous chapters, Shamir did not try to create a new utopian agenda. He championed the Zionist/pioneering utopia, also espoused by the Second and Third Aliyah pioneers, and tried to revalidate it. Shamir's significant deviation from the route taken by his predecessors manifests itself in the repository of metanarratives on which his novel's plotlines are based. Rather than metanarratives that deal with the birth of a people or the consolidation of its identity, we have here a metanarrative that deals with the question of death's place in relation to life. Is death really, as Moshe Dayan put it, not the end of life but its climax? A heroic approach, which actually assumes that there is no borderline between the living and the dead, or at least that this borderline is blurred and crossable? Or is it only the end of life, a "survivalist" approach that assumes that the pinnacle of life is life itself, and therefore that death, the element most hostile to it, should, in any given context—private or collective—be considered as an enemy, from which the human community must guard itself most vigilantly?

The heroic approach, in the spirit of Dayan's interpretation, is represented in the novel by the (failed) homecoming journey of Uri, the representative of the "sabra" generation, a journey based on two cultural narratives, one constructive and the other subversive. The first is the "axis narrative" of the literature of the period, reflecting Shamir's implied model, that is, the worldview of his generation. The other is an imported narrative, through which Shamir undermines the axis narrative, and respectively, the worldview of the Palmach Generation. The axis narrative in Uri's journey is the "living-dead" narrative, which, as many scholars and critics have noted, formed the underlying plot and thought pattern of a considerable part of the literature of the Palmach Generation. The other cultural narrative is the narrative of the "lone rider,"[32] which was created in American frontier literature, as well as, and perhaps mainly as far as Shamir and his generation are concerned, in the Wild West films (the westerns) which were very popular at the time. It is important to note that these two cultural narratives are different—and according to some writers, including Shamir, even contrasting—developments of one metanarrative: "the metanarrative of the vagabond,"[33] which had a place in ancient popular culture and spawned impressive written versions in the literature of ancient Greece.[34] The other, "survivalist" approach, is represented in the novel by the (successful) homecoming journey of Willie Cahana, the representative of the parents' generation, a journey that alludes, in its overall structure and in some of its central thematic features, to the (successful) homecoming journey of "Odysseus the Cunning," the hero of Homer's *Odyssey*.

Willie Cahana—The Intelligent, Cunning Man

Commentators on Homer's *Odyssey* have been divided over the nature and character of Odysseus the Cunning, as well as, and the two are interconnected, over the nature of his return after twenty years of wandering to his birthplace, Ithaca, and to his wife, Penelope, who had waited for him faithfully. Some commentators saw Odysseus as an element that creates upheaval and disharmony in the world,[35] while others saw him as a complex figure who faces great and contradictory forces operating on it and in it, and manages to control them by creating a harmony of oppositions.[36]

In its overall structure, Willie's return journey resembles the return journey according to the harmonistic interpretation. The central axis here is his return home and to Ruthka after twenty years dedicated to various missions. It is the return of an experienced and realistic man, who understands with a deep awareness that human life is full of painful contradictions and the way to live with them is to structure them in a configuration based on a harmony of oppositions.

Willie's trajectory, the course of his life, has a clear structure. It is based on four big movements that connect—and eventually create harmony among—four binary oppositions that represent the coordinate system of his life and his worldview, which is also the worldview of the author. These four movements branch out in dozens of ways, and include many temptations and dangers, yet for Willie—and in this he also resembles Odysseus—all the roads lead home, to Ruthka. In the course of Willie's protracted journey home he eliminates (like Odysseus) all of Ruthka's suitors, including—and here lies a fundamental difference between the *Odyssey* and *He Walked in the Fields*—his own son, whose existence is a stumbling block in Willie and Ruthka's relationship.

Willie's first big movement, which consists of emigrating to Eretz Israel and marrying Ruthka, already displays the harmonistic logic—based on opposites completing each other—that structures his life's path. Here: "Willie came with the Germans from Germany—he even went with them on Hachshara [a preparation program for Aliyah] for a few months—but in essence he was not German but Russian. His father had sent him to Germany to study, and in Berlin he met the Zionist students, a few of whom, the Movement members, went on Hachshara. He went with them and came with them to Eretz Israel" (*HWF*, 53).

The question raised by this passage—and here I am venturing into the realm of Shamir's human engineering—is why the author, Moshe Shamir, did not send his hero straight from Russia to Eretz Israel, but "bothered" to take him (with the generous aid of Willie's father) through a longer route—the route of Hachshara, in Germany of all places? But Shamir, it turns out, does not allow us time to speculate, offering a clear answer in the very same paragraph: "[Willie] had great charm. He smelled of worlds, foreign cities, or what is called in our jargon 'culture'—but he also had the warm, affable, gripping roughness of a Russian."

The logic of Willie's first big movement is very similar to the logic of Herzl's version of the Exodus from Egypt. In both cases a union, which is supposed to prosper, is made between the Jews of the East and the Jews of the West, according to the same stereotypical ethnic basic assumptions. The Jews from eastern Europe are supposed to contribute to the Zionist melting pot—human warmth, directness, and vitality—whereas the Jews from western and central Europe are meant to contribute "culture." However, between these two Aliyah movements there are significant differences. In Herzl the melting-pot stage—"the genetic crossbreeding"—occurs in the sons' generation, which "naturally" signals the next, more developed stage in the evolution. In Shamir this crucial stage occurs in the fathers' generation. Second, in Herzl each member of the central couple brings with him on the journey back to the land the traits characteristic of his community, traits that oppose and, as it eventually turns out, also complement, the traits brought by the other member of the couple to the national genetics institute. In *He Walked in the Fields* the desired merging takes place in Willie to begin with, even without Ruthka.

The first double big movement that Willie makes—emigrating to Eretz Israel and marrying Ruthka—is the crucial movement in his journey because it turns Willie into a person who has a place in the world. It is this fact that enables him to deal with all the dangers lurking in his other journeys: to overcome traps and temptations and defeat his male rivals in the struggle over Ruthka's heart.

Furthermore, Willie represents the side of light, which affirms life, as well as, and this is not obvious, the side that does not surrender to darkness, although he is strongly and darkly attracted to it. This is another sense in which there is a similarity in terms of plot and themes between Willie's life trajectory and that of Odysseus. The trajectory of Odysseus's return home is riddled with traps of various kinds, which all have in common, as shown by George E. Dimock and Jean Pierre Vernant,[37] a devouring quality, a quality that is represented by enclosed spaces, signifying the annihilation of the human body (the cyclops's cave, the palace of the king of the Laestrygones, the cave of the monster Scylla, and parallel spaces that are home to cannibalistic entities), and the extinction of memory and the loss of one's connection with one's home/wife (the home of Calypso, who hides Odysseus away from the whole world; the island of the Phaeacians, who pressure him to stay in their country; and so on). The only way for Odysseus to escape is to cling to the memory of his home at all cost, even at the price of renouncing immortality and eternal youth.

Willie, like Odysseus, clings to his country, his home, and his wife, but without the help of the gods. Already in his first big movement, he escapes and rescues Ruthka from the existential space represented by "lost romantics such as Biberman" (*HWF*, 54), a suicidal space, which the narrator compares, through Ruthka's focalization, to sands "[in which] a man gets swallowed, becoming a mere grain among their grains" (52).

Willie's second big movement, which consists of several recurrent, nonidentical moves, is the movement from Gat Ha'amakim to Tel Aviv, where Ruthka and Uri fled from the dangers of living in the kibbutz. The flight, which was perceived in the kibbutz as the "betrayal" (193) and as the "primordial sin" (45), has made it clear to Ruthka and to Willie, who "opposed it bitterly and desperately," "that Uri was at the center of the world, that he was the purpose of life" (60). Uri therefore stands between Willie and Ruthka—and not for the last time. But Willie does not give up. Unlike most of the heroes of the first aliyot's stories, who prefer the land over the woman (who is, "of course," often identified with life in the sinful city[38]), Willie moves wisely between the kibbutz and the city, until he feels that it is "time to make a decisive choice" (*HWF*, 187), and then acts firmly and resolutely.

As in his other big movements, in this context too Willie has an antagonist. Here it is Yossel Brumberg, a veteran pioneer who joined Gat Ha'amakim after Ruthka and Uri's desertion and later deserted the kibbutz himself, moving to Tel Aviv and becoming an artist/bohemian.

Although Brumberg declares he has "nothing in the world . . . but art" (184), he devotes great efforts to ensuring that Ruthka and Uri's stay in the big city is pleasant, and both of them, especially Uri who gets very little attention from his father, respond to his affection and attention.

Willie is preparing to fight with Yossel over Ruthka's heart, "and deep inside he even looks forward for the battle." Indeed, during the encounter in Yossel's room, in the presence of Ruthka, he attacks the host, repudiates his worldview, expresses disdain for his art ("you . . . increase the amount of kitsch in the world" [190]), accuses him of deceiving Ruthka and Uri and of abandoning the settlement project and the settlers, and all this in a terrible rage.

Ruthka is furious with Willie. She thinks that "he is just like an animal," but moments later she gets up, and "with no explanations, with no attempt to hide things under a veneer of politeness—she took Willie's arm and bade Yossel goodbye" (192). The following day she takes Uri and returns to the kibbutz. Willie's triumph is a personal triumph as well as an ideological one on several planes. The first is a thematic plane, whose existence is suggested by the series of binary oppositions that Willie explicitly points to ("a Tel Aviv detachment that indulges in stewing in its own psychic juices" versus "the kibbutz life and taking responsibility for all that takes place in our world" (187); the life of the artist who "increases the amount of kitsch in the world" versus "the settlement project and the settlers"; and so on). Another plane is that of language. Ruthka's choosing of Willie is also a choosing of the Hebrew language, for in contrast to Yossel Brumberg, who despite being a veteran pioneer frequently spices his conversation with Yiddish, Willie speaks fluent Hebrew that he had acquired before emigrating to the country. Remembering their first meetings, Ruthka points out that "the Hebrew he spoke was seven times better than that of the kibbutz members, ten times better than that of his friends" (53).

Willie's third big movement is his assignment to Persia to bring over the Tehran children. This assignment is described as a journey to the heart of darkness, and the author makes it clear in several ways that only a man like Willie (who has strict integrity and is convinced of the justice of the pioneering Zionist ideology, who is completely devoted to the cause before him but never forgets where he has come from—that is, where his place is), only a man like that (who here again represents the forces of light) is destined to succeed in his mission and return home safely.

Willie arrives in Tehran as a savior, and a short time after his arrival he is already "adored as much as anyone can be adored by a group that has already managed on its wanderings to despair of all the faith in the world, to offend against the laws and respectability of half a dozen states, to fondle and weigh any value in the world, only to eventually dismiss it" (105). Willie's mission seems impossible at first. He is supposed to turn this mixed human throng, wallowing in a liminal space dominated by a mixture of filth and decay and feeble signs of life,[39] into a group of human beings that will trust him and function as a resolute task force.

The way he goes about it is clear and focused. He shows sympathy for the refugees, gives them the feeling that he would do anything for them, but at the same time firmly protects his dignity and privacy. Prominent examples of this are the way in which he situates himself in the space and the manner in which he dresses. Here: "This is how Willie was at the time, when he first showed up in Tehran: buttoned-up, taut, restrained" (101).[40] And as for his accommodation: "Ze'ev [Willie's Hebrew name] Cahana kept himself to himself. He lived in the camp, with all its Jews and its orphans, as no other emissary did—but his room at the camp was like the inner sanctum. He would only receive people at the management office" (105).[41]

The hardest battle that Willie wages during his stay in Tehran is the battle over Mika's soul. Mika, and I shall return to this key issue, is a young woman with a past. She lost her family in the war, moved from place to place in suspect ways, and in the period before Willie's arrival in Tehran served as a nurse at the Polish military hospital, adjacent to the Jewish orphans' camp where Willie sets himself up. In that hospital "she lived in the shadow of that despicable dwarf, that doctor" (102), who is involved in despicable business, including trading in children and women. This doctor sleeps with her, impregnates her, and performs an abortion on her. Mika loathes him but does not dare to run away. She receives the news of Willie's arrival with mixed feelings: on the one hand she keeps dreaming "of America, at the very least of Warsaw, at the very least of tall blonds wearing boots" (103), but on the other hand she longs for "some great force [that] would shake her at will, leaving no room for her own decisions" (104), and the rumors about Willie's arrival and about his determination suggest that he is exactly the great force she has been waiting for.

Unlike her fellow group members, she refuses to appear before the committee that examines the fitness of those wishing to emigrate to Eretz Israel. Willie, who realizes he is dealing with "a difficult and insubordinate girl" (105), agrees to invite her to a private conversation. In the first part of the conversation Mika stays defiantly silent, but slowly she realizes that she is sitting opposite "a person who must be the representative of some hitherto unfamiliar force" (109). What fascinates Mika about Willie, and makes her abandon his rival, the gentile doctor, with whose aid she was planning her way up, are the same qualities that help him survive all his journeys: his unbending belief in the path that he represents and his uncompromising integrity. Here: "She felt her eyes welling up. Felt that she suddenly knew what that unfamiliar force was.—This man, this Ze'ev Cahana from Eretz Israel, believes in what he said. He is an honest man—ah, good God—an honest man! No, you don't understand, dear—imagine:—an honest man!"

The battle over Mika's soul is an intermezzo in the war over Ruthka's heart. Two other battles in this war are Willie's fight not to have erotic relations with Mika, who adores him and hopes to capture his heart during his separation from Ruthka, and at the same time his fight to push out Ruthka's last lover, Avraham Goren, whom she sees as "a new edition of Biberman [her first lover] from twenty years ago" (69).

The hardest battle of all, however—a battle that is the focus of the novel's "force field"—is the one that Willie fights with Uri. This is a battle for "life" and "death." The battle for life, for the preservation of its existence and value, is won by Willie, and therefore it is he who stands in the last scene of the story next to Mika's bed to ensure that the baby she is carrying sees the light of day. Uri, who fails to find a place of his own in the world, wins the battle for death—

a triumph, or what seems to him like a triumph that, as I will show below, he imagines, plans, and mentally stages throughout most of the story's timeline, and in the end also "produces."

The Same Cahana?

Shamir's novel encourages us, by numerous means, to create an analogy between the homecoming journey of the father and the homecoming journey of the son, which is portrayed in various ways as a distorted and castrated imitation of the father's journey.

The mechanism of a distorted and castrated imitation, which is at the same time also distorting and castrating ("mimicry" as defined by Homi Bhabha[42]), is the dominant element in the novel, or, to follow Roman Jakobson's famous definition, the structural element that gives it its unity and meaning. By means of this mechanism—or more precisely, by means of a group of literary devices that serve it—the author achieves two goals: one poetical and one ideological. He mimics, and thus reestablishes, the figure of the sabra, while at the same time casting it in a ridiculous light, neutering and destroying it. Among other things, Shamir achieve these two goals, which both complement and contradict each other, by splitting his narrating voice into two different voices, which in turn are also split in two.[43]

The first voice can be called a cracked monological voice. It is a disembodied voice, which presents itself as credible and objective. It expresses a rigid ideological position that rejects firsthand, by means of various rhetorical devices, any "foreign discourse"; that is, to follow Bakhtin, any voice that does not coincide with the period's official/dominant ideological position, including foreign discourses of whose existence, or even possible existence, the naïve reader was never aware. This exaggerated, excessive defensiveness achieves, of course, the result opposite to its overt goal. The reader begins to wonder who it is that these "rhetorical heavy guns" are turned against, and why. He starts hearing subversive voices he probably would not have registered if it weren't for the narrator's "hysterical" reaction. Thus when we turn to Uri Cahana, we hear not only the monological voice of the narrator, who wishes to give renewed validity to his community's "hero of our generation," but also the discordances in his voice, which suggest that his attitude toward the jewel in the crown of the Yishuv period has a strong ironical dimension.

The other voice of the narrator is a typical hybrid voice, both in its formal appearance and in its ideological intentions. I am referring to the "combined speech" or the "vocal aggregate" created in the encounter between the narrator's voice and the consciousness of some of his characters and, in the context of our discussion, especially to the merging between Uri's consciousness and the narrator, who frequently evokes it. This evocation has two functions that do not interfere with each other's effectiveness. The first function is socio-psycho-ideological. Shamir wished to extend Uri's characterization as a stereotypical sabra also to the level of language, that is, to present him as a person who does not say much, a person whose power is in his hands rather than his mouth, as many of the Zionist utopists imagined him.[44] The combined speech enabled Shamir to create a taciturn character and at the same time allow us, the readers, to "hear" what takes place in his head.

The second function, which is more important for our discussion, is rhetorical-ideological. The combined speech enables Shamir's narrator to present subversive positions while hiding behind the back of the hero of the generation. Uri's mind gives rise to heresies which some of the readers, especially the readers who were members of Shamir's generation, failed to listen to with the proper seriousness because they attributed them to Uri alone—rather than to Moshe Shamir who planted these heresies in his protagonist's mind—and they forgave this Uri, because as a sabra he was supposed to be at the same time both blunt and cheeky, and not really committed to his own bluntness or impudence.

A good example of the way in which the cracked monological voice operates in the novel can be found if we examine the rhetoric used by the narrator in the following passages, which were discussed at the time by Dan Miron and Gershon Shaked.[45]

> At such times of leading, leading a squad or a platoon, it was as if Uri were walking alone. The more he commanded—the more he was selfish. With straightforward simplicity he believed in and accepted his being a focal point in the lives of many....
>
> *He was* the frequent progress of pairs of blows on a line that before them was chance—and after them a new trail in the mountains.
>
> *He was* waists that tore through shrubs and flattened their dry stalks,
>
> *He was*, according to women here and there, the unknown women of his privates, an objective necessity, part of what is called in life independent causes, disturbances, external factors....
>
> *He was* a boy who perhaps could have been more successfully educated and who was certainly the subject of some injustices and mistakes, but he was, if truth be told, a hundred boys, if not more.
>
> *He was* a grape-picker. And he may go back to that one day....
>
> *He was* a young talent, especially good at field exercises and reconnaissance,

one of the lovable kibbutz kids, and they should keep an eye on him, therefore, in the after-midnight-discussions of the battalion HQ.

He was one tanned, young Jew, on the Majdal Krum road, according to a British police car speeding by, according to the Arab gasoline drivers.

He was a prankster-thief who infiltrated a few courtyards in the village of Banias, untied donkeys from their ropes and later left signs of plucked feathers all the way to Mansura....

He was a finger that pulled, firmly but only as far as was necessary, the trigger of a Bren machine gun, while it was shooting short and frequent bursts and receiving an echo from the Gilboa valleys.

He was the mystery of the sudden bestirring of being, at a time of nocturnal fatigue, or when some presented possibility of domination had not yet been realized, such as a lovers' intercourse, such as Mika. (*HWF*, 227–28; emphases and changes in typography mine)

In his introduction to these passages, which are quoted in his book *Four Aspects of Hebrew Literature*, D. Miron claims that Shamir's stories are always centered around a character whose life illustrates the hidden movement of an accumulative force, which is destined to manifest itself in the founding of some governing establishment, and that Shamir's interest in this character stems from his wish to reach a profound understanding (through analogical lenses) of the Israeli push for independence that was taking shape around him. "Shamir's vision clings, in an attitude that combines elements of both love and hate," asserts Miron, "to this role-model of a society that is in the midst of its heroic age of establishing a kingdom." Miron goes on to assert that "the individual meaning of Uri's life only serves in the book as a layer, a step on which Shamir is able to build the historical and social edifice, which is what he is mainly interested in. Paradoxically," and he adds, "one can say that Uri Cahana often becomes the hero of a historical story which takes place in the present."[46] Miron deduced this phenomenon from the fact—and here we get to the question of the narrator's voice, status and functions—that "throughout the book there is a growing effort on Shamir's part to create a distancing estrangement between the reader and the protagonist's life, so that he is able to see this life story as an instructive, symbolic, typical *detail* of the historical event from which it had been taken."[47]

Miron defines the technique with which Shamir tries to achieve Uri's comprehensive and historical estrangement as "simple, simplistic, perhaps," and goes on to remark: "In these paragraphs Shamir surrenders to the monotone, fixed sentence structure of 'He was'... with the intention to exhaust all the objective possible points of view for whom Uri constitutes an existing, tangible entity.

… This essence should be the essence of Uri, who is not a private person, with only his own experiences and development, but even the essence of Uri *the phenomenon*, the new historical factor, who emerges on the country's landscape, demanding attention. This Uri becomes alienated in experiential terms. At the moment, he is nothing but force, movement, action. In fact, he is 'a hundred boys if not more,' the New Hebrew youth."[48]

G. Shaked devoted to Shamir a substantial chapter in his study of modern Hebrew literature.[49] In that chapter he referred to the same unit of text given above, but with changes: he omitted certain sentences from Shamir's text that appear in Miron's study and included other sentences that Miron chose to omit—differences in the scholar's quoting policies that stem from their different aims. Miron examined the unit of text discussed here as part of his attempt to understand Uri as the representative of a phenomenon: Uri the sabra as representing a rising historical force. Shaked, on the other hand, examined this unit of text in order to define the distinctive stylistic characteristics of Shamir's writing. And these are his conclusions:

> The anaphora "He was" recurs in this approximately page-and-a-half long passage, which has been brought here only in part, some twenty times. Each syntactical unit comprises a sentence whose predicates describe the protagonist's qualities through synecdochical and metaphorical means. The anaphoras give the passage a rhythmic framework and create a rhetorical excess which plays a merely emotive role and does not signify anything. Uri's portrait as an ideal sabra becomes a rhythmical song of praise, which charges the character and its everyday acts with a high emotive value. To this we should add, of course . . . , that the author's language is "super-standard," and the concluding words are ridiculously exaggerated. . . .
>
> The cosmic and mystical description of the character ("the mystery of the bestirring of being") does not suit him and the circumstances he operates in. . . .
>
> The style of the description endows Uri with qualities of a "superior new Hebrew man," which are not realized in the body of the plot; whether the rhetoric in the character's description is ironic or whether it is mainly pathetic, the recipients took the words at face value.[50]

The stated aims of the two scholars are different. Their poetical-ideological basic assumptions are similar and lead to similar conclusions, which are—and this is what I wish to show—important and illuminating on the one hand, and which display an interpretive blindness, from the very same critical school, on the other.

Both scholars argue, each in his own way—and I agree with them—that Shamir is not interested in Uri in himself but rather in Uri as the signifier of a phenomenon. Furthermore, both point justifiably to a gap between the level of the signifiers and the level of the signified, and argue that it stems from a certain intention on the author's part and his failure to realize it.

Both scholars point out that Shamir has an ambivalent attitude toward the object of his description; however—and this is the main thing in terms of our discussion here—they seem to neglect this crucial observation when they turn to interpret the text. In my view, it is impossible to properly understand this unit of text in particular and Shamir's poetics and worldview in general, without taking into account the two sides of his relation to the object of his description: the side of love and the side of hate, and respectively the pathetic option on the one hand and the ironic option on the other. For these are two sides of the same coin.

As part of this approach, which actualizes the double gaze that the monological cracked voice points to, the redundancy on the level of the signifiers is perceived both as leading to a pathetic deficiency (in line with Shaked's version) or a failed attempt to create historical distance (in line with Miron's version), and, and at the same time, as deliberate pathetic deficiency and failed attempt to create historical distance! That is, the redundancy is a rhetorical lapse that has an artistic function: to signal to the reader that the sabra Uri is a descriptive object that should be treated with caution and suspicion. He is, the author hints, a descriptive object whose truthfulness we need to try and establish, either through the explicit verbal messages of the monological narrator or through the messages communicated to us through the cracks in his voice or—and this is the first level of discussion I will deal with—through the messages communicated to us by the web of intratextual relations (the relation between the citations chosen by Miron and Shaked and parallel passages in the novel) and the web of intertextual relations (the relation between the citations chosen by Miron and Shaked and parallel passages in other literary texts).

An examination of the intratextual web of relations suggests that the suspicion the rhetorical excess arouses in us is justified. This is already suggested by an examination of the passage quoted above (identical to the one cited by Miron) in its immediate narrative context. However, as I have already indicated, Miron did not quote a "natural" textual unit, that is, one that has clear graphical or grammatical borders. What might justify the boundaries of the quote cited by Miron is the existence of sentences that meet two conditions: an anaphoric pattern ("He was"), and the existence of separate vantage points (the mountain shrubs, the new recruits, etc.)—two conditions whose fulfillment enables the critic to establish his interpretive claim that Shamir intended to create "in a limited time frame a great number of impressions that would finally combine into an impressive, overall essence."

MOSHE SHAMIR, *He Walked in the Fields* (1948)

Miron's choice of this particular interpretive direction explains why he cites only twelve out of the twenty-one anaphoric sentences, as well as why he has ended the citation on this specific, sample cataloging sentence: "He was the mystery of the sudden bestirring of being, at a time of nocturnal fatigue, or when some presented possibility of domination had not yet been realized, such as a lovers' intercourse, such as Mika."

Shaked, who focused on the stylistic issue and sought to point to the rhetorical excess in Shamir's style, chose to end the quote just before the cataloguing sentence with which Miron ended his quotation. His citation ends with the sentence "He was the mystery of the sudden bestirring of being, at a time of fatigue"—a truncated sentence! About which he says, as already mentioned, "the concluding words are ridiculously exaggerated."

From the long anaphoric chain, Miron and Shaked thus chose mainly the sentences that suited their interpretive arguments: the failed attempt to create the distance of estrangement and the failed attempt to depict Uri "as an ideal man" through "a rhetorical excess which plays a merely emotive role and does not signify anything."

These theses, I wish to reiterate, are correct in marking out two dominant pairs of components: a (failed) attempt to create historical distance and a (failed) attempt to create an ideal figure. However, if we refer to the entire textual unit before us, which is based on an anaphoric concatenation of sentences whose formal subject is Uri ("He [Uri] was")—we will find that Shamir used a redundant rhetorical configuration because he wanted to tell us—in a way that bypasses external censorship (the leaders of Hashomer Hatzair), and maybe also internal censorship (the writer's ingrained loyalty to the movement, the kibbutz and the "gang")—that the "ideal sabra," the "superior new Hebrew man," is, if truth be told, a fabrication, a literary character that has no referent in the nonfictional reality. The validity of this argument can be inferred, for example, from the content of the following sentences, which Shamir placed at the end of this section; sentences that Miron and Shaked chose to ignore.

> *He was* the hater of translations of foreign literature,
> *He was* the lover of American western battle movies. His self-love was reflected in his heart an endless number of times, through all the feelings he felt and all the needs he needed—but he never reached piggishness.
> *He was* an appetite that was aroused but not satisfied and therefore became hunger—in one girl who on that day climbed up the winding steps of Har Ha'ayalot and in the end got what she got and had her day spoiled.
> *He was* filthy at times, and at times even content to be so.

He was hated,

He was considered a liar.

He was the commander of a platoon that was now finishing a trek, which started at their base camp in the kibbutz and aimed to bring them to a training camp on some desolate hills, *in a place that sadly cannot be named*, above the din of a gray sea, which, if it is not the Dead Sea must be the Mediterranean. (*HWF*, 228; Emphases mine)

In this passage, which as already mentioned concludes the anaphoric section and therefore carries special weight, the balance between the tone of apotheosis (praise) and the tone of irony in the (cracked) voice of the monolithic narrator changes.

The sentences dedicated to a coveting gaze aimed at Uri's body, which include repeated fetishistic glances at his moving body parts,[51] and the sentences dedicated to Uri's elevation beyond the boundaries of the everyday and the common are replaced at the end of this section of anaphoric characterization by a series of sentences in which the pathetic, glorifying, and elevating tone gradually turns sarcastic and even grotesque.

This series of sentences mainly underlines the consequences of the injustices and mistakes that were made in Uri's education, which the narrator enumerates. Although they preserve unconcealed affection for his rough characteristics, which conceal "a heart of gold," they also take on an increasingly derisive tone. First we hear that Uri does not like translations of foreign literature—a fact that highlights his provincialism. Then we learn that he likes cinema, and especially—and as will become clear later, this is a very important piece of information for our discussion—American western battle movies, through whose prism he presumably understands the reality around him.

Further on we discover that Uri is not a great lover either: "He was an appetite that was aroused but not satisfied and therefore became hunger—in one girl." This is an unflattering piece of information, which is highlighted here because of the unusual structure of the sentence in which it is incorporated. This sentence leads the readers to form a preliminary assumption, based on the grammatical gender of the anaphoric phrase "He was" and on the semantic pattern of the previous sentences, that the observation "an appetite that was aroused but not satisfied and therefore became hunger" refers to Uri himself. This expectation turns out to be false and is moreover attributed to a (the) girl that Uri was supposed to satisfy (Mika). This double reversal of expectations, and moreover in such a sensitive context—which I shall return to later—casts the new superior Hebrew man in a sharply ironic light. This ironic remark is joined by suspicion and doubt when we learn that "he was hated" and also "was considered a liar."

The dominant tone of the ending of this narrative section is thus different from the tone of its opening. Those who follow the modal changes in the narrator's voice discover the less admirable sides of the sabra. Moreover, and especially, the narrator's biting (ironic) voice, which hides behind his pompous (self-important) voice, signals to us that Uri the "liar" is himself a fabrication, as does the "wink" about Uri's army base, which, like Uri himself, takes on a patently risible aura of mystery: "a place that sadly cannot be named."

What is suggested by the unflattering information about Uri the sabra is also suggested, and more blatantly, by the combined speech—the hybrid medium that results from the combination of Uri's focalization and the narrator's words. One example among scores of others that portray Uri as a laughable imitation of Willie or as a literary fiction, a fake and even a deception, is included in the following excerpt, in which we follow the feelings and thoughts of Uri, who has just avoided visiting the pregnant Mika, feelings and thoughts that are brought to us through the prism of the narrator, who presents himself as a sensitive, erudite and analytical, and mainly objective mediator:

> Suddenly the feeling struck him that if he had been sitting next to the driver, facing the direction of travel, he would have surely stopped him at the right moment, but while he was still caught up in this hesitation the van kept flying forward, and at once the kibbutz disappeared behind the remains of the Arab mill—only to appear again later, very far in the distance.
>
> Now he felt that it was hopeless. No, he was not going to have the strength to go there this evening. He should have got off now, and be damned with everything else. He felt the despair taking over him with all its weight. The more the car underneath him drove on and the farther away it got, the more this bitter feeling of guilt grew in him. Something undefined, a dull sense of unease, of self-hatred, of bitter tab-keeping. And just at that moment of mixed-up confused wondering about what will happen, and how it will be. And Willie—is he at home, and maybe something will happen after all—cropped up a malignant lucidity of self-flagellation and some strange belief that now, only now, he knew his own soul fully, disgustingly.
>
> The thought that Willie is already home, and so he has betrayed him too, completed a mental process that took place in a speed typical only of processes of destruction: in the stampeding van, at the back, sat Willie's fatherless son, a boy who has recently lost all faith in himself, *it turns out it was all fake*, all the fatherless masculinity. All the heroism, the self-confidence, everything, it was all fake! (276–77; emphasis mine)

The feeling described in the first paragraph of this quotation is probably Uri's, with the narrator playing a merely technical role: that of a linguistic relay station. This distribution of roles is also preserved in the first part of the second paragraph, when the dividing line between the two narrative instances is underscored by the emphasis on the world "now," which modulates the movement of Uri's thoughts and feelings in relation to the external, chronological timeline. The ascription of these thoughts and feelings to Uri is also justified by the transition, which simulates an associative move, from the blurring that clouds Uri's consciousness to the moment of clarity and with it the sudden recollection of Willie. By contrast, it is difficult to ascribe the subtle formulation about the "malignant lucidity" that Uri experiences, and the statement regarding the quick pace that typifies only processes of destruction, to Uri, who as we may remember has not been blessed with any real capacity for abstraction.

The distribution of roles between Uri and the narrator becomes completely blurred in the last part of the quotation. Consequently, the dividing lines between their consciousnesses and between their areas of responsibility in relation to the strong statement contained in this textual unit are also erased. The reader cannot give a definite answer to the question of who is responsible for the sentence "it turned out it was all fake." Is it only the narrator who said the words that precede this sentence ("at the back, sat Willie's fatherless son, a boy who has recently lost all faith in himself"), or is it only Uri in whom the accelerated mental process produced a surprisingly comprehensive insight? Perhaps both are responsible for this sentence—with the narrator hiding behind the back of the audience favorite, Uri—a position that deepens the impression made by the shocking statement contained in this sentence, which is greatly emphasized due to being repeated twice and to the recurring word "all," which appears five times (!) in the short concluding unit.

The shocking, subversive message of this passage becomes clearer in the intertextual context, especially when Uri's portrayal is compared with the portrayal of his literary forefathers—the characters of Yoash and of Yehuda the orchard keeper. Yehuda the orchard keeper is described as a natural phenomenon and as a work of art. This effect—of a person as a sculpture—is also created through statements such as "he was like . . . a strong marble statue" (*Stories*, 55), as well as, and especially, through the descriptive technique that is based on describing the object from several perspectives, when, and this is a crucial variable, the object itself remains static at the center of the scene, whereas the characters, and through them the readers, observe him from lower or higher positions. This descriptive technique recurs in all the scenes in "Yoash" that deal with an encounter with the representatives of death. It is already in evidence in the scene in which the boy Yoash "grabs the end of the snake's tail and rolls it in the air like a strap" (63): he "stands there calmly," creating around himself a circle as wide as the span of the snake's movement, and the older workers surround him from a safe distance—"voicing their fear loudly [as] he eyes them with scorn" (64).

The scene with the snake foreshadows the scene in which Yoash gets killed. Here too he is standing still, "erect and proud," "his eyes burning with an internal fire" as he "move[s] the heavy butt of the gun over his enemy's heads" in a motion that creates a circle similar in circumference to the one he created years earlier by swinging the snake, and around this small circle there is a wider circle of Arabs "who surround Yoash" and try to kill him (89).

Like Yehuda and Yoash, Uri also serves as an object to be observed by various figures, and like them he too is described from vantage points that lend him a strong element of empowerment and glorification. Furthermore, like his literary fathers, Yehuda the orchard keeper and Yoash, and his literary grandfathers, Zalman Shneur's "Pandre the Hero" and Chaim Nachman Bialik's "Big Harry" [Arieh Ba'al Guf], Uri is presented as having a strong affinity with both the historical and the mythological aspect of the people of Israel's chronicles. Therefore, when Shamir's narrator says about his protagonist that "he was the mystery of the sudden bestirring of being" (*HWF*, 228), these are not, as Shaked put it, "concluding words [that] are ridiculously exaggerated," but rather an at once pathetic and ironic allusion to the mix from which were concocted all the heroes who "in their death bequeathed us life."[52] This element of mystery, which appears in one way or another in all of Uri's detailed descriptions,[53] joins the three elements employed in the apotheoses of Yoash and his like: (conquering) masculine potency, death, and aestheticization. Thus Shamir, like Luidor in his time, creates a hero from time immemorial; however, unlike Luidor, who was careful not to mar or damage the wondrous, mytho-historical entity he had created, Shamir refutes it and breaks it to pieces.

The essential difference in the two writers' attitude toward their protagonists manifests itself in the practices of description they each employ to create and portray them. As we have seen, in dramatic situations Luidor's protagonists are always stationary, surrounded by human beings or animals that observe them with a mixture of admiration and awe. This group of onlookers creates a circle—a geometrical shape that represents unity and wholeness—comprised of individuals that belong to one defined and distinct sociological or ethnic category, or at most to two such categories (one of whom may split in two). Thus Luidor confronts his protagonists with monolithic, or at most dualistic essences, a distinct pattern that enables him to preserve the innocence and wholeness of his protagonists both on the physical and on the existential plane.

By contrast, Shamir's protagonists are always in motion: walking, working in the field, engaged in military cross-country navigation, driving a tractor, using weapons, making love, and so on. The prism through which they are described is often composed, as in the passages we have just seen, of gazes of human beings from different places and different groups, who create fleeting, temporary circles of affiliation. Because of this decentralized, multiple-gaze situation, the protagonist is never at the clear center of one delimited and defined setting. Thus Shamir's sabra protagonist does not have a distinct place in the world—a stable place that could have perhaps enabled him to construct a clear identity.

I would like to qualify and clarify this last statement. The fact that Shamir's protagonist is characterized by motion does not in itself inhibit his mythicization. On the contrary, characterization in motion—as others have already noted—is a major component in Uri's glorification, as well as in the glorification of other protagonists in the works of Shamir and of other writers of the Palmach Generation. These writers, and chief among them Shamir, established a position in which a protagonist is watched while moving, as in a widescreen movie, across relatively large, mostly "virginal" spaces, spaces that do not yet display the marks of civilization.

What creates the demythicization of Shamir's protagonist in the passages before us and in many others is the twofold fragmentation on the level of the novel's focalization: the fragmentation on the one hand of the focalizers, that is, of the audience that observes Uri, and the fragmentation on the other hand of the focalized, that is, of the object of observation, of Uri himself.

The fact that Uri is described in such a short narrative unit from so many points of view, which have no clear common denominator—neither in terms of the semantic fields to which they may be assigned, nor in terms of the semantic fields to which they assign Uri—has two purposes that both support and contradict each other: one purpose, as Miron suggested, is "to exhaust all the objective possible points of view, for whom Uri constitutes an existing, tangible entity"; the other purpose is to highlight the multiplicity, the accidental nature, the superficiality, and the lack of commitment of Uri's contacts with the world that is represented here through shredded pieces of reality. Through the technique of the cinematic montage—or rather the pseudo-montage—Shamir fools the reader. He creates in us an expectation for an overall impressive essence (the first purpose), but leaves us with a multiple number of impressions (the second purpose).

The words with which the narrator concludes the passage before us are perceived, as G. Shaked noted, as "ridiculously exaggerated." But not because they do not befit "the actions of the character in the plot," but rather because the host of noncorresponding fragments that Shamir condenses here together do not really allow for any "concluding words." For the fragmentation of the focalizers is merely a reflection of the fragmentation that exists in the protagonist's psyche. Uri, unlike Yoash and his like, is not monolithic—a firm rock, a formidable slab of marble, and so on. He is made of numerous patches that do not connect with one another; a deliberately sloppy patchwork, which hints to the reader that the character before him is not "original," or in other words, that this character is a sociocultural fabrication.

"He had no choice but to be exposed as it were—under the cloak of darkness"

In all his movements in the world, Uri keeps having the same frustrating experience: being "the same Cahana" (*HWF*, 31, 80)—but in a failed and ridiculous version. This is already suggested by the comparison of the book's two opening units: a) the official opening (chapter 1), whose status as an opening unit is underscored by its title ("The First Day") and that is centered around Uri's return to the kibbutz after completing his studies at Kadoorie, in Ilana's truck, which picks him up on his way to the kibbutz; and b) the pre-opening opening (the prologue), whose status as an opening unit is underscored by its title ("Introduction in Qantara") and that centers around Willie's return journey to his army camp in Egypt.

Willie's journey back to the army camp, like all his journeys, is seen as a kind of venturing into "the heart of darkness" and an escape from it thanks to his devotion to life; that is, as Willie understands it (and he serves here as a mouthpiece for the author), thanks to his devotion to the "home"—an existential space that combines three interconnected and interdependent vital elements: the right physical place (Eretz Israel, the Jezreel Valley, the kibbutz), the right partner (Ruthka), and the right ideology (pioneering socialist Zionism).

"The aging, gray-haired corporal, Cahana" is in "a creaking train going out into the heavy, black Egyptian night" "with a new catastrophe in his heart" (7–8)—but at the same time, and despite this, he feels that "some warmth sneaks into your heart when you think of the camp, of the large camp-city in the desert." Willie is mourning his son's death and "what is left behind at home," yet as the reader learns both from the prologue and from the development of the events in the story, he returns to the desert with renewed energy.

The novel's official opening, which centers on Uri's return to the kibbutz after completing his studies at Kadoorie, resembles in its general outlines the passage in the prologue that describes Willie's return to Egypt. Each of the two openings describes a return that combines the commonplace with the unusual and threatening. The train that drives through the desert is replaced by the truck that drives Uri home. It seems like a completely ordinary ride: a ride home (rather than to the desert), in a familiar vehicle (the kibbutz's Fargo truck, rather than a shadowy train), driven by a kibbutz member known to Uri from childhood. However, this ride is described through Uri's eyes as a terrifying, thwarting, and castrating journey. This ride—during which we are introduced to Uri for the first time; a fact that affects the impression he leaves on us—begins "unexpectedly": Uri hears the call, "Hey, dumbbell!" and discovers that it is "Ilana"—a strange name for a man, which gives the reader (who at this stage does not know any of the kibbutz people) a feeling of formal unease (on a gender basis).

Ilana, who controls the "steering wheel of the mighty car" as it "sail[s] into the black, sizzling asphalt river" (10), is described, again through Uri's focalization, as a strange, somewhat monstrous combination of man, machine, inanimate lump, and amazing natural phenomenon. Here: "Ilana was a big man. The soft, crumpled cap on his head ridiculously but distinctly emphasized the gnarled expanses of his face. Under his chin and round and round thereafter, under his ears and under the lock of hair on the back of his neck, rose a roundly and protuberantly fattened neck. Its front could be called a double chin and its back could be called a bull's neck, and under his ears it could give the feeling of an inanimate lump. Either way the slope that led from the skull to the shoulders, the tank top, the hairy chest, and the fat belly, this slope was firm, rounded, ripe."

Ilana, who is both intimidating and ridiculous, arouses in Uri a sense of unease: "Uri was hesitant near Ilana. It was easier to start a conversation with a tractor. Like the silence of a motor that had suddenly stopped pumping, like the mountains in the night, like un-ploughed land. Like all the things in which silence is neither welcomed nor liked. Ilana was not a big talker. It was surprising that he stopped of his own accord to give Uri a lift" (10–11).

Uri finds the silence of "this big-armed man" difficult, and he tries to get him to speak. After some deliberation he asks Ilana what he is transporting in his truck. Ilana does not respond. Uri repeats the question, Ilana delays his answer, and then he finally asks, "You've been studying at Kadoorie for two years?" (11). Uri replies in the affirmative, and then Ilana delivers the following castrating line: "So you've spent two years at Kadoorie and you haven't learned to tell, when you get on a loading truck, whether it's loaded or not, huh?" (11–12).

Uri's journey evokes the opposite feeling from Willie's journey. Willie is traveling away from home, on a threatening route, but he is not threatened because home is within him. By contrast Uri is traveling home on a routine route, but he is very threatened because he has no home within him. This scene teaches us something else: we have already seen that Uri was found not to merit a room of his own and is staying in the room of his first nursemaid, Ethel, a fact that has a symbolic meaning. From Ilana's cutting remark we learn that Uri does not and will not have a place even in the realm in which he is supposed to be skilled and proficient, his generation's defining area of expertise—handling mechanical tools.

The difference in the father's and son's reactions to their parallel journeys in the opening chapters has another dimension as well: a mythological or mythopsychological dimension, which marks the relations between the two returns and prefigures their endings. Uri, like his father—and like Homer's Odysseus—finds himself swallowed by a devouring space that resembles the guts of some monster: the "hidden maw" of the desert on the one hand, and the "scorching cabin" of the "enormous" Fargo on the other. Yet unlike his father, who escapes this devouring space unscathed,[54] the "kibbutz's eldest son" is ejected from this space (*HWF*, 12)—which is merely a derisory copy of the real devouring and threatening space, which the father survives when his shameful impotence is revealed.

The first big movement made by Uri Cahana, his return to the kibbutz from Kadoorie, is thus marked by a stinging failure with regard to a crucial component of his pioneers' community's agenda: work. This failure is intensified in view of the parallelism created between Uri's attempted homecoming—which is essentially a belated return for a youth whose life trajectory as an adult has barely begun and has nevertheless already ended—and Willie's homecoming after twenty years of wandering and searching, a return that includes the reconciliation with Ruthka, following which Willie is described, through the combined focalization of himself and of the narrator, as someone who has been granted renewed powers of youth. Here: "Now look what can be generated by one reconciliation, which is like being reconciled with everything, like falling in love again: a renewed youth, with all its courage and shame and with that typical illusion that from now on—it's forever" (257). And later, when he goes to visit his elderly mother in Tel Aviv: "As Willie was walking to her house on the city streets he noted to himself that he had never felt so fresh, so in possession of a new clear-sightedness as at this hour" (259).

Uri's second big movement is related to his relationship with Mika. Here too Uri finds himself undergoing a test of his maturity, which duplicates the test his father underwent during his twenty years' journey toward Ruthka, since the two tests are modeled on the same topos: entering dark, "female," threatening spaces, and trying to escape them. As we find out, in the area of love—as in the field of agricultural work and the world of machines—it is Willie who emerges from the darkness wiser and stronger, while Uri sinks into the obscurity and is swallowed by it, all his attempts to conquer the "female space" and "come out of it in one piece," to "become a man," repeatedly exposed as failed, pitiable, and risible imitations of his father's feats.

Willie leaves his mother's home in Tel Aviv on his way back to Ruthka, another journey home and the last return in the narrated time of the novel—a journey that sums up and sheds new light on the couple's whole relationship through the prism of Willie, who has been wandering for twenty years on the way to his wife: "*Willie went out into the sunlight* . . . he was overwhelmed by the profound emotion of coming back, by the excitement at the approaching meeting. It seemed as if it was not three months that separated him from his wife but *an abyss, and the overcoming of that abyss*" (263, emphasis mine).

As in the scene in which the train enters the desert as if being swallowed by "some hidden maw," here too Willie escapes some kind of engulfment. He overcomes the abyss—that all-engulfing female entity, which according to Mesopotamian and other mythologies preceded the creation of the world—thanks to his devotion to "his eternal wife" and returns home older and richly experienced, a life trajectory that again recalls the life trajectory of Odysseus:

> He loved Ruthka because he loved the ability of his life, of life in general, to transcend itself. The purpose of love is not pleasure, but that something that is more enduring. He had to live a whole life just to get to this truth and be convinced of it. Man's nature is animalistic, and the more animalistic he is, and the more he aspires to be liberated, nothing liberates him more from the animal than love. For it is the overcoming of nature through its own power, for it is nature that love comes from and to which it returns.
>
> *And this is not a one-off conquest, but it keeps living, keeps growing.* This way you are *eternally courting the woman who has always been your wife*. This is how you must love Ruthka, this is how you must live your life with her. Thus an aging corporal sneaks into his kibbutz through the back yard, knowing that at home awaits him the culmination of an excited development—and he is still asking himself what shape this culmination will take, and how he will behave, and what his wife will be like on that occasion, and what the kibbutz will be like, and wouldn't his son also show up to say a quick hello?—and he also has a girl in the kibbutz, doesn't he? (268, emphasis mine)

Uri's relationship with women and with the "feminine essence" is completely different. This is explicitly suggested as early as his first erotic encounter, the one that takes place in the vineyard—a first meeting between him, the sabra son of a kibbutz, and Mika, the new immigrant and a novice worker:

> "Be careful not to leave panniers lying in the sun—from now on...."
>
> "And you, Uri," replied Mika, picking up an empty pannier, "try not to be a kind of commander or teacher. All right?"
>
> "One-one," Uri thought as he rode to the shed. Damn her—an attractive girl. *Is that how you say it?*—sure—an attractive girl. And the last remark, clearly, is in connection to Willie. Don't act big and don't assume your father's feathers. Your father was a teacher and lorded it over us—and you, you Uri try not to be a kind of teacher too—all right?
>
> "All right," thought Uri, "the devil take me if I remind you too much of Willie, of father Cahana. You will get to know Uri, you will learn to acknowledge Uri's existence, Uri who perhaps knows no boundaries, at first—but a very specific and very clear Uri. After all—" (98, emphasis mine)

Uri swears that he will not remind us "too much" of Willie, and that we will learn to "acknowledge his existence" and his specificity. But this is an empty promise. He continues to be "the same Cahana," albeit in a watered down version, and . . . the devil does take him.

Uri is aware that he is trying to step into his father's big shoes, but he fails to understand how big they are. He does not know what the narrator, and through him the readers know—that his father is not only Mika's teacher but also the only object of her desire, and that he, Uri, only serves her as a poor substitute for the original, for that "hitherto unfamiliar force" (109). Mika reflects, "Uri, what is he then—is he love or a way to preserve Willie's memory, as a kind of memento, a handkerchief, a manuscript he has left behind?" (165).

As I have already noted, the novel fashions Uri's status as a substitute lover, as a faint reflection of "some hitherto unfamiliar force" found in Willie, by using the same topos that serves as the poetic/semantic framework to all the father's voyages. When Willie goes to Tehran in order to bring back the children of the "remaining few" from the "Underworld," he enters the refugee camp, which is depicted as a typical liminal space, but none of that hybrid existence marked by chaos and infected with corruption and decay clings to him. Willie "keeps himself to himself," is "buttoned-up, taut, restrained," and his private space in the camp is presented as the "inner sanctum." The defining manifestation of Willie's ability to touch the "infected" experience of the Holocaust without being marred by it is his relationship with Mika. Willie triggers in Mika great emotional turmoil, as a consequence of which she becomes attached to him. But he keeps his distance: he is sympathetic, supportive, acknowledges her worth and her power, but he is not tempted to develop an erotic relationship with her.

In his attitude toward Mika, as in other human contexts, Willie is revealed as a strong source of light. The force of this light source, which is based on Willie's ability to constantly hold on to "Ruthka's thread" (as in Ariadne's thread), is felt by the "dark" Mika already in Tehran, when she wonders to herself: "Where is his nocturnal, lonely side?" (108).

By contrast Uri, whose name derives from the Hebrew root *or*—light—has no light source of his own. His light is borrowed from his father's light, and is too weak and faint to lead him through Mika's dark labyrinths. His relationship with Mika the Holocaust refugee, who is the novel's most complex and complicated character and who is perceived as a "black hole," amounts, like his relationship with other "objects" he encounters and as Eliezer Schweid already noted,[55] to a momentary and superficial conquest, after which he loses his spatial orientation.

Uri and Mika's story, or as Mika wittily puts it, their "tiny drama" (*HWF*, 98), is marked from beginning to end by the struggle between a primordial, unifying, "female" darkness and a differentiating, wounding, disassembling "male" light, and simultaneously between depth and surface, past and present, and memory and forgetting. This set of oppositions is established in the description of the kibbutz's vineyard C, where Uri and Mika first meet, which is the stage for Moshe Shamir's "type scene," in which the youths who are about to become the fathers and mothers of the nation, or their representatives (Eliezer, Abraham's slave, and Rebecca; Jacob and Rachel; and so on) meet.

The encounter between Uri and Mika during the grape harvest in vineyard C is preceded by a long description of nature, whose structural and thematic focus is the tense "dialogue" between the slowly withdrawing night and the new day, the bright conqueror emerging with its countless lights. First the vineyard is described in "the last hours of the night," under heavy dew: "The dew lay on the broad and hairy vine-leaves, slid down rounded twigs and tendrils, and hid in the folds of branches and arms. The rich and dark foliage of the vine looked like a black mass extending and receding into the night—but it was still holding many secretes" (86).

This passage overflows with a vitality that evokes an erotic game, which has an adult aspect (the vine) and a childlike aspect (the dew), and is accompanied with a sense of mystery that intensifies because of the thick darkness that blurs the scene's outlines. The same applies to the next passage:

> Darkness lay on the vineyards, and only their rows upon rows of prolonged masses were visible....

The night incorporated all the incidents that had happened yesterday so that now, before dawn, they became part of its essence, a vineyard-essence. A pannier abandoned on a pole became covered in dew and clung to the vine below it, its outline merging with its outline; pieces of paper that a last evening breeze glued and hung upright against the iron wires absorbed so much dampness that they almost dissolved and became one with the iron they were clinging to; and traces of walking feet in the dust were covered with a thin film of moisture, as if they had been imprinted there *since the six days of Creation*; and a broken branch lying where it broke . . . The evening gathered into the vineyard a rabble of guests and incidents, *the heavy night rolled over them*, and they came out from underneath it as tight as brothers, some of them hewn into a single landscape, the vineyard and everything in it, the vineyard—vineyard C." (*HWF*, 86; emphasis mine)

This unified and unifying darkness, which absorbs any object in its parameter —an absorption whose intensity is emphasized by the repeated use, rare in modern Hebrew, of verbs in the (intensive reflexive) *nitpael* stem to describe the fate of the objects that used to have a separate and distinct existence ("nit'ar'u" [happened], "nitztamed" [clung], "nitbal'u" [merging], "nitmasmessu" [dissolved])—is penetrated, as "the Eastern horizon brightened" and due to the beginning of human activity in the space, by "bright dust." The silence, darkness's ally, "was slowly being pushed aside, withdrawing to the mountaintops, to the ends of trails and roads, to the distant fields—while down below it was pushed and pushed forcefully." Later the reveille sounds, tearing "a big and cruel rift" in the world, and by then "the curtains above the Tabor had already caught fire and the sun pushed its way out and emerged" (87).

The description of the rising dawn, which brings to mind mating and a painful birth, and the subsequent supplementary description,[56] which comes across as its reduced and toned-down version, a kind of children's version of the sexual-cosmic drama, serve as a scenic/atmospheric/symbolic exposition for the first meeting between the novel's Romeo and Juliet: the "bright" Uri and the "dark" Mika.

Mika, who starts her works at an early, dusky and cool hour of the morning, is described thus: "Mika picked a bunch and lifted it up to examine it and fix its defects. She was a full girl, slightly fat as the Youth Aliyah girls tended to be, as girls who have seen a lot of suffering and who have attained peace being ravenous and voracious tended to be. *She was black all over*, not only her hair which was tied in a heavy bun on her nape but also the color of *her brownish skin*, her lips *whose darkness obscured* their freshness, *the thick and short down of hair* on her arms" (91, emphasis mine).

In contrast to Mika, who emerges in the dim dawn as a "full" and "black" girl-woman, Uri emerges thus: "In the vineyard it was already summer. Although at the foot of the vines the shadow covered their full width, above, from where Uri stood, the vineyard looked flooded all over with a *glowing and full brightness*. The heads of the grape pickers were dipped in that brightness and the last drop of dew had already evaporated away. Under the wheels [of the horse-led cart that Uri is driving] the dry clods of soil were squashed with a muffled crack together with dried twigs and pieces of chalk. At that time of day the shade became preferable to the sun, ordinary water to grape juice, and rest to work. In this ripe hour and with a full recognition of his worth, Uri rolled up and reached the rows of grape pickers" (96–97, emphasis mine).

Uri is observing vineyard C, where Mika is, from above, a position that highlights his mastery as a man and as a native of the place. His position of dominance is charged with extra power because, at least ostensibly, he is part of a rising force—here, the force of the sun, having defeated the darkness and now at the height of its power. Uri's mastery and masculinity, however, are cast in doubt. First, unlike Willie, Uri is not described as a source of light. Nor is he seen as an "illuminated object"—a status enjoyed by the vineyard and the heads of the grape pickers. Second, in this passage as well as in those preceding and following it, Uri's position of mastery and masculinity is not a mature, self-confident position but rather an adolescent, narcissistic one,[57] a thin layer of showy masculinity covering over a profound castration anxiety. Third, Uri is portrayed as someone who treats nature with arrogant mastery and whose movement across the land involves trampling and crushing.

Mika, the urban immigrant whose dreams are also entirely urban, tries, unlike the native Uri, to approach the local flora and fauna with awe and gentleness —first through her diligent grape picking, and then by slowly, hesitantly yet determinedly befriending the horse that pulls Uri's cart. The workhorse—used in this "pleasant place" scene in a role similar to the one played by animals in parallel scenes in *The Love of Zion*, *Altneuland*, and "Yoash": the representative of nature and therefore also the catalyst for the erotic relationship between the central protagonists of the nation-building plot—sinks its big teeth into the beam of the packing shed and shakes it, alarming the female packers. Uri and Mika each react in their own way: "Uri merely threw a piece of wood at the horse— but Mika became interested and excited" (113). Here follows a long description, extending over several paragraphs, whose thematic focus is the interest and excitement that Uri's horse arouses in Mika.

Mika's growing relationship with the horse accelerates the growing closeness between her and Uri and endows the "tiny drama" with an erotic character.

MOSHE SHAMIR, *He Walked in the Fields* (1948)

Uri uses the fact that Mika is feeding his horse (whose name, Tsahor [white], serves as another variable in the play of light-shade, black-white employed here as an architectural metaphor), goads the horse with a call so that it pushes Mika away, and warns her not to train the horse to eat bread; a warning that comes as a belated response to Mika's warning to Uri not to boast and pretend to be a commander or a teacher. The scene ends with a chase among the vine rows—initiated (again) by Mika. Mika runs away, Uri chases, and in the end "Uri had no choice but to really pounce and really grab her body. [And he] seized her by the waist with two trembling arms" (96).

Uri, like his literary older brother Yoash, is an expert in matters of horses, "a person who before walking on his own feet was already walking on horses and on carts" (95); he is "an esteemed," "first-rate carter." But he is also, again like Yoash, a total novice in matters of women, love, and sex. Yet Yoash was destined to die a virgin on the virgin land and so become holy betrothed to it, whereas Uri is fated to contend with a land that is no longer "virgin," as well as with a woman who is no longer a virgin, whose heart, moreover, is given to another, to his father.

The next sexual scene between the two, which again takes place within the parameters of the pleasant place in the packing shed of vineyard C, makes clear what had only been hinted at in the first scene. The one who is seen here as a sexual object—who is looked at and desired—is actually Uri, whereas Mika is identified with the voyeuristic, scrutinizing, coveting, and conquering gaze, in line with her essence: from the dark, hidden space, out into the bright expanse.

The setting for this scene takes us back to the site of the vineyard at night, as described in the exposition—an enclosed place, in which any distinct details are swallowed up by the thick darkness: "The inside of the shed had darkened and already contained some remote corners whose details were invisible, save for their heavy, ill-defined shadow" (140). Uri finds himself in an uncomfortable situation, alone with Mika: "He felt embarrassed. Now that he was not engaged in any *work*, in any manly pursuit, that there was no use exchanging bright and clever words with a girl under the *dome* of the dark shed, he had no choice but to be revealed, as it were–*under the cloak of darkness*" (141).[58]

An escape from this awkward situation is found when the loading truck arrives at the vineyard and Uri gets the job of loading the grape boxes onto the back of the truck. This job, unlike the job of courting Mika, Uri performs very skillfully. Moreover, his attitude toward the work, as can be easily inferred from the following passages, is much more erotic than his attitude toward Mika. He finds it easier to cope with the "narrow hips" of the fruit boxes than with the hips of "a full, slightly fat girl":

Again a box was noisily dragged, straining-nimble steps were heard, a bulky shadow stomped and emerged—and Uri appears: his back muscles turned to you, something wondrous moving in his shoulders as he sketches a full circle around himself—and the box flies into the car like a bundle of cotton wool.

Mika looked on covetously and felt herself watching. Felt herself doing the watching.

She began to discern Uri's movements even in the darkness of the shed....

Uri would grab the box by its two narrow hips, drag it toward him, hold it up against his chest, turn around sharply, make two-three stomping steps, jump to face the car, raise his arms—which, bathed in the light, moved like the mischief of brown, sleek puppies. Raise his arms and lift the box up in the air.

That's how he moved, with light and shadow surprises, flickering, his shoulders gleaming in the dark . . . His breath grew heavier, till it started echoing the sound of his footsteps. Dragging a box, breathing, turning his body, groaning, lifting the box, pacing, breathing, emerging into the light, stretching his muscles, breathing, hurling, breathing—panting, returning to the boxes, stooping, dim, large, groaning, and suddenly becoming larger, marching with his added shadow, bending back, loading—emerging into the light, sliding the box skyward, his arms sparkling with sweat, returning to the shed, turning his face toward you for an instant—and then shining as if he had been rubbed with oil, his eyes sunk in their sockets, strands of hair stuck to his forehead, falling all the way to his scrunched eyebrows: and his jaws wearing that hard expression worn—oh, surely it is worn!—by men in the heat of battle. (142–43)

These are Uri's big moments. Here he is revealed through the combined voyeuristic, yearning gaze of Mika and of the narrator, a gaze that, as shown by Michael Gluzman,[59] establishes the "anatomy of the Zionist body" in all its glory. Yet it is a feeble masculine glory—both, as I have already intimated, because the erotic relation is displaced here from its proper object, Mika, to a surrogate object, the fruit boxes, and because Uri is seen—like Yoash and Yehuda the orchard keeper—as an aesthetic object, an object of observation and admiration, and at the same time as someone who exists onto himself, in a kind of narcissistic, autoerotic existence ("sketches a full circle around himself"), a state of being that turns him as it did Yoash and Yehuda before him and to use the terms suggested by Robert Scholes and Robert Kellogg, from a representative figure, simulating a flesh-and-blood person, into an illustrative figure, representing an aspect of an entire human group ("that hard expression worn—oh, surely it is worn!—by men in the heat of battle."); a figure that undergoes a process of glorification ("shining as if he had been rubbed with oil") that paves the way for its exclusion from life's stage.

MOSHE SHAMIR, *He Walked in the Fields* (1948)

Shamir, however—unlike Luidor, who enables us to enjoy Yoash's radiance only for an instant before sending him in the storm of battle into the mists of myth—prolongs Uri's presence on life's stage and embroils him in its tangles. He thus deprives him of the combination of monolithicity and enigma, which, as I have already noted in relation to Yoash, is the ultimate combination for creating heroes from time immemorial. It must be emphasized here that unlike Yoash and Yehuda, who are unburdened by wives and families, "he, Uri, had no choice" but to withstand the test of real life (*HWF*, 114). And in this test he, the sabra who is supposed to represent the perfect merging of a healthy soul with a healthy body, fails completely.

After the voyeuristic scene in the vineyard shed, Uri and Mika return home on foot. Midway between the vineyard and the outskirts of the kibbutz—still outside the boundaries of the kibbutz proper, for in the kibbutz, as the narrator reminds us, they have no place[60]—they find an isolated corner: "Neither the kibbutz was visible from here, nor the fields, nor the valley—and only Har Ha'ayalot was a dim bulky mass beyond the grove" (146). Here it is Uri who makes the first move: "Uri kind of pushed Mika so she leaned against one of the cypresses." Mika acquiesces and immediately, as usual, takes the initiative: "She dropped her handkerchief and then stretched out her arms and pulled him toward her." Uri "responded to her," but immediately returns to his auto-erotic mode: he contemplates the "shower [that] would be empty by now," pulls himself together, "and is suddenly struck by a dizzying thought, that here, under his arms, there is a woman who is ready for anything."

The meaning of this loaded turn of phrase, which I shall return to shortly, is revealed in the course of the scene. Uri fondles Mika, who immediately senses his lack of experience in such matters ("She felt his fingers recoiling from the stretched, curved fabric they came across, recoiling, scuttling on her back, playing on the buttons, recoiling again") and later sees herself "as if she was looking at it all from one side" and bursts out in a light laughter, accompanied with "a teasing growl" (146).

Mika's reaction cuts Uri to the quick. He is "shocked, and for a moment feels stingingly insulted. Is this a mature woman, steeped in adulterous acts, who is mocking him? And at the same moment he desired her for a third time with such full potency, that he felt his knee joints hurting. He held her tight and tried to lower her slowly to the ground, squashing her flesh, trying to squeeze it all the way down to her belly and her buttocks" (146–47). Mika, however, halts this adolescent beginner's assault, gently but firmly: "Then she pushed him away, and said in a voice that totally contradicted this pushing: 'Stop Uri . . . not now.'"

The erotic relationship between Uri and Mika reaches its climax—and at the same time, at least as far as Mika is concerned, its failed consummation—during their walk to Har Ha'ayalot. At the beginning of the walk whose destination, as we shall see, is by no means coincidental, Uri feels like a great man. Here, in the Eretz-Israeli nature, he behaves like someone who is at home, like a master. In fact, "he loved it [the walk] in advance because he loved himself as a leader, protector, navigator, knower, and ruler" (158).

Again he impresses Mika, the immigrant and a city girl ("Uri noticed Mika's gait and saw again that it was the gait of a foreigner who was treading on unfamiliar paths for the first time" [161]), with his walking skills, his familiarity with the fauna and flora—he even "hunts for food for his woman" (156)[61]—and with his arrogant, sovereign attitude toward the locals, the Arabs they meet on the way. But Uri's feeling of control and his display of mastery and masculinity dissolve at the crucial moment: the intercourse.

> She fell backward and lay on her back. She didn't fix her skirt, only her naked legs dropped this way and that way. Here it comes—her heart beat with hope—just let him be wise, let him be wise and knowing—ah, dear God, does pure happiness really exist in your world? . . .
>
> Uri unbuttoned her shirt, but she put her hand on his hand.
>
> "It will prickle," she whispered, "on the ground without a shirt. Right, boy?"
>
> He devoured her neck. He shut his eyes and stretched his body along her body. . . .
>
> A wave of warmth surged, as he felt her hand helping him slowly and gently. As if his pounce on her had dissolved and become a loving and soft rippling. She herself, with quiet, practiced movements, with a smooth rustle and a motion of her careful hand. . . .
>
> Mika stretched her hand under his shirt and squashed the muscles between his waist and his back. Her hand was warm and moist and Uri was ready to give her anything she would ask for in life. . . . Not to give her half of what she is capable of receiving but more. Seventy-seven times more. To give her so much that it would squash her, weigh on her, that she would groan, that she would bite her lips:—Uri, stop! That she would feel a great awe. (171–72)

However, once Uri sees Mika's white belly and the sudden slope that leads to "her house of darkness"—the phrase by which Shamir chose to designate Mika's genitals, a phrase that ties in with the group of characteristics and images that depict her as the representative of some black entity—"for a brief moment he was overcome by weakness" (172), only afterward being able to muster his strength and withstand the test. But as the narrator does not neglect to report elsewhere, far from this description of the first intercourse, Uri—whom the "experienced" Mika, and not without reason, calls "boy" during the intercourse scene—did not pass the test with full success, certainly not by the standard he set himself. Here: "He [Uri] was an appetite that was aroused but not satisfied and therefore became hunger—in one girl who on that day climbed up the winding steps of Har Ha'ayalot and in the end got what she got and had her day spoiled" (228).

Uri, then, manages to arouse Mika but not satisfy her—in the first sexual intercourse as we have just seen, and as the following passage suggests, in all their other sexual intercourses: "He never slept with her in the tent, they never had a week of quiet, consecutive nights, happy, sleeping next to each other, at times content with a light caress on the forehead, with a touch. How many times did they do it together on the ground? In the wood, in the apple-garden, on a stroll. It was always bad. They didn't even reach complete happiness. He, maybe—not even he. And the deceived Mika—not even one full and pleasured time. And it is only vile and shameful that nevertheless, something must have happened" (222–23).

The next stage in Uri's journey to "the heart of darkness" is his decision to abandon Mika to her fate and devote himself to the experience of war, with all that it entails. This is a decision whose meaning on the symbolic level, as the text makes clear in a complex and impressive fashion, is Uri's renunciation of his own light—which in itself, as we remember, is borrowed from his father's light source—to be impotently swallowed by the annihilating space of darkness. This crucial stage takes place after Uri receives a note from an unnamed person of authority, saying that he must report to his battalion. He hesitates whether to share this information with his mother or with Mika, and finally chooses Mika. They leave the dining hall together, sit on the nearest public bench, and have a conversation. This conversation—if it can be called that, since Mika speaks and Uri hardly listens; or to put it differently, the "discursive plot" between the two—is integrated with descriptions of the night, which create "a descriptive plot" that maintains fascinating interrelations with the discursive plot.

The first unit in this desertion scene—just as in Uri and Mika's first encounter scene in that pleasant place of vineyard C, which began in the twilight of a new day's dawn—is descriptive and full of dramatic, pathetic elevations on the one hand, and playful light-comic revelations on the other: "It was a starry night and the stars were feverish, as if they felt they were ensconced in the ceiling of a special night, one of those nights that harbor the unexpected turning points of history. Under the trees the darkness was a single mass, as if it could be cut by a sword or by excited speech. A dog barked. The perennial dog of the perennial neighboring village that never shuts up. The two people concealed on the bench were the only beings at that time, whose ancientness was not extreme and who did not belong to the enormous giant family of the night-pillars. Nevertheless the night is this couple's habitat, and they are used to it and know it like a tree full of owls. The broad and flat fig tree's blades held a debate with the wind about the direction it had taken—whether it was good, seemingly clapping astonished hands on hearing its taunting remarks, so that the elegant and expectant night was also frequented by spirits of merriment" (195).

This passage starts with a dramatic atmosphere, which stems both from the bombastic statement ("one of those nights that harbor the unexpected turning points of history") and from the projection onto the cosmos of the already familiar topos of being swallowed (the feverish stars ensconced in the night's ceiling). The topos of being swallowed is intensified here both because of the remark that "the darkness was a single mass" and, perhaps especially, because of the reference to Uri and Mika as "the two people *concealed* on the bench" (195, emphasis mine).

This passage, however, does not offer a fatalistic worldview. On the contrary. The narrator explicitly says that it was as if the "primordial" darkness "could be cut by a sword or by excited speech"; that is, that a heart-to-heart conversation could have patched the rift between the two. The narrator adds that they still had time to save their developing relationship, precisely because they formed an excluded couple that had failed to find itself a place in the bosom of the normative, bright, everyday society. The night, the ultimate expression of otherness, would have been willing to embrace them.

Furthermore, this specific night in which the crucial encounter between the two takes place offers an example for a successful conversation between counterparts. The debate between the fig tree's blades and the wind is conducted in a relaxed, somewhat mischievous atmosphere: "The broad and flat fig tree's blades held *a debate with the wind* about the direction it had taken—whether it was good, seemingly clapping astonished hands on hearing *its taunting remarks*. So that the elegant and expectant night was also frequented by *spirits of merriment*" (195, emphasis mine).

The setting for this encounter between the story's Romeo and Juliet signals to us that this is an hour of grace. However Uri does not want or is unable to listen, being unwilling to reflect, let alone think abstract thoughts. He blocks his ears to Mika's troubles, relinquishes his responsibility as a partner and as a father-to-be, and again hangs on the phrase "but there is no choice" (199), as if he, the young sabra, has no way of controlling his destiny. With the night's mediation, Mika, who is sitting opposite him, and her troubles are replaced in his consciousness by distant, more heart-warming scenes, in which a woman/

girlfriend/partner who has to be listened to and taken into consideration has no foothold. Here: "The night rejoiced, suddenly, from every direction. Crickets hurled their insults at their rivals in the sky. Frogs sorted the shreds of silence by their various sizes, and suddenly one was reminded of the view of rocks and a wadi, the figure of stooping shadows emerging, loose stones rolling down the slope, a signal, a stealthy clacking of tongues, the smoke of Arab villages, adventures were pinching one's blood like a real 'sixty-four'" (196).

In this scene Uri finally abandons the options of Odysseus, Theseus, and Willie Cahana, who find their way through dark labyrinths thanks to their loyalty to an "eternal woman," and takes on the plot pattern of myths and tales in which the heroes are swallowed (forever) in the bowels of some "primordial entity." I am referring, as I have already noted, to myths such as Tannhäuser and popular stories such as the Pied Piper of Hamelin.

Uri renounces the pact with his beloved Mika and replaces it with a new pact: the pact with the night. Thus he finally gives up—save one last attempt, the most absurd and ridiculous of all, which I will touch on later—on his attempts to constitute a body, albeit second-handedly, as his father's light reflector. Thus the seemingly exemplary sabra relinquishes the attempt to be "a very specific and very clear Uri" (98), destining himself to be swallowed by the "eternal darkness," by the obscure and the indefinite.

"There, this is how a fine fellow falls!"

The scale of Uri's failure in all his rites of passage, he who is supposed to be the crowning glory of the Zionist revolution, is fully revealed when we compare his homecoming path and his attempt to gain his community's recognition to the paths and attempts of all the novel's other major characters. For example, when we compare Uri's homecoming to Willie's successful homecoming, we reach the same conclusion reached when we compare Uri's return to his kibbutz with Mika's attempt to be absorbed in it, an attempt that at first seems impossible—and I will expand on this later—but ends with tremendous success. And the same becomes apparent when we compare Uri's homecoming/acceptance path to the life trajectories of his mother Ruthka and of Avraham Goren, her lover.

Like Willie and Uri's paths, the life trajectories of Ruthka and Avraham Goren are doubly marked by rites of entry into the community, and by the topos of "the heart of darkness"—entering a closed, dark, warm, and tomb-like space, and exiting it as if reborn; or in Uri's case, as if spellbound by death—and these life trajectories relate, in different ways, to the same elements in the novel's fictional landscape.

Early in her career in the pioneering Zionist-project, Ruthka already finds herself in the situation of someone who does not live up to the expectations of her community. Her decision to remove the toddler Uri from the kibbutz and take shelter with him in the bourgeois, untroubled Tel Aviv is, as the narrator presents it in combination with Ruthka's consciousness, an unforgivable sin as far as the kibbutz is concerned: "There is something in the flesh and blood of the kibbutz, in its innermost essence, that would never forgive you for running away with Uri in order to save his life . . . [For] in the kibbutz a person must accept death as well, and not only life. The kibbutz takes a person from dust to dust . . . There is no opening, there is *absolutely* no opening for anyone who wishes to seek salvation from elsewhere. The kibbutz must raise children—will it agree, then, for someone to exclude their child from this rule? It must raise children in its home, with its means, with its nursemaids, with its own mistakes, with its own tragedies; and its first children must pave the way for generations of rural kibbutz children, anticipated in the necessity of the coming years" (180, emphasis in original).

The full price of this (shocking) philosophy of life is paid by Uri, even though he is not the one who decides to "run away" to the city. As for Ruthka, she navigates between the dictates of her maternal instinct and the draconian laws of the community. At first she rebels—and follows her heart's decree—but after a while she changes her mind and cooperates with the demands of the community, albeit in her own way. And so she manages to find, after years of "making guilty sacrifices" and "atoning for her sin," a niche of her own.

In the end Ruthka regains her respectable position within her community. After returning to the kibbutz, which she left because she doubted its child-raising method, she becomes (of all things) a kindergarten teacher, and is recognized as "the best of the best nursemaids, the most admired kindergarten teacher" (62). Moreover, as an educator Ruthka establishes a life path different from the one paved by all the men in her life—Biberman, Willie, Avraham Goren, and her son, Uri. The latter, each in his turn, work at conquering the land, settling it, and defending it, tasks that almost always begin with the planning and drawing of topographical maps.[62] By contrast Ruthka, and in this she faithfully represents all the women in the novel, is not concerned at all with journeys of conquest and consequently has no interest in drawing topographical maps. In her case this conquering activity is replaced with the meticulous planning and execution of embroidered serviettes for the kindergarten children. Although, as the following passage suggests, some of the novel's characters underestimate the importance of this activity, Ruthka herself and the author, "who is hiding behind her back," ascribe great importance to it: "Ruthka spread a first piece of cloth on the table. This is a serviette. People nearby bent down to take a look. What is Ruthka up to? How many important things she could decide on! Who shall have the serviette—one. In which of its corners will the name of the serviette's owner be embroidered—two. What shall be the drawing, its size, its content—three, four, five. Ruthka is sitting in the kibbutz meeting, on Saturday evening, and is occupied with her work and able to decide the appearance of figures and shapes that would later be dear to the child, she still doesn't know who this child would be, who would draw from them so many associations of images and dreams, who would learn from them a first lesson in beauty, in good taste, in grown-up culture" (*HWF*, 181).

Ruthka therefore finds some traditional, feminine avenues of activity in the kibbutz, thus joining a long list of women educators in world literature—be it written or oral—but she is not content with that. Wishing to regain the approval of the kibbutz society, she intends to be newly tested in all the initiation rites of her imagined community.

First, like Willie, she embarks on a long journey of a rejuvenated return home, to the "eternal man" in her life. True, unlike him, she has had several lovers through the years. But none of them has taken his place. The exception that proves the rule is the toddler Uri, for whom Ruthka abandoned the kibbutz and Willie. But this too is only a temporary desertion. When Uri returns home from Kadoorie, Ruthka refuses to let him keep behaving like a child, looking to hide under his mother's dress. Although she does kiss him on the lips, as if he were still a child, or as if they were a boy and a girl, she does not make room for him in her home, and he is forced to live in the house of his nursemaid. Moreover, in the end, and I will expand on this issue later, Ruthka swaps the mother-son alliance with Uri for the mother–adopted-daughter alliance with Mika. Above all, as the following passage, ostensibly dealing with her embroidery, subtly suggests, Ruthka, who according to Uri "knows everything," accepts her son's impending death, half-consciously adopting in his place "a new Uri," the one growing in Mika's womb: "She sketched 'Uri' in clear and large diagonal letters, on the fabric's corner, and definitely meant little Uri, in her kindergarten, rather than her son, although it's possible she was hearing him, tiny and tender, under the figure of some new Uri, a stranger and not a stranger at the same time" (*HWF*, 181).

Second, in contrast to Uri, who is gradually drawing away from the kibbutz and stops taking part in its rituals, Ruthka plays a central role in "the celebration of Rabbi Silo" (64), an agricultural ceremony that takes on the added aura of a religious event.[63] This ceremony is described at length and integrated with passages in which Ruthka remembers the period of her primordial sin—the period in which she deserted the kibbutz with Uri and ran away to Tel Aviv. It takes place inside the kibbutz's silo—a container which is closed and sealed from all sides, apart from a narrow opening—while a flood of corn kernels collected from the kibbutz's fields is poured through the funnel onto its central platform (*HWF*, 61).

The celebration is undoubtedly a significant event in the collective experience described in the story, and it abounds with characteristics of initiation rites in primitive and modern agricultural societies.[64] For our discussion here, it is important to note two things: a) Uri, who in his infancy was prevented by his mother from facing the dangers posed at the time by growing up in the countryside, avoids these dangers again, this time symbolically; he, the kibbutz's first native child, does not climb to the top of the tower to take part in the initiation rite, but instead hangs around at its foot in the company of a few worried mothers; and b) Ruthka, who evaded with Uri the dangers posed at the time by raising children in the countryside, this time takes part in the rite—both as an adored kindergarten teacher and as . . . the partner of Ilana, the Hebrew "Pan."

> Ruthka was greeted with applause and found herself dancing with the others. One of the guys took out a harmonica and started blowing on it, tossing about beaten, fierce and danceable shreds of dance.
>
> Ruthka took Ilana and they launched into a Polka. Her heels were caught in the corn stems and threatened to stumble, her knees buckled, and her head grew dizzy but Ilana's arms held her firmly and from time to time took on all her weight without fear.
>
> The children went crazy on seeing her. They wailed and danced around themselves and around anything that could be danced with. Ruthka, everyone's beloved Ruthka—the best of the best nursemaids, the most admired of all the kindergarten teachers, Ruthka is dancing with us. She loves us so much! Crush the silo, press the corn—Polka, Horah, Debka, yoo-la-la—forget the sweat and the dirt, take off your sandals—like this, and put them in the corner like this . . . Press up to one another, love one another, join your tiny feet and give weight, give, don't be shy, with the grown-ups together, with the whole kibbutz together. More, more. (*HWF*, 62)

Third, Ruthka—again in contrast to Uri, and as will shortly become clear, similarly to Mika—takes part in the ascent to Har Ha'ayalot, the new Nahal settlement that is being founded with the support of Gat Ha'amakim, the established kibbutz. It is an impressive ceremonial event with many participants, to which Shamir dedicates a whole chapter and which serves as a ritualistic reenactment of the first settlement in the Jezreel Valley. For Ruthka, participating in this ceremony means having a revived experience, marked by penitence for an ancient guilt, of the pact between the New Jews and the new-old land; a pact that draws its force from the ancient covenant between the people of Israel and the land of Israel.

The renewed experience of the covenant with the land, which is marked by the connection with the "primordial" past, is combined here with the feeling of sisterhood created during the ascent to Har Ha'ayalot between Ruthka and Mika—a feeling of strong feminine camaraderie that stems from the selfish behavior of the men and the women's attempt to overcome it. "There,"—thinks Ruthka, who is nursing the pregnant and hurting Mika—"Mika and Uri. How silly it is that a woman's beloved son shall turn out to be a man with all the same mistakes, rudeness and cruelty to a woman" (243).

Avraham Goren, an important figure within the range of existential possibilities in Shamir's world, who for years "has not befriended anyone in the kibbutz" (67), also finally finds his place in the pioneering settlers' community. This Goren is presented in the first part of the novel through several pairs of eyes as a typical "outsider," a person who is always in the existential gap between two defined human groups: "Since he had nothing to hold on to he was distant and detached. He lived his own life, read a lot of foreign literature, rarely took part in the general conversations and never let himself be assigned any role" (68; cf. 31, 151).

Goren is also an in-between man in terms of ethnicity and mentality. His personality combines—and in this he resembles Willie—the typical qualities of a Jew of German origin with those of a Jew of Russian origin. "He was," as Ruthka defines him, through the voice of the narrator, "a new version of Biberman from twenty years ago" (69). But there are also striking differences between the two, which explain why Ruthka has shown more interest in Goren than in Biberman: Goren has "an independent sense of humor ... [which] Biberman never had," and "Biberman never had any confidence, or at least he never inspired confidence like Goren does, he was never as bold as he is."

Goren is a European intellectual—he reads German and is knowledgeable in Western culture—but he is also connected to the "Orient." This is suggested, among other things, by the appearance of his room, as it is seen through Ruthka's eyes: "The room was both foreign and intimate. The windows were covered with thick curtains, embroidered in the Arab style. A low table, with plenty of books on it and a dagger stuck into the wood among them. In a deep armchair lay a stocky, closely shorn, and squat dog. On the walls, in big frames, hung good-quality color pictures. One of them was a famous Tahitian nude by Gauguin ... A guitar was hanging diagonally on the wall near the almost imperceptible door of a built-in closet. Avraham himself sat on his bed, leaning back on many cushions and smoking a drooping pipe" (67).

Goren's status as an intermediary figure can also be inferred from his physical features. His body does not fit the physical model of the New Hebrew Man; he is tender and gentle and feminine, and yet—and this combination surprises Uri—he is a first-rate worker: "He was a proper worker, an excellent tractor driver, and his output was shipshape—and maybe this was the surprise: at least let him be a good-for-nothing! For every evening he would extract himself from under the dust and go and seclude himself in his rooms."

Avraham is also the in-between man on the level of the plot, where he plays the role of the surrogate figure. This is true first and foremost with respect to the relationship between Ruthka and Willie. He takes Willie's place in Ruthka's bed and leisure time but, as I have already pointed out, not in her heart. It is clear the whole time to both Ruthka and Avraham that this is a temporary affair, an intermezzo within the "eternal relationship" between Willie and Ruthka.

A similar role, albeit in an interestingly different guise, is played by Avraham with respect to the relationship between Ruthka and Uri. Here he serves as a brake against the danger of Uri gaining renewed control, with his infantile domineering needs, over his mother. This is suggested by Ruthka's thoughts about the potential for upheaval in her world order upon Uri's return from Kadoorie:

> Such absorption with Uri may spell the end of the Avraham Goren affair. If Uri sneaks in during the breakfast break and tidies your room, if at noon you find wild flowers in the vase on the cupboard, if you are able to put your feet up in the evening, and he brings your meal to your room and carries the easy chair from the lawn up to the balcony—ha-ha, he may take Avraham Goren's place.
>
> If the room's intimacy is disturbed and once again there is someone in the kibbutz who enters without knocking, someone whose room this is, mom's room, *our* room—Avraham Goren may stop coming. A lesson for a respectable lady of forty, Ruthka dear, not to start falling in love with young commanders while her adult sons are already popping up under her nose? Perhaps the whole thing with Avraham is merely an illusion and a brief self-forgetfulness? And all that pretended casualness of yours and Willie's—you should have held on to each other, perhaps?" (67, emphasis in original)

Avraham Goren thus preserves a kind of psychological, ideological, and plot-level status quo between, on the one hand, Willie and Ruthka, the representatives of the older generation, and on the other hand, Ruthka (and indirectly also Willie), the representative of the older generation, and Uri, the representative of the sons' generation: first as a substitute and later as someone who finds his own place. I have already mentioned Goren's role as Willie's, and indirectly also Uri's, substitute for Ruthka. To this should be added his position as Willie's substitute as an adoptive father to Mika, and especially to Uri. This is suggested both by the dialogue that Goren tries to develop with Uri during the latter's (first and last) visit to the agricultural fields (28–31), and by the fatherly attitude he displays toward Uri and Mika during their visit to Har Ha'ayalot.[65]

Avraham Goren's personality, which combines the characteristics of contrasting groups of human beings in the novel—older and younger people, women and men, German Jews and Russian Jews, intellectuals and people dedicated to security and work—makes him the representative of a special existential option within the pioneering settlers' community. We learn of this option from his thoughts while preparing for the ascent to Har Ha'ayalot: "At that moment he understood his happiness. It was a happiness of purity and lightness. He felt cleansed, like someone who has gotten rid of a troubling internal ache. Was it the first happiness of asceticism? For he has immersed himself in a life that brings him no benefit. It looks like he is learning to do things out of some inner wisdom that guides him by pointing to deeds because they need to be done, and not necessarily, and necessarily *not* because there is joy in doing them" (150, emphasis in the original).

The path on which Goren actualizes his "ascetic option," on which he gains "an intense feeling of a masculine, dry and clean happiness" (148)—a path that parallels the paths pursued by other bachelors in modern Hebrew utopian fiction, which is "naturally" based on the dominance of heterosexual couples (for example, the explicit "ascetic options" of Avishai and Sitri on the one hand and of Zimri on the other in *The Love of Zion*, and the explicit "ascetic option" of Kingscourt in Altneuland), this path is similar in structure to the other paths of assimilation in *He Walked in the Fields*. It is the "Minotaur topos": the hero enters a space that resembles a dark cave, meets some kind of "creeping creature" (150), grapples with it, and emerges back into the light with renewed energy.

The operation of settling on Har Ha'ayalot, of which Avraham Goren is the "supreme commander," is entirely marked by the Minotaur topos. It starts in the dead of night, with a stealthy preparation that has two functions: a reality-simulating function—the fear of the watching eyes of the British authorities—and a ritualistic function. The kibbutz and the Hachsharot people are preparing for this operation as for a secret ceremony with a clear sacred dimension. The operation itself takes place during the night in a format that recalls—and I shall return to this issue when I examine the process undergone by Mika in that constitutive event—the liminal stage in "primitive" initiation rites. A mixture of people—old immigrants, new immigrants from different countries and sabras

—are making pilgrimage to Har Ha'ayalot. Some make their way on foot, some ride there in vehicles. But this is merely a technical difference. For both the former and the latter lose their private identity for a few hours and become part of a great conquering entity. Shamir—who is a grand artist of grand gestures—creates this highly impressive maneuver by describing numerous movements from various directions and by making intelligent use of elements that stem from the nature of the described activity: the heavy darkness that lends everyone a uniform appearance; the movement in long convoys on foot, which resemble caravans of camels; and the movement in covered trucks with no seats, crammed with people, most of whom have no support and often trip and fall on each other.

The overall picture of the pilgrimage operation to Har Ha'ayalot, which is the crucial stage in Shamir's version of the Zionist melting-pot narrative, is clear in advance only to Avraham Goren. For the other participants in the operation—and for the readers—it only becomes fully clear with the light of dawn:

> Now the east brightens somewhat and the convoys can be seen from afar, whether up ahead or behind. Moreover, on the mountain range, like a string of rhythmic accents against a sky-blue background, marches another convoy. And on the left can be seen running down into the wadi and coming back up again the members of a third, and the mountain, the appointed mountain—where the roadside inn is, maybe, and the end of the road—rises nearby, and from every direction there are convoys going up, and suddenly it becomes clear that we are not one long convoy but numerous camps that are storming up from all sides....
>
> The light gradually intensified... From every direction the convoys climbed up. The night atmosphere still reigned among the walkers. Those marching in the wadi looked like they were still caught in the spell of the past hours, but the moment they got to the top of the range and saw all around them, on every plateau and hill, endless caravans marching, marching—things inevitably looked different, maybe nearby and simple, in any case daytime things.
>
> The light intensified. The caravan walked on the ridge of a hill. Suddenly there stood out, a little below the walkers, a rectangular building—the inn!—and around it everything was teeming: multitudes, tasks, camps, tents, work animals. Someone said: "It's going to be hot."
>
> And all at once it was morning, and daytime, and a very hot day. (217)

The Minotaur topos that structures the mass pilgrimage to Har Ha'ayalot exists, in an embryonic form, in the introductory passage to this collective act, which describes Goren's daily routine in the days before the great ascent. This passage, from which I will quote below, includes the typical elements of the

Minotaur topos with one conspicuous change: the substitution—so characteristic of the literature of the Palmach generation—of the animal-monster with a machine-monster. Here:

> Avraham went to the *tractors' lair* to prepare some breakfast....
>
> He knew where everything was inside the lair, among the tractors; nonetheless he first stepped onto the heavy stone threshold, *and smelled the musty darkness as if abandoning himself to an unknown world* ...
>
> The darkness was primeval and damp, and only the light stench of gasoline and lubricating oils ruptured its congealed serenity. Avraham felt his way around and ran his palms over the Diesel's cool metal. He knew it was the Diesel, and he knew that in daylight it was red—however now he ran his palms over it as if he wished to calm in it some *dormant beast*....
>
> Every morning he did the same. What was easier than to take a box of matches from beside the lamp in the tent?—But he liked the moments of groping in the dark, and didn't want to put on the light in the lair other than with the matches that would be found in it. He struck a match and put on the light. Distances slid all of a sudden and crowded around him like moving shadows. *The Diesel's chimney pointed its snout upward and its tracks grew out of the ground like a single mass*....
>
> Now, at the very moment he raised his eyes and saw the *tractors' lair coming back to life in the light*, the feeling of great happiness swept over him again with wide and warm waves. From the day he settled in Gat Ha'amkim he had not lived his life to the full until he saw life here. (150–51, emphasis mine)

"Maybe what's important is not how a man lives but how a man dies?"

The fact that even Avraham Goren, the "other," the "outsider," manages to complete the initiation rite of the pioneering Zionist community, albeit by using an existential model—"the ascetic's option"—that does not coincide with the basic principle of human engineering in nation-founding fiction (the necessity of coupling women and men so that the national dynasty lives on and flourishes) puts "our Uri," who does not manage to complete this ultimate initiation rite, in an especially risible light. The way out that Uri sketches in order to escape the embarrassing situation in which he finds himself is to get killed in a heroic action in the Palmach, thus, so he hopes, gaining the recognition of his community. He is convinced that this is a wonderfully original and creative solution, as this is the only existential option that the members of the generation before him, notably his father, have not yet actualized. Through this maneuver, so he keeps imagining, he will manage to merge the two goals whose merging seems to him, and to those he is meant to represent—the members of the revolution's second generation—impossible: fulfilling the Zionist ethos that the "frontiersmen" had delineated, while at the same time challenging it.

This existential option takes shape in Uri's mind after he finds out, immediately upon returning to the kibbutz, that his father is about to join the Jewish Brigade and thus rob his son of the possibility of outshining him at least in the military domain—the domain that he naturally sees as intended for him and his sabra peers. And indeed, already in his first meeting with Willie, Uri thinks that he should have told his father directly: "Again you are quicker than me. Again I have no choice but to imitate you. When will you finally sit back and start looking at me, at how *I* make things happen in this world?" (192, emphasis in original). Once his father enlists, Uri feels that there is only one possibility left for him: to get killed before his father. This possibility becomes clear in his mind in a strange dialectic process, which begins with wishing to pay his father his dues and ends with revenge and a kind of resignation:

> Uri understood now, with a clarity sharpened by the pain, that what tormented him, perhaps, most of all in Willie's going [to the army], was that dad slipped away from all that Uri must and is going to give him, Uri making himself deserving of what he had been given by giving some of it back . . .
>
> [For] there would come a moment in which he [Willie, whom Uri is imagining in situations of distress in the Jewish Brigade] would really need you, and someone would curse him, or spit in his face, or shove a dagger into him, or steal his bread, and he would really need at that moment an eager, strong, and daring son—and you would be dragging your feet at that moment with some foul-smelling work animal among sleepy vineyards. For the first and last time in his life dad would really need you . . . But at that moment you would be starting up tractors in the machinery shed, and he, then, would also *die before you* and for you, just as so far he lived before you, and took a wife before you, and founded a kibbutz before you, and did all the hard things that you are not sure yet if you would be able do . . . And now he will also die before you . . . You couldn't live before him—but you can go before him. Leave the world with Willie, with Ruthka—and without Uri. Destroy what you believed was Being itself: the three of you . . . Be loftier and saintlier than the both of them, be a sacrifice—give them back everything at once: lie there and laugh and see how they love and walk around and make senseless gestures. Lie there, laugh, and see how they cherish and nurture anything that preserves the touch of your hand or your life: a girl, books, a fountain pen, sneakers. . . .

MOSHE SHAMIR, *He Walked in the Fields* (1948)

Uri entered the courtyard and already needed to take care in order to navigate among all the trails and the passageways and the tracks, but he was still caught up in the sweet delirium of his thoughts, imagining death as a kind of more comfortable and relaxing lie-down, believing that he knew for the first time why some people were not afraid of it, and envisaging the greatness of spirit of those who took their leave calmly, and daring a thought that was pulsating in him like dangers: *Maybe what's important is not how a man lives but how a man dies?* (130–31, emphasis mine)

Uri thus steers himself toward the existential approach that says, as Moshe Dayan put it in his preface to Alterman's selected poems *Magash Hakesef* [Silver Platter], that death is not the end of life, its point of cessation, but rather its peak. On the face of it, and if truth be told only on the face of it, Uri dies as a hero, as someone who gave his life to save his soldiers, in a scene—picking up the grenade and getting blown up with it—the likes of which (for example, lying on a "live grenade" and saving comrades) serve as the cornerstones of the IDF's heroic legacy. However, when we examine the text before us from a departure point that is free of the (legitimate) expectations of its immediate historical recipients, we discover deep undercurrents that erode the heroic interpretation, creating instead an interpretation that exposes a derisory character to this death story, as well as its subversive character.

The intertextual unit to be referred to in connection with the event of Uri's death is the event of Yoash's death in Luidor. The two death events—that of the mythological New Hebrew Man and that of his literary descendant—share essential qualities. In both the protagonists are sabras who are paragons of a healthy spirit in a healthy body, New Hebrews who feel at ease only in the open space and in the company of animals and/or Arab natives. Perhaps most importantly for our discussion, the similarity between the two protagonists can also be discerned in the status they enjoy in the stories' semiotic/symbolic configuration: both are presented as role models both for the (generations of) reading audiences and for the "internal audience," the secondary and fringe characters in the story's reality-simulating world, who watch them with admiration and try to adopt their ways. Luidor's Yoash has one private mentee at the beginning of the story (the new immigrant David, who tries to adopt his teacher's qualities) and later, at the end of the story, a group of "mentees" that reflects the different faces of the Yishuv. In *He Walked in the Fields* the semiotic/symbolic configuration (like other variables in the novel) is more formal: Uri is the official commander of a platoon of new recruits, who follow each of his movements with admiration. It is an anonymous, uniform, faceless group, except for one new recruit—"Shimon, 'Zimon Artzt,' as he was called by the gang because of his name, Shimon Artzi, and because of his origin which was, if you'll excuse me, from Germany" (282).

The similarity between the death episodes that conclude "Yoash" and *He Walked in the Fields*, which were perceived as paradigmatic of their time, underlines the highly significant differences between them. First, Yoash dies in battle, whereas Uri dies during training. Second, Yoash's death yields two clear positive results: a) following his death, "the land [was] established in perpetuity as the moshava's" (*Stories*, 90); and b) David, the new immigrant, the Old Jew, takes his place and becomes a New Hebrew Man. By contrast, Uri's death bears no positive results: a) there is no sign that Shimon Artzi, the new immigrant, the Old Jew, takes Uri's place or becomes a New Hebrew Man; and b) neither Kibbutz Gat Ha'amakim nor the whole Hebrew Yishuv enjoy any material or spiritual gain.

Moreover, the event of Yoash's death has become—together with other literary death events in works by Second Aliyah writers,[66] and with the death events of flesh and blood human beings from that Aliyah[67]—a central pillar in the Zionist ethos. A similar fate awaited Shamir's Uri and Elik, who unfortunately were destined to die at a young age, as well as the flesh and blood soldiers of the War of Liberation generation who fell in battle.[68] Uri's status among this group, however, is dubious because he, unlike Yoash and the others, did not die as a result of a noble sacrificial act—as his historical readers, who defiantly ignored the text's reading instructions, believed—but as a result of an existential feeling of being at a dead end.

In fact, the author hints through scores of reading road signs that Uri committed suicide. Some of these road signs are planted in the death scene itself. Uri suddenly deviates from the training program. On the day of his death there was supposed to be a shooting practice, and he—to the astonishment of his second in command Gabi ("Are you nuts? Today is shooting practice!" [*HWF*, 281])—chooses instead to practice with live grenades (even wondering to himself about his own decision: "What did he want from them now? And why did it occur to him just now to practice with live grenades?" [283]). Later on he chooses, of all people, "Zimon," the older new immigrant, who is described as a person masquerading as a soldier, to be the first to throw the grenade. Zimon "trembles and hesitates. He was pale and nervous." His friends tease him, and Gabi, Uri's deputy, again cannot understand his commander's decision: "'Why,' Gabi whispered, 'why him first?'" And indeed, choosing Zimon turns out to be disastrous. This Zimon, who "is in a very shabby state," fails to ignite the grenade's top (these are "striking grenades"), and when he manages to do it he is unable to throw the grenade, and when he manages that—and that is because Gabi the deputy, rather than Uri the commander, shouts at him to throw it—he drops the grenade "about two steps from the trench. [And] it [the grenade] sparked like a cigarette in the grass" (283–85).

The climax of this suicide scene is Uri's failed spectacular action. After Zimon drops the grenade outside the trench, Uri is supposed to duck in the trench like his deputy Gabi and the other soldiers, or at most reach out his hand, grab the grenade (it is "two steps from the trench"), and throw it as far as possible. Instead Uri "jumped out of the trench, grabbed the grenade, squatted back, took in for a moment the view of the gloomy sea, the wind's meanderings in the sand, remembered at once Mika of all the girls and Ruthka" and only then (after his life flashes before his eyes, like in a movie), still crouching in an impressive cinematic pose, he "forgot everything again and hurled what he had in his hand with all his force."

The episode of Uri's death/suicide is also cast in a derisory light in the romantic and intergenerational context, as is suggested by the emphasized discontinuity between the death episode and the dramatic episode that concludes the book—the moment in which Mika decides not to abort the fetus she is carrying. She makes this dramatic decision, it should be noted, without at all contemplating the father Uri's possible reaction to this decision, a reaction that will indeed not come, because at that very moment Uri is already lying dead, his body shattered, in the hospital in Afula.

Thus Uri's death remains both senseless and valueless, save the one incisive contribution, that his removal from life's stage enables the continuation of the Zionist revolution.

The Living-Dead, the Dead-Living and the Scapegoat

Uri's attempt to return to his community must be connected to the central cultural narrative of the Palmach generation—the living-dead narrative,[69] which was first established in Alterman's early poetry (*Stars Outside* and *Joy of the Poor*),[70] and which continued to underpin his late poetry ("The Silver Platter," *Summer Festival*)[71] and that of many of the poets of the Palmach Generation.[72] This narrative allowed the country's cultural establishment, during and after the War of Liberation, to present personal death as embodying the hope of national life by presenting the living-dead as a medium, a kind of bridge between the living and the dead, between the past and the future, and between the founding stage of the imagined community (the Yishuv period) and its institutional stage (the State period). This is why, for example, the boy and the girl of the burgeoning Hebrew Yishuv in Alterman's famous poem are represented as a platter—a dish for conveying products—that carries an impressive offering: the Jewish state. This narrative served (like its parallels in post–First World War Europe, and in different guises also post–Second World War Europe, as shown convincingly by George Mosse[73]) as a highly efficient tool for relieving the feelings of siege and anxiety that permeated the Yishuv during the Second World War, and for making sense of the killing of Jewish civilians in Eretz Israel all through the Mandate period, and especially of the massive killing of Jews, mainly young sabras, during the War of Independence.

Shamir, however, turned the tables: Uri Cahana, the hero of *He Walked in the Fields*, is not presented as a living-dead, but as a dead-living, as someone who already in life has become a casualty, present but absent. Shamir created this parodic reversal (whose target is not the "high" imitated object, the "frontiersmen's" way of life, but rather—and this is a parodic mechanism expanded on by Linda Hutcheon[74]—the "low," imitating object, the Palmach generation's way of life) in three parallel trajectories: a) the compositional and rhetorical trajectory, which includes plot inversions, linguistic foreshadowings, and borrowings from other genres, first and foremost from the genre of commemoration stories, which enjoyed a tremendous boom in modern Hebrew literature; b) the chronotopic trajectory, which centers on shedding a new light on the living-dead narrative by representing it through "related" narratives that carry a contradictory cultural import, the vagabond narrative and the lone rider narrative from the Wild West movies; and c) the "cinematic trajectory," which centers on a cinematic, exaggerated, and deliberately absurd production of the story of Uri's life and death.

Blowing Up the "Sabra": The Compositional and Rhetorical Trajectory

Shamir's novel is called *He Walked in the Fields*, a phrase taken from Alterman's famous poem "The Third Mother" and, more precisely, from the poem's second verse, which Shamir cites as his book's epigraph:

> My son is tall and quiet
> I am sewing a holiday shirt for my dear.
> He is walking in the fields. He will soon be here.
> And he holds in his heart a lead bullet.[75]

In this double allusion to Alterman's poem, both in the title and in the epigraph—a poem that all of Shamir's historical addressees knew, and most of them even knew by heart—Shamir sets up the novel's semantic resonance chamber. This is a book that we must read and try to understand within the Altermanian living-dead narrative. However, in Alterman the tense in which the living-dead exists is the present continuous (he is walking in the fields), whereas in Shamir it is the past (he walked in the fields). This tiny grammatical change implied a revolutionary move. Its essence: a blatant denial of the mythical, supposedly eternal status of the living-dead and its relegation to the antiquities museum of cultural icons. In other words, by changing the tense in which the dead sabra exists from the present continuous to the past, the writer declares that this narrative, which was then, at the time the novel *He Walked in the Fields* was published, at the height of its powers, is no longer relevant.

The fact that Uri seems to be dead already in life is implied by the "unnatural" relations between the novel's two opening units—the prologue and chapter 1. We are introduced to the living Uri himself only in chapter 1, after learning of his death in the prologue, which is placed at the beginning of the narrative sequence even though the events described in it—Willie's return to Egypt and his thoughts about his family and the story of his son's life and death—conclude the novel's chronological time.

Which means that we are introduced to the living, young and seemingly vibrant Uri, to whom the story's first chapter is dedicated while knowing about his death— a fact that attaches a clear dead-living streak to Uri's character. This streak is reinforced throughout the story by dozens of linguistic foreshadowings that keep reminding us what we already know from the paratext: that we are dealing with the chronicle of a death foretold, and moreover, that it is a foretold chronicle of death that results from a destructive streak that runs through the sabra from the outset.

A clear foreshadowing of this kind occurs a few minutes before Uri, who is returning from the Kadoorie school, first meets Ruthka. Uri has just finished taking a shower, and walking through the children's courtyards, which "were deserted and empty"; he comes across Yairi, who is defined "as the best of the valley's mischief-makers," "busily and whole-heartedly rummaging and digging in the earth" (*HWF*, 43). The two—Uri, who cannot find a place in his own kibbutz apart from the public places and apart from the room of Ethel, who looked after him when he was Yairi's age, and Yairi, a lonely boy like Uri, who serves as his distorted and distorting mirror—embark on the following short dialogue:

> "Hey, naughty boy [called Uri to Yairi], who are you digging a grave for here?"
>
> The boy raised his eyes to him with annoyance. It was clearly directed at some other, unrelated matter—but it was so evident and vivid, that it would have struck anything.
>
> "For you," [Yairi] muttered angrily and went back to his business. (43)

This scene, which a naïve reading may perhaps find amusing, contains the kernel of the novel's catastrophe. For Yairi, Uri's mischievous double, digs a grave for his adult double in the children's courtyard—the existential space through whose (infantile) boundaries Uri is unable to break during his short life.

This sophisticated foreshadowing, and others like it (for example, Uri's seemingly neutral announcement in response to Biberman's refusal to give him a room of his own: "Live with Mom? With someone? No way! Alone—that's the whole point! Even in the grave—but alone" [134]) charge even innocent phrases (for example, "All right, Mom. I'm really dead-tired, see you" [45]; "The devil take me [thought Uri] if I remind you too much of Willie, of father Cahana" [98]; "The world was leaving Uri" [131]) with macabre/grotesque portents.

Blowing Up the "Sabra": The Chronotopic Trajectory

The living-dead narrative's ideological basis in the culture of the Eretz-Israeli Yishuv was, as already mentioned, the continuing inclusion of the dead—especially the sabras among them—in the pioneering revolutionary community. This Gordian knot between the dead and the pioneering revolutionary community served as the metaphysical equilibrium point of the fundamentally oppositional worldview of writers of the Palmach Generation, who repeatedly tried, as Nurit Gertz has remarked, to create "harmony between two realms of life: the collective realm (the kibbutz, work, a vibrant social life, the Palmach, the war) and the personal realm (love, family, artistic creation, etc.)."[76] Shamir's work was also written on the seam between the collective and the private. However, in opposition to most of his generation, he did not wish to create harmony between the two realms, but rather to intensify the tension between them, with the aim of preserving an "eternal flame" that would fuel the Zionist revolution.

The most effective means to achieve this aim was to question the living-dead narrative, by presenting it through the prism of related but different narratives, which highlighted the tension between the collective realm and the private realm, and even erected walls of suspicion and enmity between them.

Let me elaborate. The living-dead narrative was created and gradually crystalized in the early writings of Alterman, who quickly became, not least thanks to his reworkings of this narrative, a "national poet." This narrative first crystalized in Alterman's poetry in the figures of the wanderer and the wayfarer; poetical personas free of any national defining characteristics. The prominent quality of this wanderer-wayfarer was, as D. Miron showed in his seminal essay, his being in a state of constant motion, manifested in a fleeting and faint contact with the phenomenal world, including the human world.[77] This wanderer's only commitment is to the tune, which he tries in vain to leave behind, a compulsive tune that forces him to keep walking.

As I have shown elsewhere,[78] Alterman put this universal wanderer through a fast-tracked, tribal, national-ideological conversion, whose climax is the poem "The Silver Platter," which was perceived in the Israeli society for several generation as the definitive expression of the War of Liberation period. The protagonist of this poem, which was published at the same time as *He Walked in the Fields*,[79] is the sabra, or more precisely, and I will return to this important point, its protagonists are the male and female sabras who serve as a connecting link ("a platter") between the world of the dead and the world of the living. Here is the poem:

THE SILVER PLATTER

A State is not handed to a people on a silver platter
—Chaim Weizmann

The Earth grows still.
The lurid sky slowly pales
Over smoking borders.
Heartsick, but still living, a people stand by
To greet the uniqueness
of the miracle.

Readied, they wait beneath the moon,
Wrapped in awesome joy, before the light.
—Then, soon,
A girl and boy step forward,
And slowly walk before the waiting nation;

In work garb and heavy-shod
They climb
In stillness.
Wearing yet the dress of battle, the grime
Of aching day and fire-filled night.

Unwashed, weary unto death, not knowing rest,
But wearing youth like dewdrops in their hair.
—Silently the two approach
And stand.
Are they of the quick or of the dead?

Through wondering tears, the people stare.
"Who are you, the silent two?"
And they reply: "We are the silver platter
Upon which the Jewish State was served to you."

And speaking, fall in shadow at the nation's feet.
Let the rest in Israel's chronicles be told.

The uncommitted wanderer's place is taken first by a living-dead who walks in the fields with a lead bullet in his heart, and finally by two sabras, "wearing youth like dewdrops in their hair"—"the silver platter" on which the Jewish state was served to us. The trajectory Alterman designed for his wayfarer features another change crucial to our discussion. After the fulfillment of the national dream of founding the Jewish state, the Altermanian wanderer, who never stops walking, not even for one short moment, and before whom the road always keeps opening, undergoes a crucial transformation: he stops moving. At first the young man and woman, the protagonists of "The Silver Platter," "stand" "silently," and it is unclear whether they belong to the realm of the living or the dead, or perhaps to both. At the end of the poem, however, they attain "proper rest"—they fall at the feet of the state, and turn from beings living in the middle realm between myth and history—the romance twilight zone; the one that serves, both in Mapu and in Luidor, as the breeding ground for the establishment of a nation—into historical human beings, "house-dwellers," whose story will be told in "Israel's chronicles."

The two human types that form the poles of the process described above, the "wanderer" and the "house-dweller," differ from one another fundamentally—as Hannah Naveh notes, following Bruce Chatwin:[80]

> The model of Western literature's hero was fashioned after the human types in postmedieval society, such as the bourgeois, or the rural aristocrat in his estate, or the peasant on his land, or the military man or the churchman, who are each associated with a social and cultural institution governed by law and order.... The worldview of the settled or established hero is created from the perspective of the home and the domestic territory, and the meaning of his action in the world emanates from these concepts. The home and the territory—or the establishment—are the departure point for the perception and evaluation of changes, developments, highs and lows. The home is [Naveh quotes from Sarit Shapira's book[81]] "a place where movement stops, becomes fixated and settles within borders of stability and meaning," ... to be outside the home is a temporary state, a threatening and danger-filled state, and the concept "Homeless" in modern society embodies its negativity....

MOSHE SHAMIR, *He Walked in the Fields* (1948)

The inverse figure of this literary and cultural hero is the figure of the nomad. The nomad undermines in his very existence most of the conventions, values, worldview, culture, and existential principles of the permanent settlers.... The nomad is on the periphery of settled society, and when he touches it, his touch seems to the permanent settlers more like the infiltration of a foreign tribe, of a foreign and frightening entity of an unfamiliar and unintelligible kind.[82]

The tension between the nomad and the house-dweller has accompanied modern Eretz-Israeli Hebrew literature from its early days. It enjoyed a special revival in the works of some of the "progressive" writers of the First Aliyah (those who espoused principles championed by the Second Aliyah people, mainly Moshe Smilansky and Nehama Puhachevsky) and of many of the writers of the Second Aliyah, especially the "naïve" ones (Shlomo Tzemach, Meir Wilkansky, Aharon Re'uveni in his first Eretz-Israeli stories, and others), who based many of their works on the traditional opposition between the nomads and the house-dwellers. The latter were mostly identified with the First Aliyah people, who were farmers, family people, and bourgeois. The former, on the other hand, the homeless and the wanderers, were often identified with the Second Aliyah people, who earned their livelihood doing odd jobs as unskilled laborers and watchmen, and wandered from one part of the country to the other.

Uri Cahana's character embodies the two types at once. He gradually turns from someone who is trying to go back home into a homeless person; he slowly loses all the threads that tie him to his collective (the nuclear family, the kibbutz, his new family, and even his friends and soldiers in the Palmach), becoming lonelier and lonelier—a process that manifests itself on the chronotopic plane in a gradual replacement of the living-dead narrative as an organizing pattern for his life trajectory with another organizing pattern centered on the "wandering," "foreign," "other" hero. From "our Uri" he slowly turns into a kind of ghost that resides on the fringes of society and threatens its existence.

The identity of the specific version of the wandering narrative used by Shamir to refute the argument that the sabra has turned from a wish into a real being, is signaled by the writer in the very passage that the prominent critics of the State Generation pointed to as expressing Shamir's enthusiastic attitude toward the sabra:[83] "He was a finger that pushed firmly but only as far as was necessary the trigger of a Bren machine gun, when it was shooting short and frequent bursts and receiving an echo from the Gilboa's valleys. He was the mystery of the sudden bestirring of being, at a time of nocturnal fatigue, or when some presented possibility of domination had not yet been realized, such as a lovers' intercourse, such as Mika. He was the hater of translations from foreign literature, he was the lover of American western battle movies" (*HWF*, 228).

Why does the narrator choose to tell us that Uri was the lover of American western battle movies"? Gertz claims, justifiably, that the western was by no means unfamiliar to the Yishuv culture. On the contrary: "[The western] was familiar and very popular in those years, was regularly shown in most cinemas, and was even 'replicated' in booklets themed around the Wild West. . . . The role of the western in building the ethos of the War of Liberation can also be inferred from songs that present the fighters as horsemen riding alone in deserted landscapes . . . , from street posters that tell the story of brave fighters while likening them to the heroes wanted by the law in a western, and even from the joke that was popular at the time, that said that two people founded the Palmach, Yitzhak Sadeh and Gary Cooper."[84]

One of the central characteristics of the western, Gertz adds, is the tension between the nomadic, rootless individual, and the community that tries to put down roots in a particular place. This tension often merges with the tension between the wanderer and the woman he is associated with. "His lifestyle does not coincide with the importance that the settlers' society attaches to family life, and therefore the woman, like the society, demands that he choose between his social duties and love. Sometimes he finds sympathy precisely with women who are outside the social order: dissolute women, prostitutes."[85] After defining the western's place in the inventory of artistic influences that affected the writers of the Palmach generation, and underlining the most relevant characteristics of this cinematic genre for the Yishuv culture, Gertz focuses on *He Walked in the Fields:* the book (which as already mentioned was published in 1948) and the film (which came out in 1967).

Gertz claims that while the western had a considerable influence on the film, the book, by contrast, was only slightly influenced by the genre. Here: "In the book these tensions [the tension between the wandering individual and the community that tries to put down roots in a particular place, and the tension between that nomadic individual and the woman he is associated with] are only part of a wider array of tensions between a collective/national world and a private world, they are organized according to plot stages that outline a search for harmony, in the spirit of socialist realism, and are combined with other components of the story that are also not taken from the western. In the film, on the other hand, not only do these tension take central stage, they are also accompanied with additional components of the western, and are organized, like in many other national films, according to the stages of the western's plot."[86]

In my view, the distinction that Gertz makes here between the sources that influenced the film and those that influenced the book is inaccurate. As I see it, Shamir's novel and Y. Milo's film are both based on the model of the western. The proof: Gertz's own exhaustive and convincing description of the tension that causes the novel's hero to be torn between his social and his private duties, and the refuge he finds, just like the heroes of the classic westerns, in the arms of a woman who is outside the social order: a dissolute woman, a prostitute.

The identification of the western as an influential model in the novel *He Walked in the Fields* is a crucial element in the attempt to understand Shamir's revisionist realignment in relation to the way the fate of Zionism was commonly perceived in his time. Within the narrative/interpretative model of the western, Uri is seen as an individualist, a stranger, someone who poses a threat for civilized society—a homeless person the life-seeking community must rid itself of. This narrative-interpretative model, of course, stands in complete contradiction to the model of the living-dead, in which the hero-sabra, in his life and in his death, symbolizes the Gordian knot of relations between the individual and the community.

Uri, as I have pointed out from several directions, is presented in the novel as a liability for the community, as someone whose existence hinders its own continuing existence; that is, in Shamir's eyes, as someone who threatens the possibility of a constant revolutionary renewal of the Zionist-pioneering project. Choosing the model of the western enabled Shamir to move this both hindering and disruptive element to the rear of the stage. In other words, Uri Cahana, like the heroes of the classic westerns—which Shamir and his generation (as well as the next generation, the State Generation) watched eagerly, again and again—must appear as if from nowhere, from the u-topia (and in Elik's case, "from the sea"), in order to fulfill two defined tasks: to remind the legitimate settlers of the proper norms, albeit in a distorted way; and to leave behind a "sperm donation" and return to the no-place, to the u-topia.

Blowing Up the "Sabra": Like We've Seen in the Movies

Uri dies in place of Shimon Artzi, "Zimon Artzt"; the sabra gives his life for the new immigrant. It is an important decision on the novel's ideological plane, which is also reflected, as we shall see, in the author's surprising preference for Mika, the new immigrant, over Uri, the sabra.

The choice of Shimon Artzi, whose ridiculousness the narrator repeatedly emphasizes,[87] over Uri, coincides with the ironic/macabre tone that accompanies what may be called "Uri's cinematic production," which concerns the detailed planning of his "falling," as well as, and with the same degree of elaboration, the planning of his "commemoration."

The first time Uri associates the event of his death with a cinematic production is when he fantasizes about his father's death: "So Willie will die. Army, front, the devil knows them. They let armies massacre each other and then release—how do you say it?—optimistic military announcements, he will be killed and will be lying on the side of the road as we've seen with the Russians, or the Germans, *as we've seen in the movies*" (*HWF*, 129; emphasis mine).

Later, his father's death is tied in Uri's consciousness with the possible death of the pregnant Mika and with his own death. Uri stages these death scenes, or in other words, his fantasy of his victims' deaths, in various ways. Here, in order of appearance, are the production of Mika's death scene, followed by the production of Uri's own death scene:

> Suddenly it occurred [to Uri] that Mika could die. Against his will he saw it and became engrossed in it and couldn't break free. First of all, something could happen to her even before she went to town and it seemed that this would involve blood, a stream of blood, and then she would be very sickly . . .
>
> It is not hard to imagine her lying on the ground, her face blank and white. How much would Uri cry for her! For days he would stay lying on the spot where they would bury her and everyone would be amazed at that love.
>
> The bus going into town would crash while going over the bridge, roll down the slope, catch fire. They would pull their charred bodies out of the wreckage and phone home immediately, and Uri would be tearing his clothes and sobbing and refusing to believe it, and running on foot the whole way to see her there . . . He would later pick up a gun and blow his brains out and be done with it. Later they would be amazed at that love, and Ruthka and Willie would be so despondent over the death of them both!
>
> And maybe it would be done differently. She would go up to the woods, and she would be screaming and no one would come, no one would hear and no one would know. And the next day they would find her lying among the trees, squashed, killed . . . Suddenly his mind filled with clarity. He freed himself from the procession of horror pictures that he couldn't erase and started remembering them, listing and remembering them, one after the other. (277)

The ironic-macabre contest that is played out in Uri's mind between Mika and him on the question of who would be a bigger, more noble sacrifice, more deserving of the community's attention, is clearly reflected in the following passages:

> He must share her suffering. She cannot suffer all on her own. He must suffer, must, in some way, be as miserable as her. *More than her*—be a victim of some-

MOSHE SHAMIR, *He Walked in the Fields* (1948) 209

thing terrible, of something that would make them forget all her troubles, so they would say,—who would say?—they would say:—Right, poor Mika—but Uri, look—Uri has fallen.

The funeral would be sad and wonderful. Ginger would run around among the "big shots"; of course the big shots would be there too. And in the courtyard downstairs would stand the vans of the companies and the deluxe cars of the big shots. And serious, beautiful, and sad words would be said. And they would look at Mika and point to her with interest and she would be so grieving and proud; and Pesach would be there, and Biberman, and Avraham Goren would say some restrained words to Ruthka and a whisper would go around, festive and upright:—Here you go, this is how a fine fellow falls! (278, emphasis mine)

Another fantasy imagining his death scene—very similar in its ingredients to the actual event that would take place at the end of the novel—appears right after the previous fantasy:

The van itself could blast off now like a rocket. It's enough for two explosives to rub against each other and catch fire. They would immediately make all the jam boxes explode. An explosive is always an explosive. And one grenade blowing up, that would also be enough for you.

He was sure that he would be crushed under his jaws first and from there it would tear through him and move to the rest of his body. (278–79)[88]

The most cinematic scene in Uri's direction of the event of his own death appears simultaneously with the real event; that is, in the same brief moment in which he grabs the grenade and is blown up with it. It is a magnificent cinematic scene, centered around one action: the throwing of the grenade, which the narrator—who here, as in the preceding productions of the death scenes, is both party to the exaggerated theatrical tone and at the same time questioning it—divides into two sequences: a) Uri crouching and raising his arm, and b) the throwing of the grenade. Between the two he "plants" a hackneyed scene—Uri seeing his life flashing before his eyes like in a movie: "Uri jumped out of the trench, grabbed the grenade, squatted back, took in for a moment the view of the gloomy sea, the wind's meanderings in the sand, remembered at once Mika of all the girls and Ruthka, forgot everything again and hurled what he had in his hand with all his force."

This grandiose film production, whose subject is "the death of the sabra," concludes with the author's stage instructions, which brilliantly expose the absurdity and the ridiculousness, and with them the silent scream, encapsulated in the empty gesture of the sabra, to which the grand finale of this dramatic production is dedicated. Here: "At that moment a hidden photographer flashed an enormous load of magnesium in the air. A great glare opened up like a new, reddish, soundlessly thundering heaven, like a kind of muted, inexpressible scream" (285).

The Female Living-Dead: To Be Someone from Gat Ha'amakim

The sabra's place in the living-dead category is taken in *He Walked in the Fields*—and here Shamir returns, seemingly surprisingly, to Herzl's model—by the representative of the Diaspora, or more precisely, the female representative of the Diaspora: Mika. Mika, it should be noted, is the character with the worst Zionist starting position in the novel. Her chances of integrating into the kibbutz community, with its strict rules, seem at first non-existent. This is, among other things, because she does not have "blue eyes" and "a kind of hypnotizing body" like the sabra Dinahle, "the pride of the company" (229). For Mika "was black," "a full girl, slightly fat as the Youth Aliyah girls tended to be." Furthermore, unlike Dinahle, who is nothing but an adolescent fantasy, Mika is a flesh-and-blood being with fierce libidinal urges, and moreover she is not a virgin—and this is an unforgivable sin in any society of settlers, which is by nature puritan.

In addition to this, in the first period of her absorption in the kibbutz Mika is fed up with a crucial value of the Yishuv's society—work. She only finds her place in the vineyard, where we first meet her, after having switched from one job to another and managed to make herself hated everywhere. Two more parameters stand against her: a) she is a Holocaust refugee, and as such—that is, as someone who has managed to survive—she is repeatedly perceived in the novel (in tens of places and through the eyes of numerous characters in the story, from Willie, Ruthka, and Uri, through secondary characters, to the omniscient narrator and Mika herself) as being morally dubious;[89] and b) (and the two are of course connected) the kibbutz people cannot digest the fact that it is precisely "such" a girl, with "such" a past, that becomes attached to the kibbutz's eldest son, "a favorite child," "our Uri."

And yet, despite these poor initial prospects, Mika puts herself through the entry tests of the pioneering community and passes them with honors. This becomes apparent, on the novel's chronotopic plane, when we trace her five lines of movement.

First, Mika does not realize her dreams of going to "America, at least Warsaw" (103), but emigrates instead to Eretz Israel. Moreover, in contrast to the negative reports that appear in many of the travel stories of the protagonists of modern Hebrew literature on their way to the promised land[90]—Mika refers to "the journey to Eretz Israel as a journey full of happiness" (*HWF*, 117). Mika does not stop there: unlike the other Tehran children, for whom kibbutz Gat Ha'amakim is only an interim stop on their journey of integration, she decides to leave the "group" (the youth group) and do her best to settle in the kibbutz.

Second, although Mika fails to settle in many of the Kibbutz's jobs, the work in the vineyard does her good. At first, like Ruth the Moabite in her time and Naame and Peninah in *The Love of Zion*, she "follow[s] the grape pickers" (111).[91] Later she sings "Livlevu agas ve-gam tapu'ah" [The pear and apple trees were in bloom], a Russian song that has undergone "a proper Zionist conversion." And finally we learn, through the narrator's mediation, that she "dearly wanted . . . to integrate into the unruly crude alliance of those [the male and female grape pickers, Uri included] who teased each other in such an affable, friendly, non-resentful way" (112).

Third, Mika passes the obligatory rite in all rural utopian novels: she overcomes her fear "of animals, of big teeth, of things she didn't know how to harness" (113), befriending Uri's horse, stroking it, and feeding it—thus making a pact with the representative of nature and promoting the novel's coupling plot, which is the cornerstone of its program of human engineering and nation planning.

Fourth, Mika participates in the inauguration of the settlement on Har Ha'ayalot. Har Ha'ayalot is repeatedly described in the book as a place that enjoys a special status on the existential map of its imagined community. From the ways it is represented in the book, and from the semantic connections the book weaves between all these modes of representation, it is clear that this mountain, which overlooks Gat Ha'amakim and is a destination for walking trips and pilgrimages, has the status of an objective correlative; that is, following T. S. Eliot's famous distinction, the status of an object that symbolically signifies the novel's "regulative idea," that system of values according to which are tested and judged all the places, characters, and actions in the fictional world. This structural/thematic status is similar to the one enjoyed, as we have seen in the previous chapters, by Jerusalem in *The Love of Zion*, the Temple in Jerusalem on the one hand and the turbine plant at the Dead Sea on the other in *Altneuland*, and the romantic/Nietzschean wild expanse in Luidor's stories. This, for example, is how Har Ha'ayalot appears in a conversation between Ruthka and Uri, centered, and this is a highly significant fact in this context, around the disintegration of the Cahana family: "Don't go thinking [Ruthka says to Uri] that nature has fallen apart. I know that I and Willie are nature for you, like Har Ha'ayalot" (79). Later, the mountain is referred to during the first sexual scene between

Uri and Mika: "They [Uri and Mika] were hidden at the feet of the faintly rustling windbreakers. Above the treetops, greenish stars signaled the prodigious distances between every two worlds burning in space. Beyond a plowed road crowded a fragrant apple load; Neither the kibbutz was visible from here, nor the fields, nor the valley—and only Har Ha'ayalot was a dim bulky mass beyond the grove" (146). It is therefore an ever-present landscape fixture or, in other words, as the narrator suggests in a different context, "Har Ha'ayalot is eternal" (137). The narrator also describes the "mountain's chest" as "coarse and hairy" (159), and in reference to "a rocky hill" that rises from one of the mountain's ridges, he says that this hill "leaves no room for doubt about its origin in the six days of Creation" (160).

As people start preparing to inaugurate the settlement on Har Ha'ayalot, Mika behaves as if the whole business has nothing to do with her. She observes all the "bustle in the courtyard" from afar, imagining with pleasure how the next day, at dawn, when the convoys would have only arrived at the appointed place and people would start erecting the temporary encampment, she "would get into her bed in the tent, draw its flaps against the approaching morning, sleep, sink, wait in her bed until the noon post. Tomorrow, when they ask in the courtyard: What is this—and what about Har Ha'ayalot?—she will tell the work manager that she is sick" (208).

But in the end she skips sleeping as well as waiting for the noon post (that is, for a letter from Uri, a sign of contact from her lover on which she has been dependent until that moment), and finds herself among those going up to the mountain. There, as if by chance, she meets Ruthka, who is busy packing food, and the latter asks her to help her. Mika agrees, and that is how she ends up joining the journey. However—and this is a very important point for understanding the process she undergoes during this journey—Mika does not go up to the mountain with the convoy of people she knows from Gat Ha'amakim. Again, as if by chance, she loses Ruthka and the rest of the group and finds herself joining a convoy of new immigrants from various countries who talk in a jumble of languages, strangers to the place and strangers to each other, and most of all total strangers to Mika.

Behind this chance lies a solid logic. It is the logic that validates the rite of initiation into the pioneering/settling society, which is based, like any initiation rite of this kind, on the initiate being a total novice, with no status symbols, equal in status to all the other candidates, the other novices. In this rite the novice, who is a candidate to join the community, must experience a loss of orientation and control, must feel like one instrument among others, insignificant in himself, must undergo extreme physical processes, and also—and here we reencounter the Minotaur narrative that underpinned the stories of Willie, Uri, and Ruthka—must pass through a dark space (tomb-womb) and reemerge into the light.[92] Mika's journey to Har Ha'ayalot has all these characteristics:

> It seems she had made a bad mistake when she ran, late and nervous, in the deep darkness, grabbed on to some stretched-out hands on the back of some loading truck . . . , climbed into this foreign crowd, and was forced, henceforth and for who knows how tiresomely long, to be pressed among these people, who are they, where from and from which kibbutz, who speak such bad Hebrew that even she can tell, inserting words that sound like Bulgarian, and among whom there is no one to make his way through to her and touch her arm: "Why are you so quiet, Mika?—Feeling unwell?" . . .
>
> Mika couldn't see which way they were going or what the route was like and who they were passing on their way. It was dark all around, and only once in a while the car stopped and the din of those crowded in it intensified. Women laughed, accompanied by calm remarks by a masculine bass. Where were they taking them? . . .
>
> In the car there was disorder and limb-crushing and pushing and shoving as if you were near a pen of chickens in mid sleep. . . . [They must have] passed through [an Arab village] and its oppressive smoke was suddenly suffocating, as if they had entered a sealed cave. She felt like she needed to throw up—how long are they going to transport us? (206–10)

It all changes at dawn, when Mika gets off the truck—the tomb-womb—finds Ruthka, who from now on will play the role of her "midwife" and mentor, abandons the convoy of the new immigrants, and joins the convoy of the people of Gat Ha'amakim. The subtle transition between the two convoys sheds a bright light on the process that Mika is going through. A stranger asks, "Is Pinchas from the Giv'ataim here?," and another stranger, a new immigrant, answers: "No. This is Gat Ha'amakaim. The kibbutz." And Mika, unsolicited, corrected him. "This is the kibbutz, Gat Ha'amakim" (214)—a verbal act that puts her on the side of those who are no longer novices or new immigrants, those who already know the syntactic rules of the Hebrew language and know how to pronounce the kibbutz's name properly—the kibbutz that Mika, for the first time in the novel, now feels an integral part of.

Furthermore, this is a dramatic constitutive moment of whose significance and importance Mika—who up till now, until this impressive "settling the land" rite, was the representative of the story's foreigners and rejects—is well aware. Here: "She knew that she had corrected the mistake for her own sake. Maybe she was hasty with her reply, hasty before she was even asked, but it gave her much pleasure, clearly. To be someone from Gat Ha'amakim, to be permitted to declare on behalf of everyone: 'We,' that is: 'We, Gat Ha'amakim,' to have her identity determined simply, with an anonymity that spells security; and he, the one who had asked, with the knapsack, even if they caught him and asked him a moment later—could he have told them anything else but: 'I asked, but some member of Gat Ha'amakim told me that over there, over there is her kibbutz'" (214–15).

Mika's highly successful rite of passage is ironically bound up—like the reunion between Willie and Ruthka—with Uri's absence. Mika, who frequently reflects on what she goes through, is aware of this fact and turns it over in her mind in the last moments of her climb up to Har Ha'ayalot: "If Uri had been here—he wouldn't have let her join the climb. . . . It's good, then, that Uri is gone, because he must be indispensable [in the Palmach] and his importance rises with each day of absence, but so does yours, Mika, and you're becoming more and more precious, and you're becoming someone who has taken part in the climb to Har Ha'ayalot, someone who has something to tell, and should be listened to with interest, and that night she was, with everyone, inferior to no one, like that, then, like everyone" (217).

Fifth, the event of climbing Har Ha'ayalot is combined with a no less important and symbolic event: Mika's pregnancy, of whose early manifestations we learn simultaneously with Mika herself and with Ruthka,[93] during that same constitutive national rite.

The merging of these two events has crucial significance. This pregnancy, which in the past was perceived by the kibbutz members as a possible consequence of an undesirable bond between "our Uri" and the "bad," "corrupted" Mika, receives here, during Mika's passage through the Zionist, settling, pioneering melting pot, a retroactive endorsement. This endorsement manifests itself in three important ways: a) Ruthka takes Mika under her wings and the two develop a mother-daughter alliance; b) Uri, as usual, is not around to support his pregnant girlfriend; and c) the person who drives Mika, who has just been successfully initiated into the pioneering community, from the top of Har Ha'ayalot to her bed in the tent in the kibbutz, is none other but Ilana, who as we remember drove Uri in his truck during his failed rite of initiation into the kibbutz in the novel's opening chapter.

Shamir, then, makes a double move with respect to the living-dead, his generation's foundational narrative. He strips this narrative's natural hero, the "sabra," of his respectable status, and puts in his place the representative of the Zionist revolution's antiheroes—the representative of the suffering exiles, who arrived in the country almost against their will. This twofold literary move feeds on the same revisionist logic that restores Hebrew literature to its pre-Israeli era.

MOSHE SHAMIR, *He Walked in the Fields* (1948)

Shamir categorically refuses to accept the assumption—or according to some thinkers and critics, the fact—that the sabra has been transformed from the wish of writers and thinkers into a historical being. Accepting this assumption means, in his view, admitting the end and the failure of the Zionist revolution.

Shamir must have already believed, when he was still a loyal member of Hashomer Hatzair, that Zionism had a chance only if it did not fulfill its aims; that is, only if the soteriological gap was preserved both on the level of landscape conceptualization (the place and the Place) and the level of human engineering (the Old Jew and the New Hebrew Man). In order to preserve this gap, on both levels, Shamir surrendered the sabra's birthright on behalf of himself and of his generation (Uri, as will be remembered, is the eldest son of the pioneering community described in the novel) to those who had been considered dead (both spiritually, the members of the afflicted Diaspora, and physically, the survivors of the Holocaust), and who now, with extraordinary spiritual resources that the sabras lack, were integrating into the pioneering Zionist project.

In choosing Mika to carry the banner of the Zionist revolution, Shamir associated himself with Herzl. Both place at the forefront of the struggle the Jews who have come from the Diaspora, from the no-place, from the "Elend." Both describe the Zionist move as a move of transition from the world of the dead to the world of the living. However, and this is an intriguing difference, Herzl reserved the narrative of the vision of the dry bones in its rigorous sense—the one that implies an especially harsh melting pot—for the Jews of central Europe, whereas Shamir believed that this harsh corrective process should be undergone by the Holocaust refugees.

The Person in the Rubber Boots: Female New Immigrants, Female "Sabras," and Arab Women

As I have already indicated, in *He Walked in the Fields* Shamir followed in Herzl's footsteps, but with fascinating differences. He too, like Herzl and many of the writers of the first aliyot (and the first generation of Holocaust writers: Ka-Tzetnik, Alexander and Yonat Sened, and others), placed in the front stage, as the flagship project of his genetic engineering, a "mixed couple." In Herzl's book these are Friedrich, the central European Jew, and Miriam, the eastern European Jewess. In Shamir's story these are Uri the sabra and Mika the eastern European Holocaust-survivor Jewess. Moreover, both writers placed, alongside the central couple, another (actual or potential) couple or two of the same descent (Friedrich and Ernestina, and David and Sarah and their parents in *Altneuland*; Uri and Dinahle, and Uri and Noa in *He Walked in the Fields*).

There are also, however, striking differences between the two "genetic pools" that served these writers in their grappling with the founding of the nation. I will mention two of those, which touch directly on Shamir's human engineering and landscape conceptualization. First, Shamir, unlike Herzl, presents two possible mixed couplings: that of the central couple, Uri and Mika, and that of Willie and Ruthka—he a Russian Jew who was partly educated in Germany and she a Jewess from Poland. And, as I have tried to show throughout this chapter, it is precisely the mixed couple that is supposed to be in the background, the couple that represents the parents' generation, the past, that turns out to be the successful genetic option, whereas the young mixed couple, which is supposed to represent the present and look to the future, turns out to be a failure. Second, in the works of both authors, Herzl and Shamir, there are genetic combinations that stand no chance whatsoever. In Herzl there is one such combination: the combination between two or more representatives of the young Austro-Hungarian Jewish generation, whereas the intragroup combination, the match between a man and a woman of eastern European origins, turns out to be successful. In Shamir there are two failed genetic combinations. The first failed combination is between a Jewess from Poland and Jews from Germany—such as the relationship between Ruthka and Biberman and the relationship between Ruthka and Avraham Goren. These are relationships that possess an impressive cultural dimension but not enough vitality and libido. The second failed intragroup combination in Shamir's work—and the central one for our discussion—is the "intra-sabra" combination. An examination of the members of this group on their own, and of the option of their coupling, reveals a horrible picture.

As we may remember, *Altneuland* opened with a report about Friedrich's generational/social peer group. These are three friends, young Austro-Hungarian Jews, two of whom have already been doomed—one died of fever in Brazil and the other committed suicide—and the third, Friedrich, is seemingly heading in the same direction. An examination of Uri's generational/social peer group, and in its center his immediate peer group in his kibbutz, reveals—astonishingly—a rather similar picture.

The first generation of children in Gat Ha'amakim includes "three chicks—Uri, Danny, and Noa" (59). Danny, who was born a few months after Uri, "flourished for two years—and in the third was taken" (58); that is, he died because of the conditions in the settlement, which a certified doctor declares to be unfit for raising children. Ruthka hears the doctor's words and decides to act: she leaves the kibbutz for a few years and raises Uri in Tel Aviv. As we have seen, however, this move has destructive consequences, and the one who suffers from them is

Uri. He becomes homeless and finally pays the ultimate price, at least according to the kibbutz's (horrific) deterministic logic.

But even those who have spent their childhood and youth growing up in the kibbutz are not given a real role in Shamir's human engineering. This becomes clear if we trace the life trajectory of the kibbutz children—or more precisely, the kibbutz girls of Uri's generation—who are mentioned in *He Walked in the Fields*. We find that Uri chooses Mika not only because of what she is, but also for lack of other choices; the other option he is presented with, the intragroup option, lacks a real libido, is barren. It does not enable the continuing development and nurturing of the Jewish dynasty.

In the course of *He Walked in the Fields* Uri encounters two female sabras: Noa, his peer in the kibbutz, and Dina, his company's female support soldier in the Palmach. These are two very different women, at least on the face of it. However, for the sabra Uri neither offers a real option as a match. Dinahle is "hot." She has a "hypnotizing body" and "blue eyes" (229). The problem is that Dinahle—as opposed to Mika, who is "a woman who is ready for anything" (146)—is everyone's girl, "the pride of the company," and is in fact no one's, and may even be, as the narrator implies, a literary fiction. Noa, conversely, who has spent her whole childhood in Gat Ha'amakim, may be a flesh-and-blood character, but as a woman she is completely "effaced." We learn of this phenomenon, which is richly significant in respect to Shamir's human engineering, from the details of the encounter between Uri and Noa, which takes place after Uri is won over by Mika's fierce sensuality and vitality. As Uri makes his way back from the vineyard to the kibbutz, he realizes that someone has dug a new irrigation ditch in the middle of the track that he has been using in his role as the vineyard's carter. He surveys the surrounding area to find the person who has dug the ditch and tell them off, and finally discovers the person:

> Uri stopped and called out:
> "Hey, you there—vegetable garden!—Hey!"
> The person in the rubber boots stood up. Approaching him among the rows of bent seedlings was Noa, Naftali and Deborah's Noa. Up close he saw her: her hat, a men's hat, stuck on her shapeless hair, her shirt, exposing a reddish neck, hanging over her pants, her boots heavy with mud, boring . . .
> Uri surveyed Noa again. . . . He was wondering now that her proximity, even her large cleavage, and the light strip of fabric stretched over her collar-bone, under the shirt, had not stirred any interest in him, and he seemed to be standing there with a person who was totally unconnected to him, a male-laborer, a nobody in particular. (126–27)

The blatant indifference displayed by the sabra Uri toward the sabra Noa stands in sharp contrast to his attraction to Mika, the new immigrant. Uri is aware of this contrast and dedicates to it one of his rare reflections. Here: "Uri was preoccupied with Mika. Interesting, how this Mika captures you, till you can't get her out of your mind! Noa may be flat-chested, and maybe someone will want her, and maybe someone will find her nakedness an experience—anything can happen in this world! But Mika is something else! Maybe she doesn't even realize it herself—but you can't get her out of your mind. Fact! You can't get her out of your mind. Uri imagined Mika in his mind again. How she ran from him, and how she was soft and slippery in his hands" (128).

Uri's lack of interest in Noa and his attraction to Mika may be explained by sociological and psychological reasons, which are connected, as Bruno Bettelheim has shown,[94] to the way kibbutz children lived and were raised, especially in the kibbutzim of Hashomer Hatzair, as well as, it seems, by anthropological reasons to do with the broadening and enrichment of the genetic and economical pool of the community, in the spirit of Claude Lévi-Strauss's theory.[95] However, and especially in the context of our discussion, these extreme repulsion/attraction dynamics have an ideological rationale as well.

As already mentioned, Shamir ridiculed the figure of the sabra. He divested the sabra of his previous prestigious status as a hero in the living-dead narrative and gave this status to Mika, because he refused to accept the idea that the Zionist revolution had already been realized; that is, had stopped being relevant. For the same ideological reason he did not permit the intracamp sabra coupling—that is, the erotic relationship between the New Hebrew Man and the New Hebrew Woman, which was ostensibly the obvious option in the Palmach period. For him, a match between a male sabra and a female sabra was possible only under one of the following two conditions: either the girl is a fantasy (the Dinahle option) or the sabra has a weird sexual orientation. Either way, these are options that do not enable the continuation of the dynasty.

Moreover, from the conversation of the gang, the group of Kadoorie friends, it emerges that "even" the Arab girls attract the sabras more than the sabra women:

> And Mika is, therefore, a girl that you can't get out of your mind. They used to go out—he remembered, in that agricultural school of his—to till the corn in several pairs, and at noon they would lay out their food under one of the olive trees of the Dabourieh village. An Arab woman would start crossing the landscape and already they would pierce her with their words and their eyes and start a conversation about things.
>
> "Some of them are to die for."

"Habibi, when an Arab woman is young they stay up without a bra, like tennis balls..."

"Calm down!"

"Your Mes'cha girls are better?"

"A stupid comparison!" (*HWF*, 129)

The fact that the intra-camp coupling option—the match between a sabra boy and a sabra girl—is rejected in the novel, can be explained in two ways. One way is to conclude that the author, Moshe Shamir, believed that the local Jewish pool was not self-sufficient, that is, that the project of Zionist human engineering could not rely only on the local native sabra crop and required some imported "fresh meat," even if its quality was debatable: young women like Mika, who belong to the group "that has already managed on its wanderings to despair of all the faith in the world, to offend against the laws and respectability of half a dozen states, to fondle and weigh any value in the world, only to eventually dismiss it" (105).

The second way to interpret this troubling literary fact is to assume that the author, Moshe Shamir, rejected the option of intra-camp coupling because he feared that affirming the validity of this option—just like affirming the validity of the sabra character—would mean admitting that the Zionist project was over and done with and that it could be treated as a scaffolding that could be removed now that the building itself had been erected and stood firm.

These two different interpretations can coincide. Both attest to the revisionist character of Shamir's literary/theoretical endeavor; both construct and ratify the assumptions that underpin this important novel: the necessity of keeping alive the soteriological tension (the gap between the place and The Place and between the Old Jew and the New Hebrew), and the necessity of continuing to nourish it—for the time being or forever. These assumptions are of course in stark contrast to the assumptions that underpinned, as I tried to show in the previous chapters, the works of Mapu, Herzl, and Luidor, who tried, each in his own way, to eliminate the "Jewish-diasporic" soteriological tension. Furthermore, the young Kadoorie guys' conversation includes a piece of information that may be seen as foreshadowing the future history of human engineering in Hebrew literature—I am referring to the sabras' comment about the femininity of the Arab women. Shamir, it should be recalled, preserved, like Mapu, Herzl, and Luidor before him, a "racial purity"—his repository of couplings does not deviate from the Jewish gene bank. However, in the conversation of the sabra youths, another option is hinted at—an intertribal option, which will be actualized by the major writers of the next generation: the State Generation.

5

"Nomads and Viper," Amos Oz, 1963

A Short, Patched European Jacket over a White Desert Robe

Grand dreams engender a sense of defeat
—even if there is no defeat
—AMOS OZ, *interview with Idit Zertal*

The Shaman

The *Where the Jackals Howl* stories were written in the years 1962–1964. They were published in 1965 by the Massada press.[1] In the beginning of the 1970s Oz made some amendments, and a new edition of the stories was published in 1976 by the Am Oved press.[2] Since then they were reprinted many times: first by Am Oved, and later, when the writer changed publishers, by Keter.

Immediately upon its publication, *Where the Jackals Howl* (which was, it should be remembered, the first book of a young author; Oz was then twenty-six years old) earned a great flood of reviews.[3] The critics, both those who liked the book[4]—and they were the majority—and those who liked it less,[5] positioned the young author, together with another young author, A. B. Yehoshua, at the forefront of a new literary generation. Soon Oz and Yehoshua became the almost official spokesmen, in Israel and abroad, of the group of writers called the State Generation and the New Wave.

After the publication of the novel *Elsewhere, Perhaps* (1966), and especially after the publication of *My Michael* (1968), which was enthusiastically received in Israel and abroad, the collection *Where the Jackals Howl*, in both its versions, was perceived as a foundational text and since then it has preserved its status as a cornerstone of Israeli culture. Generations of pupils studied it in state high schools in the cities and in parallel educational establishments in the kibbutzim and moshavim; generations of students in the literature departments of academic and teacher-training institutions—some of whom became teachers in high schools, seminars, colleges, and universities—used it to study the principles of the short story and the characteristics of the 1960s Israeli short story.

The status of the collection *Where the Jackals Howl* as a foundational text—in particular the stories "Nomads and Viper" and "The Way of the Wind," which were perceived, alongside A. B. Yehoshua's "Facing the Forests" and "The Yatir Evening Express," as the representative stories of the State Generation—has been preserved and even further established in the forty years that have passed since it was first published.

Numerous coefficients are responsible for this graph outlining the book's reception over the years. Among them: Oz's political activity (which included membership of political movements and parties,[6] and writing dozens of political and semi-political essays and pieces, only some of which were anthologized in books[7]), a political activity that made him one of the prominent (admired but also vilified) representatives of the Israeli Left;[8] his encounters, starting in his twenties, with state leaders; the dozens of prizes he has been awarded in Israel and abroad;[9] the fact that most of his books were bestsellers; the astonishing reception his books earned worldwide (most of them were translated into dozens of languages and were bought and read by hundreds of thousands of people); the plays and films based on his stories, novellas, and novels; his status as "a shaman," a public psycho-cultural status meriting a separate discussion, which Oz himself did quite a bit to establish and reinforce; and even the special combination of his talent, his success and . . . his physical beauty.[10] All these variables, in isolation and combined, made Oz "the most read writer in the history of Hebrew literature,"[11] as well as, it seems, the most influential Israeli author of our time.

Elsewhere, Very Far

As I have tried to show in the preceding chapters, in the literature of the Hibbat Zion period and in the literature of the Zionist period, the attempts to narrow the gap between the Place and the place on the topographic plane were made in close affinity with two kinds of earthly utopia: the garden utopia and the city utopia. The reciprocal relations between the garden utopia and the city utopia partly parallel—and this is also an issue I touched on in the beginning of the book—the reciprocal relations between two human phenomena that are also central to our discussion and that Ferdinand Tönnies called community and society.

In *The Love of Zion* Avraham Mapu created a fictional landscape that is based on a harmonious integration of "community" and "society," although the "community" element has a clear precedence. This precedence manifests itself, among other things, in the fact that the story's protagonists belong to two agrarian feudal families, which preserve their economic might and their moral power by "clinging to the land" and through marriage relations that do not allow for a cross-class pairing. The integration of the garden utopia with the city utopia in *The Love of Zion* is also harmonious, and coincides with the reciprocal relations between the community and the society in the book. The integration of these two elements shows a preference for the elements of the "garden" over those of the "city."

Theodor Herzl, like Mapu before him, also tried to take a moderate, reformatory approach. However, the reciprocal relations between the elements of the community and the society in his work, and the relations between the elements of the garden and the city, are the reverse of the parallel relations in Mapu. The garden utopia as a reflection of the natural is approached here with caution. It is represented, but always within a demarcated and enclosed frame. For example, there is room in the novel for animals (the representatives of nature), but only when they are domesticated, used for scientific experiments, or reincarnated as sculptures in front of houses or in their gardens, which are surrounded by high walls. In the reciprocal relations between the society and the community in *Altneuland*—as in the reciprocal relations between the elements of the garden utopia and the city utopia in the novel—the social element takes precedence. Herzl created an existential landscape that is deliberately founded on social agreements ("treaty") and common interests, rather than on community ties—race, tribe, family, and neighborly relations.

Eretz Israel as it is depicted in Yosef Luidor's stories is the polar opposite of Herzl's: Luidor's protagonists recognize only man's "natural will" and despise thoughts and deeds that base their authority on social agreements and common interests. And thus, in the reciprocal relations between the garden utopia and the city utopia in Luidor's work, the garden elements take clear precedence. Luidor's ultimate landscape is, we may remember, a "Nietzschean paradise"—a wild virginal landscape in which the "native," and only he, can merge in an orgiastic dance with the representatives of the "great being." For ordinary people, that is, for those who are not and will never be able to be natives (the immigrants), Luidor reserves a more temperate landscape: a moshava or a moshav. But this landscape is also portrayed under the sign of the garden utopia. It is an agricultural settlement whose livelihood, raison d'être, and chances of survival depend on one single thing (and this is where the affinity between Luidor and Mapu becomes most apparent): the sumud—the steadfast persistence of clinging to the land at any price, including the price of life itself.

Moshe Shamir in *He Walked in the Fields* continued on the path paved by Luidor, but also diverged from it. In his writing there is also a clear difference between the wild, virginal landscape, reserved for the native—the areas into which the "Tarzan" or "Wild West man" Uri occasionally strays—and the domesticated landscape, the kibbutz with its buildings, facilities, and cultivated fields. But the position of Uri Cahana, Shamir's "native," in relation to the landscape is more complicated than Yoash's. His verbal and physical expressions and his existential choices reflect a tense ambivalence toward both the natural landscape and the domesticated landscape. He tries to find his place in the domesticated landscape ("a room of his own" in the kibbutz), but at the same time fears just as much the commitments such a place entails (work routine, a relationship, fatherhood).

The presentation of nature (the garden utopia) and culture (the city utopia) in *He Walked in the Fields* as essences that are experienced ambivalently—rather than, as Luidor presents them, as discrete, monolithic, and contrasting essences—coincides with the nature of the reciprocal relations between the community and the society in the novel. The story is built on the attempt to reconcile the tension between the characteristics of the traditional family unit—blood relations, parenthood, relationship—and the characteristics and demands of the pioneering society, which tried to make the family unit redundant and take its place.

Shamir created a fictional world in which the balance between its two infrastructural utopian models and the balance between the community and society elements that constitute it are preserved through a brutal act: the removal of Uri, the "first sabra," from the stage in order to conceal the "evidence" that the Zionist-pioneering genetic experiment—the turning of the Old Jew into a New Jew (a Hebrew Man)—has succeeded, a bio-literary fact that signals the completion of the Zionist revolution and therefore also suggests that it is, as it were, no longer relevant.

Uri's place in the chronicles of pioneering-Zionist human engineering is taken by Mika, the "new immigrant," who goes—like all the new immigrants who arrived in the country before her—through all the Zionist rites of entry. Thus she fulfills the role assigned to her by the author: to be another drop of oil on the wheels of the constant Zionist revolution, specifically Shamir's Zionist-nationalist version of revolution, which has been adopted, as I have already pointed out, by the Right as well as it seems by the Center in the state of Israel.

In his first stories Amos Oz embraced the ideological and psychological-existential framework set up by the "Yishuv writers," the writers who created Eretz-Israeli fiction in the thirties and forties of the twentieth century. Like them he used the kibbutz both as the real scene in which the conflict between the garden and city elements on the one hand, and the community and society elements on the other, is waged, and as a reflection of the corresponding conflicts that are waged in the psyche of his protagonists and in the psyche of the nation.[12]

However, the attempt to create harmony between the two pairs of elements on which the old-new land is built—the garden utopia and the city utopia on the one hand and society and community on the other—is replaced in Oz, and in other writers of his generation who can be identified with the Zionist Left, by a position that reconstitutes the tension between the place and the Place by escalating to the point of explosion the tension between the two pairs of contrasting elements on the basis of which the new-old land is built, and also—and this is a dramatic move whose full repercussions are difficult to assess at this stage—by changing the direction of the stories' "vector of desire." This dynamic emerges both from exploring the identity of the geographical destinations that the characters yearn for and from examining the identity of their human objects of desire.

The double tension—the tension between the Diaspora, the "elsewhere," the "Elend," and the "Place," the idea of Eretz Israel; and the tension between the figure of the Old Jew and the figure of the New Hebrew—is replaced in Oz's formative fiction by a tension centered on the longing for a double "otherness": for an elsewhere that is always "away from here" (an open space that is beyond the security fence of the settlement or outside the parameters of the Jewish settlement in Eretz Israel [the Golan mountains, Petra and so forth] or overseas, mainly in north European landscapes: fir forests, snowy mountains, great rivers, and so forth).[13] Simultaneously, the longing for other figures—figures that belong to the local landscape but are perceived as foreign (Arabs, Bedouins) or foreign women and men in overseas countries.[14]

In Oz, this double new-old tension (a tension that characterizes many of the stories of the postclassical Hebrew writers such as Chaim Nachman Bialik, Zalman Shneur, Uri Nissan Gnessin, Micha Josef Berdichevsky, and others) is always accompanied (again, as in the postclassical writers, especially in M. J. Berdichevsky, with whom Oz felt a great affinity,[15] but also in many of the central European Jewish writers—David Vogel, Franz Kafka, Joseph Roth and others) with a yearning for some "pure spirituality," Christian in its essence,[16] as well as, and the two are interconnected, with an acute death wish,[17] or some craving for an oceanic merging with the other.[18]

AMOS OZ, "Nomads and Viper" (1963)

"The camels alone spurn meekness"

The change in the objects of human longing—or in other words, the nature of the new vector of desire—in Oz's first stories may be inferred, on the topographic plane, from a comparative description of two maps: one a map that reflects the worldview that was common among the stories' historical recipients (the Israeli readers in the first half of the 1960s, who were familiar with the fiction written in the country in the 1930s and '40s), and the second a map that reflects the new and challenging worldview of the young Oz.

In the previous chapters I called the first kind of map the background map and the second kind of map the foreground map, because the two worldviews that the texts contrasted were depicted on the topographic plane as juxtaposed with each other, as if existing on the same geographical plane, albeit, as already mentioned, in divergent versions. In Oz's *Where the Jackals Howl*, on the other hand—as in the early stories of his fellow New Wave writers—the worldviews that the texts contrast are depicted on the topographical plane, not as juxtaposed with each other, but rather as superimposed on each other, as if existing on two different geographical planes: one overt and clear and the other elusive and concealed. Therefore, I shall call the map describing the first geographical plane, which reflects the period's common, conformist worldview, the upper map (in the previous configuration, the background map), and the map describing the other geographical plane, which reflects the writer's new, nonconformist, subversive worldview, the lower map (in the previous configuration, the foreground map).

These maps are already outlined in the opening lines of the story "Nomads and Viper":

> The famine brought them.
>
> They fled north from the horrors of famine, together with their dusty flocks. From September to April the desert had not known a moment's relief from drought. The loess was pounded to dust. Famine had spread through the nomads' encampments and wrought havoc among their flocks.
>
> The military authorities gave the situation their urgent attention. Despite certain hesitations, they decided to open the roads leading north to the Bedouins. A whole population—men, women, and children—could not simply be abandoned to the horrors of starvation.
>
> Dark, sinuous, and wiry, the desert tribesmen trickled along the dirt paths, and with them came their emaciated flocks. They meandered along gullies hidden from town dwellers' eyes. A persistent stream pressed northward, circling the

scattered settlements, staring wide-eyed at the sights of the settled land. The dark flocks spread into the fields of golden stubble, tearing and chewing with strong, vengeful teeth. The nomads' bearing was stealthy and subdued: they shrank from watchful eyes. They took pains to avoid encounters. Tried to conceal their presence.

If you passed them on a noisy tractor and set billows of dust loose on them, they would courteously gather their scattered flocks and give you a wide passage, wider by far than was necessary. They stared at you from a distance, frozen like statues. The scorching atmosphere blurred their appearance and gave a uniform look to their features: a shepherd with his staff, a woman with her babes, an old man with his eyes sunk deep in their sockets. Some were half-blind, or perhaps feigned half-blindness from some vague alms-gathering motive. Inscrutable to the likes of you.

How unlike our well-tended sheep were their miserable specimens: knots of small, skinny beasts huddling into a dark, seething mass, silent and subdued, humble as their dumb keepers.

The camels alone spurn meekness. From atop tall necks they fix you with tired eyes brimming with scornful sorrow. The wisdom of age seems to lurk in their eyes, and a nameless tremor runs often through their skin.[19]

These passages, which introduce us to the fictional world and allow us to locate ourselves in its semiotic landscape, are organized in a dense network of contrasting analogies, most of which structure and qualify one central analogy: them and us. Them: a Bedouin tribe moving northward "from the horrors of the famine" and camping on the outskirts of the kibbutz, which was founded on the border between the desert and the "settled land." Us: the kibbutz members sitting safe and secure on our land—or at least, safe and secure from the horrors of the famine.

The main representative of the Bedouins in the story is a young shepherd who meets Geula, the main representative of the kibbutz in the story, in the orchard. The orchard is located on the border between the kibbutz and the open landscape. The other prominent representatives of the kibbutz in the story are Rami, the leader of the youngsters, Etkin, the kibbutz secretary, and the narrator, who used to be Geula's boyfriend, who guides us through the story's paths.

The story opens with the Bedouins' movement northward. It continues with a series of small clashes between the Bedouins and the kibbutz members, allegedly following some thefts and acts of vandalism ostensibly perpetrated by the Bedouins. The story continues with a description of Geula's encounters with various males and ends with two synchronous scenes: Geula, bitten by a snake, lies dying—hallucinating among the bushes behind the memorial hall set up in memory of her brother who "was killed in a reprisal raid in the desert" (35) and a group of youths, including the narrator-protagonist and headed by Rami, who are observed through the eyes of the dying Geula as they are "crossing the lawn on their way to the fields and the wadi to even the score with the nomads" (38).

Between the "them" and the "us" there are, on the face of it, sharply delineated relations of opposition. "They," the Arabs, belong to the south. "We," the Jewish Israelis, belong to the north. They are sinuous, hungry, dusty. We are well fed and clean. They walk on foot. We ride a tractor. They move in hidden gullies, quietly. We drive on the main road, noisily. "Their" sheep are "miserable specimens: knots of small, skinny beasts huddling into a dark, seething mass." "Our" sheep are well tended. They are meek, subdued, silent, or at most utter "a guttural syllable." We "set billows of dust loose on them," cover them with "a harsh shadow." They are dark, shady, nocturnal. We are bright and fix them with a "cold blue eye." They are feminine. Their voice has "a silken quality, like that of a shy woman." We are masculine, resolute, clear. They are protean creatures—shape-shifting, deceiving: "frozen like statues," who "feigned half-blindness from some vague alms-gathering motive. Inscrutable to the likes of you." We are honest and direct.

Most of the binary oppositions distinguishing "them" from "us" can be assembled under one pair, which Oz's narrator himself offers us: "nomads" and "town dwellers."

This binary opposition, which already came up in the discussion of *He Walked in the Fields*, reflects, as many scholars from various disciplines have noted, a fundamental pattern in the way man perceives himself and the concepts of "society" and "culture." The "house dweller" or "homeowner," remarks Hannah Naveh in her book *Male and Female Travelers*, is "a protagonist . . . who is connected to a place and belongs to a society that carries the marks of permanence, order and unified state mechanisms."[20] The inverse figure of the house dweller is the nomad:

> The nomad undermines in his very existence most of the conventions, values, worldview, culture and existential principles of the house dweller. For the nomad the journey is a permanent way of life. . . . [He] is *on the periphery of settled society*, and when he touches it, his touch seems to the house dwellers more like the infiltration of a foreign tribe, of a foreign and frightening entity of an unfamiliar and unintelligible kind. . . . the nomad's contact with the settled culture is therefore always problematic . . . The nomad comes from the desert, from the forest, from the prairie, from the frontier areas . . . [He] lives outside social conventions and

structures that seem to their owners universal, and since he does not aspire to territorialization, he does not take on the social roles that derive from these structures: roles and duties of family and home, social duties and functions, nation-state institutions—as they are defined and structured in Western society, which has built itself a permanent house. The nomad has not been socialized into these roles, and obeys another, foreign order. Western culture has adopted a romantic conception of the nomad as a free savage, as barbaric, as primitive, in order to denote his absolute and extreme otherness.[21]

In order to illustrate these assertions, Naveh refers, among other things, to the stories of *Where the Jackals Howl* and especially to the story "Nomads and Viper." Here is another excerpt from her text:

> Amos Oz's story "Nomads and Viper" . . . features an expression of the deep anxiety caused by the presence of the Bedouin nomads in the psyche of the kibbutz members, the agriculturists settled on their land within the borders of their fenced-in and floodlit kibbutz. The nomads are like the viper snake—an image that in itself is enough to open the fissure of global hostility running from time immemorial between "man" and the absolute foreigner and enemy, which is immediately defined as "no man." . . . Many of the stories in this collection feature, on the story's fringes, a migration of nomads, real or symbolic, whom the town-dwellers find it hard to control and impose law and order on. They represent an inscrutable and impenetrable culture (which is perceived in the town-dwellers' imagination as a lack of culture).[22]

The configuration that the narrator of "Nomads and Viper" presents to us is concatenated from a clear central binary opposition (nomads versus town-dwellers) and, as such, implies a clear hierarchical assumption. The artistic articulation of this assumption—the inferiority of the Bedouins (positioned "down"/"under"/"on the margins") and the superiority of the Israeli civilization (positioned "up"/"above"/"in the center")—creates the story's upper map. This is how the kibbutz and the Bedouins look from afar and from up above, from the point of view of a tourist. However, the official upper map hides another map, the lower map, the unofficial map of the kibbutz and its residents. The lower map is revealed to us through the rents in the upper map created by the story's author through his representative, the narrator, who serves, like all the narrators in Oz's early work, as a kind of double agent. On the one hand—the front side, the façade—he functions as the kibbutz's spokesman, who is supposed to present to the world and the readers the "correct picture"; that is, the pretty, prettified face of the great settling-pioneering project. On the other hand—the back, shadowy side—the narrator serves as a mouthpiece for the "kibbutz underneath," a kind of exhaust pipe for all the emotions, desires, and drives that the official upper map conceals. The loneliness, the alienation, the hatred, the sexual hunger of the women (which parallels the physical hunger of the Bedouins), the impotence of the Jewish men that masquerades as omnipotence, their latent homosexuality, and so forth.

In terms of its elements, the upper map in "Nomads and Viper" overlaps with the lower map—in this sense Oz returns to Mapu's topography. The difference between Oz's upper map and lower map lies, and here too there is a resemblance to Mapu, in the logic that organizes the various elements: the upper map is based on solid and clear borders; by contrast the lower map is based on transgression, on the crossing of borders and the mixing of domains and phenomena.

The nature of the two maps is conveyed to us, as already mentioned, through the discordance between the narrator's utterances: the "official voice" represents the kibbutz's ideological pact, and the "subversive voice" expresses dark urges and desires. The official voice creates, and is created by, the hierarchical dichotomy that organizes the fictional world. The subversive voice opens cracks in this dichotomy and erodes it, thus providing an outlet for the repressed urges and desires.

The nature of the tense dialogue between these two voices—which, as we shall see later, is a kind of vocal staging of a single split-torn voice (the voice of the kibbutz collective on the one hand and of the individuals who represent it, Geula and the narrator, on the other)—can be inferred from the paragraph that concludes the assemblage of contrasting analogies that opens the story: "The camels alone spurn meekness. From atop tall necks they fix you with tired eyes brimming with scornful sorrow. The wisdom of age seems to lurk in their eyes, and a nameless tremor runs often through their skin" (*WJH*, 22).

This paragraph suggests that not all the Jewish and Arab-Bedouin inventory can be subjected to a binary division. At least one element does not easily fit into one of the two paradigms: "The camels alone spurn meekness." The camels fracture the seemingly natural division between the subjugating Israelis and the subjugated Arabs-Bedouins. The fracture widens due to the reversal of the vertically symbolic symmetry (up versus down, ruler versus ruled): the preceding passage described the kibbutz's representative as sitting on a tractor, observing the Bedouins from above and "set[ting] billows of dust loose on them"; whereas here the camels, the representatives of the Bedouin existence, are the ones looking from above. The task of questioning the dichotomous-hierarchical "upper map" in the camel paragraph is left to the reader. The narrator, who serves as a double agent—directing us to create both the upper map and the lower map—

cannot expose himself. He therefore alerts the readers to the problematic nature of the upper map, which he is supposed to represent faithfully, through reading and interpretative instructions that are implicit in the opening and closing unit of the camels paragraph.

At the start of the passage the narrator hints that perhaps it is not the camels alone that break the hierarchical dichotomy and that the conspicuous attempt to isolate the camels suggests an anxiety of losing control, crossing borders, breaking barriers, and being swept away uncontrollably. The opening unit (the Hebrew original reads, "Only the camels, the camels alone") creates a suspicious, deliberate rhetorical redundancy. This chiastic parallelism (only/alone—the camels/the camels), which stands out against the preceding wealth of normative parallelisms, has no referential function; it does not offer any new information. Its function is, first and foremost, hermeneutic: it indicates to the reader that someone is really insisting on asserting that indeed it is "[o]nly the camels, the camels alone" that violate the dichotomous-hierarchical logic of the upper map—an insistence that suggests that the "aberrant" camels actually represent a wider phenomenon.

Another clue, with a similar function, can be found in the closing unit of the camels paragraph. Here, for the first time, the narrator removes the mask of the omniscient narrator, which he worked so hard to uphold at the start of the exposition, and shares with us his descriptive dilemmas: "and a nameless tremor runs often through their skin" [the Hebrew original has "and what name shall I give the light tremor that often runs through their skin"].

At this stage we realize that not only can the catalog of phenomena presented to us not be univocally subjected to a dichotomous-hierarchical division, but also that some of the phenomena, and not necessarily the most minor ones, cannot be named and therefore are not included in this catalog.

The obvious question here is why it is specifically the camel that serves as a metonymy for this "insubordination," and one answer is that it represents the desert, that pre-cultural, annihilating space that is perceived semantically as a "zero point."[23]

Identifying the symbolic import represented by the camel is significant, since the peculiarity of the "ship of the desert," signified here by the special expression in the camel's eyes, is connected to the peculiarity of the only real female character in the story, Geula, also signified by a special expression in her eyes, very similar to that of the camels, a gaze that the narrator also has difficulty dealing with, as he explicitly admits: "Sometimes we happen to sit together in the dining hall. I avoid her glance, so as not to have to face her mocking sadness" (*WJH*, 28).

A Reflection of a Kingdom by the Sea

The exposition of the story "Nomads and Viper" thus draws up a clear reading contract between the author and the reader. According to this contract, the reader has at his disposal two maps. One is the upper map, which presents the depicted world in accordance with a binary-hierarchical principle, and the other is the lower map, which is situated under the former and shows through its tears, and which presents the world by shattering the binary-hierarchical principle and replacing it with a longing for an area that is located beyond the story's familiar, legitimate, safe parameter—an area that is connected to darkness, death, dream, sleep, madness, etc.

Oz, it should be noted, was very aware of the nature of this spatial-existential reading contract, with all its elements and implications. This emerges clearly from the opening chapter of his first novel, *Elsewhere, Perhaps*, which is entirely devoted to the poetics and semiotics of the kibbutz space. It is a unit that exhibits a sophisticated literary topography and can serve as a source document for any study that tries to identify and demarcate the characteristics of the Israeli landscape conceptualization. Here are some of the relevant passages from this brilliant ars-poetical chapter:

A CHARMING, WELL-ORGANIZED VILLAGE
You see before you the kibbutz of Metsudat Ram:

Its buildings are laid out in strict symmetry at one end of the green valley. The tangled foliage of the trees does not break up the settlement's severe lines, but merely softens them, and adds a dimension of weightiness.

The buildings are whitewashed, and most of them are topped with bright red roofs. This color scheme contrasts sharply with that of the mountain range, which completely blocks the view to the east, and at the foot of which the kibbutz lies spread. The mountains are bare and rocky, cut by zigzagging ravines. With the sun's progress their own shadows spill gradually down these folds, as if the mountains are trying to relieve their desolation with this melancholy shadow play.

Along the lower terraces on the slope stretches the border between our land and that of her enemies.

This border, prominently marked on the maps with a thick green line, is not visible to the observer, since it does not correspond to the natural boundary between the lush green valley and the bleak, bare mountains. The soil of Israel overflows the limits of the valley and spreads up the lower slopes toward the barren heights. So the eye and the mind—or, more precisely, geology and politics—come to be at odds with one another....

The landscape, then, is rich with contrasts, contrasts between appearances and reality and also inner contrasts within the appearances. These can be described only by the terms "contradiction." There is a kind of enmity between the valley, with its neat, geometrical patchwork of fields and the savage bleakness of the mountains. Even the symmetrical architecture of Kibbutz Metsudat Ram is no more than a negation of the grim natural chaos that looks down on it from above.

The contrast inherent in the landscape naturally plays a prominent part in the works of Metsudat Ram's own poet. Sometimes it takes the form of a genuine symbol, as we shall see if we look at the poems of Reuven Harish. For the time being, let us borrow the poet's favorite contrast and apply it to matters that Reuven Harish does not write about.

Consider, for example, the striking contrast between our village and the typical village, which arouses nostalgic feelings in the hearts of city dwellers. If you are accustomed to the sight of ancient villages, their roofs soaring on high in convoluted northern shapes; if in your mind you associate the word "village" with horse-drawn carts piled high with hay and with pitchforks stuck in their sides; if you yearn for crowded cottages huddling round the rain-swept spire of an old church; if you look for cheerful peasants with brightly colored clothes and broad-brimmed hats, picturesque dovecots, chickens busily scratching in a dung heap, packs of lean, vicious dogs; if you expect a village to have a forest round about and winding dirt paths and fenced fields and canals reflecting low clouds and muffled wayfarers heading for the shelter of an inn—if this is your mental picture of a village, then our village is bound to startle you, and it is this which has compelled us to introduce the term "contradiction." Our village is built in a spirit of optimism.

The dwellings are absolutely identical, as is demanded by the ideological outlook of the kibbutz, an outlook that has no parallel in any village in the world.

The houses, as we have said, are brightly painted. They are laid out at regular intervals. Their windows all face northwest, since the architects tried to adapt the building to the climate. Here there is no agglomeration of buildings clustering or ramifying haphazardly down the ages, nor blocks of dwellings enclosing secret courtyards, for the kibbutz does not have family homes. There is no question of separate quarters for different crafts; the poor are not relegated to the outskirts nor is the center reserved for the wealthy. The straight lines, the clean shapes, the neatly ruled concrete paths and rectangular lawns are the product of a vigorous view of the world. That was what we meant when we stated that our village was built in a spirit of optimism.

Anyone who draws the shallow inference that our village is stark and lacking in charm and beauty merely reveals his own prejudice. The object of the kibbutz is not to satisfy the sentimental expectations of town dwellers. Our village is not lacking in charm and beauty, but its beauty is vigorous and virile and its charm conveys a message. Yes, it does.

The road that joins our kibbutz to the main road is narrow and in bad repair, but it is straight as an arrow in flight. To reach us you must turn off the main road at a point indicated by a green and white signpost, skirt the potholes in the road, and climb a pleasant small hill not far from the kibbutz gates. (This is a green and cultivated hill, which is not to be seen as a finger of the mountains thrust violently into the heart of the valley and lopped off, since it has nothing in common with the menacing mountain heights.) Let us pause for a moment and engrave the striking colored picture-postcard scene on our memories. From the top of the hill we can look down on the kibbutz. Even if the view does not inflame the heart, still it pleases the eye. The open iron gates, a sloping fence, and, nearby, a tractor shed. Agricultural implements scattered about in cheerful disorder. Buildings crowded with livestock—chickens, cattle, and sheep—constructed on the latest plan. Paved paths branch out in various directions, and avenues of bush cypresses trace the skeleton of the over-all shape. Farther on stands the dining hall, surrounded by well-kept flower beds. It is an outstanding modern building, whose size is relieved by its light lines. As you will discover, its interior does not belie its façade. It radiates a delicate, unpretentious elegance.

Beyond the dining hall, the settlement is divided into two separate blocks, the veterans' quarters on one side and the young people's on the other. The houses wallow in cool greenery, overshadowed by trees and surrounded by lush lawns pricked out with brightly colored flower beds. The soft sound of rustling pine needles is ever present. The tall granary to the south and the tall recreation hall to the north break the uniform lowness and add a dimension of height to the settlement. Perhaps they can compensate to some extent for the missing church spire that, whether you admit it or not, is an integral feature of your picture of the typical village.

To the east, at the farthest corner from your vantage point, is a collection of huts. This serves as a temporary home for training courses, work camps, and army units, anyone who comes to share our burden for a limited span of time. The huts bestow a pioneering character on the whole picture, the air of a border settlement ready to turn a resolute face to impending disasters. So does the sloping fence that surrounds the kibbutz on all sides. Let us pause here for a moment to evoke your admiration.

Now let us look toward the fields of crops all round the kibbutz. A heart-warming sight. Fields of bright green fodder, dark orchards, cornfields echoing the sunshine with a blaze of gold, banana plantations with a tropical air of overpowering vitality, vineyards spreading right up to the rocky heights, the vines not sprawling untidily but neatly arranged on trellises. The vineyard, delightfully, makes a slight inroad into the mountain terrain, which is indicated by the gentle curve of the ends of the rows. We shall refrain from reciting yet another of the poems of Reuven Harish, but we cannot conceal our modest pride at the marked contrast between the cultivated plain and the grim heights, between the blooming valley and the menacing mountain range, between the confident optimism below and the unruly glowering presence above.

Take your last photographs, please. Time is short. Now let us get back in the car and complete the final stretch of the journey, through the green fields.

—Ah, the Jordan river?

—We have already crossed it. Yes. That flat little bridge. In this place and in this time of year the river is very meager. You can dip your feet in it when we come back, after the guided tour of the kibbutz. We are turning into the last bend. We are passing through the gate. In a minute you will be able to cool your tired souls with refreshing cold water. Indeed, the air—as usual in these parts—is very humid and hot. Let us comfort ourselves with the warm welcome, which the kibbutz people are famous for. Welcome, ladies and gentlemen, welcome.[24]

Oz has created here a geo-literary map that has two speaker-guides and two groups of addressees. The speaker-guides are the author and Reuven Harish, a member of kibbutz Metsudat Ram and the kibbutz's "official poet," who also serves as a tourist guide—a fact that, not coincidentally, is only revealed to us, and I shall return to this issue later, in the beginning of the second chapter. The addressees are a group of tourists—probably (based on the guide's remarks and comments) urbanite Israelis—and us, the story's readers.

"Take Your Last Photographs, Please"

On the topmost topographic layer (the upper map) we are presented, in an impressive poetical effort, with "a charming, well-organized village," which is ostensibly the ultimate realization of the pioneering socialist Zionist vision; a wonderfully functional habitat, presented here as a triumphant, up-to-date response to the old existential models. But in actuality, behind this "striking colored picture-postcard scene," behind the photograph's "positive"—which is presented to us in an obsessive, and there suspicious manner (for example, we the readers are asked to "engrave" this colored picture-postcard "on our memory"—what a chilling expression—while the guide instructs the tourists where exactly to use their cameras)—hide its "negatives": here the picture-postcard is perceived as lifeless and dull, whereas the old and opposing existential models are the ones that capture the heart and the imagination.

The reversal of the status of the reciprocal relations between "the cultivated plain and the grim heights" on the one hand, and the "new village" and the "old village" on the other, is effected in the novel's exposition through a large and diverse group of rhetorical devices, all directed toward one central goal: undermining the dichotomous-hierarchical mechanism on which the novel's topmost topographic layer (the upper map) relies.

"The Menacing Mountain Heights"

The fundamental dichotomy on which the story's stated ideological map is based—"the cultivated plain," the Israeli kibbutz habitat, versus "the menacing mountain heights," the dark and hostile Arab habitat—is created by the author of *Elsewhere, Perhaps* through clusters of parallelisms and contrasting parallelisms.[25] Most of these structural-semantic units are pre-defined as such; that is, rather than letting us create a landscape picture of our own, the narrator repeatedly guides us to organize the space in symmetrical configurations that both generate the fundamental dichotomy on which the story's stated ideological map is based and are generated by it.[26] Moreover, from time to time, after constructing a few descriptive units for us, the narrator checks back to make sure that we have indeed taken in the map "properly."[27]

Some of the clusters of parallelisms are organized in syntactic chains. The others are organized in anaphoric concatenations (a series of sentences that start with the same grammatical particles). These analogical configurations create several thematic foci. One of the prominent ones is the seemingly natural-essential "striking contrast": masculine versus feminine.

The upper topographic layer offers two ethno-national spatial styles. The Arab-Syrian territory is presented as feminine. It is all "grim natural chaos" dipped in "melancholy shadow play" and so on. The Israeli kibbutz territory has a "masculine" style. It was planned and designed in a style that is geometrical ("The straight lines, the clean shapes, the neatly ruled concrete paths and rectangular lawns"; "neat, geometrical patchwork of fields"), "vigorous," and phallic ("it is straight as an arrow in flight"), and it expresses the "vigorous view of the world" and "spirit of optimism" of its founders.

But the "gender relations" between the kibbutz and the mountain are not unequivocal. Although the kibbutz breaks through its natural borders ("geology") in a clear stereotypical masculine manner—it "overflows the limits of the valley and spreads up the lower slopes toward the barren heights"—this vigorous penetration into the ravines, described as having "shadows spill gradually down the[ir] folds," ends with a feminine touch. The ends of the rows of the infiltrating vines, those already located on the mountain slopes and supposed to express the confident masculine Israeli might ("geopolitics"), reveal a "delightfully . . . gentle curve." This gentle, feminine curve coincides with the symbolic, universal elements of geology; that is, with the fact that the Israelis reside down in the valley, a "feminine" place, whereas the feminine, ostensibly weaker Arabs, reside high on the mountain, a "masculine" place. There is therefore a contradiction between the narrator's pretentious declarations and what turns out to be the case on the ground, a contradiction that conceals an ironic attitude toward the masculine Israeli pretension. It is a position that demonstrates confidence and pride, yet it is nonetheless feeble, weak, and shaky. An ironic wink relating to this supposedly super-masculine position is included in the name Oz has chosen for the kibbutz in the valley—"Metsudat Ram," a name based on a tautological denotation of strength and vigor.

The Israeli phallic infiltration (invading the territory of the neighboring country) also conflicts with the end of the sentence, in which the narrator asserts that "this color scheme [the bright red of the kibbutz's tiled roofs] contrasts sharply with that of the mountain range, which completely blocks the view to the east, and at the foot of which the kibbutz lies spread" (*Elsewhere, Perhaps*, 3). Furthermore, Oz created an equivalent to the Israeli "penetration" into the Arab territory on the geopolitical plane in the shape of the Arab "penetration" into the Israeli territory on the geological plane. The only place from which the kibbutz can be looked down at from above is a small hill about which the narrator-guide tells our tourists that it is "a pleasant small hill," "a green and cultivated hill." He also takes pains to warn us—as is his wont when he wishes to direct us toward the important map, the one underneath the official upper map–that it "is not to be seen as a finger of the mountains thrust violently into the heart of the valley and lopped off, since it has nothing in common with the menacing mountain heights."

The unclear sexual identities of the kibbutz and of the mountainous area across the border, and their reciprocal penetrative relations, as they are perceived by the kibbutz's tourist guide, point to the Israelis' profoundly ambivalent attitude toward the "elsewhere," the Arab, "foreign" space. This is an attitude that mixes strong attraction, repulsion, fear, belligerence, and blatant imperiousness, and a latent longing to be conquered.

The Missing Church Spire

A similar psychic position emerges from a close examination of the reciprocal relations between the kibbutz, the "new village" in the style of Herzl, and the "old" European village, as they are portrayed in the passage under discussion.

Here too, according to the narrator's insistent assertions, there is a clear and precise pattern: "the striking contrast between our village and the typical village." The narrator tries to establish the validity of this striking contrast—as he did in relation to the "the marked contrast between the cultivated plain and the grim heights"—through an abundance (a suspicious excess) of linguistic patterns that create different kinds of symmetrical and contrasting semantic configurations.[28]

Through this (overly) dense rhetoric tapestry, however, can be seen some subversive descriptive and interpretative units that hint at an extremely ambivalent position in which the mind and the ideology tend in one direction, and the heart and the imagination in another. The mind and the ideology tend toward the "here," the labor-settlement movement in Eretz Israel, the kibbutz. But the heart and the imagination tend toward the "there," that "elsewhere," the villages, towns, and forests of Europe; that "elsewhere" that is as entrancing as it is hostile and dangerous.

This ambivalent position in relation to the "old village" is also reflected in the collapse of the distinction that the narrator has tried with great effort to establish between the official position of the kibbutz members, which absolutely rejects the European village (a position that the narrator, as the kibbutz's "minister of foreign affairs," should faithfully reflect) and the assumed position of the urbanite tourists he is guiding; or more precisely—since none of the tourists express their position in relation to the landscape, apart from a question about the Jordan river that the narrator, referring to it and what it stands for (the old touristic map of Eretz Israel[29]) greets with obvious scorn—between the official kibbutz position and his own subversive position, which he "projects" onto the tourists.[30] In two places the narrator makes an explicit distinction between the attitude of his addressees to the European village and his own attitude, as the kibbutz's representative, to that traditional way of life. First he asserts that the "typical village" "arouses nostalgic feelings in the hearts of city dwellers," whereas the kibbutz members, including him, prefer their village to be "built in the spirit of optimism." Later he claims that the "spirit of optimism" does not mean "that our village is stark and lacking in charm and beauty." "Anyone who draws the shallow inference," the narrator adds, "merely reveals his own prejudice. The object of the kibbutz is not to satisfy the sentimental expectations of town dwellers."

Like the "old" Arab village, then, the "old" European village is rejected sharply and decisively. But in this context too, it turns out that the declarations do not necessarily correspond to the emotions. This is suggested, among other things, by the narrator's strange reference to two buildings that deviate, seemingly surprisingly, from the unified geometric pattern of the kibbutz's structures. I am referring to the narrator's ambiguous attitude toward the granary and the recreation hall, two buildings that "quote" elements from the old European village: "The tall granary to the south and the tall recreation hall to the north break the uniform lowness and add a dimension of height to the settlement. Perhaps they can compensate to some extent for the missing church spire that, whether you admit it or not, is an integral feature of your picture of the typical village."

Our narrator strongly feels the lack of the church spire, as is suggested by the word "compensate." But as the official representative of the kibbutz, he cannot allow himself to admit his longing for the other place, and therefore he projects this longing onto the official tourist guide of the kibbutz, who in turn projects it on his silent addressees. The narrator's hostility to the official upper map of the kibbutz—that is, to its stated ideology—is also well reflected in the nature of the reciprocal relations he creates between its social characteristics (which correspond to the modern, socialist, optimistic, future-oriented ideology) and its communal characteristics (oriented toward the past, laden with history, anchored in tradition; the tribal, familial, class characteristics).

The narrator repeatedly emphasizes the kibbutz's status as a society, both by positively depicting the social characteristics of the "new village," and by negatively depicting the communal characteristics of the "old village." Here is an example:

> Our village is built in a spirit of optimism.
> The dwellings are absolutely identical, as is demanded by the ideological outlook of the kibbutz, an outlook that has no parallel in any village in the world. The well-known lines of Reuven Harish convey the essence of the idea:
>> In the face of a foul world bent on doom,
>> And the lascivious dance of death,
>> In the face of sordid frenzy,
>> In the face of drunken madness,
>> We will kindle a flame with our blood.
>
> Here there is no agglomeration of buildings clustering or ramifying haphazardly down the ages, nor blocks of dwellings enclosing secret courtyards, for the kibbutz does not have family homes. There is no question of separate quarters for different crafts; the poor are not relegated to the outskirts nor is the center reserved for the wealthy. The straight lines, the clean shapes, the neatly ruled con-

crete paths and rectangular lawns are the product of a vigorous view of the world. That was what we meant when we stated that our village was built in a spirit of optimism. (*Elsewhere, Perhaps*, 5)

This passage could have served as a manifesto for the modernist international style in architecture—in its socialist-pioneering version. Opening and ending it with "in a spirit of optimism" creates a logical descriptive framework for the ostensibly clear and unequivocal pattern that contrasts the landscape of the kibbutz on the one hand with the landscape of the old village on the other. But this syntactical, logical, and ideological framework is full of cracks and breaches.

Thus, for example, the narrator repeatedly emphasizes that the topography of the village is a product of a rationalist-optimistic worldview. However, that "flame" that the kibbutz members kindle to light up the darkness that reigns in the world (a Haskalah-promethean image) is not created with thought, logic, and an intensive study of the world—the ultimate "work tools" of the enlightened person (such as David in *Altneuland*)—but rather "with our blood," the "work tool" of the nationalist-romanticist (such as in Luidor's "Yoash").

Moreover, the narrative of "us against the world" that structures Harish's poem—and which the Hebrew Yishuv embraced, as Nurit Gertz has shown, as a foundational narrative[31]—does not belong in the essentially universalist "toolbox" of the *maskil*.

The narrator's romantic tendency also undermines the "clean shapes," the ruled neatness, the "straight lines," and the "rectangular lawns" in a more indirect way: by exposing the real face of the kibbutz, which presumes to be a society based on equality but which in fact, and to the narrator's hidden joy, has some conspicuous characteristics of a community—that is, of a group of people that displays individualizing and differentiating characteristics. I am referring mainly to the presence of households, social classes, and professional affiliations.

Thus, for example, the narrator's assertion that the topography of the village is completely based on principles of equality—"the poor are not relegated to the outskirts nor is the center reserved for the wealthy"—does not coincide with a certain description of the outskirts of the village: "To the east, at the farthest corner from your vantage point, is a collection of huts. This serves as a temporary home for training courses, work camps, and army units, anyone who comes to share our burden for a limited span of time. The huts bestow a pioneering character on the whole picture, the air of a border settlement ready to turn a resolute face to impending disasters. So does the sloping fence that surrounds the kibbutz on all sides. Let us pause here for a moment to evoke your admiration" (*Elsewhere, Perhaps*, 6–7).

Thus it turns out that in the kibbutz some people are more equal than others. Some live in spacious houses, with red-tiled roofs (by the way, and this has already been pointed out, this is a construction element that has functional justification only in places where there is a considerable amount of snow), and some in "a collection of huts" located, just like the huts of the poor in the old village, "at the farthest corner from" the village center. Furthermore, it is precisely the suburban huts, which clearly disrupt the whole pioneering-socialist concept, that in the narrator's view "bestow a pioneering character on the whole picture, the air of a border settlement ready to turn a resolute face to impending disasters. So does the sloping fence" (*Elsewhere, Perhaps*, 7).

In light of this, it is clear that the narrator seeks not only our admiration but also our complicity in an offence that is essentially a betrayal of the kibbutz values and an adoption of contradicting ones. For, if it is the suburb of huts reserved for temporary and changing residents and the sloping fence that "bestow a pioneering character on the whole picture, the air of a border settlement," what exactly do the houses of the permanent residents bestow on it?

In other words, logic and ideology are one thing, and the heart another. Logic and ideology demand the effacement of the "elsewhere" and the unification of the "place" with the "Place" in the vein of Herzl's "new village." But the heart—the heart stubbornly clings to elsewheres, to enchanting and elusive non-places.

It is not surprising, therefore, that Oz chose the loaded phrase "elsewhere, perhaps" [*makom acher*—another place] for the title of his first novel, nor that he chose to preface his book with an epigraph that alludes to "Annabel Lee," Edgar Allan Poe's famous poem: a love poem for a dead woman, who is "in the beyond," "in a kingdom by the sea," which, to say the least, has nothing at all to do with the socialist-pioneering flag flown here up high.

Utopia, Dystopia and Heterotopia

The plot that Oz created in "Nomads and Viper" develops on two axes: on the "collective axis," which describes national-historical conflicts, and on the "private axis," which describes personal and interpersonal conflicts. The collective axis—the axis of the kibbutz residents as a group on the one hand and the Bedouins as a group on the other—is based on the metanarrative of enlightenment in its colonialist version. The private axis—the axis of the representatives of the story's two great ethnic-national camps, led by Geula (the single Jewish poet) and the narrator (the Jewish story writer) on the one hand, and by the Bedouin shepherd on the other—is based on a plot pattern that can be called postcolonial.

The reciprocal relations between the two plot axes in "Nomads and Viper" create a highly charged "force field" because here, more than in *He Walked in the Fields*, the narrator, the author's representative, is torn between his commitment to the collective agenda, which reflects the dominant contemporary worldview, and his private inclinations and longings, which reflect a new, competing worldview. In *He Walked in the Fields* the author manages to find a solution for the conflict between the collective axis and the private axis by means of an enforced harmonistic plot twist—the removal of Uri Cahana from the story's stage in favor of the new immigrants. In "Nomads and Viper" the conflict between the plot axes is never resolved.

Chapters 1–4 in "Nomads and Viper" outline the relations between two population groups that from the narrator's official point of view, as I have already shown, maintain clear (though not solid) dichotomous-hierarchical relations. On the one hand, the kibbutz, an established, technological, modern community of house dwellers, is closed and self-enclosed. On the other hand, the Bedouins, a poor, technologically backward nomadic tribe, move freely in the landscape.

The Bedouins are perceived, according to this dichotomous-hierarchical division, as primitive "natives" that should be educated—either "politely and respectfully" (*WJH*, 25), that is, in Etkin's patronizing way ("Eventually the elder of the tribe was brought to the kibbutz office, flanked by a pair of inscrutable nomads. The short-tempered policemen pushed them forward with repeated cries of 'yallah, yallah'"), or in the bullying way of Rami and his friends ("making an excursion one night to teach the savages a lesson in a language they would really understand" [26]). The Israelis-kibbutzniks are perceived, following the same colonial logic, as enlightened grownups who have a missionary role to "cultivate" the community of "natives"; that is, to enforce the Israeli decorum on them.

Chapter 5 is dedicated in its entirety to the description of one meeting between two human beings. Not a group against a group, as in chapters 1–4, but one woman, Geula, and one man, the Bedouin shepherd. This meeting, which, as already mentioned, is a key chapter in the entangled chronicles of human engineering and landscape conceptualization in modern Hebrew literature, requires a meticulous examination—a close reading of the text. Here it is in its entirety:

> The orchards were heavily laden and fragrant. The branches intertwined, converging above the rows of trunks to form a shadowy dome. Underfoot the irrigated soil retained a hidden dampness. Shadows upon shadows at the foot of

those snarled trunks. Geula picked a plum, sniffed and crushed it. Sticky juice dripped from it. The sight made her feel dizzy. And the smell. She crushed a second plum. She picked another and rubbed it on her cheek till she was spattered with juice. Then, on her knees, she picked up a dry stick and scratched shapes in the dust. Aimless lines and curves. Sharp angles. Domes. A distant bleating invaded the orchard. Dimly she became aware of a sound of bells. She was far away. The nomad stopped behind Geula's back, as silent as a phantom. He dug at the dust with his big toe, and his shadow fell in front of him.

But the girl was blinded by a flood of sounds. She saw and heard nothing. For a long time she continued to kneel on the ground and draw shapes in the dust with her twig. The nomad waited patiently in total silence. From time to time he closed his good eye and stared ahead of him with the other, the blind one. Finally he reached out and bestowed a long caress on the air. His obedient shadow moved in the dust. Geula stared, leapt to her feet, and leaned against the nearest tree, letting out a low sound. The nomad let his shoulders drop and put on a faint smile. Geula raised her arm and stabbed the air with her twig. The nomad continued to smile. His gaze dropped to her bare feet. His voice was hushed, and the Hebrew he spoke exuded a rare gentleness:

"What time is it?"

Geula inhaled to her lungs' full capacity. Her features grew sharp, her glance cold. Clearly and dryly she replied:

"It is half past six. Precisely."

The Arab broadened his smile and bowed slightly, as if to acknowledge a great kindness.

"Thank you very much, miss."

His bare toe had dug deep into the damp soil, and the clods of earth crawled at his feet as if there were a startled mole burrowing underneath them.

Geula fastened the top button of her blouse. There were large perspiration stains on her shirt, drawing attention to her armpits. She could smell the sweat on her body, and her nostrils widened. The nomad closed his blind eye and looked up. His good eye blinked. His skin was very dark; it was alive and warm. Creases were etched in his cheeks. He was unlike any man Geula had ever known, and his smell and color and breathing were also strange. His nose was long and narrow, and a shadow of a mustache showed beneath it. His cheeks seemed to be sunk into his mouth cavity. His lips were thin and fine, much finer than her own. But the chin was strong, almost expressing contempt or rebellion.

The man was repulsively handsome, Geula decided to herself.

Unconsciously she responded with a mocking half-smile to the nomad's persistent grin. The Bedouin drew two crumpled cigarettes from a hidden pocket in his belt, laid them on his dark, outstretched palm, and held them out to her as though proffering crumbs to a sparrow. Geula dropped her smile, nodded twice, and accepted one. She ran the cigarette through her fingers, slowly, dreamily, ironing out the creases, straightening it, and only then did she put it to her lips. Quick as lightening, before she realized the purpose of the man's sudden movement, a tiny flame was dancing in front of her. Geula shielded the lighter with her hand even though there was no breeze in the orchard, sucked in the flame, closed her eyes. The nomad lit his own cigarette and bowed politely.

"Thank you very much," he said in his velvety voice.

"Thanks," Geula replied. "Thank you."

"You from the kibbutz?"

Geula nodded.

"Goo-d." An elongated syllable escaped from between his gleaming teeth. "That's goo-d."

The girl eyed his desert robe.

"Aren't you hot in that thing?"

The man gave an embarrassed, guilty smile, as if he had been caught red-handed. He took a slight step backward.

"Heaven forbid, it's not hot. Really not. Why? There's air, there's water . . ." And he fell silent.

The treetops were already growing darker. A first jackal sniffed the oncoming night and let out a tired howl. The orchard filled with a scurry of small, busy feet. All of a sudden Geula became aware of the throngs of black goats intruding in search of their master. They swirled silently in and out of the fruit trees. Geula pursed her lips and let out a short whistle of surprise.

"What are you doing here, anyway? Stealing?"

The nomad cowered as though a stone had been thrown at him. His hand beat a hollow tattoo on his chest.

"No, not stealing, heaven forbid, really not." He added a lengthy oath in his own language and resumed his silent smile. His blind eye winked nervously. Meanwhile an emaciated goat darted forward and rubbed against his leg. He kicked it away and continued to swear with passion:

"Not steal, truly, by Allah not steal. Forbidden to steal."

"Forbidden in the Bible," Geula replied with a dry, cruel smile. "Forbidden to steal, forbidden to kill, forbidden to covet, and forbidden to commit adultery. The righteous are above suspicion."

The Arab cowered before the onslaught of words and looked down at the ground. Shamefaced. Guilty. His foot continued to kick restlessly at the loose earth. He was trying to ingratiate himself. His blind eye narrowed. Geula was momentarily alarmed: surely it was a wink. The smile left his lips. He spoke in a soft, drawn-out whisper, as though uttering a prayer.

"Beautiful girl, truly very beautiful girl. Me, I got no girl yet. Me still young. No girl yet. Yaaa," he concluded with a guttural yell directed at an impudent goat that had rested its forelegs against a tree trunk and was munching hungrily at the foliage. The animal cast a pensive, skeptical glance at its master, shook its beard, and solemnly resumed its munching.

Without warning, and with amazing agility, the shepherd leapt through the air and seized the beast by the hindquarters, lifted it above his head, let out a terrifying, savage screech, and flung it ruthlessly to the ground. Then he spat and turned to the girl.

"Beast," he apologized. "Beast. What to do. No brains. No manners."

The girl let go of the tree trunk against which she had been resting and leaned toward the nomad. A sweet shudder ran down her back. Her voice was still firm and cool.

"Another cigarette?" she asked. "Have you got another cigarette?"

The Bedouin replied with a look of anguish, almost of despair. He apologized. He explained at length that he had no more cigarettes, not even one, not even a little one. No more. All gone. What a pity. He would gladly, very gladly, have given her one. None left. All gone.

The beaten goat was getting shakily to its feet. Treading circumspectly, it returned to the tree trunk, disingenuously observing its master out of the corner of its eye. The shepherd watched it without moving. The goat reached up, rested its front hoofs on the tree, and calmly continued munching. The Arab picked up a heavy stone and swung his arm wildly. Geula seized his arm and restrained him.

"Leave it. Why. Let it be. It doesn't understand. It's only a beast. No brains. No manners."

The nomad obeyed. In total submission he let the stone drop. Then Geula let go of his arm. Once again the man drew the lighter out of his belt. With thin, pensive fingers he toyed with it. He accidentally lit a small flame, and hastily blew at it. The flame widened slightly, slanted, and died. Nearby a jackal broke into a loud, piercing wail. The rest of the goats, meanwhile, had followed the example of the first and were absorbed in rapid, almost angry munching.

A vague wail came from the nomad encampment away to the south, the dim drum beating time to its languorous call. The dusky men were sitting around their campfires, sending skyward their single-noted song. The night took up the strain and answered with dismal cricket-chirp. Last glimmers of light were dying away in the far west. The orchard stood in darkness. Sounds gathered all around, the wind's whispering, the goats' sniffing, the rustle of ravished leaves. Geula pursed her lips and whistled an old tune. The nomad listened to her with rapt attention, his head cocked to one side in surprise, his mouth hanging slightly open. She glanced at her watch. The hands winked back at her with a malign, phosphorescent glint, but said nothing. Night.

The Arab turned his back on Geula, dropped to his knees, touched his forehead on the ground, and began murmuring fervently.

"You've got no girl yet," Geula broke into his prayer. "You're still too young." Her voice was loud and strange. Her hands were on her hips, her breathing still even. The man stopped praying, turned his dark face toward her, and muttered a phrase in Arabic. He was still crouched on all fours, but his pose suggested a certain suppressed joy.

"You're still young," Geula repeated, "very young. Perhaps twenty. Perhaps thirty. Young. No girl for you. Too young."

The man replied with a very long and solemn remark in his own language. She laughed nervously, her hands embracing her hips.

"What's the matter with you?" she inquired, laughing still. "Why are you talking to me in Arabic all of a sudden? What do you think I am? What do you want here, anyway?"

Again the nomad replied in his own language. Now a note of terror filled his voice. With soft, silent steps he recoiled and withdrew as though from a dying creature. She was breathing heavily now, panting, trembling. A single wild syllable escaped from the shepherd's mouth: a sign between him and his goats. The goats responded and thronged around him, their feet pattering on the carpet of dead leaves like cloth ripping. The crickets fell silent. The goats huddled in the dark, a terrified, quivering mass, and disappeared into the darkness, the shepherd vanishing in their midst.

Afterwards, alone and trembling, she watched an airplane passing in the dark sky above the treetops, rumbling dully, its lights blinking alternately with a rhythm as precise as that of the drums: red, green, red, green, red. The night covered over the traces. There was a smell of bonfires on the air and a smell of dust borne on the breeze. Only a slight breeze among the fruit trees. Then panic struck her and her blood froze. Her mouth opened to scream but she did not scream, she started to run and she ran barefoot with all her strength for home and stumbled and rose and ran as though pursued, but only the sawing of the crickets chased after her. (30–34)

The plots in the previous texts I have discussed were all written in the spirit of the metanarrative of redemption. Their stories reconstruct the traditional plots of nation founding (the Exodus from Egypt, Isaiah's vision of the End of Times, the vision of the Dry Bones, etc.). The main protagonists and the entire community take the painful path that leads to redemption, with all its necessary stations, including the central liminal station (remember, for example, the Cook Islands, where Friedrich and Kingscourt spend twenty whole years in order to rid themselves of the characteristics of the ultimate liminal space, according to Herzl—the Diaspora, the Elend), and the last station, always celebrated in public, in a large crowd or in a small representative group.

Although, as we have seen, in some of the works only the construction of some of the elements follows the format "required" by the metanarrative of redemption—for instance, Amnon and Tamar in *The Love of Zion* and Yoash in "Yoash" do not evolve but are exposed—this "deficiency" is rectified by means of a compensatory system: in *The Love of Zion* the nation as a whole goes through a prominent "melting pot" stage (the stage of returning to the proper order—the "cleansing" that takes place in Jerusalem during Nebuchadnezzar's siege), and in "Yoash" the "historical" David replaces the "mythical" Yoash.

In the formative fiction of the State Generation, two dramatic chronotopic changes take place. The first change is the replacement of the inventory of biblical metanarratives that the authors rewrite in order to actualize their worldview. Biblical metanarratives concerned with the birth phase or the end of times phase of the people of Israel are replaced by metanarratives concerned with the birth phase of humanity as a whole.

The second chronotopic change—which is generated from and generates the former—has to do with the kind of teleology that justifies the act itself of rewriting the biblical metanarratives. All the texts I have discussed up till now were written in the spirit of the "metanarrative of redemption"; that is, from a departure point that assumes that the present (personal and national) situation is intolerable, and that the way to improve it is to embrace, in a new way, a (national) metanarrative—an existential ideological endeavor (which requires, as we have seen, some intensive emotional and intellectual training) whose expected end is the realization of a biblical metanarrative, centered on the birth phase of the people of Israel or the end of times phase it is destined for, and that, of course, in the spirit of the writer's unique vision.

By contrast, the early texts written by Oz and his fellow New Wave writers—and "Nomads and Viper" is to my mind emblematic of this phenomenon—were written in the spirit of a different metanarrative, which contrasts with the redemption narrative. I shall call this metanarrative, following Batya Shimoni in her study "The Transit Camp Story," the "threshold narrative."[32]

The threshold narrative is fundamentally anti-teleological. It is founded on a denial of the assumption of the possible existence of a future redemption (personal, social, national, and so on). The realization of the end of times vision in the texts based on the metanarrative of redemption—a realization that "naturally" takes place first and foremost on the diachronic axis (the temporal axis) of the depicted world—is replaced in the texts based on the threshold narrative by a "situation report," or, in other words, a lateral staging of a given state of affairs, carried out, again, "naturally," first and foremost on the synchronic axis (the spatial axis).

The concept of threshold narrative is relevant in various literary and cultural contexts. In terms of our topic here—the dramatic chronotopic shift in Oz's formative literature (including, and as mentioned earlier especially, in the story "Nomads and Viper")—the discussion of this concept is particularly relevant in the context of the literature and criticism referred to as postcolonial.

By the threshold plot or the threshold narrative in the postcolonial context, I am referring here to a complex cultural and cognitive situation that characterizes the encounter between the rulers and the ruled in the "colonial scene." This situation takes shape and develops in a space that Homi Bhabha has called the "third space";[33] a space that—in contrast to the Western-national melting-pot space (Israel, the United States, etc.) or the colonial space—sees the creation of a dialogue and a real mutual influence among all the participants in the colonial scene; that is, among those perceived (by everybody) as privileged and those perceived as inferior.

Through his third space, Bhabha sought, in fact, to override Edward Said's famous dichotomous presentation (the "Orient" [the "East" as the West created it] versus the "Occident" [the "West" as it is perceived by itself and by the "Orientals," following the creation of the dichotomy that distinguishes it from the "Orient"][34]), which is actually based on an internalization of the essentialist (natural) existence of the hierarchy between the "West" and the "East."

Key concepts in postcolonial works—which are written, as mentioned earlier, in the spirit of the threshold narrative, are erased or create an existential landscape in the vein of Bhabha's third space—are "hybrid culture" (a crossbreed, a mixture) and "hybrid identity."[35] These concepts replace purist concepts such as "national culture," "Western culture," "tribal identity," "authentic identity"—concepts that represent monolithic/unified ideas that form a goal to be attained and realized in many of the modern Western works written in the spirit of the metanarrative of redemption.

In other words, by works that stage hybrid cultures and hybrid identities I am referring—and here I am borrowing Peter Barry's pointed formulation concerning "hybrid societies"—to works that are characterized by "the celebration and exploration of diversity, hybridity, and difference."[36]

Furthermore, as I have already indicated, a writer's choice to be inspired by the metanarrative of redemption or by the threshold narrative has a crucial effect on the status of the work's temporal units, especially the present and the future. Thus, in works that are inspired by the metanarrative of redemption, the future is dominant, while the present, including the liminal stage, the transformative real, cognitive time-space, is relatively marginal.

A clear example of this in the future-oriented utopian corpus we have been discussing is the management of the temporal economy in *Altneuland*. The novel's narrator devotes little time to the beginning of the events (the entanglement stage) and considerable time to their end (the denouement, the redemption), skipping nonchalantly over the twenty years of the present, the years of the liminal stage (the desert stage). Conversely, in postcolonialist works, inspired by the threshold narrative, the world takes place in the middle, in a multicultural bubble. Here the narrative present—and in our context, the liminal time-space, as it was defined by comparative anthropologists, or the third space, following Bhabha's definition—is dominant, while the narrative past and the narrative future remain marginal.

A European Jacket over a White Desert Robe

The encounter between Geula and the Bedouin takes place in a landscape portrayed in the mold of the biblical Garden of Eden. It is a primordial, primeval space, inviting erotic activity regardless of differences of religion and race. We are presented with a landscape brimming with vitality, the result of a harmonious conversation between the elements of the world: "The orchards were heavily laden and fragrant. The branches intertwined, converging above the rows of trunks to form a shadowy dome. Underfoot the irrigated soil retained a hidden dampness" (*WJH*, 30). This vitality manifests itself in the laden-overflowing fecundity of the garden's fruits, dripping with "sticky juice." This place, in which the elements of the world merge orgiastically, effortlessly offers nourishment for all comers and serves as a natural arena for a masculine-feminine coupling. This is suggested by the relationship between "The intertwined . . . branches" and the soil that preserves "a hidden dampness," and by the formulation "a shadowy dome" (*chuppah*)—which recalls a similar formulation ("under the dome of the dark shed") in the parallel "type scene" in *He Walked in the Fields*.

The link with the Garden of Eden scene is also made in "Nomads and Viper" through the identity of the characters acting in the modern scene. The main characters are a young woman and a young man who, not yet having had a sexual partner, find themselves in a situation of erotic courting. The secondary characters are animals: the goats that eat from the fruit trees as well as, and especially for our discussion, the imaginary animal brought to mind by the movement of the Bedouin's foot in the dust ("His bare toe had dug deep into the damp soil, and the clods of earth crawled at his feet as if there were a startled mole burrowing underneath them")—a toe movement that our consciousness cannot help but associate with the snake that appears in parallel scenes in Genesis. Another character in the modern scene that alludes to the biblical scene is . . . God—more precisely, the God of the Bedouin shepherd ("The Arab turned his back on Geula, dropped to his knees, touched his forehead on the ground, and began murmuring fervently"). By contrast for Geula, as the narrator implies—and I shall return to this fascinating issue—there is no God: "Only a slight breeze among the fruit trees."

We have here, however, and in this Oz's scene differs from all the encounter scenes between couples I have dealt with, a young man and a young woman who seem to have clear colonial characteristics. She is the representative of the conquerors, the strong ones; he is the representative of the conquered, the weak ones. She is the representative of civilization, he the representative of nature. She represents society; he—community. She is the representative of social and cultural progress, he of primitivism and barbarism.

As already mentioned, however, these are only seemingly clear colonial characteristics, for two reasons: first, because the power relations between the entities and essences that Geula and the nomad represent in the story are not based on a one-to-one correspondence; second, and the two are interconnected, this scene is marked, in my view, by Oz's attempt—which was undoubtedly subversive for its time—to explore a postcolonial option, a gender and national hybrid option. Barry proposes to distinguish several stages in the development of postcolonial criticism, which to a large extent parallel the stages in the development of feminist criticism: "In its earliest phase, which is to say before it was known as such, postcolonial criticism took as its main subject matter white representations of colonial countries and criticized these for their limitations and their bias. Thus, critics would discuss the representation of Africa in Joseph Conrad's *Heart of Darkness* (1899), or of India in E. M. Forster's *A Passage to India* (1924), or of Algeria in Albert Camus's *The Outsider* (1942). . . . The second phase of postcolonial criticism involved a turn toward explorations of themselves and their society—by postcolonial writers. At this stage the celebration and exploration of diversity, hybridity, and difference becomes central."[37]

Following Barry's distinction I wish to claim that "Nomads and Viper" is indeed a text that displays some clear colonial traces—of the kind that the critics in the first stage of postcolonial criticism identified and denounced in the works of Conrad, Forster, Ferdinand Céline, Camus, and other European authors who wrote about "Third World" countries. However, "Nomads and Viper" also features a postcolonial or quasi-postcolonial move that should be examined.

Oz's text's twofold identity—that is, the possibility of reading it both as a colonial and a postcolonial text—is especially evident in the story's central scene: the encounter in the orchard between the kibbutznik Geula and the Bedouin shepherd. We have here a seemingly cross-camps scene—a match between Juliet and Romeo in the context of conquerors representing the Occident, and conquered representing the Orient—a basic feature of any colonial text, be it canonical (*A Passage to India*) or popular (Pocahontas). Oz, however, does not leave us with the colonial encounter in its stereotypical incarnation. He depicts the biblical type scene in a colonial vein first and foremost in order to shatter it, a shattering during which there emerges for an instant—but only for an instant—the possible existence of a new kind of Garden of Eden: a Garden of Eden that corresponds to Bhabha's postcolonial third space.

Oz makes this interesting move—which starts with great fanfare and ends with a bitter failure—using a group of literary devices that are all marked by what Barry called "diversity, hybridity, and difference."[38] Such hybrid characteristics are already hinted at in "Nomads and Viper" in the story's first description of an (anonymous) Bedouin ("His garb is a *compromise*: a short, patched European jacket over a white desert robe" [*WJH*, 22, emphasis mine]), and in the description of Geula's "mocking sadness" (28), which as mentioned earlier echoes the "scornful sorrow" (22) that the narrator discerns in the camels' eyes. In chapter 5, which is entirely dedicated to the orchard scene, parallel hybrid characteristics become a dominant descriptive feature.

The meeting between Geula and the nomad takes place in the orchard. This, as always in cross-camps encounter scenes, is a separate and isolated place. A place outside the place, a no-place, which contains characteristic elements of the respective spaces from which come the representatives of the two groups. In Oz this is the place that is between the desert and the settled land, a frontier area permanently steeped in deceptive twilight and featuring, in a muddled order, corresponding elements of a "primitive" community on the one hand, and a modern society on the other. This muddled order is especially evident here on the level of sexual identity.

Although Geula, the young Jewish single woman, has some stereotypically feminine characteristics, she also has quite a few, and maybe more, stereotypically masculine characteristics. On the one hand, when she is alone in the orchard, she behaves like a girl before a first meeting with a suitor. "She picked a plum, sniffed and crushed it," then she crushed a second plum and "rubbed it on her cheek till she was spattered with juice," as if she was putting on some rouge. "Then, on her knees . . . the girl was blinded by a flood of sounds. She saw and heard nothing." And at a later stage, when she notices the nomad standing behind her back, "silent as a phantom," she reacts to him softly, responding in a feminine way to the symbolically sexual dialogue of the cigarette-smoking ritual. She "accepted one. She ran the cigarette through her fingers, slowly, dreamily, ironing out the creases, straightening it, and only then did she put it to her lips," etc. On the other hand, she gives out signals that display some stereotypical characteristics of a masculine sexuality or a castrating feminine sexuality. She "picked up a dry stick and scratched shapes in the dust. . . . Sharp angles." When she first sees the Bedouin, "letting out a low sound . . . [she] raised her arm and stabbed the air with her twig." Then she eyes the Bedouin's desert robe and asks, "Aren't you hot in that thing?" Toward the end of the encounter the teasing sexual tone turns callous, castrating, and accompanied with the corresponding body language: "'You've got no girl yet,' Geula broke into his prayer. 'You're still too young.' Her voice was loud and strange. Her hands were on her hips, her breathing still even. . . . "'You're still young,' Geula repeated, 'very young. Perhaps twenty. Perhaps thirty. Young. No girl for you. Too young.' . . . She laughed nervously, her hands embracing her hips."

The Bedouin also displays a number of feminine characteristics. "His lips were thin and fine, much finer than her own"; "His voice was hushed, and the Hebrew he spoke exuded a rare gentleness." Some of his gestures are gentle—gentler than most of Geula's: "he reached out and bestowed a long caress on the air." He "let his shoulders drop"; "bowed politely"; "bowed slightly, as if to acknowledge a great kindness"; "He took a slight step backward," and so on. Yet the Bedouin is characterized by great strength and an extraordinary physical agility, which he demonstrates in his attitude toward his goats: "Without warning, and with amazing agility, the shepherd leapt through the air and seized the beast by the hindquarters, lifted it above his head, let out a terrifying, savage screech, and flung it ruthlessly to the ground." This physical display is joined by several prominent masculine facial features ("the chin was strong, almost expressing contempt or rebellion"), and a few physical gestures that suggest a tough stance hiding under a seemingly subdued front. For example, during his prayer the Bedouin stands on all fours—a gesture that is also associated in this scene both with the posture of the goats and with the posture that Geula takes in the beginning; two gestures that ostensibly express weakness—"but his pose suggested a certain suppressed joy."

The first part of "Nomads and Vipers'" orchard scene thus features a masculine-feminine negotiation that crosses the gender boundaries between a young woman and a young man. This is a negotiation between Geula—"a short, energetic girl of twenty-nine or so. Although she had not yet found a husband, none ... would deny her good qualities" (27)—and the shepherd, who is "perhaps twenty. Perhaps thirty," who has "got no girl yet," a negotiation that for a few long moments is almost undisturbed by historical-political factors.

These ex-territorial moments create a narrative and ideological bubble. A deliberate and conscious attempt is made here to stop and freeze history for a blink of an eye. The narrative dash toward the realization of the Zionist vision, in one version or another, which characterizes previous texts I have dealt with here, is replaced in "Nomads and Viper"—as in many of the texts by A. B. Yehoshua and Aharon Appelfeld in the formative phase of their careers—by a desperate attempt to stop the movement or its metonymies,[39] and to try to perpetuate the intermediary space, the melting-pot space—before the melting itself.

This desperate attempt to replace the (Zionist) redemption narrative with a (here binational) threshold-narrative is reflected in the abundance of devices on the level of the story's spatial-temporal organization, aimed at determining and fixing the centrality and prominence of the orchard scene, in which and only in which—and more precisely, only in the first part of which—a dialogue takes place on a human-universal basis: a courting encounter between a young woman and a young man in an ex-territorial site:

A) The scene of Geula and the nomad in the orchard takes up the graphic center of the story. The story starts on page 26 (21 in the English translation) and ends on page 42 (38 in the English translation). The scene under discussion extends over pages 34–38 (30–34 in the English translation). B) The story is divided into nine chapters. The orchard scene takes up the middle chapter, chapter 5. C) This is the most detailed and plastic scene in the story, a fact that creates an impression of prominence and centrality. D) This scene is mentioned four times in the story;[40] an unusual repetition, which highlights its centrality and its importance. E) the encounter between Geula and the nomad in the orchard is also perceived as central because it is placed in what is perceived as the estimated middle of the story's timeline; that is, between the first "historical event" (the "romantic affair" between the narrator and Geula, which was "a long time ago" [*WJH*, 28]) and the latest reconstructed "historical events" (Geula lying among the bushes after being bitten by the snake and, simultaneously, the kibbutz's youths "crossing the lawn on their way to the fields and the wadi to even the score with the nomads" [38]).

To this rich array of devices on the level of space and time that focus our attention on the orchard scene we should add the story's structure of focalization. The story begins with a bird's-eye view. We look at the reality-simulating world from above and from a very wide angle, which allows us to see from horizon to horizon—from the dry Negev, with its loess pounded into dust, to the edges of the "settled land," "the fields of golden stubble" (21). Henceforth there is a gradual zooming in, until we are looking at objects from close up in a tracking sequence: the narrator's gaze moves from one figure to the next, lingering on the general external appearance and then on the body, garb, face, and grimaces of Geula and the nomad. At this stage we detect "large perspiration stains on [Geula's] shirt, drawing attention to her armpits... and her nostrils widened," and on the other hand the nomad's blinking "good eye," his skin, which "was very dark; it was alive and warm," "creases... etched in his cheeks," and even "a shadow of a mustache" showing under his nose, which is "long and narrow."

After the close-up, detailed look at the representatives of the two camps meeting in the orchard, there is a reversed movement of focalization: a gradual soaring and zooming out. This passage is focalized through the eyes of the narrator, who finds himself among the group of youths on their way to even the score with the nomads, and from there, from within the sticky, young, masculine human collective, which erases individual consciousness while rapidly moving away and cutting itself off from the heart of the kibbutz, he reports: "Far away in the darkened orchards stood somber, dust-laden cypresses, swaying to and fro with a gentle, religious fervor. She [Geula] felt tired, and that was why she did not come to see us off. But her fingers caressed the dust, and her face was very calm and almost beautiful."

But Only the Sawing of the Crickets

The orchard scene starts with a description of a young woman enjoying a kind of Garden of Eden on her own.[41] At a certain stage her solitary stay in the garden starts overflowing with sexuality: "Geula picked a plum, sniffed and crushed it. Sticky juice dripped from it. The sight made her feel dizzy. And the smell. She crushed a second plum. She picked another and rubbed it on her cheek till she was spattered with juice." It is a masturbatory autoerotic enjoyment, which, as we shall see below, is a central element in Geula's life.

Once the Arab arrives on the scene, things change. First for the better, signaling the realization of the dialogic option; then for the worse, signaling the realization of the catastrophe option. At first the two are engaged in an unconscious courting game, an unconsciousness (as in Genesis) reflected by the couple's blindness ("But the girl was blinded by a flood of sounds," and as if responding, "from time to time he [the nomad] closed his good eye and stared ahead of him with the other, the blind one"). But the moment of grace passes as "quick as lightening," replaced by a tense and violent dialogue characterized by a set of displacements to the animalistic realm (the stereotypical metonymy of the Arab, the "native," the conquered, the "primitive") and to the mechanical realm (the stereotypical metonymy of the Jewish-Israeli Geula, the conqueror who belongs to an advanced civilization).

The most obvious example of the displacement from the interpersonal to the animalistic realm is the quasisexual action—almost a rape—that the Bedouin perpetrates on the goat leaning against one of the fruit trees, just like Geula, and munching hungrily at the foliage: "Without warning, and with amazing agility, the shepherd leapt through the air and seized the beast by the hindquarters, lifted it above his head, let out a terrifying, savage screech, and flung it ruthlessly to the ground." A parallel displacement, this time on the part of Geula in relation to the nomad, takes place when she disrupts the momentary closeness established between them on the basis of (universal) man-woman relations by anchoring it in the political-social-economical context: "What are you doing here, anyway? Stealing?" It is a question/accusation to which the nomad reacts thus: "The nomad cowered as though a stone had been thrown at him." This reaction can be linked to two other events in the text: an event that preceded the meeting with the nomad (Geula throwing a stone and hitting a glass bottle lying among the bushes behind the memorial hall in the kibbutz) and an event that follows it (Geula penetrating, in the story's concluding chapter, into the domain of the viper snake slithering among the glass shards of the smashed bottle), the "penetration" of a woman into the domain of the snake, which represents the Bedouin, the man; a penetration that ends in catastrophe.

The displacements from the interpersonal, sexual realm to the mechanical realm are also effected alternately by the "native," the shepherd, the conqueror-conquered man, and by Geula, the Israeli, the conqueror-conquered woman: first the nomad interrupts the "blind[ing] . . . flood of sounds," the innocence before eating from the tree of knowledge. He asks, "What time is it?" thus shattering the initial a-temporal and a-local nature of the orchard scene. This question shunts Geula from the preconscious track ("She saw and heard nothing") to an alternative, aloof, and alienated one: "Her features grew sharp, her glance cold. Clearly and dryly she replied: 'It is half past six. Precisely.'"

The danger posed by these two alternative forms of behavior—the narcissistic position (Geula's autoerotic actions and the Arab's strange way of communing with his God)[42] and the displacement of the libidinal energy to the animalistic and the mechanical realms—is alluded to by Oz through two rhetorical configurations.

First, this danger is alluded to through a set of sights and sounds comprising two parallel trajectories of signals that will never meet. This, for example, is the interrelation between the rhythms of the Bedouins' drums (representing the "primitive" culture) and the lights of the fighter plane (representing the "modern" culture) which is "blinking alternately with a rhythm as precise as that of the drums: red, green, red, green, red." And second, the danger posed by Geula and the nomad's alternative modes of behavior is alluded to by merging and blurring the mechanical and the living to create some terrifying hybrid entities. Such merging and blurring can be found, for example, in the narrator's description of Geula's watch as it perceived through her consciousness: "She glanced at her watch. The hands winked back at her with a malign, phosphorescent glint, but said nothing. Night."

The impending catastrophe is also alluded to in the end of the orchard scene through the linguistic split/separation—Geula and the nomad's one, universal language, the language of courting between a young man and a young woman, comes undone, and each speaks in his or her own language and to himself—as well as through the split/separation into pairs of (Arab) nationality and nature on the one hand, and (Jewish-Israeli) nationality and civilization on the other. After "the man replied with a very long and solemn remark in his own language," and "again the nomad replied in his own language"—a language that Geula does not understand—he lets out "a single wild syllable." This, it turns out, is "a sign between him and his goats," a sign that both the man and the animals understand perfectly, for "the goats responded." Immediately following that, the animals and the nomad seem to turn into one single entity: "The goats huddled in the dark, a terrified, quivering mass, and disappeared into the darkness, the shepherd vanishing in their midst." And then our gaze is turned to the parallel pairing of Geula and the fighter plane: "Afterwards, alone and trembling, she watched an airplane passing in the dark sky above the treetops, rumbling dully..."

Mimicry on Mimicry

The fact that the dialogue between Geula and the nomad ends with a linguistic breakdown is important for our discussion. No less important is the device that produces this breakdown, since it reconnects us, from another direction, with the issue of colonialism and postcolonialism.

One of the key concepts in postcolonial criticism is "mimicry," a concept developed by Bhabha and studied and expanded on by other scholars:[43] a linguistic cultural product that is generated when the colonized tries to speak in the language and style of the colonizer, a product that always displays a dimension of belittling and ridiculing. Mimicry is the dominant rhetorical mechanism in the conversation between Geula and the nomad. In fact, it is precisely once the mute dance of movements between the two stops, and they start talking to each other, that a ping-pong of mimicries and mockeries is created between them.

First the nomad asks, "What time is it?" Content-wise, it is an innocent question. The "mimicry" mechanism is activated here because of the Bedouin's tone, pointed out by the narrator: "The Hebrew he spoke exuded a rare gentleness." This tone lends the nomad's Hebrew a dimension of intimacy that highlights the alienated, clear, and dry tone of the Jewish Geula. A parallel, more subtle linguistic rhetorical move occurs after the cigarette-lighting ceremony:

"'Thank you very much,' he [the Bedouin] said in his velvety voice.

"'Thanks,' Geula replied. 'Thank you.'"

So far this mimicry consists mainly of the two echoing and mutually characterizing each other. In the following dialogue sequence, built on a series of mutual mimicries, echoing turns into distorting.

Geula begins: "What are you doing here, anyway? Stealing?" The nomad replies, "'No, not stealing, heaven forbid, really not.' [And] add[s] a lengthy oath in his own language and resume[s] his silent smile." Geula breaks the equality that characterizes the postcolonial Garden of Eden by highlighting the existence of property relations between the two: she as the landlady and he as a homeless person, an infiltrator and a potential thief.

The Bedouin rejects Geula's question/accusation with a mocking imitation. The dimension of mockery is created here both by the conspicuous redundancy of negating words—three times within one sentence—and because he uses the expression "heaven forbid," an idiomatic expression that belongs to a high linguistic register not expected from a Bedouin shepherd.

The dimension of mockery intensifies after the Bedouin abandons the Hebrew and starts speaking in Arabic. Finally the Arabic speech (the monological speech), which replaces the (impossible) Hebrew dialogue, is replaced by a facial expression: "[He] resume[s] his silent smile"—the typical reaction of him and the other Bedouins in the story, and remember the Bedouin's "placatory smile" at the beginning of the story (*WJH*, 22)—a reaction that articulates a gap between what seems to be a sign of real closeness, the smile in itself, and the improper, malicious intent ostensibly hiding behind it.

The dimension of mockery in the nomad's reaction to Geula's words also derives, as mentioned earlier, from the redundancy of negating phrases in his words. A similar redundancy, which produces a similar, and therefore doubled and intensified effect, characterizes his next retort, which refers again to the same issue: "Not steal, truly, by Allah not steal. Forbidden to steal."

Geula, it should be remembered, is a poet; she is subtly sensitive to language—she detects the mimicking character of the Bedouin's utterance and answers him in kind: "'Forbidden in the Bible,' Geula replied with a dry, cruel smile. 'Forbidden to steal, forbidden to kill, forbidden to covet, and forbidden to commit adultery. The righteous are above suspicion.'" Here the mockery becomes overt and sarcastic, widening the rift between the two. What started with a careful and gentle mutual courting has become a verbal squabble that includes all the elements of the conflict: political, economic, and religious—he swears by Allah, she "adduces" the Bible.

The verbal repartee between Geula and the nomad—the likes of which appeared in the previous books I have discussed, and in all the versions of the type scene in which the potential mother-of-the-nation and father-of-the-nation meet in the "pleasant place"—includes one more act.

The Bedouin "seized the beast by the hindquarters, lifted it above his head, let out a terrifying, savage screech, and flung it ruthlessly to the ground. Then he spat and turned to the girl: 'Beast,' he apologized. 'Beast. What to do. No brains. No manners.'" And when the goat resumes its bad behavior, he aims to hurl a heavy stone at it, but Geula seizes his arm, restrains him and scolds him in the same mocking mimicking vein: "Leave it. Why. Let it be. It doesn't understand. It's only a beast. No brains. No manners."

From now on until the end of the encounter scene, the mimicking mechanism works in only one direction. Geula continues to mimic, tease, and castrate the Bedouin. He, on the other hand, withdraws into his own language, Arabic, prays to his God, and calmly communicates with the goats.

The neutering doubling also operates in this text as an organizing principle on the level of the characters' body language, or more precisely, in one of the units that deal with this level. I am referring to the physical communication between Geula and the nomad, which takes place after the first unit of speech between them, which, as may be remembered, broke and destroyed the good communication created between them through body language alone in the first moments of their meeting in the orchard.

The courting act between the nomad and Geula takes on a positive charge, as mentioned, when the nomad draws "two crumpled cigarettes from a hidden pocket in his belt, la[ys] them on his dark, outstretched palm," and offers them to Geula, who accepts one. "She ran the cigarette through her fingers, slowly, dreamily, ironing out the creases, straightening it, and . . . put it to her lips." And then, "quick as lightening, before she realized the purpose of the man's sudden movement, a tiny flame was dancing in front of her."

This mini-scene is repeated, yet this time in a neutered version: once the verbal dialogue between the two collapses, Geula tries to renew the nonverbal dialogue. She asks the Bedouin: "Have you got another cigarette?" But her approach is blocked—"The Bedouin replied with a look of anguish, almost of despair. He apologized. He explained at length that he had no more cigarettes, not even one, not even a little one. No more. All gone. What a pity. He would gladly, very gladly, have given her one. None left. All gone." And instead of this indirect, subtle dialogue, the Bedouin resumes his sexual-aggressive "dialogue" with the goat: "The Arab picked up a heavy stone and swung his arm wildly." This, as I have already remarked, is as much a clear alternative dialogue as it is sterile. And the proof is that when Geula stops him, "seize[s] his arm and restrain[s] him," the nomad drops the stone, and immediately "dr[aws] the lighter out of his belt," the same tool with which he previously lit up the cigarette that he offered Geula and that she "ran . . . through her fingers, slowly, dreamily, ironing out the creases, straightening it," and that she "put . . . to her lips. . . . sucked in the flame." Now, in the second enactment of this symbolic sexual act, the nomad holds the lighter and toys with it "[w]ith thin, pensive fingers"—like Geula who scratches shapes in the dust with the dry stick at the start of the scene. And then: "He accidentally lit a small flame, and hastily blew at it. The flame widened slightly, slanted, and died."

The future of the two camps' representatives—as the concluding part of the scene implies—is just as gloomy. As we may remember, the shepherd's appeal to his God is perceived, through the combined focalization of the narrator and of Geula, more as a sign of illness (an epileptic fit) than as a prayer. As for Geula, the representative of the third generation of the people of Israel's redemption on its land, her situation is even graver—at least according to the semantic elements implied in the following figurative expressions, which are used to describe her after the failure of the dialogue with the Bedouin: "The hands winked back at her with a *malign*, phosphorescent glint"; "then panic struck her and *her blood froze*"; "he recoiled and withdrew as though from a dying creature" (34, emphasis mine).

And when the human dialogue is extinguished, when Adam/Romeo and Eve/Juliet fail to make contact, it is the end of the Garden of Eden option, even in its postcolonial version. God's voice is no longer heard in the garden. Nor are appeals to him: "There was a smell of bonfires on the air and a smell of dust borne on the breeze. Only a slight breeze among the fruit trees." And in the garden itself, devastation begins to take place: "The rest of the goats, meanwhile, had followed the example of the first," which was munching hungrily at the fruit trees, "and were absorbed in rapid, almost angry munching." This is a process that returns a cultivated, fertile landscape to a state of desolation and barrenness; a state that cannot but recall the fate of parallel landscapes in other early works by Oz and in the works of other writers of that generation—especially in the first stories of A. B. Yehoshua.[44]

Rape, Madness, and Death

The jarring failure of the option of postcolonial erotic encounter heralds the renewed establishment of the romantic, destructive colonial option, with all its various characteristics.

The mimicking linguistic pattern, which recurs in the dialogue between Geula and the nomad—a dialogue that is blocked almost as soon as it starts—is replaced by an imagined and distorted plot pattern. Geula stands in the kibbutz's communal showers—the place represents in the story the strange and impossible combination between the private-intimate and the general-collective—and rewrites the story of her encounter with the Bedouin shepherd in a strictly orientalist manner:

> What can that Etkin understand about savages. A great socialist. What does he know about Bedouins. A nomad sniffs out weakness from a distance. Give him a kind word, or a smile, and he pounces on you like a wild beast and tries to rape you. It was just as well I ran away from him.
>
> In the showers the drain was clogged and the bench was greasy. Geula put her clean clothes on the stone ledge. I'm not shivering because the water's cold. I'm shivering with disgust. Those black fingers, and how he went straight for my throat. And his teeth. And the goats. Small and skinny like a child, but so strong. It was only by biting and kicking that I managed to escape. Soap my belly and everything, soap it again and again. (*WJH*, 35)

The plot that Geula weaves in the showers—the criminal actions she attributes to the nomad, the "savage," the "native," the "other," the "stranger," which are merely the projections of her own intentions and desires—display, as suggested by Hannah Herzig's concise and clear summary, a mixture that is highly characteristic of colonial literature: "Another tendency of the representation of the non-European in Eurocentric literature is to ascribe to it *the denied aspects of Western culture itself,* in a way that provokes contrasting feelings of both threat and attraction. The non-European is identified with a lack of maturity, primitivism and chaos, as opposed to the maturity, rationality and culture attributed to the Western white man. To protect European selfhood, the non-European was placed on the other side of the barricade, at a safe distance from the threat. This distance was also necessary because of the attraction to the other—seen as exotic, libidinal, uninhibited by rationality and culture: the Westerner attracted to such libidinality comes dangerously close to madness and chaos."[45]

Madness and chaos as diseases transmitted by "contagion" from the Bedouins to the kibbutz are mentioned by the narrator of "Nomads and Viper," as a kind of foreshadowing sign at the end of chapter 1: "The nomads' tents are made up of dark drapes.... Lean, vicious nomad hounds dart out of the camp to challenge the moon all night long. Their barking drives our kibbutz dogs insane. Our finest dog went mad one night, broke into the henhouse, and massacred the young chicks. It was not out of savagery that the watchmen shot him. There was no alternative. Any reasonable man would justify his actions" (*WJH*, 23).

What happens to "our finest dog" "one night," even before the start of the "narrative present," also happens to the story's two central characters, Geula and the narrator, as well as to the kibbutz as a collective. All the above "catch" the "madness" and "chaos" transmitted, allegedly, by the Bedouins as they move from one place to the other, like a kind of tribe of carriers of physical and mental diseases.[46]

The process of Geula's psychic collapse is signified by a web of prefiguring motifs. One of them, which I shall briefly trace here, is the coffee-making motif. First we hear that the Bedouins' elder and his people, brought in for a "conciliatory meeting" at the kibbutz office, were offered "steaming coffee prepared by Geula at Etkin's special request" (*WJH*, 25). Later, in the dense characterization paragraph that the narrator devotes to Geula, the coffee-making takes on the connotation of death. The narrator asserts that one of Geula's "good qualities" is that "no one could rival her in brewing strong coffee—coffee to raise the dead, we called it" (27). This is undoubtedly a hackneyed linguistic expression. But in a second reading of the story, when we already know Geula's fate, this expression becomes revitalized (literalized). Soon after, the narrator hastens to blur and tone down the association between Geula and death. He restores the coffee-making ceremony to its routine social context—"On summer evenings ... Geula would shut herself up in her room and not join us until she had prepared the pot of scalding, strong coffee. It was she, too, who always took pains to ensure that there was no shortage of biscuits" (27–28). The troubling connection between coffee making and death, however, reemerges extensively in the beginning of chapter 6. Here: "She returned to her room and made coffee for all the members of the secretariat, because she remembered her promise to Etkin. Outside the cool of evening had set in, but inside her room the walls were hot and her body was also on fire ... She stood and counted the number of times the coffee boiled—seven successive boilings, as she had learned to do it from her brother Ehud before he was killed in a reprisal raid in the desert. With pursed lips she counted as the black liquid rose and subsided, rose and subsided, bubbling fiercely as it reached its climax" (35).

But Geula never makes it to the meeting, and "no coffee" is served (37)—two events that, had they happened, the narrator guesses, could have maybe prevented the disintegration of the secretariat meeting: "If only Geula had come to the meeting and brought her famous coffee with her, it is possible that tempers might have been soothed. Perhaps, too, her understanding might have achieved some sort of compromise between the conflicting points of view. But the coffee was standing, cold by now, on the table in her room. And Geula herself was lying among the bushes behind the memorial hall, watching the lights of the planes and listening to the sounds of the night. How she longed to make her peace and to forgive. Not to hate him and wish him dead. Perhaps to get up and go to him, to find him among the wadis and forgive him and never come back. Even to sing to him" (38).

Geula's last wish succinctly reflects the desire of the "house dweller"—the Jewish/Israeli/Kibbutznik—for what can be called, following Gilles Deleuze and Felix Guattari, the minor-nomadic existential option as it is portrayed in the consciousness of the representatives of the major culture.[47] This desire—which characterizes many texts that can be classified as both "colonialist" and "postcolonialist," and whose distinctive sign is strange combinations of attraction and repulsion and displays of beauty and ugliness—manifests itself in "Nomads and Viper" in, among other things, Geula's reference to the Bedouin being "repulsively handsome," and in this description's echo in the narrator's pathetic/sarcastic reference, which concludes the story, to the appearance of Geula's face as she lies dying among the bushes: Geula was "tired . . . and her face was very calm and almost beautiful" (*WJH*, 38).

Geula's gradual psychic collapse is described in terms of suffocation, overabundance, bursting, and eruption.[48] The parallel collapse of the narrator, the only (relatively) well-rounded figure in the story apart from Geula, is described in terms of an unbearable tension between contradicting existential and emotional options, cracks in the definition of self-identity, and finally a complete rupture and split of personality, which carries destructive consequences.

The narrator in "Nomads and Viper" is, like the narrator in *Elsewhere, Perhaps*, a "double agent." On the one hand he feels duty bound, as someone who mediates between the fictional world and the readers, to represent the kibbutz and the Israeli society and state. On the other hand he repeatedly indicates, whether intentionally or not, that he, like Geula, is sick of the suffocating collective and its values. Between these voices of the narrator rages a harsh battle, which ends with him losing his identity.

In the beginning of the story the narrator makes a considerable effort to present himself as a reliable narrator. He recounts the events from an "Olympian" viewpoint characteristic of the omniscient narrator, and his report about the flight of the Bedouins northward sounds as if it had originated from an objective narrative entity, which has all the information and controls both the overt and the hidden, and whose narrative and moral authority we therefore tend to accept, while "laundering" a few suspicious descriptions (for example, the description of the Bedouins' movement as an unstoppable liquid mass: "*Dark, sinuous, and wiry*, the desert tribesmen *trickled*"; "a persistent *stream* pressed northward"; and the use of incriminating adjectives to describe the flocks' eating activity—"The dark flocks spread into the fields of golden stubble, tearing and chewing with strong, *vengeful* teeth" [*WJH*, 21; emphases mine]). But then we find out, to our surprise, that the information we have been getting has originated not from an omniscient, unnoticeable, and uninvolved narrator, but from a narrator-protagonist who is deeply involved in the story's plot.

The fact that this is an involved narrator-protagonist is revealed to us with calculated gradualness. First the speaker conceals his existence as a character in the world of events by reporting from an Olympian point of view. Then he uses the general second person ("you passed them on a noisy tractor") and then the first person plural ("How unlike our well-tended sheep were their miserable specimens" [22]), and only in the end of the introduction does he reveal himself by using the first person singular ("and a nameless tremor runs often through their skin") [The original Hebrew has "and what name shall I give the light and frequent tremor that runs through these camels' skin"].

This calculated, manipulative use of the telling technique gives the narrator only a short-term reliability. For once we discover that he is an involved narrator-protagonist, who had tried to pretend, at least at the beginning of our encounter (a critical time in terms of acquiring/bestowing narrative reliability), that he was an omniscient narrator, we become suspicious of his statements, especially of those that relate to the conflict between the rival camps, the kibbutz, and the Bedouins, to one of which the narrator belongs.

A meticulous examination of the narrator's statements, however, reveals a more complex picture: we are dealing here again, as in the opening chapter of the novel *Elsewhere, Perhaps*, with a double agent or a mole of a special kind: his first, "natural" loyalty, is to the members of his community, the kibbutz members, but his heart and his desire lead him—just like they do Geula—to identify with the ultimate "others," the nomads.

The rift between the narrator's natural loyalty to his community and his desire for and identification with the other is reflected in a remarkable chain of internal contradictions that repeatedly riddle his statements. We realize this, for example, when we examine the narrator's remarks regarding the existent/nonexistent link between the Bedouins' presence and "a dimension of poetry" (23), at the beginning of the story's second chapter: "You might imagine that the nomad incursion enriched our heat-prostrated nights with a dimension of poetry. This may have been the case for some of our unattached girls. But we cannot refrain from mentioning a whole string of prosaic, indeed unaesthetic disturbances, such as foot-and-mouth disease, crop damage, and an epidemic of petty thefts."

Here, as in other places in this text and in *Elsewhere, Perhaps*, the narrator not only shows us the world but also explains exactly how we should understand it. First he reports what seems like a fact: the nomad's invasion. Then he explains that there are two ways of interpreting it: a) as a phenomenon that adds a poetic dimension to the hot summer nights of the kibbutz members, and b) as a serious economic, security, and moral problem: foot-and-mouth disease, crop damage, an epidemic of petty thefts, and so on.

Moreover, the narrator hints to the reader that in choosing one of these interpretations, he places himself in one of two clear positions: a) if the reader believes that the nomad's invasion adds a poetic dimension, then he is either wrong or is an unattached girl (like Geula)—that is, as is obvious from the context, a young woman yearning for love and therefore suffering from a defective understanding of reality; or b) if he believes that the nomads' invasion is a problem, then he is right and confirmed not to be an unattached girl—that is, his understanding of reality is sound. All this is ostensibly fine. However at reading these lines the reader is reminded of other statements the narrator has made only a few paragraphs earlier: "And then, their singing in the night. A long-drawn-out, dolorous wail drifts on the night air from sunset until the early hours. The voices penetrate to the gardens and pathways of the kibbutz and charge the nights with an uneasy heaviness. No sooner have you settled down to sleep than a distant drumbeat sets the rhythm of your slumber like the pounding of an obdurate heart. Hot are the nights, and vapor-laden. Stray clouds caress the moon like a train of gentle camels, camels without any bells" (23). That is—and this, we should say, is a typical example of Oz's sophisticated "double-edged narrative" technique—that the narrator himself is either an unattached girl or someone who has a faulty understanding of reality.

Furthermore, it suggests, in a way that leaves no room for doubt, that the narrator, again like Geula, is orientalistically attracted to the world of the Bedouins, an attraction that the author, "Amos Oz," as he indicates to us behind the narrator's back, finds kitschy. This is suggested by the deliberately saccharine formulation included in the passage I have just quoted: "No sooner have you settled down to sleep than a distant drumbeat sets the rhythm of your slumber like the pounding of an obdurate heart. Hot are the nights, and vapor-laden. Stray clouds caress the moon like a train of gentle camels, camels without any bells."

This description's deliberate excess of pathos gives rise to bathos; a situation in which the reader moves away from the object of observation and views it with irony, instead of getting closer to it and identifying with it. The bathos is created here because of the combination of two literary devices: (a) the gap between the basic/banal nature of the action (a person going to sleep) and the overly elevated way of describing this action, and (b) the greasy-gooey mixture of descriptive routines in the style of Song of Songs on the one hand ("No sooner have you settled down to sleep . . .") and in the style of the Eretz-Israeli naive writers and painters on the other.

The narrator's attempt to serve two mutually hostile masters becomes even more complicated when he needs to tell us about Geula and her deeds, which are at the center of the story's plot. Here too, as in the beginning of the story, we find out that the person who is reporting the affair and is supposed to enable us to judge it—and it should be remembered that we are talking about a false rape charge—is up to his neck involved in it; a fact whose relevance the narrator tries to dismiss, or at least blur: "What had passed between Geula and me is not relevant here, and I shall make do with a hint or two. Long ago we used to stroll together to the orchards in the evening and talk. It was a long time ago, and it is a long time since it ended" (28). Also: "On such days Geula likes to walk to the orchards in the early evening. She goes alone and comes back alone. Some of the youngsters come and ask me what she is looking for there, and they have a malicious snicker on their faces. I tell them that I don't know. And I really don't."

Between these two passages there is an analogical proximity that casts a risible light on the narrator and severely dents his reliability as someone who is charged with mediating between us and the fictional world. For, as both the youths who tease the narrator and the readers well realize, there is an acute ironic link between the meetings of the narrator and Geula in the orchards in days gone by—meetings that were marked by the narrator's impotence ("Sometimes I would dare to rest a conciliatory hand on her neck, and wait for her to calm down. But she never relaxed completely. If once or twice she leaned against me, she always blamed her broken sandal or her aching head. And so we drifted apart")—and Geula's frequent, feverish journeys to that no man's land that calls for erotic encounters.

The narrator's attempt to reconcile the contradictory voices battling within him—the official voice of the seemingly sane and balanced community on the one hand, and the subversive voice of the individual in the kibbutz, which reflects the community's hidden desires on the other—reaches a point of crisis in the story's concluding chapter, a crisis that manifests itself in the narrator's mode of telling.

Up to this chapter the narrator has kept an orderly temporal and spatial division between the position of the omniscient narrator and the position of the "witness" narrator/protagonist narrator. Some of the passages have been told by an omniscient narrator or an omniscient-like narrator, and others by a witness narrator. Thus, for example, chapter 5, the story of the encounter between Geula and the Bedouin, is entirely told from the position of the omniscient narrator. Conversely chapter 8, the story of the broken-up secretariat meeting, is told in its entirety from a position of a witness narrator, who starts with the first-person plural and ends with the first-person singular. By contrast in chapter 9, the last chapter in the story, one passage, which forms a considerable part of the chapter, features a strange and jarring hybrid combination of two different narrative positions: "She was very tired. And the pain was vague, almost pleasant. A distant ringing in her ears. To sleep now. Wearily, through the thickening film, she watched the gang of youngsters crossing the lawn on their way to the fields and the wadi to even the score with the nomads. *We were carrying short, thick sticks. Excitement was dilating our pupils. And the blood was drumming in our temples*" (38, emphases mine).

The first section of this passage, displayed here in roman type, is undoubtedly under the authority of an omniscient narrator because it tells us things that only Geula could know (the pleasant pain, the distant ringing, the youngsters seen through the thickening film) and because it includes the phrase "to sleep now," which is very similar, syntactically and semantically/psychologically, to the phrases that Geula used in the narrative past: "must get out" (29), "must go now" (ibid.), "go to the showers" (35), and "now I must get outside" (ibid.). The second section, on the other hand, marked here in italics, which in the original is not distinguished from the preceding linguistic section by any graphic or semantic demarcation, is undoubtedly under the authority of a witness narrator, who reports the events in the first-person plural.

The existence of such conspicuous hybridity between the two narrative positions, which represent distinct and competing prisms, can be explained, it seems to me, in one of the two following ways: a) asserting that the young Oz had not yet mastered the secrets of the narrator's craft, or b) assuming that this conspicuous deviation from the then-dominant norm of managing the ensemble of voices in fiction is deliberate, and aims at "forcing" the reader to try and understand its significance.

In my view, this deviation from the dominant norm of managing the ensemble of voices is deliberate and calculated, and has a twofold aim—to shatter the uniform-conformist chorus of voices that ostensibly dominated the cultural and political field of the 1950s and at the same time to reflect the psychic fracture and the loss of emotional balance suffered at the end of the story by the two young people who had tried in various ways to preserve the balance between the drive, on the one hand, and order and conscience, on the other. One is Geula, who was charged, as already mentioned, with cooling down tempers with her intelligence and with the Arab black coffee she specialized in preparing; and the other is the narrator, who mediates between us and the fictional world and who confesses that "although in age I belonged with the younger men, I did not agree with their proposals. Like Etkin [the kibbutz secretary who represents the 'elders' generation' and the 'old' kibbutz morality and ideology] I was absolutely opposed to answering the nomads with violence" (*WJH*, 37).

Throughout most of the story, then, Geula and the narrator serve as mediators and arbitrators between the two contradictory and extreme positions in the kibbutz: the socialist-Zionist position of the "veterans"—perceived here as sanctimonious or at least anachronistic—and the militant-thuggish position of the youngsters led by Rami. But toward the end of the story, the pair's power to try and connect the extremities fails, and they disintegrate and fall to pieces: the narrator's voice splits in two, and Geula loses touch with reality and gives in to a destructive romantic fantasy.

Between them, Geula and the narrator encompass the central opposing elements of the kibbutz collective in general. Their ability to preserve some kind of balance between these elements reflects the existence of a similar balance in the kibbutz as a whole. The breaking of the balance between the opposing elements in the pair's psyche (she "giving herself" to the snake and he being dragged into a retaliatory action) signifies the breaking of this balance in the kibbutz as a whole and, through it, the breaking of this balance in Israeli society in general.

Back to the Shtetl?

The story, you may remember, opens with a few passages in which the kibbutz people and the Bedouins are presented, the ones against the others, from various points of view: first from an Olympian position in wide-angle, then with a zooming-in motion, in a position of "they" against a general "you," "they" against "us," and finally in an alternating description of the elder of the tribe who "was brought to the kibbutz office" (*WJH*, 25), on the one hand, and the secretariat members led by Etkin, on the other.

The direction of movement in this opening unit (the first two chapters) is from the Bedouin space (open, hungry, natural, uncultivated) to the kibbutz space (enclosed, well-fed, mechanized, modern), and it is entirely marked by the impression of the Bedouins' invasion.

After this exposition we are told of a few encounters between a man and a woman, or between a woman and a masculine metonymy, based on a pattern of tension and release. I am referring to all those surrogate erotic events that take place on the "narrated time" axis—the story's overall chronological span. These are Geula and the bottle among the bushes behind the kibbutz's memorial hall (first time); Geula and the narrator in the orchard, in times gone by (several times); Geula and the bottle among the bushes behind the kibbutz's memorial hall (second time); and Geula and the nomad in the orchard—the same orchard in which Geula and the narrator used to meet in the past.

The story concludes with two pairs of scenes on the private and collective plane—pairs that are also based on the pattern of surrogate erotic tension and release. The pairing here results from the fact that—as the narrator repeatedly points out—these are units that take place simultaneously. I am referring to the shower scene in which Geula reconstructs/rewrites her meeting with the nomad on the one hand, and the secretariat meeting that relates to this fantasy on the other; and to the scene that intersects Geula's fatal encounter with the snake among the bushes on the one hand, and the violent encounter/invasion that is about to take place between the Jews and the Bedouins on the other—this time moving from the kibbutz toward the Bedouin space.

The question that emerges from this chain of encounter units is, of course, what is the nature of the link between the story's opening unit—the one dealing with the movement of the Bedouins toward the kibbutz—and its ending unit—the one describing a group of Jewish Israeli youths making their way "to even the score with the nomads" (38). Is it a link of action (cause) and retaliation (effect), a link that gives the sequence of events the logic of natural law? Or is it an offensive hostile action by one side (the Bedouins), which generates a defensive hostile action ("a defensive offensive") by the other side (the kibbutz youngsters), a link that gives the sequence of events both a "natural" logic and a moral justification?

Or perhaps these two movements—imitating, of course, the "border skirmishes" between Israel and its neighbors, which took place in their dozens in the period in which the tale takes place (Benny Morris lists two hundred and twenty-eight such border skirmishes in the years 1949–1956[49])—are connected by a different link?

The answer to this question—on the collective plane of events—remains obscure, as the story does not provide us with any proof that the Bedouins had indeed invaded the kibbutz. There is no proof of any damage to property ("We had to admit that we had never managed to catch one of the nomads in the act" [23–24]), let alone any injury to person.

How then can the kibbutz youths' decisive "retaliatory action" be explained? The answer to this question can be garnered from a description and an analysis of the ensemble of linkages created by the author in the literary space-time between the encounter units on the private and public planes. As we know, in literary space-time two events cannot be described simultaneously; this is true even when the author wishes to describe events that took place simultaneously in reality or in an imagined reality. In literary space-time the author must always decide which of the events or scenes will be described first.

This decision carries great importance because the reader, based on life experience and reading conventions, tends to think that the later event derives from the earlier event and is its result. The author is aware of this (often mistaken) tendency of the reader and uses it for his own needs. For example, in the story before us, the author uses it to create the impression that a certain action on the collective (social/national) plane stems from an event on the private (personal/psychological) plane. Thus the narrator of "Nomads and Viper" describes the following two series of events to us one after the other, even though they happen simultaneously. The first series of events takes place in Geula's mind on the way to the showers and in the showers. This series of events has, as we remember, two versions. The first version: "What can that Etkin understand about savages. A great socialist. What does he know about Bedouins. A nomad sniffs out weakness from a distance. Give him a kind word, or a smile, and he pounces on you like a wild beast and tries to rape you. It was just as well I ran away from him." And the second version: "I'm not shivering because the water's cold. I'm shivering with disgust. Those black fingers, and how he went straight for my throat. And his teeth. And the goats. Small and skinny like a child, but so strong. It was only by biting and kicking that I managed to escape." This version is followed by the private/intimate reaction ("Soap my belly and everything, soap it again and again"). And immediately after by the transition to the collective plane: Geula's expectation that the "boys" would take revenge on the Bedouins (on all of them rather than the particular Bedouin/"rapist"): "Yes, let the boys go right away tonight to their camp and smash their black bones because of what they did to me" (35).[50] The second series of events takes place in the very same moments in the secretariat room. Etkin holds forth on "the social gospel we had adopted" (37), on the fact that "it was essential to break the vicious circle of hostility" (36), and so on. Rami, the representative of the militant youngsters, repeatedly interrupts him. Etkin takes offense, accuses the younger members "of planning terrorist activities," and the atmosphere becomes heated. At this stage the narrator, who up to that moment has served as the intermediary ("Although in age I belonged with the younger men, I did not agree with their proposals"), decides to present his position and give his reasons for it: "Like Etkin, I was absolutely opposed to answering the nomads with violence—for two reasons . . . In the first place, nothing really serious had happened so far. A little stealing perhaps, but even that was not certain . . . Secondly, there had been no rape or murder." At this, Rami detects the narrator's weakness and asks derisively, "What I was waiting for? Was I perhaps waiting for some small incident of rape that Geula could write poems about and I could make into a short story?" (37).

The fact that the narrator and Rami dismiss the possibility that a female member of the kibbutz could be hurt in the orchards—immediately after Geula experiences rape and then re-experiences it again, if only in her feverish mind—brings an ironic smile to the reader's lips. This smile turns into a grimace of horror, when we learn that the youngsters are leaving the secretariat and going out "to even the score with the nomads" (38). The source of this horror is that the actions perpetrated in the narrated world on the collective interpersonal plane—actions of destruction and maybe even killing—are devoid of justification from a factual standpoint. Worse, they are seen as stemming from caprice and groundless fantasy: a rape that never happened and that even the rumor, or the false report, of which has not reached those embarking on the retaliatory action.

Through this literary manipulation, the story's author leads us to think that the most dramatic action on the story's collective plane (and its presumed equivalents in reality: the various "reprisal raids") is not the result of a rational decision taken by level-headed people in the appropriate institution—the secretariat, the place that serves as a metonymy for the Jewish collective in its most official and authoritative expression—but the fulfillment of a personal wish formulated in a very different place from the secretariat, because Geula, who never arrives at the secretariat meeting with her famous coffee, hallucinates the rape on her way to the communal showers and in the shower itself, a place that symbolizes narcissistic Eros and in which the protagonist supplants the option of dialogue or mature sexual contact with alienated masturbation (the compulsive soaping motion).

The conclusion to which the narrator leads us through the diachronization of these two scenes, which in reality took place simultaneously, is revalidated and acquires further chilling significances when we follow the author's reading instructions concerning the creation of connections between similar and different scenes, close to or far from each other in the narrative sequence.

A central association of this kind is the complex connection the author establishes between the last encounter scene in which Geula takes part—the one in which she meets the snake while lying among the bushes behind the memorial hall—and all the encounter scenes that have preceded it.

Here, first, is Geula's last encounter scene:

> If only Geula had come to the meeting and brought her famous coffee with her, it is possible that tempers might have been soothed. Perhaps, too, her understanding might have achieved some sort of compromise between the conflicting points of view. But the coffee was standing, cold by now, on the table in her room. And Geula herself was lying among the bushes behind the memorial hall, watching the lights of the planes and listening to the sounds of the night. How she longed to make her peace and to forgive. Not to hate him and wish him dead. Perhaps to get up and go to him, to find him among the wadis and forgive him and never come back. Even to sing to him.
>
> The sharp slivers piercing her skin and drawing blood were the fragments of the bottle she had smashed here with a big stone at the beginning of the evening. And the living thing slithering among the slivers of glass among the clods of earth was a snake, perhaps a venomous snake, perhaps a viper. It stuck out a forked tongue, and its triangular head was cold and erect. Its eyes were dark glass. It could never close them, because it had no eyelids. A thorn in her flesh, perhaps a sliver of glass.
>
> She was very tired. And the pain was vague, almost pleasant. A distant ringing in her ears. To sleep now. Wearily, through the thickening film, she watched the gang of youngsters crossing the lawn on their way to the fields and the wadi to even the score with the nomads. We were carrying short, thick sticks. Excitement was dilating our pupils. And the blood was drumming in our temples.
>
> Far away in the darkened orchards stood somber, dust-laden cypresses, swaying to and fro with a gentle, religious fervor. She felt tired, and that was why she did not come to see us off. But her fingers caressed the dust, and her face was very calm and almost beautiful. (38)

This encounter scene relocates to the front of the picture all the elements that were portrayed in the background of the previous encounter scenes. The dramatic shift in the foreground-background relations among these elements marks the climactic moment in a disastrous personal and collective process.

The clearest expression of the move I am delineating here is the change in the identity of the participants in the encounter scenes in the orchard on the one hand and among the bushes behind the memorial hall on the other,[51] and in the way these participants function in the scene. As in the previous encounter scenes, we meet Geula, but the narrator and the nomad, Geula's human partners, and even the bottle and the dry stick, the phallic objects, are replaced by "a snake, perhaps a venomous snake, perhaps a viper" (*WJH*, 38). This snake is a new-old factor in the encounter scenes, on the literary/metaphorical level, on the psychological level, and on the ideological/political level.

On the literary/metaphorical level its existence was hinted at, in various ways, in the preceding encounter scenes. Thus, for example, this "living thing slithering among the slivers" is connected to the nomad's toe, which in the orchard encounter scene "had dug deep into the damp soil, and the clods of earth crawled at his feet as if there were a startled mole burrowing underneath them" (30–31). This "living thing" is also connected to the nomad because of the resemblance between the man (described as an animal) and the snake: the nomad has a blind eye, which he probably can never shut; the snake's "eyes were dark glass. It could never close them, because it had no eyelids."

The snake, which was always there at the back of the stage, now moves to the front and takes the place of the nomad, who has taken the place of the narrator. For, as we remember, the series of encounters between the narrator and Geula ended with naught. Only after the failure of these encounters does Geula return to the orchard, and "she goes alone and comes back alone," circumstances that put "a malicious snicker" on the faces of the kibbutz youngsters of Rami's gang (28), who repeatedly tease the narrator on this sensitive and embarrassing matter.

The double change in the background-foreground relations among Geula's "partners"—the replacement of the a kibbutz member, an impotent Jewish writer, with an Arab, a potent Bedouin shepherd, who Geula manages to chase away, and the replacement of the Bedouin with a snake whose triangular head is "cold and erect," the ultimate male representation of sex and death—this double change in the status of the males with whom Geula meets during the course of the story marks the major junctures in the suicidal path of our heroine and of the nation she represents.

The existence and nature of this suicidal path are indicated by the author through another narratological shift—this time on the plane of the story's order of events. I am referring to the late mention of the relationship between Geula and the narrator. The series of orchard encounters between the two, of which we are told only midway through the story, had taken place long before the sequence narrated from the beginning of the story, dealing with the relations between the two collectives. This conspicuous deviation from chronological order, which the narrator further underlines by a deliberately crude obfuscation, highlights from another direction the narrator's unreliability, which stems from the problematic link between the personal plane and the collective plane in the represented world, as well as, and especially, from the gradual intensification of Geula's series of sexual encounters.

The first encounter, chronologically, is between Geula and the narrator. This is a weak erotic encounter between a woman bursting with sexual energy and an impotent man:

> Sometimes I would dare to rest a conciliatory hand on her neck, and wait for her to calm down. But she never relaxed completely. If once or twice she leaned against me, she always blamed her broken sandal or her aching head. And so we drifted apart....
>
> I always buy her a new book of poems for her birthday. I creep into her room when she is out and leave the book on her table, without any inscription or dedication. Sometimes we happen to sit together in the dining hall. I avoid her glance, so as not to have to face her mocking sadness. (28)

The second encounter between Geula and a man, the encounter with the nomad—which takes place after Geula's two "encounters" with the bottle filled with "the remains of a greasy liquid" (27), which brought no relief (29)—is much more sexual, but also ends with naught. Here the sexual energy that was previously directed to throwing stones at the bottle splits, as I have shown earlier, into displacements onto the animal world (the Bedouin) and the mechanical realm (Geula). In the third encounter, which concludes the story, there are no longer any displacements or sublimations. The impotent Jewish man, with his ridiculous adolescent gestures, and the Arab, who is as gentle and potent as he is brutal (at least toward the goat), are replaced by "the thing itself," the illustration of the pure phallic symbol, the viper snake.

What began then with sandaled walks to the orchard with a member of the same camp and with literary/cultural conversations, becomes a tense and violent encounter with the representative of the "other" camp, the "enemy camp," this time barefooted, and ends with a "thorn in her flesh" and "drawing blood." The representative of the society that has fenced itself in from nature achieves her moment of redemption, which is also the moment of her death, only after shedding her cultural attires.

The third spatial-temporal association relevant to our discussion is created in the story's last scene through another diachronization of simultaneous events. We have seen how the author directs us to think that the dramatic action on the story's collective plane was the result of a false fantasy; the kibbutz youngsters go out to even the score with the nomads ostensibly to fulfill Geula's wish for revenge. However, at the end of the story the author neutralizes even this reasoning.

In the final scene we are told of two other, similar series of events that took place at the same time: one in Geula's mind and one in the reality-simulating world. First we read a new script of the relations between Geula and the nomad: Geula not only wants to make peace and forgive but is also willing to leave her tribe and join the Bedouin; only later does the narrator tell us about the retaliatory action getting under way—and points out that Geula "did not come to see us off" because she "felt tired" (38). This is a blatantly false explanation—because, as we have just read, Geula, in her current emotional state, is opposed to the retaliatory action—which probably responds to another fantasy (that of the boys).

Moreover, at the end of the unit that concludes the story the author presents Geula lying among the bushes and the youths going out to even the score with the nomads almost simultaneously. This is a calculated poetic move, whose structural result is a kind of merging of the two distinct action scenes, and which holds crucial significance. For this merging of Geula and her painful/pleasurable meeting with the snake, on the one hand, and the youths going out to even the score with the nomads while "carrying short, thick sticks. Excitement ... dilating [their] pupils. And the blood ... drumming in [their] temples," on the other, evokes a picture that combines clear elements of homosexuality and incest. The group of youths going out to even the score with the nomads is described as being in the midst of a thrilling sexual experience. At the same time, they are identified both with the Bedouins (the linguistic link between the descriptions of the eyes) and with the snake (the short and thick sticks), which is identified with the nomad. This sticky and disgusting psycho-cultural mess does not, of course, allow for a real outlet. Geula is caught in a kind of total orgiastic dance, an extreme version of the "love death" motif (the romantic Liebestod), and is unable to burst the narcissistic/masturbatory bubble she is trapped in, as is also suggested by the sentence with which the author chooses to conclude the story: "But her fingers caressed the dust, and her face was very calm and almost beautiful." The caressing fingers, it should be remembered, are the same fingers that hold the dry stick in the opening section of the orchard scene, when Geula is in a narcissistic/masturbatory state, and the same fingers that hold the soap in the shower and repeatedly soap her belly, again and again. As for the phrase "her face was very calm," it seems to invite thoughts of death no less than of rest. And although the adjective "beautiful" embodies a kind of promise of some sort of reconciliation between Geula and the world, one cannot ignore the modal word "almost" with which the author precedes it, a word that attenuates it and casts it in a cruel, ironic light.

In other words, after the failure of the "natural" intratribal option, the postcolonial option—existing in a multicultural Garden of Eden—is examined.

This option fails as well, and then the colonial option (which was there the whole time in the plot's background) is examined, only to be revealed as a clear and unequivocal existential recipe for catastrophe for all involved.

Like an Extended Family

The fact that the kibbutz was perceived at the time as a paragon of the "Zionist genetic laboratory" dealing with the creation of a "new community," a "new man" and a "new place," can be learned both from the writings of known kibbutz scholars and from the remarks of Oz himself, who was seen, in his first years as a writer, as one of the leaders of the young generation in the kibbutzim. Both the scholars and the writer repeatedly speak of a "scientific experiment," centered on the attempt to create a new hybrid entity that would harmoniously merge binary oppositions that belong, in F. Tönnies's terms, to the community on the one hand and the society on the other.

In the Second Aliyah period and at the beginning of the Third Aliyah, a monolithic conception of the kibbutz prevailed. Thinkers and writers espoused an approach that asserted that the kibbutz's cohesion should be based on a full commitment of all the kibbutz members to a constitutive social treaty. Such cohesion (solidarity)—as we have seen in the story of the raising of Uri Cahana in Shamir's *He Walked in the Fields*—was supposed to replace the family cohesion, or in the writer Zvi Shatz's famous words: "The family will be resurrected not on the basis of blood relations, but on the basis of spiritual intimacy."[52] Through the years, however, and in light of the changes that took place in the Israeli society, the kibbutz thinkers and the writers describing life in it had become more flexible. The literary and theoretical texts that dealt with the kibbutz in the 1950s began to depict a framework that offered cohesion based on a combination of blood ties and spiritual intimacy. Here is what Oz himself wrote in this context: "[The kibbutz is] a unique attempt, for better or for worse, to reconstruct or revive the extended family—that clan where brothers and nephews, grandmothers and aunts, in-laws, distant relations, relations of relations, all live close together—the loss of which may turn out to be the greatest loss in modern life."[53]

Similar words—this time with an evident tone of sadness over what had been realized or almost realized and had gone wrong—were said by Oz, years later, in an interview with Ari Shavit in *Haaretz*. Oz claimed there that the kibbutz could have been a kind of extended family at the center of modern society, thus offering an answer for some of the malaises characterizing this society—malaises such as alienation and anonymity.[54]

The power of that "modern clan" is that it forms a kind of "extended I." This is what various kibbutz scholars believed,[55] and this is also what Oz believed: "In a kibbutz, when you are hurt the whole community reacts like a single organism. It is hurt with you. When you hurt someone else, the whole kibbutz can feel hurt. Of course, within this intimacy bad characteristics also thrive, whether in disguise or out in the open . . . And yet, they are all part of you and you are part of the kibbutz. Flesh of its flesh. And this is all before we have even begun to talk about values, principles, beliefs."[56]

The interdependence between the individual's and the collective's situation is very apparent in "Nomads and Viper." As mentioned earlier, the retaliatory action of the kibbutz youngsters is perceived, on the level of artistic explanations, as a realization of the hidden desires of Geula who, standing in the communal showers, imagines a rape and "invites" revenge on all the men of the Bedouin tribe. The other aspect of this interdependence is evident in that the individual in the kibbutz always represents, willy-nilly, his "extended family." Geula's urgent need to break through the real and symbolic fences by which the kibbutz has surrounded itself, and her longing to join the "other," the "foreign," the "enemy," are a metonymic expression of the deep need of the entire community. Geula, like the narrator in "Nomads and Viper," and like Reuven Harish, the tourist guide in *Elsewhere, Perhaps*, are at one and the same time figures that represent the entire kibbutz community with all its different aspects, and maybe even the entire Hebrew nation in its modern journey toward redemption, and anomalous marginal figures in the pioneering Zionist "human laboratory."

This violent merging of the expressions of the general/typical and those of the individual/unique (or atypical) in separate characters leads, as Oz shows us, to destructive results. No wonder then that the one-off meeting between Geula and the nomad in the orchard is prefigured by a series of intimate encounters among individuals who represent the camps metonymically. All these encounters are portrayed through "telling," and are perceived, retrospectively, as kinds of preparations/rehearsals for the story's central encounter: the one between Geula and the specific nomad in the orchard, which is portrayed through 'showing.' A very similar analogical configuration, albeit in the opposite direction, structures the important events that take place from the orchard scene between the nomad and Geula, in chapter 5, to the end of the story. The orchard scene (which, as already mentioned, has four echoing reenactments: two by Geula, who spends the time between eight-thirty and nine in the evening at the communal showers, one by Rami and one by the narrator, who at that very time, each in his own way, present the possibility of "some small incident of rape") prefigures the story's last encounters of the same kind. I am referring to the encounters—which have by now become real/fatal—between Geula, who is lying among the bushes behind the memorial hall, and the viper that bites her to death on the one hand, and the anticipated violent encounter between the kibbutz youths and the Bedouins on the other.

The repeated encounters between the representatives of the kibbutz and the representatives of the Bedouins create a centrifuge-like movement. The foundations of the kibbutz community's existence and, analogically, the elements comprising the "I" of the central characters, gradually separate and recede from each other until they disintegrate and then fall apart. A clear example of this phenomenon, on the collective plane of the kibbutz community, is the process of the disintegration and collapse of the communal elements ("blood relation") and the social elements ("spiritual intimacy"), whose delicate balance is a necessary condition for the creation, existence and survival of the entire community.

The social aspects in the kibbutz portrayed in "Nomads and Viper" are represented in a crystallized way by Etkin, the secretary. This Etkin belongs to the generation of the founders, the ideological generation. He is "a socialist," and holds "Tolstoyan ideas and such like" (*WJH*, 24). Etkin wishes to resolve the conflict with the Bedouins peacefully. By contrast Rami, the representative of the youngsters, reflects in a crystallized way the communal/tribal aspects, based, as is suggested by his verbal and physical expressions, on ties of blood, race, and nationality. Rami and his friends have a simple and clear philosophy of existence, "eye for an eye"—or in an updated formulation, "retaliatory actions." Those who strike you must be paid back in kind and preferably with greater force.

In the middle, between these two camps, stand Geula and the narrator; the only characters in the story who, as already mentioned, receive a relatively fully rounded portrayal. Geula and the narrator serve as pressure valves. Both belong by age to the youngsters, but by their views to the founders' generation. Both are charged with the responsibility of calming tempers. Geula (who functions as the kibbutz's "minister of internal affairs," a mother and a girl hungry for love all wrapped in one) does so at the secretariat meetings with her level-headed words and her famous black coffee. The narrator (who is supposed to function as the kibbutz's "spokesman" or "minister of foreign affairs") does so with his reports on the events—supposedly balanced reports, which in truth represent both the official position formulated by the founders' generation and the position of the youngsters, his biological peer group.

Already at the beginning of the story, a precarious equilibrium is maintained between the contradictory forces that operate on the kibbutz as a "single organism." The youngsters repeatedly break the delicate balance of power with violent actions against the Bedouins, while the narrator repeatedly attempts to excuse these actions—attempts that further undermine his already shaky reliability in the readers' eyes: "We are not the kind to take such things lying down. We are no believers in forbearance or vegetarianism. This is especially true of our younger men. Among the veteran founders there are a few adherents of Tolstoyan ideas and such like. Decency constrains me not to dwell in detail on certain isolated and exceptional acts of reprisal conducted by some of the youngsters whose patience had expired, such as cattle rustling, stoning a nomad boy, or beating one of the shepherds senseless. In defense of the perpetrators of the last-mentioned act of retaliation I must state clearly that the shepherd in question had an infuriatingly sly face. He was blind in one eye, broken-nosed, drooling; and his mouth—on this the men responsible were unanimous—was set with long, curved fangs like a fox's. A man with such an appearance was capable of anything. And the Bedouins would certainly not forget this lesson" (24).

The dissimilation and disintegration of the forces operating in the kibbutz are easily inferred from a comparison between the two secretariat meetings described at length in the story.

The first meeting, described in chapter 2, focuses on the conversation with the Bedouin tribal elder after he is brought to the office and the reactions of the representatives of the principle forces to this conversation. At first, the narrator tells us, the meeting was held amidst a show of unity in the kibbutz camp: "We, the members of the secretariat [a forum that includes the representatives of the founders' generation, the representatives of the youngsters, and Geula and the narrator, the intermediaries], received the elder and his men politely and respectfully. We invited them to sit down on the bench, smiled at them, and offered them steaming coffee prepared by Geula at Etkin's special request" (25). But this temporal equilibrium is disturbed right after the end of this meeting, which yielded nothing: "Some of our young men suggested making an excursion one night to teach the savages a lesson in a language they would really understand . . . Etkin rejected their suggestion with disgust and with reasonable arguments," and they "applied to [him] a number of epithets," which the narrator, as usual, refrains from elaborating on out of "decency" (26). The second meeting is described in chapter 8, and ends with a bust-up. It is meant to start at eight-thirty p.m., but starts close to nine because those assembled are waiting in vain for Geula and her coffee. At five minutes to nine Etkin opens the meeting, noting that "he could not imagine what had happened; he could not recall her ever having missed a meeting or been late before" (36), and then presents the agenda:

> He began with a summary of the facts. He gave details of the damage that had apparently been caused by the Bedouins, although there was no formal proof,

and enumerated the steps that had been taken on the committee's initiative. The appeal to good will. Calling in the police. Strengthening the guard around the settlement. Tracking dogs. The meeting with the elder of the tribe. He had to admit, Etkin said, *that we had now reached an impasse*. Nevertheless, he believed *that we had to maintain a sense of balance and not give way to extremism, because hatred always gave rise to further hatred. It was essential to break the vicious circle of hostility.* He therefore opposed *with all the moral force at his disposal* the approach—and particularly the intentions—of certain of the younger members. *He wished to remind us, by way of conclusion, that the conflict between herdsmen and tillers of the soil was as old as human civilization,* as seemed to be evidenced by the story of Cain, who rose up against Abel, his brother. It was fitting, *in view of the gospel we had adopted,* that we should put an end to this ancient feud, too, just as we had put an end to other ugly phenomena. *It was up to us, and everything depended on our moral strength.* (36–37, emphases mine)

Etkin's speech, full of clichés and hackneyed, elevated expressions in the style of the clichés and elevated expressions used by the "movement leaders" in the 1950s and early 1960s, is interrupted by Rami "twice . . . and on one occasion [he] went so far as to use the ugly word 'rubbish.'" Etkin takes offense and accuses the young members "of planning terrorist activities," saying in conclusion, "We're not going to have that sort of thing here" (37).

Then, as we may remember, an "exchange" breaks out between the narrator and Rami. The narrator supports Etkin's position, Rami erupts and asks the narrator if he is "waiting for some small incident of rape that Geula could write poems about and [he] could make into a short story." The narrator flushes and finds no answer. At this stage Etkin deprives both Rami and the narrator of the right to speak. He presents his position again and asks "how it would look if the papers reported that a kibbutz had sent out a lynch mob to settle scores with its Arab neighbors." At hearing the phrase "lynch mob" all the youngsters get up and walk out on the meeting. The narrator follows them out, remarking, "True, I did not share their views, but I, too, had been deprived of the right to speak in an arbitrary and insulting manner."

The breakup of the secretariat meeting, the kibbutz's symbolic representative body, marks the split of the community into its principle elements: the carriers of the social/universal banner on the one hand (Etkin and the other members of the founders' generation), and the representatives of the communal/tribal instincts on the other (Rami's group). This split is also marked by the disintegration of the adhesive units—the human bridging and conciliatory units: Geula who "had not arrived," and the narrator who picks a side against his nature. Even though he agrees with Etkin and opposes a violent reaction, he eventually reacts "from the gut": he walks out on the secretariat meeting and joins the act of reprisal against the Bedouins.

Giants and Duds

In writing about the kibbutz experience Oz joined a rich discursive field, with a long and relatively extensive tradition brimming with ideological and psychological tensions, and it served him as a laboratory for examining fundamental processes in the Israeli society. This examination traces a process that is different from those outlined in the previous texts. In the literary laboratories of Mapu, Herzl, Luidor, and Shamir, a clear prominence is given to centralizing/unifying (centripetal) forces. Although, as I have shown, each of the texts also features decentralizing (centrifugal) forces, these acts of exclusion are aimed, in the end, at reinforcing the centripetal effort.

Conversely, in "Nomads and Viper" all the intra-communal centripetal efforts (in the kibbutz) fail and are replaced by efforts whose "vector of desire" is directed from within the kibbutz camp outward—to the "others"; and this, it should be emphasized, happens in violent or hallucinatory ways.

I am referring to Geula's rape fantasies on the one hand, and to her budding wish, on the verge of dying, "to get up and go to him [the Bedouin], to find him among the wadis and forgive him *and never come back*" (38, emphasis mine), and "even to sing to him." I refer as well, of course, to the retaliatory action of the kibbutz youngsters, who are seen "on their way to the fields and the wadi to even the score with the nomads" like a group of thugs heading toward a violent homoerotic sexual act.

The kibbutz also served Oz as a laboratory for examining the status and place of the "New Jew." This can be learned, for example, from the following fascinating exchange between him and Yitzhak Ben-Aharon, who was one of the leaders of the pioneering Zionist movement in Israel:

> AMOS OZ: Ben-Aharon, you took everything from your mom and dad, everything you could take, and then you closed the door for the grandchildren. For them it doesn't exist. Then you came to the grandchildren, your children, and said, Where is the world of grandpa and grandma? What is this? The world began yesterday? The people of Israel began yesterday? It was you who had closed this door.
>
> YITZHAK BEN-AHARON: Actually, it should be said, there is this dialectic: because we didn't want... this double being. You talked about a *sheigetz*. It's true

we wanted the farmer, the fighter, the soldier. We wanted the Hebrew gentile in Eretz Israel. Not the intellectual, because he was sick.... Ambivalent, complicated, messed up, assimilated.

[But] we didn't want only the muscle man; we really wanted a new figure. And when the new figure started to emerge, we were suddenly shocked, because we asked, Where is the *yiddishkeit*, where is the Jew, where is the idealism as well? Where is the intellectual, ideological idleness? Where is the ideological leader? Where is this idleness? He [the sabra] is skilled with his hands, with manual intelligence, but he is impotent or disabled in a spiritual sense, in the sense of using the imagination to build his society.

AMOS OZ: Golem, Ben-Aharon. You made a Golem and then you got scared. You wanted—you would be the Maharal and we would be the Golem.

YITZHAK BEN-AHARON: This is the verdict?

AMOS OZ: No. This is, how do you say, this is an interim summation, not the verdict.[57]

This chilling dialogue becomes more chilling when we compare the words of Ben-Aharon, the Third Aliyah man, with the thoughts of Shimshon Sheinbaum, the Third Aliyah man in another foundational story by Oz, "The Way of the Wind":

> Having made up his mind, Sheinbaum closed his notebook. The months of military training have certainly toughened the boy [his son Gideon, a gentle boy who, following his father's order, joined the paratroopers]. It is hard to believe, but it certainly looks as though he is beginning to mature at last. He still has to learn how to handle women. He has to free himself once and for all from his shyness and his sentimentality: he should leave such traits to women ... As long as he doesn't up and marry the first girl who gives herself to him. He ought to break one or two of them in before he gets spliced. In a few years he'll have to give me some grandchildren. Lots of them. Gideon's children will have two fathers: my son can take care of them, and I'll take care of their ideas. The second generation grew up in the shadow of our achievements; that's why they're so confused. It's a matter of dialectics. But the third generation will be a wonderful synthesis, a successful outcome: they will inherit the spontaneity of their parents and the spirit of their grandparents. It will be a glorious heritage distilled from a twisted pedigree. (*WJH*, 49–50)

Ben-Aharon and Sheinbaum discuss the same "genetic laboratory" and the same "working method" (dialectics), and they also agree about the "sons' generation" being a bad vintage.

The position of the sons' generation—Oz in the dialogue with Ben-Aharon and Gideon Shenhav encouraged by the narrator who is standing behind his back in the dialogue with his father, Shimshon Sheinbaum—can be deduced from the leading images in both contexts. In the conversation with Ben-Aharon, Oz claims: "*Golem*, Ben-Aharon. You made a Golem and then you got scared. You wanted, you would be *the Maharal* and we would be *the Golem*." Whereas in "The Way of the Wind," when Gideon parachuted onto high-voltage lines and could not release himself, his father, looking at him from below, picked up a little stone, "straightened up, and threw it furiously at his son's back" and lashed out at him: "Pinocchio, you're a wet rag, you're a miserable coward!" (57, emphasis mine). Shimshon Sheinbaum believes in the "wonderful synthesis" that will come about in the third generation. But it seemed, at least according to the stories written by Oz and his colleagues in that formative period, that he has nothing to base this belief on. These stories are full of "dud-children," biological and spiritual mutations of various different kinds, who do not even produce descendants.

In other words, the ever-improving genealogy in the vein of Charles Darwin's evolutionary chain is replaced by a clear trend of loss and decline. This is suggested, for example, by the composition of the second generation's "genetic pool" in "The Way of the Wind." On the one hand there is Gideon Shenhav, a boy with no "ego" and no will to power—in short, a marionette. And on the other hand there is his younger brother, the bastard Zaki (Zachariah/Ezekiel)—a name that (perhaps) betrays the origin of his mother, (perhaps) a Mizrahi Jew, who has here a similar status to that of the Bedouin in "Nomads and Viper," and his description leaves no doubt about the direction of Zionist genetic engineering according to Oz: "This spectacle [Gideon hanging on the electricity lines "like a dead lamb suspended from a butcher's hook"] provoked hysterical glee in the watching children. They *barked* with laughter. *Zaki slapped his knees, choking and heaving convulsively. He leapt up and down screeching like a mischievous monkey*" (58, emphasis mine).

We are not dealing here with a dialectical process, as Sheinbaum imagines, but with a regressive one: the fathers are presented as human beings, whereas the sons are presented as marionettes or monkeys. This is an evolutionary picture similar to the one we saw in *He Walked in the Fields*. There as here, the fathers are presented as human beings and the sons as monkeys in two senses: both as those who have reverted to a more "primitive" stage in the evolutionary ladder and as those whose main distinguishing feature is mimicry, mimicry that turns into mockery.[58]

The clear resemblance between Shamir and Oz's "genetic engineerings" also highlights the differences in some of their characteristics. The following differences are especially important to our discussion: first, the different portrayal of the parents' generation. In both texts the parents are perceived as more worthy than the sons, however while Shamir presents his value assessment with a sense of acceptance and resignation, Oz expresses fury and defiance; second, Shamir, as we have seen in the previous chapter, continues to give the Zionist revolution a chance. Although Uri Cahana is a dud who represents a whole generation of duds, he is deemed worthy, at least, of serving as the semen carrier, the biological father of the fetus in Mika's womb. Gideon Shenhav, by contrast, is found unfit even to serve as a link in the Zionist genealogical chain, both in the spiritual sense—a task that here, as in *He Walked in the Fields*, is left for the father ("I'll take care of their ideas")—and on the biological plane, as the semen carrier.

A similar fate—a regressive trajectory and a death without offspring—awaits the single woman Geula. Her erotic narrative, you will remember, is marked by an intensifying dehumanization. First she meets a young Jewish man, an impotent member of her kibbutz. Then she meets a young Bedouin, at once gentle and potent, who is seen through her eyes (and through the eyes of the narrator) as half-man half-animal, and she chases him away and then fantasizes about being raped by him. Finally, she has an encounter with a viper snake that "bites" her—and only then does she achieve her redemption.

A Kind of Epilogue: House-Dwellers, Nomads, and Viper Snakes

The coupling of Geula with the viper snake; the many parallels that the text establishes between the viper snake and the nomad/s; the obvious connection between the viper snake and the short, thick sticks in the hands of the kibbutz youngsters, who are on their way to smash the "black bones" of the Bedouins (*WJH*, 35); the fact that these literary linkages are made in the context of a story anchored by the metanarrative of the Garden of Eden story—all these elements and the myriad connections that the text establishes among them refocus the attention on the question of the place of animals and monsters in this foundational text.

The cutting up of monsters that symbolize chaos and the killing of wild, predatory, and poisonous animals that symbolize a powerful combination of life and death, knowledge and blind terror in one entity are structured and portrayed, as I have repeatedly noted in previous chapters, in hundreds of mythological, religious, historical, and literary texts that serve as foundational texts in the establishment of new or renewed communities.

The military leader's sword, the prophet's staff, the wizard's wand, the cane in which fire is transmitted from the realm of the gods to the realm of human beings, the pipe of the wondrous piper are all, as we have been taught by various scholars, objects that symbolize the glare of consciousness that is supposed to light up the darkness/chaos of the unconscious and create order in the world.[59]

King Arthur reunites the divided England with the Excalibur sword (which is taken from him once he completes his national mission); Moses turns a submissive nation of slaves into the people of Israel through repeated use of the staff (to call the Plagues, sunder the Red Sea, draw water out of the rock); Gandalf, the "White Wizard" in J. R. R. Tolkien's *Lord of the Rings*, was famous for his staff; the Pied Piper of Hamelin founds a new town through the melodies he produces from his magic flute,[60] and so on. However—and this is also a phenomenon we are familiar with from hundreds of texts foundational to nations, cultures, and religions—some of the representations of the monster, the hybrid creature that belongs to several zoological or botanical classes at once, must also be symbolically represented in the world after a separation between a chaos phase and an order phase. The link with the monstrous, chaotic, unconscious, and animalistic is perceived (again, in all cultures) as a condition for the community's survival.[61] No wonder then that in many culture-founding stories the snake—whose figure is almost always associated with knowledge and medicine on the one hand and death and mystery on the other—is connected to the sword and the staff.

This is what happens in the context of Hebrew culture in the Garden of Eden story. Here the text guides us to link the snake, which makes Adam and Eve eat from the Tree of Knowledge, to the flaming sword that flashes back and forth in the gates of the Garden and prevents them from returning to the space of blindness and innocence, at the same time forcing them to take charge of their destiny and establish human society and culture. A similar link is suggested by the metamorphoses of Moses's staff. This is a staff that can turn into a snake and that functions as a sword—a magical accessory that has the ability both to annihilate life (the Plagues, the drowning of the Egyptians in the Red Sea) and create it (drawing water from the rock). As Moses's story suggests, exercising control over this special metamorphic ability is one of the most vital skills of a leader charged with turning a mixed multitude of slaves into a chosen nation.

This twofold attitude to the precultural or animalistic predatory/poisonous entity—that is, waging all-out war against it while simultaneously preserving it on the symbolic level (for example, through a cyclical or annual reenactment of the battle against it and its eradication)—can be clearly found in the first nation-founding text I discussed, *The Love of Zion*.

As we may remember, Mapu splits the dragon-like monstrous/hybrid being into three parts: the lion whose hair sticks out like iron bristles, which stands between Amnon and Tamar in their first meeting in the Bethlehem fields; the vulture with its iron-like claws, which stands between them in their second meeting on the Mount of Olives; and the snake in the figure of Zimri and the cobra venom he offers Tamar on behalf of Amnon, which stands between them at Tamar's home in Jerusalem.

So the dragon has been cut to pieces. But the presence of its parts—the predatory animals that each represent an entire class: mammals, birds, and reptiles—and the rituals of killing each of them separately are described and perceived as indispensable elements in the realization of the erotic/national coupling. Furthermore, Amnon shoots the lion that threatens to devour Tamar and kills it, but insists on flaying its skin, which he places on the back of his war horse as he enters Jerusalem.

Herzl's *Altneuland* is a domesticated, almost sterile world. Yet even the author of the most well-known national utopia did not neglect to preserve a representation of the animalistic. The entrance to the home of the president of the New Society, David Littwak, is flanked by two stone lions, alluding to the lion from the child David's foundational story, "Androcles and the Lion." Also, and no less importantly, little Friedrich, the representative of the New Society's future generation, survives thanks to Kingscourt, the animal-loving Prussian cavalry officer.

Conversely, Yoash's world in Luidor's "Yoash" entirely revolves around the contact with the animalistic and with what is perceived by him and his creator as animalistic. The story of his growing up is a story of learning to deal with animals: first with a toad, later with a snake and a donkey and a horse, and later still with . . . Arabs. However—and here lies the seed of trouble that would grow into the tree from whose fruits Uri and Geula would eat—Luidor, unlike Mapu and Herzl, does not leave room for the animalistic in the historical world. Yoash does not spare the snake, in whose eyes he seeks "the secret of life and death" (*Stories*, 64). Thus he traces the trajectory of his own existence: a brief appearance on the stage of history and a disappearance into the mists of myth. By contrast David, the new immigrant, knows his limits. He treats his horse with respect, and the latter repays him in kind. The same goes for the new immigrant Mika in Shamir's *He Walked in the Fields*. She too—like David in "Yoash"—is scared of the horse, but she learns to control her fear. Uri, on the other hand, can controls the animals but cannot control mechanical tools, which are his generation's substitute for the animals. This becomes clear in the incident with "Ilana's" truck, as well as in the grenade-throwing incident. His lack of control over the work tools and the death tools is equivalent, in terms of its result, to Yoash's total contact with nature: in both cases the heroes have no place in the "place" and are destined to die. Yoash must die mentally pure, sexually a virgin and with his body intact, because he must remain in the collective memory as "unblemished," as "whole." Uri must die in a schlemiel way, because he must remain in the collective memory as "defective," "partial," "castrated"—thus enabling the continuing operation of the national/Zionist laboratory.

In the formative fiction of the State Generation, the web of relationships between the protagonists and the predatory and poisonous animals in modern Hebrew literature undergoes a dramatic shift. The attempts to control the forces of the hybrid creatures and the predatory animals, which embody—in various combinations—new possibilities of life and mortal dangers, are replaced by a desire for a suicidal merging with the "other," or more precisely, with the animalistic or mechanistic essence attributed to it.

This astonishing new phenomenon has dozens of manifestations. Thus, for example, many of Oz's early female protagonists turn their backs on the men in their national peer group and associate instead with the "other" (Arabs-nomads, older Holocaust refugees, and so on) and even, as we have seen in "Nomads and Viper," with the "ultimate other"—the viper, which is the distilled expression of the merging between sex (life) and death.

Geula's "communion" with the snake in the last scene of "Nomads and Viper," which, it should be noted, has many parallels in Western narrative tradition,[62] creates a grotesque, ridiculous, and alarming mirror image of the biblical Garden of Eden story. It turns out that the attempt by Oz and his generation to shift the departure point of the narrative world from the first stage of metanarratives that deal with the founding of the people of Israel (the stage cited, as I have shown in the previous chapters, by most of the Revival writers) to the first stage of the metanarrative that deals with the foundation of the human race and human society—the story of the Garden of Eden and the expulsion from it—has failed and imploded. The cross-camp encounter between Adam-Romeo (the nomad) and Eve-Juliet (Geula) in the "pleasant place," the "shadowy dome" (*WJH*, 30), ends with a "a note of terror" (34), and with signs that herald a catastrophe. The mutual sexual courting, performed "unconsciously" (31), is replaced by the rhythm of the Bedouins' drums on the one hand and the rhythm of the fighter planes' lights on the other, complemented by "a smell of bonfires on the air and a smell of dust borne on the breeze" (34). And the God of the original story is replaced in Oz's Garden of Eden by "only a slight breeze among the fruit trees."

The failure and collapse of the State Generation writers' attempt to start the modern settlement story as if *ab ovo*, on a universal humanist basis, has many causes. One of them, re-evoked by a careful examination of Oz's early writing, is the internal contradiction that characterizes some of the redemption hopes dreamt up by the early exponents of the Zionist movement—first and foremost the contradiction between the wish to abandon Western culture and take hold of or be reborn in the primordial East, and the wish to form an advanced outpost of Western civilization in the "Levant."

This fundamental contradiction, as it is embodied in Oz's early work, was pointed to long ago by Zfira Porat in an important and suggestive essay. Here is an excerpt from her text:

> At first the Jews and Judaism were at home in the world, and their God was the Lord of this world, and the life he ordained was life in this world, and the reward he promised was longevity and sons and grandsons devoted to the Torah and to work and to good deeds.
>
> But in two thousand years of suffering in the Diaspora, years of encounter with foreign and strange dreams of redemption—Platonic, Gnostic, Christian and Romantic—the wine of the original Jewry of Eretz Israel had been mixed with an alien infusion of distaste for the corporeal world and with foreign longings for a world which is all spirituality. In the Zionist incarnation of the idea of redemption, Oz believes, this wine has gone sour. Mutually alien dreams can live under one roof as long as they remain dreams. But once the dream had been realized, the realizers found themselves plagued by contradictions and tensions stemming from the very nature of the mutually-contradictory hopes of redemption—to redeem the people from its excessive spirituality and restore it to a natural corporeal life, and at the same time to elevate the revival of the people on its land and the working of the land and the worshipping of the sun and suntan to the level of a religious calling.[63]

The writers of the State Generation thus found themselves in the formative stage of their writing in a state of ideological and existential difficulty caused by the contradictions and tensions between the conflicting redemption hopes that created and fed the Zionist redemption narrative. They tried to resolve this difficulty (especially Oz and Appelfeld) through an identity split (we are in the East and our hearts are in the West) that replicates the age-old Jewish-diasporic identity split (my heart is in the East and I in the uttermost West) while reversing its vector of desire.

To be sure, we should note that the desire for the West or for the Arab other—that is, an orientalized Arab, an Arab seen through the lenses of a European—is often portrayed ambivalently, with a strange combination of longing, suspicion, and animosity. For the writers of that generation could not and did not wish to ignore the Holocaust that had only recently taken place or more than fifty years of a bloody conflict with the Arab neighbors.

However, and this is the assertion with which I would like to end this study, the formative literature of the State Generation—which shaped, no less than it reflected, the essence of Israeliness—reversed the direction of the vector of desire that had dominated Hibbat Zion and Zionist literature, thus establishing our status, if we can put it this way, precisely at the moment in which we gained sovereignty after two thousand years of exile, as exiles in our own land.

Notes

A complete list of notes may be found in the Hebrew edition.

Introduction

Epigraph: Brenner, "Self-Evaluation in Three Volumes," 1265.
1. Baum, *Annotated Wizard of Oz*, 75–76.
2. Gurevitch and Aran, "On the Place," 9–10.
3. Baudrillard, *America*.
4. A notable exception in this context is the corpus of Haskalah literature (especially its later part). The direction of desire in this corpus was not Eretz Israel, but the European centers of knowledge. And respectively—and this is an existential position that had anticipated the existential position that, as we shall see, characterized a major and significant part of the literature of the "State Generation"—the split between body (West) and heart (East), characteristic of pre-modern Hebrew literature in the European Diaspora, is replaced in the Haskalah literature with a split between Jew and man; a split implied in the phrase that became the catchphrase of the Hebrew Haskalah movement: "Be a Jew in your home and a man when you go out."
5. Gertz, *Shvuya ba-Haloma*, 9–12; Lyotard, *Postmodern Condition*.
6. Cf. Schwartz, "Holocaust Literature."
7. Cf. Roskies, *Against the Apocalypse*; Alan Mintz, *Responses to Catastrophe*.
8. Rimmon-Kenan, "Story of 'I,'" 11.
9. Jameson, *Postmodernism*, 143. See also Hayden White's famous observations in "Foucault Decoded" (230–60).
10. Rimmon-Kenan, "Story of 'I,'" 9.
11. Several fascinating studies have been written on the subject of social communities returning or, rather, seemingly returning to their inventory of metanarratives that deal with the birth phase or the end of times phase, see for example, Megged, *Ha-Atstekim*, 63–72; and Pardes, *Countertraditions*.
12. Elboim-Dror, *Ha-Machar shel Etmol*, 1:17.
13. Ibid. As I understand it, the story of the Garden of Eden is the ultimate existential story. Already here, at the beginning of days, Adam (more precisely Eve, followed by Adam) chooses to eat from the Tree of Knowledge, thus sealing his fate with his own hands—even at the price of giving up immortality.
14. Ibid. For the city, see also Mumford, *City in History*; Wheatley, *Pivot of the Four Quarters*.
15. Elboim-Dror, *Ha-Machar shel Etmol*, 1:17.
16. Tönnies, *Community and Society*.
17. Cf. Bauman, *Community*; Simmel, Park, and Wirth, *Urbanism*.
18. Shamir, *He Walked in the Fields*, 277; hereafter *HWF*.
19. Oz, *Where the Jackals Howl*, 38.

1. Avraham Mapu, The Love of Zion (1853)

Epigraph: Mendele Mocher Sforim, *Fishke the Lame*, 99.

1. Tzemach, "A Conversation."
2. The link S. Tzemach makes between the awakening national sentiment and the appearance of landscape descriptions in Hebrew literature coincides with the link made by Lennard Davis (*Resisting Novels*, 52–101). Similar arguments are made by scholars identified as postcolonialists.
3. Fichman, "Avraham Mapu."
4. Miron, *Arba Panim*, 17–18.
5. Mapu, *Love of Zion*, 14; hereafter *LZ*.
6. The fact that from childhood, Tamar is defined as having equal rights to the sons in the family indicates that Mapu granted her a privileged status in the feminine wing of the group of characters populating his fictional world.
7. Or, in Zoran's terminology, the structural-thematic relations between "the total place" or "the background" and "the scene of events" ("Towards a Theory," 27–32, esp. 30–32).
8. Using the terminology I employed elsewhere (Schwartz, 1989), we can say that "the surrounding area" represents the text's "implied map" (the "old" worldview), whereas "the central area" represents the text's "portrayed map" (the author's worldview—as the reader, of course, understands it). This dichotomous distinction relies on the distinctions made by Slawinsky (*Literature als System*) and Jauss (*Toward an Aesthetic*).
9. The connection between the fictional plot and the historical period it is set in is significant both in the context of a single author and a single work, and in the context of a group of authors and a defined corpus of books. Thus, for example, we can note the affinity of Hebrew Haskalah poets with biblical times, the affinity of Romantic writers with "primitive" cultures, and the affinity of postmodernist writers with the Middle Ages. The choice of different groups of writers in different periods to relate to certain sections of the extra-literary timeline reflects—and to a large extent also dictates—the character of the generic pool of that time. In periods in which writers stick to the present or the recent past, we witness a thriving of the realistic story in its different guises; in periods of clinging to the twilight zone between myth and history, the Romance thrives; utopias and dystopias thrive when writers pin their hopes on the future. In any case, the answer to the question of what "historical" space-time the story takes place in always has a crucial interpretive function. Cf. Lukács, *Historical Novel*.
10. It is easy to see that, alongside the opposition between the city of God and faith and the pagan city, which has a clear moral dimension, Mapu posits another opposition, to which his moral attitude is less unequivocal; this is the opposition between the young, pleasant and refined city, and the ancient brutal city—a city that carries tidings of death but is nonetheless fascinating. Mapu's fascination with Nineveh, which "is like a leopard adorned with a fine skin—pleasant to look at and fierce with the roar issuing from its mouth" (151–52) and with Sennacherib, who is like "a lion from the heights on the Jordan"—is in keeping, as we shall see, with one of the basic principles of his human engineering, that is, that to create a dynasty with real chances of survival it must include an erotically potent, as well as (and one depends on the other) a thanatically potent natural element.
11. This is, of course, a particular implementation—one of several possible implementa-

tions—of the potential-symbolic pool of relations between the two places. See—and I shall return to this issue in the following chapters—the completely different implementation of the same symbolic pool of relations in Herzl's *Altneuland*.

12. As claimed by Fishel Lachover, who compared *The Love of Zion* and *Migdal Oz* ("A Tower of Strength"), on the one hand, with *LaYesharim Tehilla* ("Praise Be to the Upright"), on the other. In contrast, Joseph Klausner rejected this view, claiming a connection between Mapu's story and the French novel in the tradition of Alexandre Dumas and Eugène Sue (*The Mysteries of Paris*).

13. Suleiman, *Authoritarian Fictions*.

14. Isaiah 2:1–4. In most cultures, holy sites are located in high places.

15. As well as during other national-religious events: *LZ*, 37, 38, 257, 260, 267.

16. Similar things are said by Zimri (*LZ*, 26) and by one of the prophets' sons (*LZ*, 69).

17. In her groundbreaking article "The Utopian Novel and the Zionist Utopia," Leah Hadomi addresses the utopian genre's casting principles, noting that "in the utopia there are usually two main characters: the 'stranger'—who happens to arrive at the place ['the approving other' is my terminology] and finds himself surprised and impressed by its organization and achievements; and the 'host'—one of the locals, who shows him around the place and introduces him to his colleagues, their logic, their morals and their way of life" (14). See also Elboim-Dror, *Ha-Machar*, 1:71.

18. Cf. Miron, "Shining Veneer," 27.

19. Ibid.

20. Amnon chooses to keep his vow to Tamar and leave Jerusalem—thus becoming party to the desertion of "God's city." Or as he puts it: "If I had not sworn to Tamar to obey all her commands, I should never have thought of leaving Zion in these troubled times. I would choose rather to suffer cold and hunger in Zion during the siege than to live in a palace in a strange land . . . Oh, how I wish that Tamar had not forced me to leave the city! I would pour out my blood for Zion and I would die in peace, and my life would end in the arms of my dear mother!" (*LZ*, 191). Likewise Tamar, preoccupied with her private grief (over Amnon's leaving), is unwilling to concern herself with the suffering of the besieged residents of Jerusalem (241).

21. For a survey of the literature on Mapu's stories in relation to this debate see Miron, "Shining Veneer," 75–94. For a survey of the descriptions of Eretz Israel in Mapu's work as they are reflected in this literature, see Cohen, *Me-Halom le-Metsi'ut*, 94–103.

22. Wright, *Aids to Geographical Research*.

23. Pocock, *Humanistic Approaches*, 9–19.

24. Davis, *Resisting Novels*, 52–101.

25. Interrelations of this kind characterize, for example, the group of writers known as Dor Hamdina (the State Generation) (Amos Oz, A. B. Yehoshua, Amalia Kahana-Carmon, Aharon Appelfeld, and others) in their formative phase—the first half of the 1960s. It is a spatial system consisting of three concentric circles. The first circle is the central area—an enclosed and isolated space, populated by characters identified as Jewish and/or Israeli or characters who, though unidentified, can be understood from their characteristics to be Jewish and/or Israeli. The second circle is the front setting—a space that surrounds the central area, more open in character and populated by "others": gentiles and jackals in Appelfeld, Arabs in Oz, etc. This space is comparatively thinly populated and is considered dangerous

by the characters from the first circle. The third circle is the circle of the elsewhere—a primordial space situated on the imaginary edges of the map. This is the back setting, seen by the characters from the inner circle as "the Place": a primeval, ideal, sublime space. Cf. Nurit Gertz, 1979, 1980, 1983.

26. Zoran, "Towards a Theory," 25.

27. Cf. Meinig, who discusses some of the symbolic landscapes of the American nations (*The Interpretation*, 164–92).

28. Miron, "Shining Veneer," 24–25.

29. Ibid., 25.

30. Pocock, *Humanistic Approaches*, 9–19.

31. Alter, *Art of Biblical Narrative*, 50.

32. Ibid., 51.

33. The deer's masculinity is also suggested by its being linked with the lion: "as if he was proud of his big horns, crowning his head like that of the king of the forest."

34. Cohen, *Me-Halom le-Metsi'ut*, 93–153.

35. Bakhtin, "Discourse in the Novel."

36. Moretti, "The Comfort of Civilization."

37. Beer, *The Romance*, 13.

38. This attempt, as we learn from Joseph Campbell (*Hero with a Thousand Faces*) and Northrop Frye (*Anatomy of Criticism*), has deep mythological roots. I am referring to the mythical struggle between the winter/god of winter and the spring/god of spring. It is an annual/cyclical/perennial struggle—which will continue to occupy us at later points in this chapter, as well as in the chapters on Herzl, Luidor, Shamir, and Oz—used here to frame the narrative. The narrative present opens with Tamar and Teman leaving for the villages, on "one of the first spring days" (*LZ*, 37). It ends in the spring, exactly a year later, with the double wedding celebration on the Mount of Olives (257).

39. Miron, "Shining Veneer," 32–36.

40. *Translator's note:* While the Hebrew original has *Rosh Ptanim* (cobra venom), Marymount's translation simply has "poison."

41. Miron, "Shining Veneer," 40.

42. Shir ha-Shirim Rabbah, section 2, 30; cited in Miron, "Shining Veneer," 41.

43. For a detailed discussion of the Exodus from Egypt from a similar standpoint see Pardes, *The Biography of Ancient Israel*, 2000. A similar use of the same foundational myth is made by Herzl in *Altneuland* (see chapter 2).

44. Werses, "Avraham Mapu's Narrative Strategies"; Miron, "Shining Veneer"; Cohen, *Me-Halom le-Metsi'ut*.

45. Some famous monstrous-hybrid creatures are, for example, the Chimera—part lion, part goat, and part snake—and the griffin, which has the body of a lion, the head of a goat or horse, and the wings of an eagle—a creature that, because of its lion's body and eagle's wings, denotes the domination of both land and sky.

46. A notable example: the flying dragons ridden by the Nazgûl in J. R. R. Tolkien's *Lord of the Rings*.

47. Bachelard, *Psychoanalysis of Fire*.

48. See for example, Lawrence Coupe, 1997; David Leeming with Margaret Leeming, 199. The act of slaying the hybrid creature and tearing it to pieces is frequently performed

with a spear, a sword, a bow and arrow, etc.—weapons that, as Ruth Netzer (*Massa el ha-Atsmi*, 390–415) points out, symbolize "power, kingship, masculine power, the active power of the will, phallic power, insight, intellect and spirituality—which all enable an incisive decision.... The sword"—she adds [and likewise the other incisive instruments, in both senses of the word, to which we can add the pen]—"separates, divides, classifies, and cuts up; therefore it is the symbol of consciousness. When the sword serves in the development of human consciousness toward higher fulfillment, it is considered sacred" (393). "In the myths the sword serves the hero in his struggle against the dragons, that is, it serves in the struggle of the I's consciousness against the negative force of the unconscious" (395).

49. Eliade, *Myth of the Eternal Return*, 3–48. Eliade cites scores of examples. Thus, regarding the link between the act of settlement and the act of creation, he cites the following story, the likes of which are very important for the present study, which deals exclusively with stories of actual and potential settlers: "When the Scandinavian colonists took possession of Iceland, landnáma, and began to cultivate it, they regarded this act neither as an original undertaking nor as human and profane work. Their enterprise was for them only the repetition of a primordial act: the transformation of chaos into cosmos by the divine act of Creation. By cultivating the desert soil, they in fact repeated the act of the gods, who organized chaos by giving it forms and norms. Better still, a territorial conquest does not become real until after—more precisely, through—the ritual of taking possession, which is only a copy of the primordial act of the Creation of the World" (10). Similarly, Eliade cites scores of examples that show that marriage rites in "primitive" cultures had a divine model and that "human marriage reproduces the hierogamy, more especially the union of heaven and earth" (23). Thus, for example, in "Brhadaranyaka Upanisad" the groom says "I am Heaven" and "thou art Earth," and in the procreation ritual that appears in these sixth-century BCE Indian philosophical texts, the generative act becomes "a hierogamy of cosmic proportions, mobilizing a whole group of gods: 'Let Visnu make the womb prepared! Let Tvashtri shape the various forms! Prajapati—let him pour in! Let Dhatri place the germ for thee!'"

2. *Theodor Herzl*, Altneuland *(1902)*

Epigraph: Le Corbusier, *Towards a New Architecture*, 45.

1. As noted by Bein, *Theodor Herzl*; Dinur, *Benyamin Ze'ev Herzl*; Elon, *Herzl*; and Avineri, *Making of Modern Zionism*, 88–100.

2. Elboim-Dror, *Ha-Machar shel Etmol*, 1:13–17.

3. Herzl, it should be added, was closely familiar with the tradition of utopian literature as well as with the literature dealing with the histories of communities that tried to realize social utopias. This is also reflected in *Altneuland*, especially—though not exclusively—in the programmatic chapter dealing with the link between the inherently universal vision of human progress and its specific local realizations. This chapter mentions, on pp. 145–46, for example: "Cabet, the dreamer of Icaria" (Etienne Cabet, *Voyage en Icarie*, 1840); "Bellamy, who outlined a noble communistic society in his *Looking Backward*" (E. Bellamy, *Looking Backward, 1878–2000*, 1888); "*Freiland*, a utopian romance by the publicist Hertzka, . . . a brilliant bit of magic" (Theodor Hertzka, *Freiland: Ein Socials Zukunftsbild* [Freeland: A social anticipation], 1890).

4. See Herlitz, "Notes for the New Hebrew Edition," 289–99.

5. Hayuta Bussel's memoirs of her father in Tamir and Sharet, eds., *Anshei ha-Aliyah ha-Shniya*, 160–61. I would like to thank Dr. Tamar Hess for referring me to this testimony.

6. Max Nordau, "Ahad Ha'am on 'Altneuland,'" 111.

7. On the reactions to *Altneuland* in the Jewish and Zionist camp see, among others: Bein, *Theodor Herzl*, 394–410; Elon, *Herzl*, 347–54; Elboim-Dror, *Ha-Machar shel Etmol*, 1:76–80.

8. Herzl, *Old New Land (Altneuland)*, 3; hereafter *ONL*.

9. See especially Ben-Arieh's essays "The Literature of Western Travellers" and "Perceptions and Images of Eretz Israel and Jerusalem"; see also Ben-Arieh, "Pioneer Scientific Exploration"; Nathan Schor, *Sefer ha-Nosi'im le-Eretz Isra'el*.

10. On the connection between culturally dependent aesthetic sensibilities and colonialism, there is a fascinating literature. See, for example, Popkin, *High Road*, 102–29.

11. See note 9 above. The typical itineraries of the eighteenth- and nineteenth-century Christian pilgrims and tourists in the Holy Land, and the parallel itineraries of famous Jewish figures visiting the country through the generations (Judah Halevi, Rabbi Nachman of Breslov, and others), also serve as a model in the large corpus of the literatures of the first aliyot.

12. On manmade structures serving as sacred sites (a phenomenon whose emblematic expression is the Mesopotamian cities and whose matching myth is the Tower of Babel or the great Ziggurat), see Armstrong, *Short History of Myth*, 58–78.

13. See above, in the introduction chapter 1.

14. George Stephenson, the inventor of the steam locomotive, is called here "the harbinger of a new era." The members of the New Society decide that in 1925, on the hundred-year anniversary of the building of the first railway, "locomotives in every part of the world, wherever they may happen to be, shall stop and whistle slowly three times" (*ONL*, 261).

15. For example David, who explains the secret of the planning of the modern city of Haifa to his guests (*ONL*, 61–70), and Steineck, "our [the New Society's] chief architect. He made the city plans" (68, 118–26).

16. This literary-ideological combination of features also explains the existence of the only non-polar (gradual) opposition in this passage—the one between the European city and the utopic Haifa, which resembles the European city, but is more modern: better planned, better lit, cleaner, less noisy etc. The upgrading of the European origin is seen here as the product of the same logic that also "necessitated" the erasure of the "old" life forms. The settlement project that Herzl suggests, it turns out, has a double justification: it propagates "the right culture" to "the backward regions," and at the same time also enhances it.

17. Baron Maurice de Hirsch (1831–1896) was a leading Jewish philanthropist and "the father" of the Jewish agricultural settlement in Argentina. He founded the JCA., the Jewish Colonization Association, whose aim was to facilitate the emigration of Jews from all the countries of Europe and Asia (especially countries where the rights of Jews were being threatened) to all parts of the world.

18. According to Bein (*Theodor Herzl*, 9–11), Heinrich is the fictional incarnation of Herzl's boyhood friend, who in 1890 took his own life after despairing of life as a writer and a Jew.

19. See, for example, David Littwak at the Seder meal in Tiberias (*ONL*, 190), Professor Steineck (212), and Kingscourt (49).

20. On this matter see also Jean Baudrillard's remarks (*America*, 6–7, 120–28). For more on the issue of the desert in this context, see chapter 5.

21. The sea as a liminal space is discussed by Michel Foucault in his *History of Madness* (11). See also Braudel, *Mediterranean*; Naveh, *Nos'im ve-Nos'ot*, 80–92. On the sea in the context of the Zionist narrative, see Hever, "We Didn't Come."

22. Eliade, *Myth of the Eternal Return*.

23. The literary expression of this belief—as we learned from Mikhail Bakhtin ("Discourse in the Novel") and Franco Moretti ("Comfort of Civilization")—is the bildungsroman. This is *the* genre par excellence of the age of the Enlightenment, and perhaps of the modern age in general.

24. A similar impression will strike Friedrich in the ruined Jerusalem (*ONL*, 26). The analogy between the Littwak family in the Diaspora and the ruined Jerusalem of 1902, which is maintained by the parallel descriptions of the family home on the one hand and the ruined Jerusalem on the other, in daytime and at night ("The Littwaks' room by daylight looked even drearier than at night" [35]; "Jerusalem by daylight was less alluring" [44]) reveals from another direction Herzl's implied assumption that it will be the vitality inherent to the eastern European Jewish diaspora that will ensure the continuing (physical) existence of the people of Israel.

25. The Muslim "Lovers of Zion" are represented in the book by Reschid Bey, who rejects any attempt by (the seemingly matter-of-fact, cynical, and misanthropic) Kingscourt to find some fault, as far as the Arabs are concerned, with the return of the Jews to Palestine. Thus, for example, when Kingscourt wonders, " . . . you Moslems. Don't you regard these Jews as intruders?" Reschid Bey replies with a negative, long and carefully argued answer, which begins with the sentence: "You speak strangely, Christian" (*ONL*, 124). As Homi Bhabha has shown (*Location of Culture*), the representation of the "locals," "the people of the Orient," as having only benefited from the actions of the emissaries of Western culture, and even welcomed them, is a typical representation of the subjugated subject in the colonialist discourse.

26. Gurevitch and Aran, "On the Place."

27. *ONL*, 53.

28. This seems like the appropriate place to mention that "the presidential mansion" of the New Society, which will be the future residence of David Littwak, the former Ostjuden beggar, "reminded them of the palazzi of the Genoese Patricians" (*ONL*, 271).

29. Another newly acquired aristocratic class referred to in the novel is "the nouveaux riche." Herzl repeatedly, directly, and blatantly expresses his loathing of this class—for example in the description of the engagement party at the Loefflers' home (*ONL*, 10–18) or, by way of negation, in the description of all those filling public posts in the New Society. For instance, when Dr. Marcus explains why he and Joe Levy propose David Littwak for the post of president, he points out that although Littwak came from humble beginnings, he is not one of the nouveaux riche (286).

30. See Boyarin, "Colonial Drag" and *Unheroic Conduct*; Elon, *Herzl*; and Bardenstein, 1997.

31. We learn of Kingscourt's status also from an external testimony—the dramatic changes this character underwent during the course of the book's writing. Hadomi mentions that "in the Zionist Archive there are eight pages outlining the novel's plan, as noted down by the author while on a train ride from Paris to Frankfurt on 21 July 1899" ("Utopian Novel,"

154). She notes that "one of the significant changes made by the author between the initial and the final, printed version concerns the character of Kingscourt. In the first draft he is called Torpedofabrikant, that is, a weapon's manufacturer, and his involvement in the plot ends with his death. Loewenberg mourns his death, and on his way back revisits Eretz Israel, where he finds the New Society. In *Altneuland* this character's association with the weapons industries is abandoned, and he isn't 'killed,' but rather continues to play an important role in the remainder of the plot." Of course, the new name given to this character (Kingscourt) adds an aristocratic-royal touch.

32. See Boyarin, "Colonial Drag"; Boyarin, *Unheroic Conduct*; Gluzman, "Longing for Heterosexuality."

3. Yosef Luidor, "Yoash" (1912)

1. Almost all those who did refer to Luidor's stories, both before and after the publication of his collection of stories (1976), did so because he had been connected, at the time, to places, people, and events that were seen in retrospect, in the memories of his contemporaries, as having historical-national importance. The only literary-critical references are those of Dov Landau in the 1976 introduction to Luidor's collection of stories and of Gershon Shaked, who dedicates to Luidor two pages (including more than a page of illustrative quotes) out of his entire discussion of Hebrew literature (*Ha-Siporet ha-Ivrit*, 59–61).

2. By "period novel" I mean a novel that is based on a combination of two literary models: "a novel of a period" and "a novel about a period." In a novel of a period I mean a novel that seeks to express the period, to look at it as it were through its own eyes. In a novel about a period I mean a novel that seeks to examine the period, to observe it from afar with a critical eye. For a detailed discussion of this issue, see my book *Living for Living* (99–230).

3. Brenner, "Eretz Israel Genre and Its Artifacts," 569–78.

4. See Shaked, *Ha-Siporet ha-Ivrit*, 15–154.

5. Anderson, *Imagined Communities*, 9.

6. See the studies by Bartal, "'Old Yishuv'"; Shilo, *Princess or Prisoner?*; Alroey, "Lost Pioneers?"

7. Tamar Hess points out that "The Second Aliyah is an ambiguous term: it denotes a historical period (1904–1914) and refers to a certain prominent social group among those who arrived in Eretz Israel during those years (about thirty thousand men and women). The social group which the term 'Second Aliyah' refers to was a small group—about two thousand people" (3–4). Hess cites Bartal, Tzahor, and Kaniel, *Ha-Aliyah ha-Shniya: Mechkarim*, 5–6. Frankel argues that the term "Second Aliyah" refers to an even smaller group: "the more or less permanent force of labor youth—the group considered synonymous in popular parlance with the 'Second Aliyah'—was no more than a few hundred strong" (*Prophecy and Politics*, 367).

8. See in this context Gish Amit's fascinating essay "The Nation and the Hope" on Naphtali Herz Imber, the little-known writer of the national anthem.

9. This novel's other leading characters—Meir Tziprofitz, the accountant, the bookkeeper, who is defined as "one of the crowd" (the "hero" of the first part of the trilogy, *In the Beginning of Confusion*), and Gedaliah Branchuk, the writer who records the events (and the "hero" of the second part of the trilogy, *The Last Ships*)—live on the periphery of the period. See my book *Lichyot Kedei Lichyot* (175–92).

10. According to another version he came from Łódź.

11. Kressel, "Yosef Luidor," 174.

12. Incidentally, the volume "Personages" published as part of a three-volume study called *The Second Aliyah* (I. Bartal, Y. Kaniel and Z. Tzahor, eds.), printed in a lavish edition by Yad Ben-Zvi Press (1997), depicts the portraits of more than ninety people—but Yosef Luidor is not among them. It seems, then, that even for academia Luidor was an unknown soldier/writer.

13. This genre was already well established by the first decade of the previous century. See Rabinovich's *Yizkor*, published in 1911. The book's full title in English is "Yizkor, a Memorial for the Fallen Hebrew Workers in Eretz Israel." The collection is a memorial booklet for eight "pioneers-saints" who died "for the love of the Yishuv" (4–5). The booklet opens with a list of the deceased to whom it is dedicated. See also Frankel, "Yizkor Book of 1911."

14. Rabinovich, "On Our Dead," 11.

15. The writers Y. H. Brenner, Z. Shatz, and Y. Luidor, as well as Zvi Gugik, the father Yehuda Yitzkar, and his son, Avraham.

16. The murder took place in a secluded house in an orchard near Jaffa, which was the residence of Y. H. Brenner and where Luidor and Shatz were staying, on 2 May 1921 (according to Kressel ["Yosef Luidor"] the date was 1 May, 1921). Ben-Gurion ("Letter 306") writes that, "already on the first day of the riots, efforts were made to obtain a military guard to accompany those who were rushing to the place to save the Jews from the Arab environment, but these efforts were unsuccessful. It only became possible on the second day. When they came they found five casualties. The Jews asked the [English] soldiers to load the dead bodies into the car, but the soldiers were afraid to stay on the narrow path of the orchard and claimed that they received an order to take only living people and not dead ones. Thirty meters away from the place they saw another dead person, Yosef Luidor, and returned to town. After some appealing, another guard was provided. The sixth body which was apart was not found." This information is included as an addendum in a letter that Ben-Gurion wrote to Moshe Luidor, Yosef's father, which adds a dimension of horror to this affair. Here it is:

To Moshe Luidor, Łódź

Jerusalem, 24.3.1922

We have received his last letter.

What can we tell him and we have no news. It is true that two trusty sons of Israel managed to discover, after much searching, the traces of the murder, and even to find some of the murderers. It is true that the Eretz-Israeli government has finally been forced, by public pressure from here and from abroad (in the English parliament the government was also asked about the murder of the writers Y. H. Brenner and Yosef Luidor), to seek justice, and it is true that the World Zionist Organization, which has taken on the task of managing the trial, has appointed the two most famous attorneys in Eretz Israel. However, 'The earth is given into the hand of the wicked; He covers the faces of its judges.' The trial that took place at the end of Tevet in Jaffa released all six Arabs who were put on trial. The Arab and Christian judges found they had done no wrong.

And as for his son's body we are encountering difficulties, but the rumor that has reached him about his son's body being found is untrue. Indeed a few months ago some human bones were found in the vicinity of that killing-place, and the government did what it did with them. Whether they were the remains of his son's body was left unclear.

It is very difficult and almost impossible now to get a certificate [a permit to immigrate to Israel] for his younger son, however we will do our utmost to obtain this certificate. And the moment we manage to obtain it we will send it to him. It is a pity he didn't specify how old he is. Of the letters of his deceased son only a few are left, not even enough for one collection. Those that are left are still kept with us. (96)

17. See Kushnir, "Last Times," 218–28. All six people who were murdered were found naked, but only Luidor was found naked and tied up with ropes. This is also confirmed by Y. Rabinovich ("On Our Dead"). For more on this murder story from an angle that centers on the other "unknown writer" who was "found worthy" (as Y. Rabinovich puts it) to die with Brenner, see Menachem Poznanski's introduction to Zvi Shatz's collection of Stories *On the Edge of Silence*, which was published in 1929 (v–xiv), and then edited by Muki Tzur in 1990 (13–22). This is another matter on which there have emerged new testimonies that, generally speaking, coincide with the previous information. A significant testimony in this context is the report by Bechor Sheetrit, a British police officer and the future police minister in the Israeli government, who was appointed special investigator in this affair. See Qedar, "Pale, Taciturn, Feeble-Bodied Young Man."

18. See for example Tzur, "Second Aliyah People," 286–87.

19. Yaari-Polskin, "Yosef Luidor," 473–76.

20. Ben-Zvi, "Ein Hai in the Old Days," 472–73.

21. Yaari-Polskin concludes his piece on Luidor with the sentence "in his life as in his death he was alienated from man" ("Yosef Luidor," 476)—a sentence that echoes the opening sentence of Luidor's best known story, "Yoash": "Since childhood Yoash had *alienated* himself in his actions" (*Stories*, 63; emphasis mine).

22. Luidor, "Pan," 9.

23. Luidor, "Robinson Crusoe," 10b.

24. Ibid., 11a.

25. Ibid., 11a.

26. Davis, *Resisting Novels*.

27. Luidor, "Robinson Crusoe," 11a.

28. This is at least the way they saw it. In fact, they were almost the first. The credit in this context is due, as in several other contexts, to the people of the First Aliyah. For different reasons, which this is not the place to go into, they were not seen as founding fathers, as members of a "foundational generation"—at least not until the end of the seventies.

29. See Cohen, *Me-Halom le-Metsi'ut*, 96–97.

30. See Ofrat, *Adama, Adam, Dam*; Sadan-Lowenstein, *Siporet Shnot ha-Essrim be-Erets Isra'el*; Shaked, *Ha-Siporet ha-Ivrit*, 17–154.

31. See Zach, *Kavei Avir*, 11–19.

32. Yaari-Polskin testifies, in his essay on Luidor, that this lonely, strange and tormented man always vacillated "between life and non-existence," giving as an example a "typical event" that happened to Luidor, and about which he heard from him after a while:

He went to bathe in the sea. He was an excellent swimmer, and started swimming, and got very far from the shore without realizing it, since he was absorbed in his own thoughts, as usual. Thus he kept swimming, farther and farther away, and suddenly, when he awoke from his dreams and looked back, he saw with great fear that the shore was almost invisible. How will he swim back such a distance? And at that moment, when he was lying on his back, resting on the water's surface, an idea occurred to him and he started thinking thus: to begin with, he wouldn't have found the courage to settle his accounts with life in such a way, although at some point he would finally be forced to choose, one way or another. Now, in retrospect, since he is already here, and the shore is very far, almost impossible to return to, and the opportunity has presented itself—why should he not use it? What has he got to lose? His bed with the holey and bare straw mattress in Lifshitz's hotel in Neve-Shalom, where he hasn't paid his three grushes per night for over a month? And where, and what should he return to? Maybe to copy another of Brenner's manuscripts, a kind of new 'Breakdown and Bereavement,' which he had been copying until now? To start dealing again with those anguished and tormented Brenner types, who bang their heads against the wall and tear their hair out and scratch their bleeding wounds?—Or maybe he should go back to work and to nature, as has always been his wish?—But he will be laughed at, because he is odd and strange, he walks about like a foreigner.

No, he has no place in this world! The abyss, it is his only savior, one moment—and he would be saved. Thus he was taking his mental stock, lying supinely far out at sea, rocking on the waves, still contemplating like a sick child in his cradle, ready to plunge into the abyss, when suddenly his eyes opened, and he saw, as he had never seen them before, the light blue sky and the brightly shining sun. His ears heard the sound of the waves and everything merged into a powerful voice calling him to life, to love, to happiness!—He heard a kind of surging, strong and powerful echo from the distant shore:—To life!

—To life!—an echo from his own heart burst out in reply, and in a moment he mustered his strength and started to swim, all the way back to the shore. He swam to a rock far from the shore, rested on it for a few moments and then swam further, until he was finally near the shore, as the sounds of the night were already taking over the land." ("Yoseph Luidor," 474–75)

33. As we shall see in the next chapter, the writers of the Palmach Generation, and chief among them Moshe Shamir, intensified this process while at the same time undermining it.

34. Luidor, *Stories*, 72–74. [All translations of citations from this book into English are by M. S.]

35. Gurevich and Aran, "On the Place," 9–10. Cf. Eliade, *Myth of the Eternal Return*, 3–6.

36. As in the title of Eliezer Shmueli's famous book (1933) about Alexander Zaid, a prominent Second Aliyah figure.

37. For more on this issue, see chapter 4.

38. For more on this issue, see chapter 5.

39. This is a notable phenomenon in the genre/naïve corpus of the period's affirmative literature; that is, in works by writers, poets, and playwrights in which the gap between the official Zionist ideology and the worldview suggested by their works is relatively small. In works by writers of the anti-genre/ironic corpus, the picture is more complex, but it displays the same topographical-ideological trend. Although they feature central places from the implied map of the period, these places are granted, through various stylistic methods, a new status in the existential hierarchy of the Yishuv. This phenomenon is especially evident in

the attitude to Jerusalem, which all the important writers of that generation (Y. H. Brenner, S. Y. Agnon, Aharon Reuveni, Dov Kimchi, L. A. Arieli-Orloff, and others) engaged with from a belittling or distorting starting point.

40. See chapter 1.

41. The semiotics of food is a crucial ingredient in acclimatization/settlement stories. This is the case both in the ancient Hebrew acclimatization/settlement stories (the reference to the fruit of the land in the Torah) and in modern acclimatization/settlement stories. In the corpus of modern literature this phenomenon is evident both in the attitude toward the fruits of the land, either fresh or dried, in the literature written in the Diaspora or about the Diaspora (for example, in S. Y. Agnon's *Guest for the Night*) and in the attitude toward local fruits that are less familiar to the new immigrants (for example, the status of bitter olives, tomatoes, prickly pears, and watermelons in Moshe Smilansky, M. Wilkansky, A. Reuveni, Y. H. Brenner, Z. Shatz, and others).

42. Also: "When his father sent him to school in the sixth year of his life, the boy's eyes expressed great amazement. What business does he have with school? All these boring lessons that the teacher teaches him, what are they for?" (ibid., 66).

43. An exception (in Hebrew fiction; in Yiddish fiction the situation is different) is the group of stories by the new writers (Ben Avigdor, Yitzhak Goida, and others), for whom venturing outdoors, mainly to the urban street, was part of their ideological/literary agenda.

44. On American frontier stories, see Rosowski, *Birthing a Nation*; Hall, *Performing the American Frontier*.

45. On this important issue as well, there is no essential difference in my view between "naïve" and "ironic" writers. Both complied with the period's "conversion directive" regarding the meaning of the Place.

46. This attempt, and its subsequent failure, are events with symbolic importance. That is because according to the story's implied map, the committee building is parallel to the synagogue. Therefore, as the author directs us to think, Yoash's request, at the age of thirteen(!), to be in charge of guarding the granary is natural and legitimate. The analogy implied here between the two coming-of-age occasions has another aspect, which becomes clear when we examine the essence of Yoash's argument before the committee members. Yoash wants to take over the guarding of the granary not from the people of the moshava, but from the Arab guard. He justifies this wish by arguing, "It is I who was born in this moshava, and not the negro Abu-Kassim! It is I who love this land and the granary, not Abu-Kassim! I should be the granary's guard, I and no other!" (68). In the semantic context created here (the analogy made between guarding the land and being called up to read the Torah in the synagogue), the committee members' refusal to grant Yoash's request has a clear and serious meaning: abandoning the "Holy Ark"/"Holy Land" and inviting a stranger to desecrate it.

47. See Miron, *Mul ha-Ach ha-Shotek*, 61–119.

48. Dayan, "Voice and the Echo," 5–6. I am grateful to Yehonatan Geffen for referring me to this document.

49. Gurevich and Aran, "On the Place," 10. Cf. Armstrong, "Short History of Myth," 22–23.

50. Otto, *Idea of the Holy*.

51. Ofrat, *Adama, Adam, Dam*, 20.

52. On this issue see, among others, Almog, *Hatzabar*.

53. Biale claims that "Zionism often used the German voilcisch language of 'blood and soil' before that language became irretrievably corrupted by the Nazis" (*Eros and the Jews*, 189).

54. See Leeming with Leeming, *Dictionary*, 83–83; Frazer, *Golden Bough*, 366–74.

55. Among other things, by turning it into a moral act of faith and a historical, that is, unique, noncyclical event. The link between the myths of the killing and reviving of gods in ancient civilizations and the fundamental rituals of Judaism and Christianity has been noted by numerous culture scholars. See among others, Shoham, *Ha-Mitologia* and *Valhalla*; Campbell, *Masks of God*, 90–94.

56. Campbell (*Masks of God*) claims that moving from a low rank to a higher rank in any social order cannot be performed without a real or symbolic cessation of life. Similar claims are made by classical anthropologists who dealt with the structure of rites of passage in "primitive" cultures: Turner, *Ritual Process*; van Gennep, *Rites of Passage*; Eliade, *Rites and Symbols*.

57. See also Biale, *Eros and Jews*; Miron, *Imahot Meyasdot*.

58. The scope of women's movements in literature and its meanings has been the subject of several brilliant recent studies. See Naveh, *Nos'im ve-Nos'ot*; DeKoven, *Booking Passage*; Moretti, *Atlas of the European Novel*; and Mazali, *Maps of Women's Goings and Stayings*. For more on this see also chapter 4.

59. A. D. Gordon and Z. Shatz tried to develop models of family life that would ensure the future of the dynasty, but their views were unusual among the Second Aliyah people. See Biale, *Eros and Jews*.

60. Eliade, *Myth of the Eternal Return*, 17–21.

61. Ibid., 11. In the religions of nationalism, of course, the equivalent of erecting the cross is planting/erecting/flying the national flag.

62. See Friedländer, *Reflections of Nazism*.

63. Ofrat, *Adama, Adam, Dam*.

64. Eliade, *Myth of the Eternal Return*, 93–137. Cf. Smith, *Illustrated World Religions*, 235.

65. This is a point that Clint Eastwood, as an actor and a director, brilliantly exposed and portrayed. See especially his film *High Plains Drifter* (1973); for more on this, see chapters 4 and 5.

66. Schiller, *Naïve and Sentimental Poetry*.

67. About the myth of Tannhäuser, see Elisabeth Frenzel, *Stoffe Der Weltliteratur* 612–14.

68. Most of the male settlers in the pioneering Hebrew literature, throughout the first half of the twentieth century (as well as later, although, as I shall show in the following chapters, in a different form), overwhelmingly prefer to disappear into mother nature than to build a home, live with a woman, and raise children. About the misogyny in the literature of the first aliyot, see among others: Melman, "From the Periphery to the Center"; Hess, "Autobiographical Writings"; Schwartz, *Ma she-Ro'im Mikan*, pp. 125–47.

69. David's profound fear of the sea sheds an ironic light on his description as "lay[ing], enjoying the place's magnificence to the full. Looking and enjoying—and that was enough" (*ONL*, 78). This ironic perspective, which is intensified because of the hackneyed phrase "here he has found a safe haven," reaches its peak in the scene that follows immediately after the sea scene, in which David meets two Arab youths. These youths beat him up and almost steal his horse and his weapon (the "savior," Yoash, appears in the nick of time). This is a hu-

miliating scene, which ridicules all of David's declarations in the preceding scene, in which he feels "that he is the son of this land," where "his soul can finally rest," etc.

70. Seede Vries and Pfefferman, "Henya Pekelman"; Hess, "Henya Pekelman."
71. See Even-Zohar,"Israeli Hebrew Literature"; Eyal, "Discursive Origins."
72. Shaked, "Narrative of Persecution,"144–60.
73. Both here and in the previous passage I quoted, the horse is seen as representing the lion, the king of the animals, in the portrayed world. The parallelism suggests, of course, that Yoash (who, incidentally, is a typical Samson-like character, and not only because in the end he dies with the "Philistines") controls the "lion," which attacks at the will of his master like "a lion's cub," whereas David has a great fear of it.
74. See Avraham Shaked, *Ha-Aborijinim*, 31–37, 69.
75. Naveh, *Nos'im ve-Nos'ot*, 103.
76. Deleuze and Guattari, *A Thousand Plateaus*, 381.
77. Naveh, *Nos'im ve-Nos'ot*, 104–5. Similar claims are made by Shulamith Shahar in her book about the gypsies (*Ha-Tso'anim*).
78. Naveh, *Nos'im ve-Nos'ot*, 103.
79. Reuveni, *Even to Jerusalem*, 405.
80. Biale wrote about the Zionist revolution that "never has a national revolution been accompanied by such a culture of pessimism in which a mythological ideal of virile national revival coexisted improbably with a poetics of impotence" (*Eros and the Jews*, 200).
81. Agnon, *Only Yesterday*, 641–42.
82. See Y. Schwartz, "Omanut ha-Sipur"; G. Shaked, *Shmuel Yosef Agnon*.
83. Shaked, *Shmuel Yosef Agnon*.
84. The similarity between the two texts is even more profound. In Isaac's burial ceremony, as in the pagan ceremony, the transition from season to season is also a reenactment of Creation—the great confrontation between chaos and order. In S. Y. Agnon this conflict is expressed in the temporary ambiguity about the nature of the rains: favorable rains or a flood. First the rains came down incessantly, "the water flowed from above and from below" (*Only Yesterday*, 641). Moreover, as a kind of distorted and self-replicating repetition of Creation, the water came down "for six or seven days . . . and when they stopped they started coming down again." Only "finally, the rains stopped and the clouds dispersed and the sun shone. And when we came outside we saw that the earth was smiling with its plants and its flowers."

4. Moshe Shamir, He Walked in the Fields *(1948)*

Epigraph: Oz, "The Lost Garden," 153–64.
1. Halperin, "Literature, Biography and Politics," 380.
2. Ben-Amos, "*He Walked in Fields* in 1948," 46n67.
3. Zonder, "Moshe Shamir."
4. See Gur, "First Original Play," 598.
5. The data is from Ben-Meir, "Normot Itsuv-Bima," 6.
6. Shaked, *Ha-Siporet ha-Ivrit*, 235.
7. Bartov, "On Moshe Shamir," 37.
8. Gamzu,"'He Walked in the Fields'—at the 'Cameri.'"
9. Achi-Neeman, "He Walked in the Fields."

10. Aran, "On Three Books." See also Zilbertal, "The Heroism"; Sha'anan, "On the Hebrew Story," 243.

11. Halperin, "Literature, Biography and Politics."

12. Shamir in an interview with E. Mohar (2 March 1973).

13. See Halperin, "Literature, Biography and Politics," 386–87.

14. Yoseph Yadin, *Kol Israel*, 1988; cited in Feingold, "1948 in the Theater," 239.

15. Ben-Amos, "*He Walked in the Fields* in 1948," 143. A similar picture is depicted by Y. M. Neiman: "There was no division between the stage and the audience. The audience included many Palmachniks and soldiers, and it was as if Uri and Willie and Ginger and Mika and Ruthka had come down into the audience, and some of the audience members got onto the stage. Total identification" ("*He Walked in the Fields* at the Cameri Theater," 13). A similar description appears in Uri Avneri's *1948: A Soldier's Tale—The Bloody Road to Jerusalem*.

16. Gilula ("'He Walked in the Fields,'" 87) touches on this issue, hinting that Shamir was aware of his recipients' "clamor" for a heroic protagonist, and that he responded to it in the story's stage version, in the play—where Uri died not "in a needless training accident, in a grenade-throwing practice he himself initiated unnecessarily," but "in an important action—blowing up a bridge," replacing a partisan whose wife had given birth. Similar claims, from related points of departure, were made by Nurit Gertz ("No Longer the Same Fields") in an article that deals with the affinities between the novel and the 1967 film that was based on it, and by A. Ben-Amos ("*He Walked in the Fields* in 1948").

17. See Sivan, *Dor Tashach*; Ne'eman, "Fields of the Dominant Fiction."

18. Sivan, *Dor Tashach*, 56.

19. Rancière, "Interview: The Image of Brotherhood," 26, 28. The concept "dominant fiction" is analogous to the concept "implied model" as I use it here and in previous works.

20. Ne'eman, "Fields of the Dominant Fiction," 401. The film based on Shamir's novel, directed by Yosef Milo and starring Assi Dayan as Uri, was made in 1967.

21. "Kadoorie"—the name of two agricultural schools founded in Israel with the funds from the estate of Sir Ellis Kadoorie, a Jewish merchant in Hong Kong. The first school was founded in 1930 in Tulkarm, for the agricultural education of the Arabs. The second school, for Jewish students, was founded in 1933 at the foot of Mount Tabor; many of the commanders of the Haganah and the Palmach received their education there.

22. The "Tehran Children"—around a thousand children, mostly orphans, who survived the war and arrived in Tehran, which was at the time under British rule, in the months of April–August 1942, following an agreement between the Polish government in exile and the Soviet authorities. When word about the Jewish children's arrival in Tehran reached Eretz Israel, the Jewish Agency sent two emissaries, Reuven Shefer and Avraham Zilberberg, to set up a Palestine Office there. In October 1942 Tzipora Shertok arrived in Tehran to direct, with a group of pioneers who arrived with the refugees, the orphanage called Jewish Child Home. The children finally made it to Eretz Israel, through Karachi, India (today Pakistan), and Suez, on 18 February 1943. The children's journey created great excitement in the Yishuv. Thousands of people waited along the route of the train that brought them to Atlit and gave them a warm and enthusiastic welcome. Soon, however, a heated and prolonged debate began among the various religious factions and the Histadrut and Labor movement on the question of in what schools the children should receive their education. See Dina Porat, the entry "Tehran Children," 571–72; Tomer (ed.), *Adom ve-Lavan*.

23. Arbel, "Masculinity and Nostalgia," 58.

24. *He Walked in the Fields*, 49; hereafter *HWF*. All the citations from *He Walked in the Fields* refer to the Am Oved edition, 1998 [1948]. [All translations of citations from this book into English are mine—M. S.].

25. The Jewish Brigade (The Jewish Infantry Brigade Group) was a brigade in the British Army, comprising Jewish volunteers from Eretz Israel, was formed in September 1944, following many debates in the British government and army. The three infantry battalions of the Palestine Regiment were assembled near Alexandria, and in the beginning of November sailed to Italy and took part in the first stages of the Allies' final offensive in Italy in April 1945. After the fighting ended, many of the Brigade's soldiers were engaged in helping Holocaust refugees, organizing illegal immigration to Palestine, acquiring weapons for the Haganah, and so forth.

26. Parodic overtones can also be detected in the letter he writes Ruthka on his way to Egypt: "Here we are sailing to the land of the Ten Plagues, and this must be the eleventh plague not written in the Torah" (*HWF*, 147).

27. "Uri didn't get a room and the girls had returned to Mika's tent. They would have their meetings, therefore, in the wood, in the apple grove, in the vineyards" (*HWF*, 158). Also, according to Mika: "He never slept with her in the tent, they never had a week of quiet, consecutive nights, happy, sleeping next to each other, at times content with a light caress on the forehead, with a touch. How many times did they do it together on the ground? In the wood, in the apple-garden, on a stroll" (222).

28. See, for example: Goldberg, "He Walked in Fields"; Shaham, "What Do You Think"; Shaked, *Ha-Siporet ha-Ivrit 1880–1980*, 230–66.

29. See, for example, Tochner, "Change of the Guard"; Miron, *Arba Panim*, 449–52.

30. For the similarity between the fictional map and the real map in the fiction of S. Yizhar, see Ma'apil (Itsuv ha-Metsi'ut) and Nevo (*Shiv'ah Yamim ba-Negev*).

31. This was noted by Schweid, *Shalosh*, 185–201; Miron, *Arba Panim*, 439–71; and others. Shaked wrote the following pertinent words in this context: "Shamir's hero is a romantic figure. These are Byronic figures, powerful in love and war. Rather than by sexual impulses, they are driven by the urge to conquer; sex is the reward of the conqueror, and the hero is the fighter who wins the woman" (*Ha-Siporet ha-Ivrit*, 241).

32. See Wright, *Six Guns and Society*.

33. An extensive literature has been written on the nomads in Western literature and culture. See among others, Naveh *Nos'im ve-Nos'ot*, 96–120; Shahar, *Ha-Tso'anim*; Islam, *Ethics of Travel*.

34. See Bakhtin, "Forms of Time."

35. For example, Dimock, "Name of Odysseus."

36. For example: Howard Clarke, *Return of the Hero*; Vernant, *Universe*, 87–134.

37. See Dimrock, "Name of Odysseus"; Vernant, *Universe*, 87–134.

38. On this issue, see Y. Schwartz, *Lichyot Kedei Lichyot*, 155–58; Hess, "Autobiographical Writings."

39. The camp is described through the focalization of Mika, who expresses her revulsion toward it, for example, through the triple repetition of the phrase "such a degeneration" (*HWF*, 101–3).

40. Willie's appearance is described through Mika's focalization, in which it is contrasted

with Uri's appearance, as it seemed to her at the start of their relationship: "His shirt was hanging loosely, baring to the sun a blackish, strong and self-confident triangle" (*HWF*, 100).

41. On the ship on the way to Palestine Willie is also revealed—through Mika's (adoring and at the same time perceptive) eyes—as a person with an exemplary harmonic personality: "... This person lived in complete maturity: a kind of stern yet enlightened equilibrium between what should be refrained from and how to take.... Realizing in his life the dreams he is preaching... he combines the strictness of the ascetic who is enslaved to his teachings, with the sense of having the right to come to the other with bitter demands, which belongs to someone who has gone far with his internal and conscientious discipline, as well as the sobriety of a wise man who has already seen all sides, as well as the knowledge of a man who no longer errs, as well as the integrity of someone who no longer has anything to look for among you, and to whom it's not in your power to offer any benefit..." (*HWF*, 116).

42. Bhabha, *Location of Culture*, 85–92. This is the place to remark—and I will elaborate on this fascinating issue later—that the mocking-ridiculing figure, the "mimicker," is in H. Bhabha the "native," and the object of ridicule is the colonizers as a group. By contrast in Shamir, and in this he was followed by some of the writers of the State Generation, the "mimicker" is the native-sabra (rather than the Arabs or the Bedouins), and the object of ridicule is the settling parents as a group, "the frontiersmen" of the Zionist project.

43. A number of literature scholars, and in particular N. Gertz, have claimed that Shamir's narrator, like most of the narrators in the Palmach Generation, has a monolithic and authoritative voice, in contrast with the multivocality and ambivalence of the narrators in the fiction of the State Generation writers. This is an inaccurate assertion, which probably originates from these scholars' wish to distinguish the fiction of the State Generation writers from that of the preceding generation. This and other poetical comparative contexts of discussion raise an important question, which has so far not been discussed extensively enough in the literature: Is there an essential, "real" difference, between the writers of these two generations?

44. For an exhaustive discussion of this issue, see Shapira, *Yehudim Hadashim*, 155–74.
45. G. Shaked, *Ha-Siporet ha-Ivrit*, 242–45.
46. Miron, *Arba Panim*, 445.
47. Ibid., 445–46; emphases in the original.
48. Ibid., 446–47; emphasis in the original.
49. G. Shaked, *Ha-Siporet ha-Ivrit*, 230–68.
50. Ibid., 243–44.
51. "He was the frequent progress of pairs of blows ... He was waists that tore through shrubs" (*HWF*, 227), and so forth. This fascinating phenomenon was astutely noted by Gluzman, "Aesthetics of the Mutilated Body."
52. See the songs composed as part of the myth of Tel Hai and Yosef Trumpeldor: "Hayo haya / gibor echad, / libo amitz / velo pachad. // 'Tov lamut al hamishmar / be'ad artzenu!' koh amar. / Hayo-haya gibor chidah, / lo zro'ah yechidah" [Once upon a time there was/ one hero,/ his heart was brave/ and he was not afraid. // "It's good to die on the watch, / for our land!" so he said. / Once upon a time there was an enigmatic hero, / who had only one arm] (from a 1950s schoolbook for first graders [Tel-Hai stories], p. 136). And also: "Hayo haya gibor atik / tzurim baka, sla'im he'etik" [Once upon a time there was an ancient Hero/ He smashed rocks, he moved boulders], "Be'ad amenu be'ad artzenu gibor Yosef nafal... ki nil-

chamti ve-gam nafalti be'ad moladeti" [For our people for our land the hero Yosef fell ... For I have fought and also fell for my homeland]. See Laskov, *Trumpeldor*, 252–53.

53. Thus, for example, in the scene in which Mika watches him loading the boxes of grapes onto the truck: "From her dark corner Mika watched Uri so tensely and excitedly that a suddenly heard sound or the bang of a box could give her a stroke. Uri also felt, along with the discomfort of his great effort, the preciousness of the passing moments, the inspired *festivity and mystery* in which Mika was immersed behind him, surreptitiously—and kept a total silence the whole time" (*HWF*, 143; emphasis mine).

54. The ability to escape devouring spaces in one piece is reserved in mythology for celebrated people with noble qualities. On this issue see the entry "Man-Eating Monster" in Cirlot, *A Dictionary of Symbols*, 204.

55. Schweid, *Shalosh Ashmorot ba-Sifrut ha-Ivrit*, 185–201.

56. "The vineyard was flooded with lights, and all its countless dewdrops, at once, with an unstoppable mischievousness, started waving her good-morning with the radiant handkerchiefs in their hands, and they were so excited they didn't know what to do but to wipe their wet cheeks. The vineyard glittered with stripes and myriad droplets. Its land was divided into camps of light and shade, which immediately started battling for every clod and tiny wrinkle" (*HWF*, 87).

57. See for example: "Uri stampeded inside [into the pannier shed] on the rubber wheels of his rectangular cart while arrogantly holding the reigns in his fist loosely and doing with the horse as he pleased. . . . Uri appeared, demonstrating his indifference toward pedestrians and making his horse gallop right up to standing . . . An arrogant entrance that almost squashed him [Yozek] against the beam" (*HWF*, 95).

58. It should be remembered that "Uri was not fond of reflection for its own sake. Sometimes he would get caught in it when something bothered him or was so important to him that he couldn't get it out of his mind; but reflections exercising the thinking power for its own sake, an original and independent life of emotion, reaction, analysis—all these were something to be avoided" (125).

59. Gluzman, "Aesthetics of the Mutilated Body."

60. "Uri didn't get a room, and the girls had returned to Mika's tent. They would have their meetings, therefore, in the wood, in the apple grove, in the vineyards" (*HWF*, 158).

61. This formulation portrays Uri once more as an ape-man, a modern Tarzan.

62. See Avraham Goren (*HWF*, 152); Willie (*HWF*, 105); Biberman (*HWF*, 263), and Uri (*HWF*, 160). Incidentally, the novel's stage versions are much more masculine and military. Thus, for example, in the second version of the play (1956), the narrator was given an additional task: he became a kind of military commentator and during one of the transitions between scenes he even used a map and a stick to indicate the route Uri's platoon had taken on its way to the action.

63. The phrase "the celebration of Rabbi Silo" is derived from the phrase "the celebration [hillula] of Rabbi Shimon bar Yochai," the popular celebration that takes place on the night of Lag BaOmer on the tomb of Rabbi Shimon bar Yochai at Meron near Safed. The transformation of religious holidays into agricultural festive days was, as has already been noted by scholars from various disciplines, a fundamental element in the creation of the Yishuv's culture.

64. This is, in fact, a symbolic rite in which the human fruits of the community, the little

sabras, are sacrificed to the God of fertility, which is represented in the modern agricultural community (the kibbutz) by that huge "spilling pipe" that releases the abundance of corn kernels collected in the fields. Subtler versions of this rite—whose religious equivalent in Judaism is the ceremony of Pidyon Haben (redemption of the first born son)—are the ceremonies of bringing in the first fruits that were (and still are) celebrated in the kibbutzim and moshavim. See on this matter Oz Almog, *Hatzabar*, 96–97, 353.

65. "He [Avraham Goren] pulled his blanket off his unmade bed and into the light. He picked it up carefully, walked toward those sleeping [Mika and Uri] and very gently spread it over them" (150).

66. Including the death events of major and minor characters in the "anti-generic" wing of the period's literature: first and foremost, the event of Hanoch Hefetz's death in Y. H. Brenner's *Breakdown and Bereavement*, the death of Meyer Ponek in Aharon Reuveni's *Even to Jerusalem*, and that of Isaac Kumer in S. Y. Agnon's *Only Yesterday*.

67. These death events were already institutionalized in the collection "Yizkor," published in 1911, and later on in scores of documentary and semidocumentary publications—for example, in the written portraits included in the Second Aliyah Book (1947). This sensitive issue was touched on, from another angle, by Alroey, "Lost Pioneers?"

68. The commemoration of the War of Liberation soldiers took various forms: songs ("Bab el Wad," "Dudu," "Elifelet," and so forth), stories of heroism and/or exemplary personal behavior (the thirty-five soldiers who spared an old Arab shepherd who later revealed their location to the enemy soldiers), commemorative monuments (for example, the armored vehicles on the road to Jerusalem), and the names of many settlements and institutions (Netiv HaLamed-Heh [Path of the Thirty-Five], Kfar Achim [Brothers' Village], Metzudat Yoav [Fort Yoav], Sdeh Yoav [Yoav's Field], Netiv HaShayara [Path of the Convoy], Ein HaShlosha [The Threesome's Spring], and so on).

69. On the centrality of this narrative in the corpus under discussion see Arpaly, *Avotot shel Hoshech*, 29–58; Miron, *Mul ha-Ach ha-Shotek*.

70. On this matter, see Schwartz, "The Person, the Path, and the Melody."

71. See Kartun-Blum, *Ha-Lets ve-ha-Tsel*, 117–36.

72. See Hever, "Majority as a National Minority"; Oppenheimer, "Living Dead Model."

73. Mosse, *Fallen Soldiers*.

74. Hutcheon, "Modern Parody and Bakhtin."

75. Alterman, *Kochavim Bachutz*, 141–42.

76. Gertz, "No Longer the Same Fields," 65.

77. Miron, *Arba Panim*, 14–30, 150–64.

78. See Schwartz, *Ma she-Ro'im Mikan*, 235–64.

79. N. Alterman, "Magash Hakesef."

80. Chatwin, *Anatomy of Restlessness*, 75.

81. S. Shapira, *Routes of Wandering*, 67.

82. Naveh, *Nos'im ve-Nos'ot*, 103, 104–5.

83. See Miron, *Arba Panim*, 446–52; Shaked, *Ha-Siporet ha-Ivrit*, 243–44.

84. Gertz, "No Longer the Same Fields," 70–71.

85. Ibid., 72.

86. Ibid.

87. See, for example, "At exactly three thirty Uri surveyed his platoon. The guys were

very tired and disheveled. The most ridiculous of all, as usual, was Shimon, 'Zimon Artzt,' as he was called by the gang because of his name, Shimon Artzi, and because of his origin which was, if you'll excuse me, from Germany." And also: "Immediately a long line of Khaki-wearers was running in the adjacent ravine, climbing near the orchard's fence up the slow slope—on the way to the areas of the desolate hills. Just behind it chased one creature [Shimon Artzi], holding a binoculars with long leather straps, which was tossing about restlessly" (*HWF*, 282).

88. In the sculpture he made after Uri's image, Y. Tumarkin sensitively incorporated both the sabra figure's element of explosion (the figure is composed of reassembled metal shards) and his pathetic masculinity/sexuality (his sex organ is represented by a hollow and rusty pipe).

89. The collective with which Mika is affiliated before the ceremonial ascent to Har Ha'ayalot, the Tehran Children, is defined by the omniscient narrator as "a group that has already managed on its wanderings to despair of all the faith in the world, to offend against the laws and respectability of half a dozen states, to fondle and weigh any value in the world, only to eventually dismiss it." Mika herself wonders, "Is it not possible to see all her shame in her" (*HWF*, 237). Uri wonders, "Is this a mature woman, steeped in adulterous acts, who is mocking him?" (146). Even Willie privately calls her "this nerve-ridden girl" (285), and referring to the abortion, he tells Ruthka: "By the way, I'm not sure that this is her first time. After all I know what human material I brought from there" (286).

90. See Hever, "We Didn't Come"; Naveh, *Nos'im ve-Nos'ot*, 80–95.

91. The creation of this linkage between Mika, the Holocaust refugee, and Ruth the Moabite seems to have two aspects. One aspect highlights her "otherness." The other aspect hints—and I will elaborate on this matter later—at her status as the one who is embodying the future of the revived nation. This double status differs from the double status of Naame and Peninah in *The Love of Zion*. For Naame and Peninah are "others," "foreigners," only in appearances, whereas Mika is described and perceived as a real "other" who undergoes a conversion.

92. Initiation rites of this kind are a crucial element in every national project that is based on a "melting pot" policy. On this issue, see Tzameret, *Melting Pot in Israel* and *Alei Gesher Tsar*; Bernier and Williams, *Beyond Beliefs*, 274–70.

93. "A slow, creeping and bad bout of nausea, tiredness, headache, dizziness, and the devil knows what else" (*HWF*, 206).

94. Bettelheim, *Children of the Dream*.

95. See Lévi-Strauss, *Savage Mind*.

5. Amos Oz, "Nomads and Viper" (1963)

Epigraph: Zertal, "A Generation's Strong Weaknesses—An Interview with Amos Oz."

1. The story "Nomads and Viper" (hereafter *NV*) was first published in *Haaretz* on 7 February 1964.

2. On the differences between the two editions, see Brifman, "'Artsot Hatan'"; Ben-Baruch, "Lands beyond the Fence," 12–14; Navot, "Tell It Not."

3. See the comprehensive bibliography prepared by Yosef Yerushalmi (*Amos Oz—Bibliografia*).

4. I have been especially intrigued by a piece by Yehoshua Kenaz, a very important writer of Oz's generation, who in later years consigned himself to public silence—he stopped writing reviews and strictly refused to give interviews for newspapers and literary periodicals. The piece contains some perceptive observations. Here are two of them: "Amos Oz's collection of stories is characteristic of the young prose that has appeared in recent years, [one of] whose features . . . is dealing with 'a-social' protagonists, with repressed and eruptive drives, with a wild world in the bosom of a disciplined and sublimated civilization." And also: "With all the differences among the various stories . . . you always find in them the double vision of a civilized world set against a primeval, animalistic world, two worlds that are merely projections of one psychic complex" ("Where the Jackals Howl," 175).

5. Kurzweil, who heaped scorn on many of the Israeli works published in those years, wrote the following: "an incessant repetition of the same technique with variations is the entryway to the epic wasteland. It happens [even] with a real talent like Amos Oz. The single story allows one to listen, captures the heart with its linguistic talent. The sum total of the stories is tiresome, disappointing, discouraging and annoying, because the reader becomes weary of the richness of scarcity. Again and again the same situation. Again and again the virtuosity to skillfully evoke the putrid mire in the landscapes of animalistic man. If Satan had literary talent, he would write using Oz's formula" ("Israeli Story").

6. For instance, in the beginning of the 1960s Oz was active in the social-democratic "Min Hayesod" group. Since the Six-Day War he has been active in various groups and organizations of the Israeli peace movement advocating the existence of two states, Israel and Palestine, side by side. He was part of the Committee for Peace and Security (1967), the Moked and Shelli Movements, and has been among the principle spokespersons for the Peace Now Movement since its founding. In 2003 he was one of the initiators of the "Geneva Document," an Israeli-Palestinian peace initiative. Oz was one of the editors of the collection *Siach Lochamim* ("A Conversation of Fighters," published in English as *The Seventh Day*), which was published in 1968 by the kibbutz movement, together with Muki Tzur, Avraham Shapira, and others, and was a collection that served as a platform for conversations and testimonies of kibbutz members after the Six-Day War.

7. See *Under This Blazing Light* (1979), *In the Land of Israel* (1983); *The Slopes of Lebanon* (1987); *Kol HaTikvot* (All the Hopes, 1998); *Be'etzem Yesh Kan Shtei Milchamot* (Actually There Are Two Wars Here, 2002); *Al Midronot Har Ga'ash* (On the Slopes of a Volcano, 2006). These collections have been translated into many languages. In addition, six collections of articles and essays that were not published in Hebrew were published in various languages. Additionally, Oz published two collections of literary essays: *The Silence of Heaven: Agnon's Fear of God* (2000) and *The Story Begins* (1999).

8. See for example: Reuveni, *Ad-Yerushala'im*; Calderon, "Amos Oz."

9. The prizes awarded to Oz in Israel include the Kugel Award (1965), the Brenner Prize (1976), Ze'ev Award for Children's Literature (1978), the Bernstein Prize for literature (1983), the Blalik Prize (1986), and the Israel Prize for literature (1998). The prizes awarded to Oz internationally include the Hans Christian Andersen Medal for Children's Literature, Denmark (1978); Officer of the Order of Arts and Letters of the French Republic (1984); Prix Femina, for best foreign novel appearing in France (for *Black Box*) (1988); Peace Prize at Frankfurt International Book Fair, awarded by German Publishers' and Booksellers' Association (1992); Hamoré Prize for Children's Literature, France (for *Soumchi*) (1993); Knight's

Cross of the Legion D'Honneur of the Republic of France (1997); Blue Cobra Award, Switzerland (1997); Prix "France Culture," France (2004); International "Ovidius Literary Prize," from Romania's writers union, for literary merit and peace work (2004); Catalonia International Prize (shared with Sari Nusseibeh) (2004); International "Die Welt" Literary Award, Berlin (2004); Bruno Kreisky Prize for Political Literature, Vienna (2005); KORET Jewish Book Awards, San Francisco (for *A Tale of Love and Darkness*) (2005); Goethe Prize for lifetime literary and essayistic work, Frankfurt (2005); nominated "Commander of the Order of Arts and Letters," French Republic (2005).

10. Dov Sadan, one of the most important critics to appear in Hebrew culture, wrote, among other enlightening things about Oz, the following bizarre sentences: "I knew him from infancy, and he was a beautiful boy, just as he became in time a beautiful youth, and he is now a beautiful man (and I do not adhere to the belief of my friend, Zvi Kesseh, that man's beauty is his danger)" ("Mountain and Its Slopes," 43). The connection between the talent, success, and physical beauty that were also to Oz's detriment was wonderfully delineated by Aviad Raz ("Why Do People").

11. Inbari, "Bringing Some Relief."

12. In this context I believe that justice lies with the critics who highlighted the common ground between the writers of the Yishuv literature and the writers of the State Generation.

13. This is already true in the dream that Gideon Shenhav "had nestled in" in "The Way of the Wind" on the night prior to his death/suicide on Independence Day. Here: "Gideon Shenhav's last day began with a brilliant sunrise. He felt he could even see the beads of dew evaporating in the heat. Omens blazed on the mountain peaks far away to the east. This was a day of celebration, a celebration of independence and a celebration of parachuting over the familiar fields of home. All that night he had nestled in a half-dream of dark autumnal forests under northern skies, a rich smell of autumn, huge trees he could not name. All night long pale leaves had been dropping on the huts of the camp. Even after he had awakened in the morning, the northern forest with its nameless trees still continued to whisper in his ears" (47).

14. The most prominent expression of this phenomenon in Oz's early prose is the longing of some of the protagonists of his first novel, *Elsewhere, Perhaps*, for Germany. In an interview that Y. Kenaz conducted with Oz on Kol Israel (1966), which was also printed that year in *Shdemot* to coincide with the novel's publication, he asked him, among other things, what the Germany in the novel means for him. Oz replied: "Germany in the novel *Elsewhere, Perhaps* is neither a political Germany nor a historical Germany, it is a Germany of a hallucination or a dream that exist in the hearts of several of the protagonists. It is in fact an 'elsewhere,' it is a name that expresses deep-lying forces that threaten some of the protagonists in this book and burst out of them, sometimes as longings, sometimes as terror, sometimes as an eruption of emotion" (106–7).

15. See Oz, *Under This Blazing Light*.

16. A paradigmatic example of this move in Oz's fiction is the novella *Unto Death* (1970), which describes a group of Crusaders making their way to Jerusalem, or more precisely, to the heavenly Jerusalem. And see on this matter Zfira Porat's profound remarks in her article "The Golem of Zion: About Amos Oz" (1976), as well as A. Balaban's important remarks in his book *Between God and Beast* (79–137) and in the preface to his book *A Different Wave in Israeli Fiction* (18–28).

17. Oz's two main Romantic guides in Hebrew literature in Eretz Israel are, it seems, S. Y. Agnon and Nathan Alterman. On the affinity between Alterman and Oz in this context, see Kartun-Blum, "Instead of an Epilogue," 175–82.

18. On Oz's affinity with Carl Jung's teachings, see Balaban, *Between God and Beast*, 79–137, 27–30, 33, and 139–41, as well as the preface to his book *A Different Wave in Israeli Fiction* (18–28).

19. *Where the Jackals Howl*, 21, 22; hereafter *WJH*.

20. Naveh, *Nos'im ve-Nos'ot*, 103.

21. Ibid., 104–6; emphasis mine.

22. Ibid., 105.

23. See on this issue Baudrillard, *America*; Zerubavel, *Recovered Roots*; Nir, "Perception of the Desert."

24. *Elsewhere, Perhaps*, 3–7. [The passage from "through the green fields" to "Welcome" is missing from de Lange's translation, and therefore the translation is mine.—M. S.].

25. The abundance of parallelisms in this unit is reflected by the rich inventory of grammar particles that compare and contrast. Let me demonstrate. A) X and Y. Example: "So the eye and the mind—or, more precisely, geology and politics—come to be at odds with one another" (*Elsewhere, Perhaps*, 4). B) On one side and on the other. Example: "the veterans' quarters on one side and the young people's on the other" (6). C) Does not/do not . . . but merely. Example: "The tangled foliage of the trees does not break up the settlement's severe lines, but merely softens them" (5). D) If . . . then. Example: "If you are accustomed to the sight of ancient villages . . . if you expect . . . then our village is bound to startle you, and it is this which has compelled us to introduce the term 'contradiction'" (6–7). E) In the face of. Example: "The well-known lines of Reuven Harish . . . : In the face of a foul world bent on doom, / And the lascivious dance of death, / In the face of sordid frenzy, / In the face of drunken madness, / We will kindle a flame with our blood" (7).

The abundant parallelisms have two contradictory functions, which coincide with the double-layered structure of the story's topographic plane. On the one hand, almost all the mentioned landscape details are organized in a symmetrical pattern—which lends the represented world an orderly, disciplined character, supported by the logical aspect of most of the verbal patterns that connect the different wings of the analogical configurations (example: "Anyone who draws the shallow inference that . . . merely reveals his own prejudice" [7]). On the other hand, the fact that the narrator is unable to relate to any landscape detail without immediately assigning it a place in the ideological descriptive order hints at his great anxiety and at the same time his secret longing for this order to fall apart and collapse.

26. Starting with the chapter's title ("A Charming, Well-Organized Village"), which creates an equivalence (later revealed as false) between an advanced civilization and emotional welfare; continuing with the story's first two sentences, which direct us to organize all the kibbutz buildings "in strict symmetry" (*Elsewhere, Perhaps*, 3), and with the many sentences that echo the opening sentences (for example: "Beyond the dining hall, the settlement is divided into two separate blocks" [ibid., 7]).

27. The opening chapter's fifth paragraph, which serves as a rhetorical transition link between the verbal sequence that preceded it and the one that follows it, concludes thus: "if this is your mental picture of a village, then our village is bound to startle you, and it is this which has compelled us to introduce the term 'contradiction.' Our village is built in a spirit

of optimism" (*Elsewhere, Perhaps*, 6). And the immediately following paragraph ends with an echo of the same leading analogical-contrasting term: "That was what we meant when we stated that our village was built in a spirit of optimism" (ibid.).

28. For example, in the following paragraph, which is entirely based on the symmetrical contrast that seemingly exists between the kibbutz and the "old" European village: "The houses, as we have said, are brightly painted. They are laid out at regular intervals. Their windows all face northwest, since the architects tried to adapt the building to the climate. *Here there is no* agglomeration of buildings clustering or ramifying haphazardly down the ages, nor blocks of dwellings enclosing secret courtyards, *for* the kibbutz *does not* have family homes. *There is no question of* separate quarters for different crafts; the poor *are not* relegated to the outskirts *nor is* the center reserved for the wealthy. The straight lines, the clean shapes, the neatly ruled concrete paths and rectangular lawns *are* the product of a vigorous view of the world. That was what we meant when we stated that our village was built in a spirit of optimism" (*Elsewhere, Perhaps*, 6; emphases mine).

29. For more on this see chapter 2.

30. The "tourist guide" position characteristic of the texts before us parallels the "local host" position characteristic of utopian texts—such as Herzl's *Altneuland*. Oz uses the utopian descriptive convention in order to turn it on its head. The pioneering-Zionist utopia (the implied model) is replaced here by a Zionist dystopia (the portrayed model).

31. Gertz, *Shvuya ba-Haloma*, 13–34.

32. Shimoni, "Sipur ha-Ma'abara," 149–52. Shimoni refers to Bakhtin, "Forms of Time," 247–50.

33. Bhabha, *Location of Culture*.

34. Said, *Orientalism*.

35. The assertion that nations are fundamentally hybrid constructions is, it seems, the basic assumption in all of Homi Bhabha's works. This is true already for the book *Nation and Narration* (1990).

36. Barry, *Beginning Theory*, 196. Cf. Ashcroft, Griffiths and Tiffin, *Empire Writes Back*; *Postcolonial Studies*, 183–84.

37. Barry, *Beginning Theory*, 196.

38. Ibid.

39. Here belong the heroic-pathetic attempts of many of the protagonists in A. B. Yehoshua's first stories (in the collections *Mot Hazaken* [The Death of the Old Man] and *Mul HaYe'arot* [Facing the Forests]) to stop movement/time/history. I am referring, for example, to the derailing of the train in "The Yatir Evening Express," the great siesta in the middle of building the national project in "Tardemat Hayom," the attempt to spoil/prevent Galia's wedding in "Galia's Wedding," the attempt to delay the implantation and enrooting of the Zionist project in "Facing the Forests," and so on. All of Aharon Appelfeld's early stories are marked by a denial and refusal of the historical reality in which the protagonists find themselves after the Holocaust. Prominent examples: "A Serious Attempt," "Slowly," "Love Story," and "Bertha" (in the collection *Ashan* [Smoke]), "Andriko's Journeys" (in the collection *Bagay HaPoreh* [In the Fertile Valley]), "By the Beach" (in the collections *Ashan* and *Bagay HaPoreh*), and "St. George Islands" (in the collection *Kfor al Ha'Aretz* [Frost on the Ground]). See Schwartz, *Kinat ha-Yachid*, 24–27; *Ma she-Ro'im Mikan*, 201–14.

40. One explicit allusion appears in the shower scene in which Geula "creatively" re-

constructs the orchard scene as a rape that requires an act of vengeance. A second explicit allusion is in the scene at the end of the story, when Geula lies among the bushes behind the memorial hall and reflects again on the "rape," this time from a conciliatory position. These are joined by two implicit allusions conveyed by the author to the reader "above the heads" of the narrator and other kibbutz members, who do not know what happened to Geula in the orchard or what she imagines in the shower. These are the allusions incorporated into the narrator and Rami's words at the secretariat meeting. The narrator claims that they should not react violently toward the Bedouins for the time being, because "there had been no rape or murder," to which Rami responds by asking, "Was I perhaps waiting for some small incident of rape that Geula could write poems about and I could make into a short story?" (*WJH*, 37).

41. Oz's inversion of the order of appearance of the man and the woman in his Garden of Eden story is significant on several levels. For our discussion here, it adds to the text's hybrid dimension (Geula/the woman "takes" the place of the man, and the Bedouin/the man "takes" the place of the woman). On the significance of Adam and Eve's order of appearance in the biblical scene, from a feminist point of view, see Pardes, *Countertraditions in the Bible*. See especially her presentation of the interpretations of Elizabeth Cady Stanton, Phyllis Trible, and Mieke Bal.

42. "The Arab turned his back on Geula, dropped to his knees, touched his forehead on the ground, and began murmuring fervently" (*WJH*, 34). This description brings to mind the spasms of man having an epileptic fit rather than the gestures of a Muslim praying.

43. See Bhabha, *Location of Culture*, 85–92; and Parry, "Problems in Current Discourse Theory."

44. First and foremost in "Facing the Forests," which deals with the planting and burning of (Jewish National Fund) forests, as an allegory for, among other things, the renewal of Jewish settlement in Eretz Israel and the processes of its destruction, originating here in a collaboration between an old Palestinian Arab and a Jewish Israeli student. See also Zerubavel, "Desert as a Mythical Space."

45. Herzig, *Torat ha-Sifrut ve-ha-Tarbut*, 363; emphasis in the original.

46. For example, the foot-and-mouth disease, whose origin the narrator explicitly attributes to those coming from the frontier space of the desert: "We cannot refrain from mentioning a whole string of prosaic, indeed unaesthetic disturbances, such as foot-and-mouth disease ... [The] disease came out of the desert, carried by their livestock, which had never been subjected to any proper medical inspection. Although we took various early precautions, the virus infected our sheep and cattle, severely reducing the milk yield and killing off a number of animals" (*WJH*, 23).

47. Deleuze and Gauttari, *Kafka*.

48. This descriptive concept also encompasses the bottle that Geula repeatedly tries to smash (*WJH*, 29), and her phrases that express an urgent need for an outlet: "Must get out," "Must go now," and "Now I must get outside" (35).

49. Morris, *Israel's Border Wars*.

50. Here the colonialist tendency in the story reaches its most extreme expression: in her feverish mind, Geula turns the Bedouins' dark skin color to black, a color that ostensibly also symbolizes their bones—that is, as she sees it, black is their essentialist (inherent-biological) quality. The significance of skin color in the colonialist context was brilliantly delineated by Franz Fanon (*Black Skin, White Masks*).

51. The backyard of the memorial hall serves as a smaller extension of the orchard inside the kibbutz. In this sense it has the same spatial/semantic status that was preserved for the green hill in the introductory chapter of *Elsewhere, Perhaps*, which was defined, as mentioned earlier, as "a finger of the mountains thrust violently into the heart of the valley" (*Elsewhere, Perhaps*, 6).

52. Quoted in Eliberg-Schwartz, *People of the Body*, 291.

53. Oz, *Under This Blazing Light*, 128–29.

54. See Shavit, 13.7.1990.

55. See on this issue Nir, "I-You-We"; Miron, "Kibbutz"; Achituv, "Kibbutz."

56. Oz, *Under This Blazing Light*, 129.

57. Oz and Ben-Aharon, "Sicha," 11–12.

58. A paradigmatic example of the replicating-ridiculed status of the sons' generation in the formative stories of the State Generation is the status of the developmentally disabled son in the story "The Continuing Silence of a Poet" by A. B. Yehoshua. The story ends with a poem that is "crazy, without metre, twisted, lines needlessly cut off, baffling repetitions, arbitrary punctuation," with the father's name "plastered across" its top (*The Continuing Silence of a Poet*, 34).

59. See, for example, Netzer, *Massa el ha-Atsmi*, 390–415.

60. See Zaarur, "Matzeva le-Shnaim."

61. It seems that it was this insight that motivated M. J. Berdichevsky when he created his anthology *Mimakor Israel*. It is a kind of "inverted canon" that connects, deliberately, with the pagan, hybrid, groundbreaking, and taboo-violating elements in the Jewish narrative tradition. It stands in sharp contrast to the canonical, normative, Jewish-monotheistic anthology—*Sefer Ha'agada*—created by Chaim Nachman Bialik and Yehoshua C. Ravnitzky.

62. Starting with the Hebrew midrashim on the Garden of Eden story and continuing with the various cover versions in medieval Christian literature. On this issue see Sax, *Serpent and the Swan*.

63. Zifra Porat, "Golem of Zion," 483.

Bibliography

All titles with English translations appeared originally in Hebrew unless otherwise noted. Complete bibliography may be found in the Hebrew edition.

Abramovich, S. Y. (Mendele Mocher Sforim). *Fishke the Lame.* Trans. Gerald Stillman. New York: Thomas Yoseloff, 1960 [1888].

Achi-Neeman, Y. "He Walked in the Fields" [in Hebrew]. *Bamaale* 18, no. 13 (9 July 1948): 260–61.

Achituv, Yosef. "The Kibbutz as a Community" [in Hebrew]. *Shorashim* 7 (1992): 63–73.

Agnon, S. Y. *Only Yesterday.* Trans. Barbara Harshav. Tel Aviv: Schocken, 2000 [1945].

Ahad Ha'am. "Altneuland" [Crime and punishment]. In *Kol Kitvey Ahad Ha'am* [The collected writings of Ahad Ha'am], 313–23. Jerusalem: Dvir and Hotza'a Ivrit, 1950.

Almog, Oz. *Hatzabar: Dyukan* [The sabra: A profile]. Tel Aviv: Am Oved, 1997.

Almog, Shmuel. "The Second Aliya in Its Own Eyes and in Ours" [in Hebrew]. In *Ha-Aliyah ha-Shniya: Mechkarim* [The Second Aliyah: Studies], 38–59. Ed. Israel Bartal, Zeev Tzahor and Yehoshua Kaniel. Jerusalem: Yad Yitzhak Ben-Zvi, 1997.

Alroey, Gur. "Lost Pioneers? The Issue of Suicide in the Second and Third Aliyot" [in Hebrew]. *Yahadut Zmanenu* 13 (1999): 209–41.

Alter, Robert. *The Art of Biblical Narrative.* New York: Basic Books, 1981.

———. "New Israeli Fiction." *Commentary* 47, no. 6 (1969): 59–66.

———. "The World of Oz." *The New Republic*, 29 July 1985:38–39.

Alterman, Nathan. *Kochavim Bachutz: Shirim* [Stars outside: Poems]. Tel Aviv: Yachdav, 1938.

———. "Magash Hakesef" [The silver platter]. *Davar*, 19 December 1947.

———. *Magash Hakesef: Mivchar Shirim* [The silver platter: Selected poems]. Tel Aviv: Ministry of Defense Press, 1974.

Amit, Gish. "The Nation and the Hope: How We Remembered and Why We Forgot Naftali Herz Imber" [in Hebrew]. *Mikan*, 6 (2005): 86–105.

Anderson, Benedict. *Imagined Communities: Reflections on the Origin and Spread of Nationalism.* New York: Verso, 2006 [1983].

Aran, David. "On Three Books—and Their Authors" [in Hebrew]. *Massa* 7, no. 19 (13 May 1952).

Arbel, Michal. "Masculinity and Nostalgia: A Reading of Moshe Shamir's *He Walked in the Fields* against the Backdrop of his Generation" [in Hebrew]. *Madaei Hayahadut* 39 (1999): 53–66.

Armstrong, Karen. *A Short History of Myth.* Edinburgh: Canongate, 2005.

Arpaly, Boaz. *Avotot shel Hoshech: Tisha'a Prakim al "Simchat Ani'yim" le-Natan Alterman* [Bonds of darkness—Nine chapters on Nathan Alterman's poetry]. Tel Aviv: Porter Institute and Hakibbutz Hameuchad, 1983.

Ashcroft, Bill, Gareth Griffiths, and Helen Tiffin. *The Empire Writes Back: Theory and Practice in Post-Colonial Literatures.* London: Routledge, 1989.

Ashcroft, Bill, Gareth Griffiths, and Helen Tiffin, eds. *The Post-Colonial Studies Reader*. London: Routledge, 1995.

Avineri, Shlomo *The Making of Modern Zionism: Intellectual Origins of the Jewish State*. New York: Basic Books, 1981.

Avneri, Uri. *1948: A Soldier's Tale—The Bloody Road to Jerusalem*. London: Oneworld Publications, 2008 [1949].

Azaryahu, Maoz. *Pulchanei ha-Medina: Hagigot ha-Atsma'ut ve-Hantsachat ha-Noflim be-Isra'el, 1948–1956* [State Rituals: Celebrations of Independence and the Commemoration of Fallen Soldiers in Israel, 1948–1956]. Kiryat Sde Boker: Ben-Gurion Heritage Center, Ben-Gurion U in the Negev Press, 1995.

Bachelard, Gaston. *The Psychoanalysis of Fire*. Trans. Alan C. M. Ross. Boston: Beacon, 1964.

Bakhtin, Mikhail. "Discourse in the Novel." In *The Dialogic Imagination: Four Essays*. Ed. Michael Holquist and trans. Caryl Emerson and Michael Holquist, 269–360. Austin: University of Texas Press, 1981.

———. "The Forms of Time and the Chronotopos in the Novel: From the Greek Novel to Modern Fiction." *PTL* 3 (1978): 493–528.

———. "Forms of Time and the Chronotope in the Novel." In *The Dialogic Imagination: Four Essays*. Ed. Michael Holquist and trans. Caryl Emerson and Michael Holquist, 84–258. Austin: University of Texas Press, 1981.

Balaban, Avraham. *Between God and Beast: An Examination of the Fiction of Amos Oz*. University Park: Pennsylvania State University Press, 1993.

———. *Gal Acher Basiporet Haivrit: Siporet Ivrit Postmodernistit*. [A different wave in Israeli fiction: Postmodernist Israeli fiction]. Jerusalem: Keter, 1995.

Bardenstein, Carol. "Territorialism and Desire in Palestinian and Israeli Discourses of Exile and Return." *European Journal for Semiotic Studies* 9 no. 1 (1997): 87–114.

Barry, Peter. *Beginning Theory: An Introduction to Literary and Culture Theory*. Manchester, UK: Manchester University Press, 2002.

Bartal, Israel. "'Old Yishuv' and 'New Yishuv'—The Image and the Reality" [in Hebrew]. *Catedra* 2 (1976): 3–19.

Bartal, Israel, Zeev Tzahor, and Yehoshua Kaniel, eds. *Ha-Aliyah ha-Shniya: Mechkarim* [The Second Aliyah: Studies]. Jerusalem: Yad Yitzhak Ben-Zvi, 1997.

Bartana, Orzion. *Ha-Fantasyah be-Siporet Dor ha-medina* [Fantasy in the narrative fiction of the State Generation]. Tel Aviv: Papyrus, 1989.

Bartov, Hanoch. "On Moshe Shamir: Once in a Blue Moon" [in Hebrew]. *Maariv*, 9 July 1973: 37.

Barzel, Hillel. *Shisha Mesaprim: 16 Sipurim* [Six authors: 16 stories]. Tel Aviv: Ministry of Education and Culture with Yachdav, 1972.

Baudrillard, Jean. *America*. Trans. Chris Turner. New York: Verso, 1989.

Baum, L. Frank. *The Annotated Wizard of Oz*. Ed. Michael Patrick Hearn. W. W. Norton, 2000 [1900].

Bauman, Zygmunt. *Community: Seeking Safety in an Insecure World*. Cambridge: Polity, 2001.

Beer, Gillian. *The Romance*. London: Methuen, 1970.

Bein, Alex. *Theodor Herzl: A Biography*. London: East and West Library, 1965.

Ben-Amos, Avner. "*He Walked in the Fields* in 1948: Bereavement, Memory and Consolation" [in Hebrew]. In *Ha-Cameri shel Tel Aviv: 50 Shnot Te'atron Isra'eli* [Tel Aviv's Cameri: 50 years of Israeli theater], 140–47. Tel Aviv: Daniela Di-nur, 1997.

———. "*He Walked in the Fields* in 1948: Bereavement, Memory and Consolation" [in Hebrew]. In *Ha-Cameri: Te'atron shel Zman u-Makom: Iyunim be-Toldot ha-Tetron ha-Cameri* [The Cameri: A theater of time and place: Studies in the history of the Cameri Theater], 25–47. Ed. Gad Kaynar, Eli Rozik, and Freddie Rokem. Tel Aviv: Tel Aviv University, 1999.

Ben-Amos, Avner, and Ilana Bet-El. "Holocaust Day and Memorial Day in Israeli Schools: Ceremonies, Education and History." *Israel Studies* 4 no. 1 (1999): 258–84.

Ben-Arieh, Yehoshua. "The Literature of Western Travellers to Eretz Israel in the 19th Century as a Historical Source and a Cultural Phenomenon" [in Hebrew]. *Catedra* 40 (1986): 159–88.

———. "Perceptions and Images of Eretz Israel and Jerusalem in the Literature of 19th-Century Western Travellers" [in Hebrew]. In *Tmurot ba-Historya ha-Yehudit ha-Hadasha: Kovetz Ma'amarim Shai le-Shmuel Etinger* [Transformations in modern Jewish history: A collection of essays presented to Shmuel Etinger], 89–114. Jerusalem: Zalman Shazar Center for Jewish History, 1987.

———. "Pioneer Scientific Exploration in the Holy Land at the Beginning of the Nineteenth Century." *Terrae Incognitae* 4 (1972): 95–110.

Ben-Baruch, Yossi. "The Lands beyond the Fence: A Renewed Look at Amos Oz's Collection *Where the Jackals Howl*" [in Hebrew]. *Alei Siach* 12–14 (1982): 269–86.

Ben-Gurion, David. Letter 306 (24 March 1922). In *Igrot* [Letters], 96. Vol. 2. Tel Aviv: Am Oved and Tel Aviv University, 1972.

Ben-Meir, Orna. "Normot Itsuv-Bima be-Hatsagat Machazot Dor-ba-Aretz bein ha-Shanim 1948–1956" [Conventions of Stage-Design in the Staging of Palmach-Generation Plays in the Years 1948–1956]. Master's thesis, Haifa University, 1995.

Ben-Zvi, S. "Ein Hai in the Old Days" [in Hebrew]. In *Sefer ha-Aliyah ha-Shniya* [The Second Aliyah book] Ed. Bracha Habas, 472–73. Tel Aviv: Am Oved, 1947.

Bernier, Normand R., and Jack E. Williams. *Beyond Beliefs: Ideological Foundations of American Education*. Englewood Cliffs, NJ: Prentice-Hall, 1973.

Bettelheim, Bruno. *The Children of the Dream*. New York: Macmillan, 1969.

Bhabha, Homi K. "Cultural Diversity and Cultural Differences." In *The Post-Colonial Studies Reader*, 206–9. Ed. Bill Ashcroft, Gareth Griffiths, and Helen Tiffin. London: Routledge, 1995.

———. *The Location of Culture*. London: Routledge, 1994.

Bhabha, Homi K., ed. *Nation and Narration*. London: Routledge, 1990.

Biale, David. *Eros and the Jews: From Biblical Israel to Contemporary America*. Berkeley: University of California Press, 1997.

Biedermann, Hans. *Dictionary of Symbolism*. New York: Penguin, 1994.

Boyarin, Daniel. "The Colonial Drag: Zionism, Gender, and Mimicry." In *The Preoccupation of Postcolonial Studies*. Ed. Hamid Naficy, Fawzia Afzal-Khan, and Kalpana Seshadri. Durham, NC: Duke University Press, 2000.

———. *Unheroic Conduct: The Rise of Heterosexuality and the Invention of the Jewish Man*. Berkeley: University of California Press, 1997.

Braudel, Fernand. *The Mediterranean*. University of California Press, 1996.

Brenner, Y. H. "The Eretz Israel Genre and Its Artifacts" [in Hebrew]. [1911] In *Kol Kitvei Y. H. Brenner* [The collected works of Y. H. Brenner], 3:569–78. Tel Aviv: Hakibbutz Hameuchad—Sifriat Poalim, 1985, 569–78.

———. "Our Self-Evaluation in Three Volumes" [in Hebrew]. In *Kol Kitvei Y. H. Brenner* [The collected works of Y. H. Brenner], 4:1223–96. Tel Aviv: Hakibbutz Hameuchad—Sifriat Poalim, 1985 [1914].

Brifman, Erella. "'Artsot Hatan' le-Amos Oz: Iyun Mashveh bi-Shnei Nosachim al-pi Hamisha Sipurim" [Amos Oz's "Where the jackals howl": A comparative study of two versions through five stories]. Master's thesis, Haifa Uuniversity, 1979.

Brinker, Menachem. *Ad ha-Simta ha-Tverianit: Ma'amar al Sipur u-Machshava bi-Yetsirat Brenner* [Narrative art and social thought in H. Y. Brenner's work]. Tel Aviv: Am Oved, 1990.

Calderon, Nissim. "Amos Oz: The Debate" [in Hebrew]. *Mikarov* 2 (1998): 173–80.

Campbell, Joseph. *The Hero with a Thousand Faces*. Princeton, NJ: Princeton University Press, 1973.

———. *The Masks of God: Creative Mythology*. London: Secker and Warburg, 1968.

Chatwin, Bruce. *Anatomy of Restlessness*. New York: Penguin, 1997.

Cirlot, Juan Eduardo. *A Dictionary of Symbols*. Trans. Jack Sage. New York: Dover, 2002 [1971].

Clarke, Howard W. "The Return of the Hero." In *The Art of the Odyssey*, 67–85. Englewood Cliffs, NJ: Prentice-Hall, 1967.

Cohen, Tova. *Me-Halom le-Metsi'ut: Eretz-Isra'el be-Sifrut ha-Haskala* [From dream to reality: Descriptions of Eretz Israel in Hebrew Haskalah literature]. Ramat Gan: Bar Ilan University Press, 1982.

Coupe, Lawrence. *Myth*. London: Routledge, 1997.

Davis, Lennard J. *Resisting Novels: Ideology and Fiction*. New York: Methuen, 1987.

Dayan, Moshe. "The Voice and the Echo" [in Hebrew]. In *Magash Ha-Kessef: Mivchar Shirim* [The silver platter: Selected poems], 5–7. Ed. Nathan Alterman. Tel Aviv: Ministry of Defense Press, 1974.

Deleuze, Gilles, and Felix Gauttari. *Kafka: Toward a Minor Literature*. Trans. Dana Polan. Minneapolis: University of Minnesota Press, 1986.

———. *A Thousand Plateaus: Capitalism and Schizophrenia*. Trans. Brian Massumi. Minneapolis: University of Minnesota Press, 1987.

De Vries, D., and T. Pfefferman. "Henya Pekelman: The Ordeal of a Female Construction Worker." In *Struggle and Survival in Israel and Palestine*. Ed. M. Levine and G. Shafir. University of California Press, 2011.

Dimock, George E. "The Name of Odysseus." *Hudson Review* 9, no. 1 (Spring 1956): 52–70. Rpt. in Homer. *The Odyssey*, 406–24. Tr. Albert Cook. New York: Norton, 1967.

Dinur, Ben-Zion. *Benyamin Ze'ev Herzl: Al ha-Ish, Darco u-Dmuto, Hazono u-Poalo* [Benjamin Zeev Herzl: The man, his path and personality, his vision and work]. Ramat Gan: Masada, 1968.

Elboim-Dror, Rachel. *Ha-Machar shel Etmol* [Yesterday's tomorrow]. Vol. 1, *The Zionist Utopia*; Vol. 2, *A Selection from Zionist Utopias* [both vols. in Hebrew]. Jerusalem: Yad Yitzhak Ben-Zvi, 1993.

Eliade, Mircea. *The Myth of the Eternal Return: Or, Cosmos and History*. Princeton University Press, 2005 [1954].

———. *Rites and Symbols of Initiation: The Mysteries of Birth and Rebirth*. Trans. Willard R. Trask. San Francisco and London: Harper Torch Books, Harper and Row, Hagerstone, 1975.

Eliberg-Schwartz, Howard. *People of the Body: Jews and Judaism from an Embodied Perspective*. Albany: State University of New York Press, 1992.

Elon, Amos. *Herzl*. New York: Holt, Rinehart and Winston, 1975.

Even-Zohar, Itamar. "Israeli Hebrew Literature: A Historical Model." In *Papers in Historical Poetics*. Tel Aviv: Porter Institute, 1978.

Eyal, Gil. "The Discursive Origins of Israeli Separatism: The Case of the Arab Village." *Theory and Society* 25, no. 3 (July 1996): 389–429.

Ezrahi DeKoven, Sidra. *Booking Passage: Exile and Homecoming in the Modern Jewish Imagination*. Berkeley: University of California Press, 2000.

Fanon, Franz. *Black Skin, White Masks*. Trans. Charles Lam Markmann. Grove Press, 1967 [1952].

Feingold, Ben Ami. "1948 in the Theater" [in Hebrew]. *Sadan—Mechkarim Besifrut Ivrit* 5 (2002): 233–53.

Fichman, Yaakov. "Avraham Mapu, His Life and Work" [in Hebrew]. *Kol Kitvei Mapu* [Mapu's Collected Writings]. Tel Aviv: Dvir, 1964, iii–xxiii.

Foucault, Michel. *History of Madness*. Trans. Jonathan Murphy. Routledge, 2009.

Frankel, Jonathan. *Prophecy and Politics: Socialism, Nationalism, and the Russian Jews, 1862–1917*. London: Cambridge University Press, 1981.

———. "The Yizkor Book of 1911—A Note on National Myths in the Second Aliyah." In *Religion, Ideology, and Nationalism in Europe and America*. Ed. H. Ben-Israel et al. Jerusalem: Historical Society of Israel and Zalman Shazar Center for Jewish History, 1986.

Frazer, James George. *The Golden Bough: A Study in Magic and Religion*. New York and London: Oxford University Press, 1994.

Frenzel, Elisabeth. *Stoffe Der Weltliteratur*. Stuttgart: A. Kroener, 1963.

Friedländer Saul. *Reflections of Nazism: An Essay on Kitsch and Death*. Indiana University Press, 1993.

Frye, Northrop. *Anatomy of Criticism: Four Essays*. Princeton, NJ: Princeton University Press, 1957.

Gamzu, Haim. "'He Walked in the Fields'—at the 'Cameri'" [in Hebrew]. *Haaretz*, 11 June 1948.

Gertz, Nurit. *Ha-Siporet ha-Isra'elit bi-Shnot ha-Shishim* [Israeli narrative fiction in the sixties]. Units 1–3. Tel Aviv: Open University, 1982.

———. *Hirbet Hiz'aa ve-ha-Boker she-le-Macharat* [Hirbet Hiz'aa and the morning after]. Tel Aviv: Porter Institute and Hakibbutz Hameuchad, 1983.

———. "No Longer the Same Fields—'He Walked in the Fields'" [in Hebrew]. In *Sipur me-ha-Sratim: Siporet Isra'elit ve-Ibude'ah la-Kolnoa* [Motion fiction: Literature and cinema], 63–94. Tel Aviv: Open University, 1993.

———. *Shvuya ba-Haloma: Mitosim ba-Tarbut ha-Isra'elit* [Captive of a dream: National myth in Israeli culture]. Tel Aviv: Am Oved, 1995.

———. "Transformations in Hebrew Literature: The Transition from the Palmach Generation to the Generation of the Sixties Based on Positions and Expressions in the Work" [in Hebrew]. *Hasifrut* 29 (1979): 69–75.

Gilula Dvora. "'He Walked in the Fields': On the 50th Anniversary of the Stage Show" [in Hebrew]. *Bama* 152 (1998): 84–88.

Gluzman, Michael. "The Aesthetics of the Mutilated Body: On the Culture of Death in *He Walked in the Fields*" [in Hebrew]. *Sadan—Mechkarim Besifrut Ivrit* 5 (2002): 347–77.

———. "The Longing for Heterosexuality: Zionism and Sexuality in *Altneuland*" [in Hebrew]. *Teoria Ubikoret* 11 (1997): 145–62.

Goldberg, Leah. "He Walked in the Fields" [in Hebrew]. *Itim*, 20 February 1948, 2–3.

Golden, Stephanie. *The Woman Outside: Meanings and Myths of Homelessness*. Berkeley: University of California Press, 1992.

Gur, Israel. "The First Original Play in the State of Israel" [in Hebrew]. *Hauma* 5, no. 20 (1967): 592–99.

Gurevitch, Zali, and Gideon Aran. "On the Place (Israeli Anthropology) " [in Hebrew]. *Alpayim* 4 (1991): 9–44.

Hadomi, Leah. "The Utopian Novel and the Zionist Utopia" [in Hebrew]. *Bikoret Uparshanut* 13–14 (1979): 131–68.

Hall, Roger A. *Performing the American Frontier, 1870–1906*. Cambridge, MA: Cambridge University Press, 2001.

Halperin, Hagit. "Literature, Biography and Politics: The Ban on *He Walked in the Fields* and How It Was Reflected in Moshe Shamir's 'On His Horse on Saturday'" [in Hebrew]. *Sadan—Mechkarim Besifrut Ivrit* 5 (2002): 378–400.

Herlitz, Georg. "Notes for the New Hebrew Edition of *Altneuland*" [in Hebrew]. In Theodor Herzl, *Kitvey Herzl, vol.1, Ha-Hazon* [Herzl's writings, vol. 1., The vision]. Jerusalem: Zionist Library, World Zionist Organization, 1960.

Herzig, Hanna. *Torat ha-Sifrut ve-ha-Tarbut—Askolot Bnot Zmanenu: Tse'adim Nosafim* [Literary and cultural theory—Contemporary schools of thought: Further steps]. Tel Aviv: Open University, 2005.

Herzl, Theodor. *Old New Land (Altneuland)*. Trans. Lotta Levensohn. Princeton, NJ: Markus Wiener, 1997 [1902].

Hess, Tamar. "'Klum Tish'al Mahu Shi'ur-Koma shel Marvad'": Dimuyim shel Nashiyut ba-Kovetz "'Kehiliyatenu' u-ba-Roman 'Yamim ve-Lelylot'" [Images of femininity in the collection *Our Community* and the novel *Days and Nights*]. Master's thesis, The Hebrew University, 1995.

———. "Ktavim Otobiografy'im Me'et Nashim Bnot ha-Aliyah ha-Shniya" [Autobiographical writings by Second Aliyah Women]. PhD dissertation, The Hebrew University, 2003.

———. "Henya Pekelman: An Injured Witness of Socialist Zionist Settlement in Mandatory Palestine." *Women's Studies Quarterly* 36, no. 1–2, (Spring-Summer, 2008): 208–13.

Hever, Hanan. "A Majority as a National Minority in Israeli Narrative Fiction from the Beginning of the Sixties" [in Hebrew]. *Siman Kria* 22 (1991): 328–39.

———. "We Didn't Come from the Sea: Outlines for a Mizrahi Literary Geography" [in Hebrew]. *Teoria Ubikoret* 16 (2000): 181–95.

Hovav, Gil. "The Road from Jerusalem" [in Hebrew]. *Politika* 23 (1988): 30–31.

Hutcheon, Linda. "Modern Parody and Bakhtin." In *Rethinking Bakhtin: Extensions and Challenges*, 87–103. Ed. Gary Saul Morson and Caryl Emerson. Evanston, IL: Northwestern University Press, 1989.

Inbari, Assaf. "Bringing Some Relief to the Whole Tribe" [in Hebrew]. *Proza* 103–4 (1988): 72–80.

Islam, Syed Manzurul. *The Ethics of Travel from Marco Polo to Kafka*. New York: Manchester University Press, 1996.

Jameson, Fredric. *Postmodernism: O ha-Higayon ha-Tarbuti shel ha-Capitalism ha-Me'uchar* [Postmodernism or the cultural logic of late capitalism]. Trans. Adi Ginzburg-Hirsch. Tel Aviv: Resling, 2002.

———. *Postmodernism or the Cultural Logic of Late Capitalism*. Durham: Duke University Press, 1991.

Jauss, Hans Robert. *Toward an Aesthetic of Reception*. Trans. Timothy Bahti. Minneapolis: University of Minnesota Press, 1982.

Kartun-Blum, Ruth. *Bein ha-Nisgav la-Ironi: Kivunim ve-Shinuyei Kivun bi-Yetsirat Natan Alterman* [The sublime and the ironic]. Tel Aviv: Hakibbutz Hameuchad, 1983.

———. *Ha-Lets ve-ha-Tsel: Hagigat Kayits—ha-Po'emah ha-Menipa'it shel Natan Alterman* [The darkling jester: Hagigat Kayits (summer revelry)—Nathan Alterman's Menippean poem]. Tel Aviv: Zmora-Bitan, 1994.

———. "Instead of an Epilogue—Searching for the Mother Spaceship: On Amos Oz's 'The Same Sea'" [in Hebrew]. In *Sefer Amos Oz* [The Amos Oz book]. Ed. Aharon Komem and Yizhak Ben-Mordechai. Beer Sheba: Ben-Gurion University in the Negev Press, 2000.

Kenaz, Yehoshua (S. R.). "Where the Jackals Howl" [in Hebrew]. *Keshet* 8, no. 2 (30) (1966): 175–76.

Kenaz, Yehoshua, and Amos Oz. "A Dialogue on 'Elsewhere, Perhaps'" [in Hebrew]. *Shdemot* 24 (1966): 104–7.

Kressel, Gezel. "Yosef Luidor" [in Hebrew]. *Lexicon ha-Sifrut ha-Ivrit ba-Dorot ha-Achronim* [Lexicon of Hebrew literature], 2:174 Merchavia: Sifriat Poalim, 1967.

Kurzweil, Baruch. "The Israeli Story in Recent Years" [in Hebrew]. *Haaretz*, 9 March 1966:10.

Kushnir, Mordechai, ed. and author. "The Last Times on the Way to Brenner's House" [in Hebrew]. *Yosef Haim Brenner—Mivchar Divrei Zichronot* [Y. H. Brenner—Selected memoirs], 218–28. Tel Aviv: Hakibbutz Hameuchad, 1944.

Landau, Dov. "Introduction" [in Hebrew]. In Yosef Luidor, *Stories*, 5–38. Ramat Gan: Writers' Association Press and Masada, 1976.

Laskov, Shulamit. *Trumpeldor: Sipur Hayav* [Trumpeldor: The story of his life]. Jerusalem: Keter, 1995.

Le Corbusier. *Towards a New Architecture*. Translated by Frederick Etchells. New York: Holt, Rinehart and Winston, 1986 [1927].

Leeming, David, with Margaret Leeming. *A Dictionary of Creation Myths*. New York: Oxford University Press, 1995.

Levinger, Esther. *Andartot la-Noflim be-Isra'el* [War memorials in Israel]. Tel Aviv: Hakibbutz Hameuchad, 1993.

Lévi-Strauss, Claude. *The Savage Mind*. Trans. John Weightman and Doreen Weightman. University of Chicago Press, 1966 [1962].

Lord, Amnon. "The Highway from Dimona to Oslo" [in Hebrew]. *Tchelet* 4 (1998): 93–105.
Luidor, Yosef. "Pan" [in Hebrew]. *Hapoel Hatzair* 13, no. 33 (2 June 1920): 9–10.
———. "Robinson Crusoe" [in Hebrew]. *Hapoel Hatzair* 14, nos. 20–21 (11 March 1921): 10–11.
———. *Stories* [in Hebrew]. Edited and introduction by Dov Landau. Ramat Gan: Writers' Association Press & Masada, 1976.
Lukács, Georg. *The Historical Novel*. Trans. Hannah Mitchell and Stanley Mitchell. University of Nebraska Press 1983.
Lyotard, Jean-François. *The Postmodern Condition: A Report on Knowledge*. Trans. Geoffrey Bennington and Brian Massumi. Minneapolis: University of Minnesota Press 1984 [1979].
Ma'apil, Avi. "Itsuv ha-Metsi'ut ba-Siporet shel S. Yizhar" [The portrayal of reality in S. Yizhar's narrative fiction]. PhD dissertation, The Hebrew University, 1988.
Mapu, Avraham. *The Love of Zion*. Trans. Joseph Marymount. Toby Press, 2006. Originally published as *The Sorrows of Name*. New York: National Book Publishers, 1919.
Mazali, Rela. *Maps of Women's Goings and Stayings*. Redwood City: Stanford University Press, 2001.
Megged, Nahum. *Ha-Atstekim: me-Hanit ha-Shemesh le-Hanitot Shvurot* [The Aztecs: From the sun spear to the broken spears]. Tel Aviv: Dvir, 1996.
Meinig, Donald William, ed. *The Interpretation of Ordinary Landscapes: Geographical Essays*. New York: Oxford University Press, 1979.
Melman, Billie. "From the Periphery to the Center of Yishuv History: Gender and Nationalism in Eretz Israel (1890–1920)" [in Hebrew]. *Zion* 62, no. 3 (1997): 243–78.
Mintz, Alan. Hurban: *Responses to Catastrophe in Hebrew Literature*. Columbia University Press, 1985.
Miron, Dan. *Arba Panim ba-Sifrut ha-Ivrit Bat-Yamenu: Iyunim bi-Yetsirot Alterman, Ratosh, Yizhar, Shamir* [Four aspects of contemporary Israeli literature: Studies of the works of Alterman, Ratosh, Yizhar, Shamir]. Jerusalem: Schocken, 1975.
———. *Ha-Shira ha-Ivrit ba-Me'ah ha-Kaf* [Hebrew poetry in the twentieth century]. Jerusalem: Academon, 1996.
———. *Imahot Meyasdot, Achayot Horgot: Al Shtei Hatchalot ba-Shira ha-Eretz-Isra'elit ha-Modernit* [Founding mothers, stepsisters: Two beginnings in modern pre-state Israeli poetry]. Tel Aviv: Hakibbutz Hameuchad, 1991.
———. *Mul ha-Ach ha-Shotek: Iyunim be-Shirat Milchemet ha-Atsma'ut* [Facing the silent brother: Essays on the poetry of the War of Independence]. Jerusalem: Keter, 1992.
———. "The Shining Veneer—Avraham Mapu's Elevated Art in *The Love of Zion*" [in Hebrew]. In *Bein Hazon le-Emet: Nitsanei ha-Roman ha-Ivri ve-ha-Yiddi ba-Me'ah ha-Tsha-Esreh* [From romance to novel: Studies in the emergence of the Hebrew and Yiddish novel in the nineteenth century], 15–151. Jerusalem: Bialik Institute, 1979.
Miron, Stanley. "The Kibbutz as a Familial Community" [in Hebrew]. *Yaad* 3 (1990): 81–88.
Mohar Eli. "Novels are Difficult—A Conversation with Moshe Shamir" [in Hebrew]. *Davar*, 2 March 1973:10–11, 35.
Moked, Gabriel (Gershon Maor). "'Where the Jackals Howl'" [in Hebrew]. *Achshav* 15–16 (1966): 150–51.

Moretti, Franco. "The Comfort of Civilization." In *The Way of the World: The Bildungsroman in European Culture*, 15–74. London: Verso, 1987.

———. *Atlas of the European Novel, 1800–1900*. London and New York: Verso, 1999.

Morris, Benny. *Israel's Border Wars, 1949–1956: Arab Infiltration, Israeli Retaliation, and the Countdown to the Suez War*. New York: Oxford University Press, 1997.

Morrison, Toni. *Playing in the Dark: Whiteness and the Literary Imagination*. Cambridge, MA: Harvard University Press, 1992.

Mosse, George L. *Fallen Soldiers: Reshaping the Memory of the World Wars*. New York: Oxford University Press, 1991.

Naveh, Hannah. *Nos'im ve-Nos'ot: Sipurei Massa ba-Sifrut ha-Ivrit ha-Hadahsa* [Male and female travelers: Travel stories in modern Hebrew literature]. Tel Aviv: Ministry of Defense Press, 2002.

Navot, Amnon. "Tell It Not in Ofra, Publish It Not in the Streets of Kdumim" [in Hebrew]. *Maariv*, 20 March 1998, 31.

Ne'eman, Judd. "The Fields of the Dominant Fiction" [in Hebrew]. *Sadan—Mechkarim Besifrut Ivrit* 5 (2002): 401–15.

Neiman, Y. M. "*He Walked in the Fields* at the Cameri Theater" [in Hebrew]. *Davar*, 10 June 1948:12–13.

Netzer, Ruth. *Massa el ha-Atsmi: Alchimiyat ha-Nefesh—Smalim ve-Mitosim* [The quest for the self: Alchemy of the soul—Symbols and myths]. Ben Shemen: Modan, 2004.

Nevo, Gidi. *Shiv'ah Yamim ba-Negev: Al 'Yemei Tsiklag' le-S. Yizhar* [Seven days in the Negev: On S. Yizhar's 'Days of Ziklag']. Tel Aviv: Hakibbutz Hameuchad, 2005.

Nir, Dov. "The Perception of the Desert in Modern Hebrew Literature: Illustrations from the Writings of Agnon, Shenhar and Yizhar" [in Hebrew]. *Lashon Veivrit* 6 (1990): 15–20.

Nir, Henry. "I-You-We: Buber's Theory of Companionship and the Kibbutz" [in Hebrew]. *Hakibbutz* 12 (1988): 195–211.

Nordau, Max. "Ahad Ha'am on *Altneuland*." *Ktavim Tsioni'im* [Zionist writings]. Vol. 2, *Speeches and Articles (1901–1904)*, 110–19. Trans. Y. Yeivin and H. Goldberg. Jerusalem: Zionist Library, World Zionist Organization, 1960.

Ofrat, Gideon. *Adama, Adam, Dam: Mitos he-Halutz ve-Pulchan ha-Adama be-Machazot ha-Hityashvut* [Land, man, blood: The myth of the pioneer and the cult of the land in settlement plays]. Tel Aviv: Cherikover, 1980.

Oppenheimer, Yochai. "The Living Dead Model in the Poetry of the War of Independence" [in Hebrew]. *Sadan—Mechkarim Besifrut Ivrit* 5 (2002): 416–42.

Oren, Yosef. *Ha-Sipur ha-Isra'eli ha-Katsar* [The Israeli short story]. Rishon Lezion: Yachad, 1987.

Otto, Rudolf. *The Idea of the Holy*. Trans. John W. Harvey. Oxford: Oxford University Press, 1958 [1919].

Oz, Amos. *Elsewhere, Perhaps*. Trans. Nicholas de Lange. New York: Harcourt Brace, 1973 [1966].

———. *The Silence of Heaven: Agnon's Fear of God*. Trans. Barbara Harshav. Princeton, NJ: Princeton University Press, 2000.

———. *Under This Blazing Light*. Trans. Nicholas de Lange. Cambridge, MA: Cambridge University Press, 1995 [1979].

———. *Where the Jackals Howl and Other Stories*. Trans. Nicholas de Lange. New York: First Mariner, 2012 [1965].

Oz, Amos, and Yitzhak Ben-Aharon. "Sicha" [A conversation], 11–12. Amos Oz Archive, 167-1-4, 1983.

Pardes, Ilana. *Countertraditions in the Bible: A Feminist Approach*. Cambridge, MA; Harvard University Press, 1992.

Pardes, Ilana. *The Biography of Ancient Israel: National Narratives in the Bible*. Berkeley: University of California Press, 2000.

Parry, B. "Problems in Current Discourse Theory." *Oxford Literary Review* 9 (1987): 27–58.

Pocock, Douglas Charles David, ed. *Humanistic Approaches in Geography*. Newcastle upon Tyne: University of Durham, 1988.

Popkin, Richard Henry. *The High Road to Pyrrhonism*. San Diego: Austin Hill Press, 1980.

Porat, Dina. The entry "Tehran Children" [in Hebrew]. In *Ha-Entsiclopedya shel ha-Sho'ah* [The Holocaust encyclopedia], 571–72. Ed. Israel Gutman. Tel Aviv: Yad Veshem and Sifriat Poalim, 1990.

Porat, Zfira. "The Golem of Zion: About Amos Oz" [in Hebrew]. *Molad* 7, nos. 37–38 (1976): 481–89.

Poznanski, Menachem. Preface to *Zvi Shatz, Al Gvul ha-Dmama* [On the edge of silence]. Ed. Muki Tzur, 13–22. Tel Aviv: Davar, 1990 [1929].

Qedar, Yair. "A Pale, Taciturn, Feeble-Bodied Young Man" [in Hebrew]. *Haaretz*, 6 May 2003, E1.

Rabinovich, Alexander Ziskind, ed. *Yizkor: Matsevat Zikaron le-Halalei ha-Po'alim ha-Ivri'im be-Erets Isra'el* [Yizkor book]. Jaffa: A. Atin, 1911.

Rabinovich, Yaakov. "On Our Dead" [in Hebrew]. *Hapoel Hatzair* 14, no. 26 (6 May 6 1921): 11.

Rancière, Jacques. "Interview: The Image of Brotherhood." *Cahiers du Cinema* 268, no. 9 (1976).

Raz Aviad. "Why Do People Love to Hate Amos Oz? Reflections Following the Last Collective Attack" [in Hebrew]. *Haaretz*, 3 March 1989, B8.

Reuveni, Aharon. *Ad-Yerushala'im: Roman mi-Yemei Milchemet ha-Olam ha-Rishona* [Even to Jerusalem]. Jerusalem: Keter & Hakibbutz Hameuchad, 1987 [1954].

Rimmon-Kenan, Shlomith. "The Story of 'I': Illness and Narrative Identity." *Narrative* 10, no. 1, (2002): 9–27.

Roskies, David. *Against the Apocalypse: Responses to Catastrophe in Modern Jewish Culture*. Harvard University Press, 1984.

Rosowski, Susan J. *Birthing a Nation: Gender, Creativity, and the West in American Literature*. Lincoln: University of Nebraska Press, 1999.

Sadan, Dov. "A Mountain and Its Slopes" [in Hebrew]. *Davar, Massa* 24 (September 1976): 43–44.

Sadan-Lowenstein, Nili. *Siporet Shnot ha-Essrim be-Erets Isra'el* [Israeli prose in the twenties]. Tel Aviv: Sifriat Poalim, 1991.

Said, Edward W. *Orientalism*. New York: Pantheon Books, 1978.

Sax, Boria. *The Serpent and the Swan: The Animal Bride in Folklore and Literature*. Blacksburg, VA: McDonald and Woodward, 1998.

Schiller, Friedrich. *On Naïve and Sentimental Poetry*. Trans. Helen Watanabe O'Kelly. Manchester: Carcanet New Press, 1988 [1795].

Scholes, Robert, and Robert Kellogg. *The Nature of Narrative*. New York: Oxford University Press, 1968.

Schwartz, Yigal. "The Concept of Place in Post-Classical Hebrew Narrative Fiction: M. Y. Berdichevsky's 'Across the River'" [in Hebrew]. In *Sifrut ve-Hevra ba-Tarbut ha-Ivrit ha-Hadasha—Ma'amrim Mugashim le-Gershon Shaked* [Literature and society in modern Hebrew culture—Essays presented to Gershon Shaked]. Ed. Yehudit Bar-El, Yigal Schwartz, and Tamar S. Hess. Tel Aviv: Keter and Hakibbutz Hameuchad, 2000.

———. "Holocaust Literature: Myth, History and Literature." In *Literary Responses to Mass Violence*, 97–108. Waltham, MA: Brandeis University Press, 2004.

———. "'Human Engineering' and Landscape Conceptualization in Modern Hebrew Culture" [in Hebrew]. *Mikan* 1 (2000): 9–24.

———. *Kinat ha-Yachid ve-Netsach ha-Shevet: Aharon Appelfeld—Tmunat Olam* [From individual lament to tribal eternity: Aharon Appelfeld's worldview]. Jerusalem: Magnes and Keter, 1996.

———. *Lichyot Kedei Lichyot: Aharon Reuveni—Monografia* [Living for living: Aharon Reuveni—A monograph]. Jerusalem: Magnes and Yad Yitzhak Ben-Zvi, 1993.

———. *Ma she-Ro'im Mikan: Sugiyot ba-Historiografia shel ha-Sifrut ha-Ivrit ha-Hadasha* [Vantage point: Issues in the historiography of modern Hebrew literature]. Or Yehuda: Dvir, 2005.

———. "Omanut ha-Sipur shel Aharon Reuveni" [Aharon Reuveni's narrative art]. PhD dissertation, The Hebrew University, 1989.

———. "The Person, the Path, and the Melody: A Brief History of Identity in Israeli Literature." *Prooftext* 20, no. 3 (2000): 318–39.

Schweid, Eliezer. *Shalosh Ashmorot ba-Sifrut ha-Ivrit* [Three watches in Hebrew literature]. Tel Aviv: Am Oved, 1964.

Sha'anan, Avraham. "On the Hebrew Story: A Review of S. Yizhar's 'The Wood on the Hill,' Moshe Shamir's 'He Walked in the Fields' and Yigal Mossinson's 'Who Said He's Black'" [in Hebrew]. *Molad* 1, no. 4 (1948): 241–43.

Shahar, Shulamith. *Ha-Tso'anim: Am ha-Navadim shel Eropa* [The gypsies: The nomads of Europe]. Tel Aviv: Mapa, 2006.

Shaked, Avraham. *Ha-Aborijinim: Massa el Zman ha-Halom* [The aborigines]. Tel Aviv: Mapa, 2004.

Shaked, Gershon. *Ha-Siporet ha-Ivrit 1880–1980* [Hebrew narrative fiction 1880–1980]. Vol. 2, *Ba-Aretz u-ba-Tfutsa* [In Eretz Israel and in the Diaspora]. Tel Aviv: Keter and Hakibbutz Hameuchad, 1983.

———. *Ha-Siporet ha-Ivrit 1880–1980* [Hebrew narrative fiction 1880–1980]. Vol. 4, *be-Hevlei ha-Zman: ha-Re'alism ha-Isra'eli 1938–1980* [Israeli realism 1938–1980]. Tel Aviv: Keter and Hakibbutz Hameuchad, 1993.

———. "The Narrative of Persecution" [in Hebrew]. *Partial Answers* 4, no. 2 (2006): 239–49.

———. *Shmuel Yosef Agnon: A Revolutionary Traditionalist*. New York University Press, 1989.

Shaham, Nathan. "What Do You Think, My Friend?: With the Publication of Moshe's Book" [in Hebrew]. *Bashaar*, 25 March 1948, 4.

Shamir, Moshe. *Hu Halach ba-Sadot* [He walked in the fields]. Tel Aviv: Am Oved, 1998 [1948].

Shapira, Anita. *Land and Power: The Zionist Resort to Force, 1881–1948*. Tr. William Templer. Oxford University Press, 1992.

———. *Yehudim Hadashim Yehudim Yeshanim* [New Jews old Jews]. Tel Aviv: Am Oved, 1997.

Shapira, Sarit. *Routes of Wandering: Nomadism, Journeys and Transitions in Contemporary Israeli Art* [in English and Hebrew]. Exhibition catalogue. Jerusalem: Israel Museum, 1991.

Shatz, Zvi. *Al Gvul ha-Dmama: Ktavim* [On the edge of silence]. Preface by Menachem Poznanski and introduction by Muki Tzur. Tel Aviv: Am Oved, 1990 [1929].

Shavit, Ari. "An Expert in Romantics." *Haaretz*, 13 July 1990, 4–9, 17.

Shilo, Margalit. *Princess or Prisoner?: Jewish Women in Jerusalem, 1840–1914*. Waltham, MA: Brandeis University Press, 2005.

Shimoni, Batya. "Sipur ha-Ma'abara—Bein ha-Kol ha-Shalit la-Kol ha-Hatrani" [The transit camp story—The dominant voice and the subversive voice]. PhD dissertation, Ben-Gurion University in the Negev, 2005.

Shoham, Shlomo Giora. *Ha-Mitologia shel ha-Ro'ah* [The mythology of evil]. Tel Aviv: Ministry of Defense Press, 1990.

———. *Valhalla, Calvary & Auschwitz*. Bowman and Cody, 1995.

Simmel, Georg, Robert E. Park, and Louis Wirth. *Urbanism: Ha-Sociologia shel ha-Ir ha-Modernit* [Urbanism: The sociology of the modern city]. Ed. Oded Menda-Levi. Trans. Miriam Krauss. Tel Aviv: Resling, 2004.

Sivan, Emmanuel. *Dor Tashach: Mitos, Dyukan ve-Zikaron* [The 1948 generation: Myth, profile and memory]. Tel Aviv: Ma'arachot, 1991.

Slawinsky, Janusz. *Literature als System und Prozess*. Munchen: Nymphenburger Verlagshandlung, 1975.

Smith, Huston. *The Illustrated World Religions: A Guide to our Wisdom Traditions*. San Francisco, 1991.

Suleiman, Susan R. *Authoritarian Fictions: The Ideological Novel as a Literary Genre*. New York: Columbia University Press, 1983.

Tamir, Nachman, and Yaakov Sharet, eds. *Anshei ha-Aliyah ha-Shniya: Pirkei Zichronot* [The Second Aliyah people: Memoirs]. Tel Aviv: Center for Culture and Education of the Histadrut with "Culture and Education," 1970–1974.

Tochner, Meshulam. "A Change of the Guard" [in Hebrew]. *Bchinot Bebikoret Hasifrut*, 3 (1953): 30–34.

Tomer, Ben-Zion, ed. and tr. *Adom ve-Lavan ve-Rei'ach Tapuchei Zahav ("Yaldei Tehran")* [Red and white and the smell of oranges ("The Tehran children")]. Jerusalem: Zionist Library, World Zionist Organization, 1971.

Tönnies, Ferdinand. *Community and Society*. Trans. and ed. Charles P. Loomis. East Lansing: Michigan State University Press, 1957 [1887].

Turner, Victor. *The Ritual Process: Structure and Anti-Structure*. Chicago: Aldine, 1968.

Tzameret, Tzvi. *Alei Gesher Tsar: Itsuv Ma'arechet ha-Hinuch bi-Yemei ha-Aliyah ha-Gdola* [Across a narrow bridge: Shaping the education system during the Great Aliyah]. Kiryat Sde Boker: Ben-Gurion Heritage Center, Ben-Gurion Unniversity in the Negev Press, 1997.

———. *The Melting Pot in Israel: The Commission of Inquiry Concerning Education in the Early Years of the State*. Albany: State University of New York Press, 2002 [1993].

Tzemach, Shlomo. "A Conversation" [in Hebrew]. In *Eruvin: Massa u-Bikoret* [Essays and criticism], 177–224. Tel Aviv: Dvir, 1964.

Tzur, Muki. "The Second Aliyah People, the Immigrant Types and their Socio-Cultural Profile" [in Hebrew]. In *Ha-Aliyah ha-Shniya: Mechkarim* [The Second Aliyah: Studies], 282–93. Ed. Israel Bartal, Zeev Tzahor, and Yehoshua Kaniel. Jerusalem: Yad Yitzhak Ben-Zvi, 1997.

Van Gennep, Arnold. *The Rites of Passage*. Trans. Monika B. Vizedom and Gabrielle L. Caffee. London: Routledge and Kegan Paul, 1960 [1909].

Vernant, Jean-Pierre. *The Universe, the Gods and Mortals: Ancient Greek Myths*. Trans. Linda Asher. London: Profile Books, 2002.

Werses, Shmuel. "Avraham Mapu's Narrative Strategies in 'The Love of Zion'" [in Hebrew]. In *Sipur ve-Shorsho: Iyunim be-Hitpatchut ha-Proza ha-Ivrit* [A story and its root: Studies in the development of Hebrew prose], 46–59. Ramat Gan: Writers' Association Press and Masada, 1971.

Wheatley, Paul. *The Pivot of the Four Quarters: A Preliminary Enquiry into the Origins and Character of the Ancient Chinese City*. Chicago: Aldine Publications, 1971.

White, Hayden. "Foucault Decoded." In *Tropics of Discourse: Essays in Cultural Criticism*, 230–60. Baltimore, MD: Johns Hopkins University Press, 1978.

Wright, John Kirtland. *Aids to Geographical Research*. New York: Columbia University Press, 1947.

Wright, Will. *Six Guns and Society: A Structural Study of the Western*. Berkeley: University of California Press, 1975.

Yaari-Polskin, Yaakov. "Yosef Luidor" [in Hebrew]. In *Holmim ve-Lochamim* [Dreamers and fighters], 473–76. Tel Aviv: Masada, 1946.

Yehoshua, A. B. *Between Right and Right: Isreal—Problem or Solution?* Trans. Arnold Schwartz. New York: Doubleday, 1981.

———. *The Continuing Silence of A Poet: The Collected Stories of A. B. Yeshoshua*. Trans. Marsha Pomerantz. Syracuse, NY: Syracuse University Press, 1998 [Penguin, 1991].

———. *Mul HaYe'arot: Sipurim* [Facing the forests: Stories]. Tel Aviv: Hakibbutz Hameuchad, 1968.

Yerushalmi, Yosef. *Amos Oz—Bibliografia: 1953–1981* [Amos Oz—A bibliography, 1953–1981]. Tel Aviv: Am Oved, 1984.

Zaarur, Shlomit. "Matzeva le-Shnaim: 'Bo-Zmaniut ke-Mangenon Parshani, Poeti ve-Temati ba-Roman *Tmol Shilshom* le-S. Y. Agnon" [A tombstone for two: 'Simultaneity' as an interpretive, poetic and thematic mechanism in S. Y. Agnon's novel *Only Yesterday*." Manuscript.

Zach, Nathan. *Kavei Avir: al ha-Romantika ba-Siporet ha-Isra'elit ve-al Nos'im Acherim* [Air lines: On romanticism in Israeli narrative fiction and other subjects]. Jerusalem: Keter, 1983.

Zertal, Idit. "A Generation's Strong Weaknesses—An Interview with Amos Oz" [in Hebrew]. *Davar*, 9 July 1965:24.

Zerubavel, Yael. *Recovered Roots: Collective Memory and the Making of Israeli National Tradition*. Chicago: University of Chicago Press, 1995.

Zerubavel, Yael. "The Desert as a Mythical Space and a Site of Memory in Hebrew Culture" [in Hebrew]. In *Ha-Mitos ba-Yahadut* [Myths in Judaism], 223–36. Ed. Moshe

Idel and Ithamar Gruenwald. Jerusalem: Zalman Shazar Center for Jewish History, 2004.

Zilbertal, Moshe. "The Heroism of the Walkers in the Fields" [in Hebrew]. *Itim* 23 (April 1948): 2–4.

Zonder, Moshe. "Moshe Shamir: Cause of Death: An Ideal" [in Hebrew]. *Maariv*, 1 June 2001, 26–32, 96.

Zoran, Gabriel. "Towards a Theory of Space in the Story" [in Hebrew]. *Hasifrut* 30–31 (1981): 20–34.

Index

Title abbreviations are: *LOZ* for *The Love of Zion*; *ALT* for *Altneuland*; YOA for "Yoash"; *HWF* for *He Walked in the Fields*; NAV for "Nomads and Viper."

acclimatization stories, 107–11, 122–23, 124, 125–32, 136, 300n41
Achi-Ne'eman, Y., 145
aesthetization, 119, 128, 129, 169, 172, 182, 183
Agnon, S. Y., 98, 99–100, 122, 138–41, 307n66, 311n17
Ahad Ha'am, 50–52
Akedah metanarrative: Agnon, 141; *HWF*, 10; nomad/settler tensions, 133–38; Second Aliyah, 116–17, 141; YOA, 9, 116–18, 120, 121–22, 123, 132, 133–34
alienation, 104–6, 137, 298n21
Alter, R., 33, 34
Alterman, N., 119, 133, 200–205, 311n17
Altneuland (Herzl): chronotopic plane, 70–71, 74, 249; city/country opposition, 64–65, 116; critical reception, 50–52, 87; as foundational text, 4, 49–50, 65; human engineering, 67, 72, 85–93, 107, 124–25, 159, 216–18, 220; influence of, 50; landscape, 52–70, 74–75, 107, 295n28; nature, 285; plot, 73–78, 80–85, 296n31; renaissance narrative, 9; sexuality, 81, 84, 87–88, 89, 91–92, 217; utopias, 8, 9, 49–50, 64–65, 223, 293n3; vector of desire, 7, 9, 50
Anderson, B., 98–99, 100
Androcles, 78, 94, 95, 285
animals: *ALT*, 69, 70, 93–96, 223, 285; *HWF*, 181–82, 212, 282, 285; *LOZ*, 36–37, 38, 39, 40, 43–48, 93, 292n33; Luidor, 126, 127–29, 133–34, 223, 285, 302n73; NAV, 230–31, 250, 255, 256, 258, 259–60, 272, 282, 283–86, 292n45; as the "other," 141, 286; Reuveni, 100, 138; type scenes, 35

anonymity, 98–101, 140, 141, 297n12
anti-genre fiction, 98, 299–300n39, 300n45, 307n66
antisemitic metanarrative, 71, 74, 76–79, 80–85, 125
Appelfeld, A., 253, 287, 312n39
Arabs: *ALT*, 51, 58, 68, 69, 70, 80, 87, 295n25; animals and nature, 11, 70, 115, 127, 129, 250, 255, 256, 272, 285; desire for, 12, 225, 237, 274, 287–88; femininity, 228, 236, 252; *HWF*, 153, 220; Luidor, 112; NAV, 227–31, 242–46, 252, 254–56, 261, 263, 313n46, 313n50; Reuveni, 138; YOA, 126, 153, 301–2n69
Aran, D., 145
Aran, G., 2–3, 82, 110, 120–21
aristocracy, 86–87, 89–93, 295–96n31
assimilation, 50, 53–54, 56, 63–64
auto-antisemitic syndrome, 50
axis narrative. *See* living-dead narrative

Barry, P., 250
Bartov, H., 144
Baum, L. Frank, 2–3
Ben-Aharon, Yitzhak, 280–81, 282
Ben-Gurion, David, 297–98n16
Ben-Zvi, S., 102–3
Berdichevsky, M. J., 43, 52, 314n61
Bethlehem, 18, 30, 32–35, 36, 44
Bhabha, H., 248, 295n25, 305n42, 312n35
Biale, D., 301n53, 302n80
Bialik, C. N., 42–43, 314n61
biblical metanarratives: *ALT*, 9, 70–76, 79, 80–85, 159, 216; collective/private plotlines, 26–27; End of Days, 9, 27–28, 30, 71, 73, 246; false messianic, 72–73;

"from tending the flock," 28–29; *HWF,* 10, 151–52, 304n26; *LOZ,* 6, 8, 19, 27–29, 33–35, 34, 45; Luidor, 9, 116–18, 120, 121–22, 123, 132, 133–34, 135; Nebuchadnezzar Syndrome, 19; replacement, 247; Saul, 8, 28–29; Valley of the Dry Bones, 9, 71, 74, 80–85, 216. *See also* Akedah metanarrative; Exodus from Egypt metanarrative; redemption narrative

bildungsroman, 42, 295n23

birth phase metanarratives, 5–6, 247, 286–87, 289n11

blood and soil language, 301n53

blood covenant. *See* Akedah metanarrative; covenants

Brenner, Y. H.: *Breakdown and Bereavement,* 98, 99–100, 118, 122, 307n66; death of, 101, 297–98nn15–17; genre/anti-genre dichotomy, 98; on home and identity, 1, 2; influences on, 16; status, 106

buildings: *ALT,* 65–66, 84, 88–89, 295n28; Oz, 233–34, 238–41, 311–12nn26–28; as sacred sites, 294n12; YOA, 300n46

Campbell, Joseph, 292n38, 301n56

Carmel, 18, 30, 35, 36, 37, 75

castration anxiety, 132, 175, 181, 252, 286

celibacy, 81

central/eastern European Jews: comparison, 52, 56–57, 67–68, 86–87, 89, 95–96, 159; Enlightenment metanarrative, 76–79; human engineering, 93, 151, 158–59, 216–18, 220; settlement narrative, 71–72; vitality, 78, 80–81, 82, 295n24

Chimera, 292n45

Christianity: *ALT,* 80, 86–87, 89–93; Osiris, 301n55; possession-taking, 124; spiritual longing in Oz, 225; YOA, 119, 121, 124

chronotopic plane: *ALT,* 70–71, 74, 249; birth phase narratives, 247; *HWF,* 150–51, 201, 203–8, 211–16; *LOZ,* 26, 29–31, 35–36, 44; Luidor, 116–24, 134–35; NAV, 247–48

cinematic effect in *HWF,* 201, 208–11

city/country opposition: *ALT,* 64–65, 116; *HWF,* 150, 160–61, 224; *LOZ,* 21–24, 30, 31, 116, 222–23; Oz, 232–35; pleasant places, 33, 43–44; YOA, 116

city planning, 65–67, 68, 294n15

city utopias. *See* utopias

class: *ALT,* 54, 65–66, 67, 69, 86–87, 295n29; *LOZ,* 8, 31, 35, 38–39, 40; NAV, 255; nomad/settler tensions, 133; pleasant places, 33

collective/private plane opposition: *ALT,* 65; *HWF,* 155, 203, 207–8; *LOZ,* 19, 30, 41–42, 44; NAV, 230–31, 241, 260–68, 272–73, 276–80

colonialism: *ALT,* 59, 67, 70, 71, 79–80; Defoe, 105–6; desire for, 260–61, 295n25; Herzl, 52; land rights, 123–24; mimicry, 305n42; NAV, 241, 242, 250–51, 254–56, 260–67, 313n50; skin color, 313n50; South America, 294n17; women, 122; YOA, 123

community/society opposition: *ALT,* 8, 9, 223; *HWF,* 10, 224; *LOZ,* 8, 222–23; NAV, 11, 12, 279–80; will and, 7–8; YOA, 8, 9, 223

country/city opposition. *See* city/country opposition

covenants: *HWF,* 10, 192; Luidor, 10, 120, 121–22, 123, 141, 199

cracked narrator, 163, 164–66

creation myths, 46–48, 123, 124, 284, 293n49

cultural narratives, 5–6. *See also* biblical metanarratives; European metanarratives; metanarratives

cutting-up of the monster, 43, 45–48, 283–85

dark/light opposition: *HWF,* 179–81, 182–83, 185–88, 195, 211, 214, 306n56; *LOZ,* 25; NAV, 228, 263, 313n50

Dayan, Moshe, 119, 198

day/night opposition, 179–80, 181, 186–88, 195, 306n56
Dead Sea, 18, 21, 22–24, 62, 63, 64
death: *HWF,* 156, 162–63, 171, 189, 190, 198–216; living-dead narrative, 156, 200–216; NAV, 261–62, 271–75, 286; YOA, 117–18, 123, 156, 171, 198–99
death, love of: *HWF,* 162–63, 196–200; Luidor, 107, 298–99n32; Oz, 142, 274; Second Aliyah, 106, 107, 138–41, 199, 307nn66–67; YOA, 138. *See also* memorial culture
Defoe, Daniel, 104–6, 129, 137
demythicization, 169–74, 201–3, 206–7, 208–11, 224
dragons, 45, 292n46, 292–93n48
Dry Bones metanarrative, 9, 71, 74, 80–85, 216, 246–47
dynastic concerns. *See* human engineering
dystopias, 290n9, 312n30

eagles, 44, 47, 292n45
eastern European Jews. *See* central/eastern European Jews
East/West opposition: *ALT,* 53, 60–61, 70; pre-modern literature, 4–5, 289n4; State Generation, 287–88; third space and, 248
education: *ALT,* 56, 77, 79–80, 92; *HWF,* 148, 155, 189–90; Kadoorie school, 148, 155, 303n21; NAV, 242; Tehran Children, 303n22; YOA, 114, 153, 155, 300n42
Elboim-Dror, R., 7, 49–50
Eliade, M., 47, 124, 293n49
Elsewhere, Perhaps (Oz), 12, 221, 232–41, 276, 310n14, 311–12nn25–28, 312n30
encounter scenes: *HWF,* 179–80, 212; *LOZ,* 34–36, 43–44, 285; NAV, 242–46, 249–60, 271–77, 283–86, 312–13n40
End of Days metanarrative: *ALT,* 9, 71, 73; community identity, 6, 289n11; *LOZ,* 27–28, 30; as redemption narrative, 246
Enlightenment metanarratives. *See* European metanarratives

Eretz Israel, 4–5, 7, 9–10. *See also* acclimatization stories; First Aliyah; Second Aliyah
Europe: *ALT,* 50, 51, 52, 58–59, 65–66, 68, 69–70, 79, 88, 294n16; kibbutz/village comparison, 232–35, 238–41, 311–12nn25–28; vector of desire, 9, 11, 50, 225, 289n4, 310nn13–14
European metanarratives: *ALT,* 71, 73–85, 125; bildungsroman, 42, 295n23; holy grail, 29; liberal/universal, 71, 76–79; neoromantic antisemitic, 71, 74, 76–79, 80–85, 125. *See also* colonialism
Even to Jerusalem (Reuveni), 98, 99–100, 118, 122, 138, 296n9, 307n66
Exodus from Egypt metanarrative: *ALT,* 9, 71, 73–76, 79, 80–85, 159; *LOZ,* 34, 45, 47; as redemption narrative, 246

faith/paganism opposition, 18, 21–22, 24
false messianic metanarrative, 72–73
family: *ALT,* 56, 77; First Aliyah literature, 301n68; Luidor and Second Aliyah, 107, 111, 113, 114; NAV, 275–80; westerns, 207. *See also* fathers and sons
fathers and sons: *HWF,* 150, 152–53, 158, 160, 162–63, 170–71, 174–76, 193–94, 197–98; mimicry of sons by fathers, 282, 314n58; Shtetl literature, 113
femininity. *See* masculinity/femininity
fertility, 29, 218, 259–60, 293n49, 306–7n64. *See also* Osiris
Fichman, F., 15
First Aliyah, 99, 206, 298n28, 301n68
food and drink, 261–62, 300n41
founding metanarrative. *See* birth phase metanarratives
"from tending the flock" metanarrative, 28–29
frontier stories, 115, 130, 156, 201, 301n65

Gamzu, H., 144
Garden of Eden: *ALT,* 84; multicultural, 274–75; NAV, 11, 249–50, 251, 254, 283, 286, 313n41; as theme, 7, 289n13, 314n62

garden utopias. *See* utopias
genre fiction, 98, 299–300n39, 300n45
geography. *See* landscape
Germany: *ALT,* 217; *HWF,* 148, 150, 158–59, 192; *LOZ,* 89, 92, 95–96; Oz, 310n14
Gertz, N., 203, 207–8, 303, 305n43
Gilula Dvora, 303n16
Golem, 281, 282
Gordon, A. D., 301n59
griffins, 292n45
Gugik, Zvi, 297n15, 298n17
Gurevitch, Z., 2–3, 82, 110, 120–21

Hadomi, L., 291n17, 295–96n31
Haifa, 60, 61, 66–67, 69–70, 112, 153, 294nn15–16
Hamsun, K., 104, 129, 137
"Harvest Days" (Luidor), 136
Haskalah literature, 52, 111, 133, 289n4, 290n9
Hazan, Y., 145
Hebrew literature, 3–4. *See also specific works*
Herzig, H., 260–61
Herzl, Theodor: Eurocentricism, 58–59; influence of, 50, 99; *The Jewish State,* 49; as non-immigrant, 106; suicide of friend, 249n18; utopias, 293n3. *See also Altneuland* (Herzl)
He Walked in the Fields (Shamir): chronotopic plane, 150–51, 201, 203–8, 211–16; city/country opposition, 150, 160–61, 224; critical reception, 144–46; demythicization of sabras, 169–74, 201–3, 206–7, 208–11, 224; film, 147, 207–8, 303n20; as foundational text, 4, 144–47; heroic death narrative, 196–200; homecoming, 157–63, 174–76; human engineering, 148, 158–59, 192, 207, 212, 216–20, 224, 282–83; influence of, 143–44; landscape, 149–56, 212–13, 216, 230; living-dead narrative, 157, 201–16; narrator's voice, 163–74, 305n43; play, 143, 144, 145–46, 303n15, 306n62; plot, 148–49, 158–63; renaissance narrative, 9–10; Ruthka's and Goren's trajectories, 188–96; sexuality, 154–55, 162, 169, 176, 177–86, 211, 212–13, 218–19, 304n27, 304n31, 306n56, 308nn88–89; survivalist narrative, 157–63; vector of desire, 10; YOA comparison, 152–56, 171–72, 198–99
Hirsch, Baron Maurice de, 71, 294n17
Holocaust refugees, 146–47, 149, 150, 151, 211–16, 304n25, 308n89. *See also* Tehran Children
holy grail metanarrative, 29
home: *ALT,* 53, 55; *HWF,* 148, 150, 152, 153–54, 157–63, 174–76, 206–7, 218; immigrants, 2–3; love of homeland, 14; *LOZ,* 18–19, 24; Shtetl literature, 112–13; *The Wizard of Oz* (Baum), 1–3; YOA, 113–14, 153. *See also* nomad/settler tensions
homoeroticism: acclimatization stories, 122–23, 124; *ALT,* 91–92; *HWF,* 123; *LOZ,* 40–41; NAV, 123, 274, 280; YOA, 122
human engineering: *ALT,* 67, 72, 85–93, 107, 124–25, 159, 216–18, 220; axis description, 6; *HWF,* 148, 158–59, 192, 207, 212, 216–20, 224, 282–83; *LOZ,* 7, 30, 93, 107, 124–25, 290n10; Luidor, 98, 122–23, 124, 125, 126, 136; Oz, 242–46, 280–83; State Generation, 220
hybrids: monsters, 43–48, 284, 292n45, 292–93n48; nations, 312n35; NAV, 11–12, 251, 256, 274–75; postcolonialism, 248–49, 250
hybrid voice, 163–64, 170–71, 266–67

identity and narrative, 5–6. *See also* biblical metanarratives; European metanarratives; metanarratives
immigrants. *See* acclimatization stories; First Aliyah; Second Aliyah
impotence: Agnon, 139; *HWF,* 169, 176, 185–86; NAV, 258–59, 265, 272, 273; YOA, 132; Zionist culture, 302n80

individuation/socialization opposition, 76–79, 80, 102, 103
initiation stories. *See* rites of passage
ironic fiction. *See* anti-genre fiction
ironic/pathetic opposition, 163, 167, 169–70, 172, 208–10
Israel, emigration from, 99. *See also* landscape; place/Place gap

Jaffa, 57, 101–2, 112, 297–98n16
Jerusalem: *ALT,* 58, 60–62, 295n24; genre/anti-genre fiction, 299–300n39; *HWF,* 150, 153; *LOZ,* 18, 19, 20–21, 22–25, 29–30, 212; Luidor, 112; siege of, 44. *See also* place/Place gap
Jewish Brigade, 149, 197, 304n25
The Jewish State (Herzl), 49
Jung, Carl, 311n18

Kadoorie school, 148, 152, 155, 303n21
Kenaz, Y., 309n4
kibbutz: *HWF,* 150–51, 152, 153, 156, 160–61, 189, 217–19, 224, 275; Oz, 11, 226–31, 232–41, 275–80, 311–12nn25–28, 314n51
Kressel, G., 101, 297–98n16
Kurzweil, B., 309n5
Kushnir, M., 102

Lachover, F., 291n12
landscape: *ALT,* 52–70, 74–75, 107, 295n28; axis description, 6; frontier stories, 130, 301n65; genre/anti-genre fiction, 299–300n39; *HWF,* 149–56, 189, 212–13, 216, 230; limited, 111–12, 116, 152–53; *LOZ,* 7, 14, 17–27, 31–37, 64, 107, 290n10; Luidor, 98, 111–16, 124, 125, 130–31, 132, 134–35, 136, 152–54, 155–56; Oz, 225–32, 232–38, 242–46, 249–50, 311–12nn25–28, 314n51; Palmach Generation, 112; Second and Third Aliyahs, 111–12; secondary, 32, 291–92n25; State Generation, 112, 291–92n25; United States, 292n27; Yizhar, S., 155, 304n30
liberal/universal subnarrative, 71, 76–79

light/dark opposition. *See* dark/light opposition
lions: *ALT,* 78, 94, 95, 285; Chimeras and griffins, 292n45; *LOZ,* 20, 43–44, 45–46, 47, 285, 292n33; YOA, 134, 302n73
living-dead narrative, 156, 200–216. *See also* memorial culture
lone rider narrative, 156, 201
"The Lost Garden" (Oz), 142
The Love of Zion (Mapu): biblical metanarratives, 6, 8, 19, 27–29, 33–35, 34, 45; chronotopic plane, 26, 29–31, 35–36, 44; city/country opposition, 21–24, 30, 31, 116, 222–23; cutting-up of the monster, 43, 45–48, 283–85; as foundational text, 4, 14–16, 48; human engineering, 7, 30, 93, 107, 124–25, 290n10; influence of, 15–16, 42–43; landscape, 7, 14, 17–27, 29–30, 31–37, 64, 107, 290n10; otherness in, 308n91; plot, 16–17, 27–31, 35–36, 41–42; "primitive" metanarrative, 42–48; redemption metanarrative, 247; renaissance narrative, 6–7, 8; sexuality, 30, 37–41, 87; utopias, 5, 7, 8, 21–22, 222–23; vector of desire, 5–8, 30
Luidor, Moshe, 104–6, 137, 297–98n16, 298n21
Luidor, Yosef: anonymity, 98–101, 297n12; character, 102–4; death, 101–2, 107, 298–99n32; as immigrant, 106–7; influences on, 104–6; "Malaria," 114, 120, 122–23; recruitment by, 107–11; status, 97–98, 99, 106, 296n1; "Yehuda the Orchard Keeper," 113, 119, 120, 123, 134–36, 156, 171–72. *See also* "Yoash" (Luidor)
Luzzatto, M. C., 21, 291n12

"Malaria" (Luidor), 114, 120, 122–23
maps: *ALT,* 52–59, 62, 68, 74; *HWF,* 150–54; *LOZ,* 18, 25–26; Oz, 226, 229–32, 235–39; YOA, 111–16
Mapu, Avraham: conservatism, 41–42; as non-immigrant, 106; status, 99. *See also The Love of Zion* (Mapu)

masculinity/femininity: acclimatization stories, 122; *ALT,* 55, 84, 87; Arabs, 220, 228, 236, 252; ascetic option, 194; Garden of Eden, 249–50; *HWF,* 155, 179, 181, 183, 185, 189–90, 192, 193, 213, 218, 220, 306n62; *LOZ,* 39–40, 87; nature, 87, 236–37; Oz, 228, 236–37, 249–50, 251–52, 281; YOA, 132, 172

melting-pot narrative: *HWF,* 159, 194–95, 213–14, 215, 308n91; *LOZ,* 57, 82, 247; stopping time and, 253; third space, 248

memorial culture: Agnon, 140, 307n66; living-dead narrative, 156, 200–216; Luidor, 101; rise of, 108, 118–19, 141, 297n13, 299n33, 307nn67–68; YOA, 119–20

metanarratives: birth phase metanarratives, 5–6, 247, 286–87, 289n11; "primitive" metanarrative, 42–48. *See also* biblical metanarratives; European metanarratives

Metsudat Ram, 232–35
Milo, Yosef, 143, 146, 303n20
mimicry, 163, 256–60, 282, 314n58
Minotaur, 194–96, 214
Miron, D., 15–16, 32–33, 43–44, 164–68, 173
Mizrahi Jews, 12, 282
mockery. *See* mimicry
monological narrator, 163, 164–66
monsters, 43, 45–48, 194–96, 214, 283–85, 292n45
Moses, 34, 74–76, 284. *See also* Exodus from Egypt metanarrative
mothers, 193, 215
music, 84–85, 88–89, 305–6n52, 307n68
My Michael (Oz), 12, 221
myths: cutting up monsters, 43, 45–48; demythicization, 169–74, 201–3, 206–7, 208–11, 224; frontier stories, 130, 301n65; heroes, 172, 173, 184; Tannhäuser, 132, 139, 188; YOA, 123

naive fiction. *See* genre fiction
narrator: *Elsewhere, Perhaps* (Oz), 236–41, 262, 263, 264; *HWF,* 163–74, 305n43; NAV, 229–36, 242, 262–67, 270, 277–90

national memorial genre. *See* memorial culture

nativeness: concept of place, 2–3, 110, 115, 120–21; indigenous peoples, 105–6, 305n42. *See also* Arabs; sabras

nature: Agnon, 138; *ALT,* 68, 81, 83, 87, 88, 285; destruction of, 259–60, 313n44; *HWF,* 152, 212; *LOZ,* 33; Luidor, 9, 114–16, 115, 129, 130–32, 135; NAV, 250; as the "other," 141

Naveh, H., 137–38, 205–6, 228–29
Nebuchadnezzar Syndrome, 19
Ne'eman, J., 147
neoromantic antisemitic metanarrative, 71, 74, 76–79, 80–85, 125
new/old opposition, 225, 232–35, 238–41, 311–12nn25–28
night/day opposition, 179–80, 181, 186–88, 195, 306n56
1948 Generation. *See* Palmach Generation; Shamir, Moshe
Nineveh, 18, 19–20, 57, 290n10
nomads: gypsies, 137, 302n77; living-dead narrative, 203–4, 205–7; sabras as, 108; in westerns, 207. *See also* nomad/settler tensions

"Nomads and Viper" (Oz): chronotopic plane, 247–48; colonialism, 241, 242, 250–51, 254–56, 260–67, 313n50; critical reception, 221–22, 309nn4–5; as foundational text, 4, 221–22; human engineering, 242–46, 282–83; kibbutz as family, 275–80; landscape, 225–32, 242–46, 249–50, 314n51; order of events, 269–70, 272–74; plot, 227–28, 241–46; postcolonialism, 241, 242–46, 250–51, 256–60, 274–75; renaissance narrative, 9, 11–12; sexuality, 123, 249–50, 251–52, 254–56, 265, 273, 274, 280; threshold narrative, 253; vector of desire, 11, 12, 225–26, 280, 286, 310nn13–14

nomad/settler tensions: acclimatization stories, 133–38; *HWF,* 206–7; Luidor,

334 INDEX

125–32, 133–34, 136; NAV, 226–31, 242, 257, 262, 263–65; Naveh on, 137–38, 205–6, 228–29
Nordau, M., 51–52

Odyssey, 157–60, 176, 177
Oedipus, 111, 112, 116, 141
Only Yesterday (Agnon), 98, 99–100, 122, 138–41, 307n66
open spaces. *See* outdoor spaces
Osiris, 46, 121–22, 132, 139, 140–41, 301n55, 302n84
the "other": animals as, 141, 286; Arab women, 219–20; desire for in Oz, 12, 225–26, 237, 238, 260–61, 262, 263–65, 274, 276, 280, 310nn13–14; desire for in State Generation, 287–88; *LOZ*, 308n91; nomads as, 229
outdoor spaces: as dangerous, 291–92n25; as empty, 67, 79; *HWF*, 155–56, 173; Luidor, 113, 114–16, 126–27, 129, 137, 153, 156, 212; Oz, 225, 236–38
Oz, Amos: on dreams, 221; *Elsewhere, Perhaps*, 12, 221, 232–41, 276, 310n14, 311–12nn25–28, 312n30; influence of, 10, 222, 309–10n9; influences on, 224–25, 311nn17–18; on kibbutz as family, 275, 276; "The Lost Garden," 142; *My Michael*, 12, 221; political activity, 222, 309nn6–7; on sabras, 280–81, 282; on Tarzan, 142; *Unto Death*, 310n16; "The Way of the Wind," 222, 281–82, 310n13. *See also* "Nomads and Viper" (Oz)

paganism/faith opposition. *See* faith/paganism opposition
Palmach Generation: centrality of gangs, 155; landscape, 112; living-dead narrative, 156, 200, 203; machine monsters, 196; mythification, 147, 299n33; narrators, 305n43; nomad/settler tensions, 133. *See also* Shamir, Moshe
Pan (Hamsun), 104, 129, 137
parody, 152, 169–70, 201–11, 304n26. *See also* mimicry

picaresque romance, 107, 108, 125–32
pilgrimages: *HWF,* 191–92, 194–96, 212–15; itineraries, 294n11; *LOZ,* 27, 30; Luidor, 135
pioneers. *See* settlers/pioneers
place, pleasant, 33, 35–37, 43–44
place, symbolic, 31–37, 292n27
place/Place gap: *ALT,* 52–61, 70–71, 74–75, 86–93, 216; genre/anti-genre dichotomy, 98, 300n45; *HWF,* 10, 149–51, 216, 220; immigrants and natives, 2–3; *LOZ,* 5, 13–14, 31–37; Oz, 225, 241; pre-modern literature, 5, 13; State Generation, 291–92n25; YOA, 98, 107–11, 116–17, 125, 129, 130, 136
Porat, Z., 287
postcolonialism: hybrid culture, 248–49, 250; love of homeland, 14; NAV, 241, 242–46, 250–51, 256–60, 274–75; nomad/settler tensions, 262
postmodern literature, 290n9
power plant, 60, 62–64, 66, 94, 212
pregnancy, 200, 215, 308n89. *See also* fertility
"primitive" metanarrative, 42–48
private/collective plane opposition. *See* collective/private plane opposition
public/private opposition, 150, 151, 152, 154–55, 161–62, 176, 178–79, 207

Rabbi Silo celebration, 190–92, 306–7nn63–64
Rabinovich, Y., 101, 297n13, 298n17, 307n67
Rancière, J., 147, 303n19
rape, 255, 260–67, 269–70, 276–80, 312–13n40
Ravnitzky, Y. C., 314n61
Raz, A., 310n10
recruitment by Luidor, 107–11
redemption narrative, 80, 85, 246–48, 249, 276, 287
refugees. *See* Holocaust refugees; Tehran Children
renaissance cultural narrative, 6–7, 8, 9–10, 11–12, 30, 42–48

INDEX   335

Reuveni, A., 98, 99–100, 122, 138, 296n9
Revival literature, 111, 133
reward narratives, 27–28
Rimmon-Kennan, Shlomith, 5–6
rites of passage: changes in status, 301n56; *HWF*, 190–92, 194, 211–16, 308n91; liminal spaces, 82; Luidor, 107–11, 300n46
Robinson Crusoe (Defoe), 104–6, 129, 137
Romantic literature, 30, 33, 41, 43, 290n9
romantic metanarrative, 71, 74
Russia, 59, 148, 150, 158–59, 192, 217
Ruth, 34, 212, 308n91

sabras: animals and nature, 115–16, 126, 127–29; demythicization, 169–74, 201–3, 206–7, 208–11, 211–16, 218–19, 224, 305n42; love of death, 138–41; Luidor, 108, 113–16, 119, 125–32; mythification, 108, 147, 299n33; nomad/settler tensions, 132–38; Oz, 217–20, 280–82; sculpture, 308n88; YOA, 126
Sadan, D., 310n10
Samaria, 18, 19, 20–21
Saul metanarrative, 8, 28–29
schools. *See* education
seas, 60, 75, 130–32, 301–2n69
Second Aliyah: anonymity, 98, 99–100; death attitudes, 138–41, 199, 307nn66–67; defined, 296n7; denial of place/Place gap, 116–17; lack of parents, 107; landscape, 111–12; nomad/settler tensions, 132–38, 206; sanctifying land, 121; status of kibbutz, 275; writers as immigrants, 106–7
settlement stories, 71–72, 141, 287, 300n41
settlers/pioneers: anonymity, 99–100; homoeroticism, 123; lack of parents, 107; mimicry of, 305n42; risk of death, 106, 107. *See also* nomad/settler tensions
sexuality: *ALT*, 81, 84, 87–88, 89, 91, 217; creation myths, 47, 293n49; cutting up the monster, 285; *HWF*, 154–55, 162, 169, 176, 177–86, 211, 212–13, 218–19, 304n27, 304n31, 306n56, 308nn88–89;

LOZ, 30, 37–41, 87; NAV, 249–50, 251–52, 254–56, 258, 259, 265, 273, 274, 280; YOA, 122–23, 124, 128, 182, 286. *See also* homoeroticism; human engineering
Shahar, S., 302n77
Shaked, G., 98, 143–44, 164, 166–68, 173–74, 296n1, 304n31
Shamir, Moshe: death of brother, 145, 172–73; Luidor comparison, 142–43, 145; mythification of sabras, 299n33. *See also He Walked in the Fields* (Shamir)
Shatz, Zvi, 101, 275, 297nn15–16, 298n17, 301n59
Shtetl literature, 112–14, 115
"The Silver Platter" (Alterman), 119, 200–201, 204–5
Sivan, E., 147
snakes: Chimeras, 292n45; creation myths, 46; Garden of Eden, 284, 286; *LOZ*, 43, 44, 45–46, 47, 284–85; NAV, 11, 250, 271–75, 283, 286; YOA, 127–29, 285
socialization/individuation opposition, 76–79, 80, 102, 103
society/community opposition. *See* community/society opposition
socio-economics. *See* class
soteriological tension. *See* place/Place gap
South America, 71, 124, 294n17
space: devouring, 176, 306n54; liminal, 82, 247, 249; metonymic, 54, 55; oppositions in *LOZ*, 25; third, 248, 251
split-torn voice, 230–31
State Generation: birth phase metanarratives, 247, 286–87; human engineering, 220; influences on, 310n12; landscape, 112, 291–92n25; mimicry of sons by fathers, 314n58; narrator's voice in, 305n43; nomad/settler tensions, 133; otherness, 286; vector of desire, 287–88, 289n4. *See also* Oz, Amos; Yehoshua, A. B.
Stories (Luidor). *See* "Yoash" (Luidor)
suicide: *ALT*, 54, 55, 71, 77, 81, 217, 249n18; *HWF*, 10, 146, 199–200; in Luidor,

298–99n32; merging with the "other," 286; NAV, 272–74; in Reuveni, 100, 138
survivalist narrative, 157–63
swords, 284, 292–93n48
synagogue space in YOA, 112, 113, 114, 300n46

Tannhäuser myth, 132, 139, 188
Tarzan, 142, 224, 306n61
technology: *ALT,* 60, 62–64, 65, 66–67, 68, 69, 70, 83, 84, 93, 294n14; *HWF,* 155–56, 175, 196, 285–86; NAV, 255, 256
Tehran Children, 148, 161–62, 174, 178, 303n22, 304n39, 308n89
Tel Aviv, 150, 153, 160
Temple, 27, 60, 62–64, 94, 212
temporal plane: *ALT,* 52, 53, 249; *LOZ,* 18–19; NAV order of events, 269–70; redemption narrative, 249; stopping time, 253, 312n39; utopias, 249, 290n9
Third Aliyah, 111–12, 275
"The Third Mother" (Alterman), 201–2
threshold narrative, 247–49, 253
Tiberias, 60, 61, 88, 112, 153
Tönnies, F., 7–8. *See also* community/society opposition
topography. *See* landscape
trains, 65, 67, 84, 294n14
Tumarkin, Y., 308n88
type scenes, 33–36, 179–80. *See also* encounter scenes
Tzemach, S., 13–14, 118

United States, 1–3, 71, 292n27
unknown soldiers. *See* anonymity
Unto Death (Oz), 310n16
utopias: *ALT,* 8, 9, 49–50, 64–65, 223, 293n3; future orientation, 249, 290n9; Haskalah literature, 52; *HWF,* 224; *LOZ,* 5, 7, 8, 21–22, 222–23; Oz, 11, 12, 225; roles, 28, 291n17, 312n30; YOA, 8, 9, 223–24

vagabond narrative, 157, 201. *See also* nomad/settler tensions

vector of desire: *ALT,* 7, 9, 50; East and West, 4–5; *HWF,* 10; *LOZ,* 5–8, 30; NAV, 11, 12, 225–26, 280, 286, 310nn13–14; State Generation, 286–87, 289n4; type scenes, 35; YOA, 7
Vienna, 53–57
villages compared to kibbutz, 232–41, 311–12nn25–28
vipers. *See* snakes
virginity, 128, 182, 184, 286
Vision of the Dry Bones metanarrative, 9, 71, 74, 80–85, 216, 246–47
vocal aggregate. *See* hybrid voice

wanderers. *See* nomads
"The Way of the Wind" (Oz), 222, 281–82, 310n13
West. *See* East/West opposition
westerns, 156, 168, 169, 201, 207–8, 224
Where the Jackals Howl. See "Nomads and Viper" (Oz)
The Wizard of Oz (Baum), 1–3
women: acclimatization stories, 122; *ALT,* 87; First Aliyah literature, 301n68; *HWF,* 176–77, 179, 189, 218–20; *LOZ,* 16, 290n6; Oz, 231, 286, 313n41; Second Aliyah literature, 141; westerns, 207, 208; YOA, 132

Ya'ari, M., 145
Ya'ari-Polskin, Y., 102, 298n21, 298–99n32
Yadin, Y., 146
Yehoshua, A. B., 11, 12, 221, 222, 253, 260, 312n39, 314n58
"Yehuda the Orchard Keeper" (Luidor), 113, 119, 120, 123, 134–36, 156, 171–72
Yitzkar, Avraham and Yehuda, 297n15, 298n17
Yizhar, S., 155, 304n30
Yizkor (Rabinovich), 297n13, 307n67
"Yoash" (Luidor): biblical metanarratives, 9, 116–18, 120, 121–22, 123, 132, 133–34; chronotopic plane, 116–24; city/country opposition, 116; compared to *HWF,* 152–56, 171–72, 198–99; critical recep-

tion, 97, 296n1; as foundational text, 4, 97–98; human engineering, 98, 125, 126, 136; landscape, 98, 111–16, 124, 125, 130–31, 132, 134–36, 152–54, 155–56; nomad/settler tensions, 125–32, 133–34, 136; plot, 125–32; recruitment intent, 107–11; redemption metanarrative, 247; renaissance cultural narrative, 9; sexuality, 122–23, 124, 128, 182, 286; utopias, 8, 9, 223–24; vector of desire, 7